39470 -2

GV
342
I59

Introduction to
physical educa-
tion

| DATE DUE | | |
|---|---|---|
| MAY 1 '80 | | |
| OCT 18 '82 | | |
| 5-21-07 | | |
| | | |
| | | |
| | | |
| | | |
| | | |
| | | |
| | | |

*Introduction
to
Physical Education*

Argus Africa News Service

**JOHN CHEFFERS**
*Boston University*

**TOM EVAUL**
*Temple University*

*Authors / Editors*

# Introduction

# to

# Physical Education

## Concepts of Human Movement

PRENTICE-HALL, INC., Englewood Cliffs, New Jersey 07632

*Library of Congress Cataloging in Publication Data*
Main entry under title:

Introduction to physical education.

   1. Physical education and training—Philosophy.
2. Human mechanics.  3. Movement, Psychology of.
I. CHEFFERS, JOHN T., (date)  II. EVAUL, TOM,
(date)
GV342.I59      613.7′01    77-23507 ✓
ISBN 0-13-493031-2

Printed in the United States of America

10  9  8  7  6  5  4  3  2  1

PRENTICE-HALL INTERNATIONAL, INC., *London*
PRENTICE-HALL OF AUSTRALIA PTY. LIMITED, *Sydney*
PRENTICE-HALL OF CANADA, LTD., *Toronto*
PRENTICE-HALL OF INDIA PRIVATE LIMITED, *New Delhi*
PRENTICE-HALL OF JAPAN, INC., *Tokyo*
PRENTICE-HALL OF SOUTHEAST ASIA PTE. LTD., *Singapore*
WHITEHALL BOOKS LIMITED, *Wellington, New Zealand*

# Contents

## Section B

### The Quality and Quantity of Human Movement Affect and Are Affected by Factors within the Individual and the Environment   49

## PART III

## HUMAN MOVEMENT:   APPLIED

### Section A

### Human Beings Help Others Function through Movement: Professionally   199

# Introduction:
# What Is the Difference between Human Movement
# and Physical Education?

Most people conceive of physical education as a school subject centered around the teaching and learning of sports, exercise, and possibly dance. The images of jumping jacks in the gymnasium and varsity games on Friday night predominate. The recent explosion of professional sports, with all its connotations of "jockism," have clouded the conception of physical education even more.

Alternative names have been proposed that more aptly describe the endeavors pursued by the diverse group of people known as physical educators. The names that most frequently appear are kinesiology, biokinetics, and human movement.

This last term, *Human Movement*, has gained favor with many serious-minded physical educators in recent years. There are several reasons for this. First, the term *physical education* no longer accurately represents the diverse growth that has taken place in this field. Individuals specializing in exercise physiology, sports sociology, motor learning, and exercise therapy have difficulty coping with the "gym teacher" image that pervades the concept of a "physical educator." The study of *Human Movement* has become a more acceptable umbrella under which this diverse group can huddle.

Second, despite efforts to the contrary, physical education has perpetuated the concept of dualism—the separation of mind and body. Such well-intentioned movements as the President's Physical Fitness Council have tended to perpetuate this myth. Human Movement, with its strong emphasis on the psychological and sociological aspects of human beings in motion, more accurately conveys the total-person concept of the field.

Finally, physical education, by the very nature of its name and predominant practice, has become an associated branch of the education profession. While by no means undesirable, this association has limited the acceptance of the field by those outside the profession of education.

Human Movement is not a profession, but a body of knowledge applicable to many professions ranging from teaching to therapy. Human Movement may be more suitably classified as a discipline like Biology, History, Anthropology, Psychology, Sociology, and others. Physical education should remain a profession which makes use of this body of knowledge in teaching movement to youngsters.

Some physical educators, wary of faddism and flippant innovation, believe that physical education and Human Movement are one and the same. This is no more accurate, however, than equating the practice of medicine with the discipline of Biology or the profession of teaching with the discipline of Psychology.

## WHAT IS A DISCIPLINE?

Ever since the dawn of history, human beings have been preoccupied with learning. Being endowed with the ability to observe, remember, and think, human beings have been able to amass knowledge and develop symbolic systems to communicate this knowledge to others. As this body of knowledge increased, people began to organize it into systems that could be studied and expanded. With the development of universities in Europe around the eleventh century A.D., scholars began to crystallize these systems into disciplines.

Although the term *discipline* derives from Latin roots meaning "teaching" and "learning," present-day definitions elaborate on this concept. Schwab[1], for example, suggests that a discipline must have (a) a substantive structure, conceptual in nature, that both guides inquiry (what questions should be asked) and organizes the results of such inquiry (gives meaning and interpretation to knowledge), and (b) a syntax that defines the types of evidence necessary to verify knowledge in the discipline and the pathway to be followed in moving from raw data to conclusions. Kenyon[2] maintains that a discipline is characterized by having a particular focus of attention, a unique body of knowledge, and a particular mode of inquiry.

[1] Joseph J. Schwab, "Problems, Topics, and Issues," *Education and the Structure of Knowledge*, Fifth Annual Phi Delta Kappa Symposium on Educational Research (Chicago: Rand McNally, 1964).

The present writers propose that any scholarly pursuit can claim the status of a discipline if it meets three criteria:

1. It must have an identifiable body of substantive knowledge that has some degree of uniqueness.
2. It must use systematic and validated procedures for collecting, processing, and interpreting data.
3. It must not be dependent on any specific means of application for its existence, but must be capable of being applied in many personal and professional pursuits.

Traditionally, such subjects as Mathematics, Chemistry, Physics, Biology, Sociology, Psychology, Anthropology, and History have been called disciplines. If one carefully examines the body of knowledge underlying Human Movement, it is apparent that it, too, meets the criteria for a discipline.

The body of knowledge that has been generated about human beings in motion has substance and is, to some degree, unique. Such concepts as the adaptation of the human organism to functional overloading, the retention of motor skills that have been overlearned, and social mobility through sports participation are examples of substantive knowledge in the discipline of Human Movement.

Arguments questioning the uniqueness of the knowledge about Human Movement claim that much of it may be found in subdivisions of other disciplines such as Biology (Exercise Physiology), Psychology (Motor Learning), and Sociology (Sports Sociology). However, the same question may be raised about other disciplines such as History, whose very existence depends on the multidisciplinary approach to past events. Indeed, History often prides itself on being the supreme integrative discipline[3]*.

The reverse question may also be raised about other disciplines. Does the psychologist's investigation of personality factors related to human movement represent the journey of psychology into the discipline of human movement in an effort to explain the observed phenomenon? Can the resultant movement be ascribed to personality, as the psychologist suggests, or is personality a result of movement activities?

It is our contention that both disciplines have a perfect right to inves-

[2]Gerald Kenyon, "On the Conceptualization of Sub-Disciplines within an Academic Discipline Dealing with Human Movement," Proceedings of the NCPEAM, 1968.

[3]Schwab, *op. cit.*

*Hereafter, citation numbers in parentheses refer to works listed in the "References Cited" sections at the end of each chapter.

tigate the relationship of personality to human activity from their individual perspectives. Virtually all disciplines overlap others in certain areas, and all have knowledge that is uniquely their own. The discipline of Human Movement is no exception.

All disciplines are dynamic—that is, they are constantly changing. Both scholars and practitioners change the field by observing, hypothesizing, researching, and forming conclusions. One example of this is the change that has taken place in both the theory and application of progressive resistance exercise (weight training) over the past two decades. Men involved in weight lifting and body building thirty years ago tended to be "muscle-bound" (lacking flexibility and coordination). Some concluded that weight training caused this phenomenon. Knowing that strength was a major component of human performance, some began to research the problem. As a result of this and the voluminous research by others that followed, the "muscle-bound" myth was dispelled and new concepts of weight training were developed. It was hypothesized that people who inherently lacked coordination for traditional sports turned to weight training to express their masculinity. The observed lack of coordination was not an effect of the weight training, but was a characteristic of the people who participated in the field.

All disciplines attack problems, discover new knowledge, and sometimes dispel traditional "truths" with their new revelations. In so doing, researchers adopt, adapt, and create procedures for collecting and analyzing data and drawing conclusions. Since Human Movement is a relatively young discipline, it has rested heavily on the techniques used by others. But some of its procedures are characteristic of it alone.

Human Movement has been hard pressed to meet the third criterion of a discipline—independence of specific professional applications. Until recently, virtually everyone trained in physical education has entered the teaching or coaching profession. With an expanded and more sophisticated body of knowledge, more opportunities have been opening up for the trained physical educator. Therapeutic rehabilitation (particularly in the cardiovascular area), research, athletic training, adult fitness, public and commercial recreation, equipment design, and observation of crowd behavior at sport gatherings are a few of the areas opening up to physical educators (persons trained in the area of Human Movement). As people become better prepared with the body of knowledge about Human Movement, opportunities for its professional application will increase.

The study of Human Movement is not only important for its professional application in helping others, but is also useful to individuals in making meaningful decisions about their own lives. Knowledge about themselves and their environment—and about how movement affects each —can enable individuals to make personal decisions that may enhance their growth and maturation, and consequently increase their satisfaction with life.

## WHAT IS A PROFESSION?

The term *profession* has as many definitions as *discipline*. Some say that a professional is one who has an assured competence in a particular field. Others would narrow the professions to those occupations that require advanced study in a college or university. The present writers believe that the application of the knowledge and skill generated by one or more disciplines to a socially defined occupation that helps meet human needs comprises a profession. People who carry out this application, professionals, besides having a command of the body of knowledge of one or more disciplines, develop technical skills in the application of this knowledge. Professions tend to be self-certifying and self-regulating (and, to some degree, self-serving). That is, a profession usually has some control over who it admits to its ranks, it has some rules and ethics governing its members in their practice, and it tends to benefit the members of the profession as well as society. To find examples of all these criteria in differing degrees, one may examine the professions of medicine, law, communications, management, education.

Physical education, by its very name, is a branch of the education profession. Until recently virtually all graduates of such professional preparation programs were certified to teach in public schools. In the past few years, as a result of the shrinking teaching market and the expanding opportunities in other areas, colleges and universities have begun to offer programs designed for purposes other than teacher training; which has increased concern over the appropriateness of the term *Physical Education*.

The writers contend that both *physical education* and *Human Movement* are appropriate terms when properly used. If Human Movement is the discipline that incorporates a body of knowledge about human beings in motion, then physical education is a profession that applies that knowledge.

One may study the discipline of Human Movement just as one may study Anthropology, Chemistry, or History. Perhaps it rivals History for the claim to being "Supreme Integrative Discipline."

In addition to studying the discipline, students may develop technical skills that will enable them to apply this knowledge in some professional pursuit. One of these ways is in education. Thus, a physical educator (perhaps more appropriately named a movement educator) would be a person who has studied Human Movement and also developed skills in teaching. Here lies the difference—and here lies the future. When Human Movement becomes accepted as a discipline with all the rights and privileges thereof, when persons who study this discipline become well versed in the body of knowledge, and when professionals who apply this discipline begin making broader and more significant contributions to society, the full potential of this field in meeting human needs will be realized.

## ACKNOWLEDGMENTS

We wish to acknowledge the invaluable assistance of the following people for their contributions to this text: Eleen Dunn for the chapter 10 art; Jody Ayers for help in chapter 13; Miriam Serman for her help with the text; and Carolyn Champion for her artwork.

We would also like to thank the contributing authors for their efforts.
Barbara Burris, East Stroudsburg State College
Victor Mancini, Ithaca College
Arne Olson, East Stroudsburg State College
Lois Smith, University of Texas at the Permian Basin
Leonard Zaichkowsky, Boston University
Linda Zaichkowsky, Boston University

TOM EVAUL
JOHN CHEFFERS

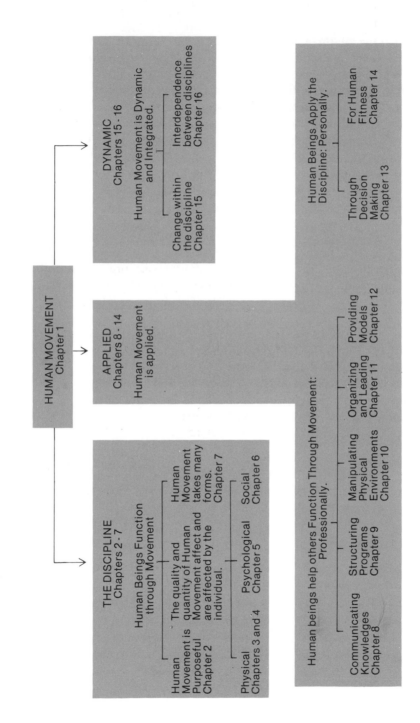

HUMAN MOVEMENT
Chapter 1

THE DISCIPLINE
Chapters 2 - 7

Human Beings Function
through Movement

Human
Movement is
Purposeful
Chapter 2

The quality and
quantity of Human
Movement affect and
are affected by the
individual.

Human
Movement
takes many
forms.
Chapter 7

Physical
Chapters 3 and 4

Psychological
Chapter 5

Social
Chapter 6

APPLIED
Chapters 8 - 14

Human Movement
is applied.

Human beings help others Function Through Movement:
Professionally.

Communicating
Knowledges
Chapter 8

Structuring
Programs
Chapter 9

Manipulating
Physical
Environments
Chapter 10

Organizing
and Leading
Chapter 11

Providing
Models
Chapter 12

Human Beings Apply the
Discipline: Personally.

Through
Decision
Making
Chapter 13

For Human
Fitness
Chapter 14

DYNAMIC
Chapters 15 - 16

Human Movement is Dynamic
and Integrated.

Change within
the discipline
Chapter 15

Interdependence
between disciplines
Chapter 16

# PART I

*The Discipline of Human Movement and Its Applications*

# 1

## What Is Human Movement?

*Tom Evaul / John Cheffers*

Having identified Human Movement as an academic discipline in the introduction to this text, we shall now describe its substantive structure, explore its personal and professional applications, develop an understanding of its interrelationships with other disciplines, and explain its dynamic capacity for change.

### HUMAN BEINGS FUNCTION THROUGH MOVEMENT

The discipline of Human Movement stems from a single basic concept: human beings function through movement. This idea can be validated daily by observing the activities of people. Be it so simple as the blinking of an eye or so complex as propelling one's body into the air to clear a high-jump bar, human beings accomplish everything through movement.

This concept gives rise to three basic questions:

*Why* does a human being move?

*What happens* when a human being moves?

*How* does a human being move?

The answers to these questions reside in the multitude of empirical research and logical conclusions generated by numerous scholars and practitioners in a diverse range of professional settings, and they can be summed up as follows:

Human movement is purposeful.

The quality and quantity of human movement affects and is affected by factors within the individual and the environment.

Human movement takes many forms.

The chart below outlines these three concepts, which are more fully explained in this chapter. The subconcepts derived from each of these are enumerated and defined in Chapters 2 through 7.

## Why Does a Human Being Move?

Many theories have been proposed to explain why people do what they do. Human movement, essentially human behavior, is motivated by a variety of factors: tangible rewards, desire for acceptance, curiosity, self-satisfaction, and many others. Common to all these theories, however, is the existence of a powerful urge or need which all human beings attempt to satisfy. Skinner's operant conditioning would not work if the individual being conditioned did not need the reinforcer. Nor would Rogers's self-directed education function if the learner had no desire or purpose in life.

Every human being seems to have a basic need to grow and mature. This need is not confined to the physical dimension, but exists in the social, emotional, intellectual, and spiritual dimensions as well. Nor is

### The Discipline of Human Movement(2)

| Human beings function through movement |
|---|

| Human movement is purposeful | The quality and quantity of movement affect and are affected by factors within the individual and the environment | | | Human movement takes many forms | |
|---|---|---|---|---|---|
| Purposes | Physical Factors | Psychological Factors | Social Factors | Fundamental | Complex |
| Physical | Structure | Learning | Structure | Locomotion | Sport |
| Social | Function | Motivation | Function | Stability | Dance |
| Intellectual | Mechanics | Readiness | Processes | Manipulation | Exercise |
| Emotional | Environment | Personality | Dynamics | | Aquatics |
| Spiritual | | | Culture | | Drama |
| | | | | | Work |

this need limited to childhood and adolescence, for people continue to grow and mature throughout their lives. Virtually everything people do represents attempts to fulfil this need (1).

Sometimes, because of insufficient or distorted experiences, individuals misinterpret their needs and behave in a manner that fosters growth and maturation in one dimension at the expense of other dimensions (1). Consider, for example, the athlete who becomes engrossed in perfecting his skill in a certain sport during his youth. In the process, he may neglect his intellectual and social growth. Later in life, his skills in these areas may be insufficient to meet his needs.

History provides numerous examples of human movement as a means of satisfying multidimensional needs: primitive man, whose physical survival depended upon his ability to move; the ancient Greeks, who virtually worshipped the Olympic champion; medieval knights, whose social status was determined by their skills in combative activities; early explorers, whose curiosity opened the New World; and modern mountainclimbers, who achieve emotional satisfaction from scaling dangerous peaks.

The existence of physical, emotional, social, intellectual, and spiritual needs and people's attempt to satisfy them provide the answer to the question "Why do human being move?" All movement is *purposeful.*

## What Happens When A Human Being Moves?

Movement does not exist in a vacuum. People move in an environment. The particular environment in which an individual finds himself at a given moment partially determines how well he moves (quality) and how much he moves (quantity). The physical, intellectual, social, emotional, and spiritual condition of the individual at that moment also influences the quality and quantity of his movement.

Not only do these external and internal factors influence the movement, but the movement in turn influences them.

Consider a ballerina performing an intricate ballet. It is obvious that her physical condition, neuromuscular skill, and emotional excitement influence her performance. Likewise, the surface of the stage, lighting, air temperature, and response of the audience also influence her dancing.

Many of the factors that influence her movement may in turn be influenced by it. The quality of her performance, for example, will certainly have an effect upon those watching it, creating either excitement or boredom, happiness or sadness, admiration or pity. Each practice and performance in turn may improve her physical ability and increase her confidence and resolve to become even better.

A reciprocal relationship exists between individuals and their environment, and human movement. Much has been learned about this relationship. This knowledge may be classified as physical, psychological, and sociological. Portions of it are traditionally studied in such courses as exercise physiology, kinesiology, motor learning, and sport sociology.

The concept that the quality and quantity of human movement affects and is affected by factors within the individual and his environment lies at the very heart of the discipline of Human Movement.

## What Form Does Human Movement Take?

Many forms of movement have evolved as human beings have attempted to satisfy their needs. Once the primate stood on two feet, new forms of locomotion were discovered. As the superior mind of *Homo sapiens* began to conceive and create tools, new manipulative forms evolved. With the onset of civilization, new symbolic forms of movement, such as sport and dance, were initiated.

The activities of modern man are quite different from those of his prehistoric ancestors. However, the movement forms have changed little. Ancient dance, for example, most probably included gyrations to elicit responses of gods thought to control the elements of nature. Today such highly structured activities as ballet include similar movements.

*Forms* of movement are permanent structures. Activities within these forms consist of skills organized around specific purposes. The form of movement called *sport* has existed for ages. The activity of gladiatorial combat, where movement frequently continued until the death of one participant, was quite popular under the Roman Empire. As humanity advanced, this activity has been refined to include more symbolic forms of combat such as fencing, boxing, and wrestling.

Many classifications of movement forms have been developed over the years as the body of knowledge of Human Movement has expanded. These classifications have ranged from Jewett's sophisticated taxonomy of the psychomotor domain to the simple grouping of play, sports, and games presented by sports sociologists. It is not the purpose of this book to present yet another classification of movement forms. A review of a number of existing schemes will serve to illustrate the diversities and commonalities of thinking in this unique aspect of the discipline of Human Movement.

When movement occurs, the factors affecting and affected by movement become operational. As a person moves in one form or another, things happen to the individual, to his environment, and to the movement itself. Different forms cause different things to happen. The form of movement known as exercise, and a specific activity in this form known as weight lifting, provides an example. As the individual exerts the energy to lift the weight, certain things happen to him. Blood pressure rises, muscles strain and concentration on the task increases. The weight moves and, if others are watching, their perceptions may cause a change in their feelings and attitudes. The strength, balance, and skill of the lifter will determine how far the weight will move. Success in this movement will undoubtedly affect the lifter, both physically and psychologically. So may failure. Whatever form of movement is used, things will happen—to the individual, to his environment, and to his movement.

## HOW DOES ONE APPLY THE
## DISCIPLINE OF HUMAN MOVEMENT?

A discipline is of little practical value if it cannot be applied to improving the human condition. Zoology, for example, is a discipline which has applications in medicine, physical therapy, animal husbandry, and many other areas. Psychology is a foundation for mental health professions, advertising, education, and so on.

The discipline of Human Movement has its applications, too. The professional applications are aimed at helping people. The major function of the teaching application, most commonly known as the profession of physical education, is the communication of various knowledges and skills in the discipline. This includes knowledges about why people move, what happens to people physically, psychologically, and socially when they move, and how various physical, psychological, and social states and situations affect people's movement, as well as the various forms of movement themselves. A more intense and specialized type of teaching—coaching—also draws heavily upon the discipline of Human Movement.

Other applications of the discipline result from the structuring of various programs designed to improve the human condition. Such programs include the physical education curricula of elementary and secondary schools and colleges; recreation programs conducted by both public and private agencies; fitness, therapy, and rehabilitation programs raised in diverse institutions ranging from "Y's" to hospitals; and manipulative skills training programs found in vocational schools and apprenticeship programs.

There are many individuals and groups that use information from Human Movement in creating and manipulating various environments for movement. These include manufacturers of various types of sporting, recreational and safety equipment and designers and builders of apparatus and facilities that aid movement. Virtually every human endeavor, particularly those that become institutionalized, require organization and leadership. By their very dynamic nature, activities involving considerable human movement frequently require more and better organization and leadership than other ventures of less kinetic energy. A thorough understanding of why people move, what happens when they move, and how they move can contribute much to the structuring of successful organizations and the provision of sound leadership for successful programs.

Models for movement abound in society. One need only observe youngsters emulating their favorite sports hero, teenagers dancing to the latest rock group, or adults scampering to learn lifetime activities for which they had no opportunity during their youth. Individual models for movement are usually provided by groups that may be, to various degrees, open or closed to the masses of society. The descriptions of Human Movement provide a basis for examining and altering such models.

Various aspects of the discipline of Human Movement are applied in numerous professions that render a variety of services to people. Physical therapists, athletic trainers, human engineers, environmental planners, commercial recreation leaders, dance teachers, drama coaches, rescue squads, and drama producers, all have gained some knowledge, either formally or empirically, from the vast discipline of Human Movement, which they have applied to their specific professional endeavors.

Not only can the discipline be applied in helping others, but it also provides a basis for making many personal decisions. Each of us is continually faced with decisions to be made in an attempt to satisfy our many needs. The decisions we make are based on the knowledge and attitudes we have and on the pressures brought to bear upon us by the environment. There is little we can do about the latter, but much we can do about the former. As people gain more knowledge and experience, they are capable of making more decisions; decisions that will meet their needs as total individuals. The more people know about the discipline of Human Movement, the better and more informed their personal decisions about movement become.

For example, if people have the need to improve their strength to perform a task, they may look for various ways to develop this. They may try long bouts of exercise, intricate equipment advertised for this purpose, special vitamins recommended by friends, or they may behave in other trial and error activities with no guaranteed success. However, if they have some knowledge of the effects of various forms of movement on the structures and functions of the organism, they will be able to select forms of movement (weight training) and apply specific principles (overload, progression, resistance, etc.) to designing efficient and effective programs for meeting their needs (strength development).

The more people know about various disciplines, including the discipline of Human Movement, the better they are prepared to make personal decisions that will meet personal needs and professional applications to help others satisfy their needs.

No discipline is static. Each changes as researchers and practitioners discover new information and processes. The discipline of Human Movement is no exception. Formal research conducted in universities, government, industrial laboratories, and in clinical and field settings has continued to expand the parameters of knowledge in this area. Empirical observation of ongoing movement has led to the generation of hypotheses and principles that add to the fund of information and technique. Synthetic playing surfaces, new safety shoes for construction workers, new rehabilitative exercises for post-operative patients, and improved training methods for athletes are all examples of changes that have added to or resulted from changes in the discipline. As needs arise and resources become available, the discipline will continue to change, both in adding new understandings, skills, and processes, and in expelling ideas exposed as false in light of new knowledge.

No discipline exists in a vacuum. All interrelate with one another to some degree. Human Movement, because of its focus on the human being, integrates more with other disciplines than do most others. Examination of the model of the discipline proposed and diagrammed in the preface evidences this fact. Concepts of History, Philosophy, Psychology, Sociology, Physiology, Physics, and Chemistry can all be seen in this model. Not only does Human Movement draw upon other disciplines, but other disciplines draw upon it for their existence and application. Psychology must examine the role of vigorous, purposeful movement in understanding the role of emotions and behavior. Chemistry cannot avoid studying the physiology of exercise in its quest for new understanding of the effects of compounds on human functioning. And as the psychologists and chemists seek answers to questions that may not seem directly related to movement, they must move themselves, often in very precise ways, to discover the tenets of their discipline and new applications.

Indeed, Human Movement may well be the cornerstone of all other disciplines. When people cannot move, they have difficulty examining, manipulating, and discovering their total environment.

## References Cited

1. HOMEL, STEVEN R., AND TOM EVAUL. *Understanding Human Behavior: A Needs Approach.* Philadelphia, 1968.
2. EVAUL, TOM. "Where Are You Going? What Are You Going to Do?" *Curriculum Improvement in Secondary School Education.* Washington, D.C.: American Alliance for Health, Physical Education and Recreation, 1972, pp. 73–82.

# PART II

*Human Beings Function
Through Movement*

# 2

## Why Do Human Beings Move?

*John Cheffers / Tom Evaul*

### THEORIES OF MOVEMENT

People spend most of their waking hours moving—working, communicating, exercising, creating, playing, grooming, eating; sustained movements and brief ones; gross movements and fine ones; slow movements and fast ones.

The question "Why do human beings move?" may seem to have obvious answers. Yet the reasons underlying a given movement will vary among individuals. Ask a number of tennis players why they play the game, for example, and you will hear such answers as "for fun," "to meet others," "for exercise," and "to win." Some may even respond with a quizzical look and the words "I don't know," for people are not always aware of why they make many movements.

Many theories have been developed to explain why people do what they do. These theories, expounded by psychologists, sociologists, anthropologists, and other behavioral scientists may be categorized into four general groups.

### Homeostatic Theories

According to *homeostatic theories*, people do things in an attempt to maintain or restore a balance, or homeostasis, to their lives. That is, when some internal or external influence, either natural or contrived, acts to cause some aspect of life to get out of balance, the individual is motivated to do something in an attempt to restore homeostasis.

One of the earliest theories of this kind was the *surplus-energy theory*. Proponents of this theory (1, 2, 3) hold that the human organism generates energy which must be expended, some of it in work, the surplus in play.

A variation on this theme suggests that activity deprivation results in the building up of energy which must be expended through movement.

The *catharsis theory*, which stems from research in the area of aggressive behavior (4, 5), postulates that physical activity can serve as a cathartic release for aggression. Once released, homeostasis is regained.

Festinger (6) proposed that a *cognitive dissonance* or disturbance is created when a person meets a problem calling for a solution. Once the solution is found, the disturbance is removed and homeostasis returns. This theory of cognitive dissonance can explain one of the reasons people move to solve problems (7).

A kindred theory advanced by Berlyne (8) is concerned with conflicts that arise in the mind of individuals because of inconsistencies in their past experiences. The reconciliation of these inconsistencies requires both the acquisition of new knowledge and rethinking past experiences. When completed, the conflict is eliminated and homeostasis is achieved. Although this process, called *epistemic behavior*, deals primarily with cognitive activity, the seeking of new information can motivate a person to move.

## Developmental Theories

People pass through certain stages of development from birth to death. Intrinsic to the individual during these stages are certain motivations and facilitators for movement.

Many *developmental* or *learning theories* are predicated upon the influence of the environment. Jean Piaget believes that psychological development is self-generating, "activated by innate tendencies toward adaptation" (9, 10): the human being's curiosity, probing, and interacting with the environment initiates development within the individual. As the outside world influences the child, he or she develops, adapts, copes.

Piaget (10) has identified four stages of development through which all persons pass:

1. *Sensorimotor* (birth to two years)—During this stage a considerable amount of movement is used to explore the environment and respond to it.

2. *Preoperational* (two to seven years)—The child begins to form internal representations of the world and make movements based on these ideas.

3. *Concrete operations* (seven to eleven years)—At this stage the child's cognitive ability develops sufficiently to permit the planning and carrying out of concrete operations.

4. *Formal operations* (eleven onward)—The ability to think and communicate in abstract and theoretical terms characterizes this final stage. Planning and implementing movements for a wide range of purposes is now possible.

The basic premise underlying Piaget's theory is that with maturation and the accumulation of experiences, the individual's way of thinking about the world changes, which, in turn results in different behavioral or movement patterns.

Another theory, developed some time ago by Groos (1), suggests that people move in order to prepare themselves for later life. This theory is particularly applicable to children's play. Closely related to this is the *mimicry theory*, which describes play movement as an imitation of real-life experiences in a less threatening environment. Supporters of this theory have suggested that competitive sporting events such as the Olympics perhaps serve as substitutes for war.

One particularly interesting development theory is the *developmental task theory* suggested by Robert Havighurst (11).

The tasks an individual must learn—the developmental tasks of life
are those things that constitute healthy and satisfactory growth in our
society.

Havighurst defines a developmental task as a challenge which arises at a certain period in an individual's life and which is crucial to his continued growth and happiness: success will continue the growth pattern, failure will produce side effects tantamount to demotivation and stagnation. Havighurst identified six major developmental stages in life with appropriate task challenges:

1. *Developmental tasks of early childhood (birth–6 years)*—e.g., learning to walk, learning to talk, learning sex differences, learning to distinguish right from wrong.

2. *Developmental tasks of late childhood (6–12 years)*—e.g., learning tasks of games skills (throwing, catching, kicking, etc.), forming concepts, learning peer adjustment, developing a conscience, developing attitudes through social groups and institutions.

3. *Developmental tasks of adolescence (12–18 years)*—e.g., achieving patterns of motor development (sporting roles), achieving emo-

tional satisfaction, achieving masculine/feminine social roles, achieving career direction.

4. *Developmental tasks of adulthood (18–30 years)*—e.g., selecting a mate, rearing children, assuming civic responsibilities, achieving maximum physical skill development.

5. *Developmental tasks of middle age (30–60 years)*—e.g., developing leisure time activities, adjusting to physiological changes, achieving career maturity and success, dealing with adolescent children and aging spouse.

6. *Developmental tasks of later maturity (60– onward)*—e.g., adjusting to tasks needed to maintain health, adjusting to deaths of friends and spouse, maintaining enthusiasm for goal achievement after retirement, maintaining physical living arrangements.

Havighurst emphasizes that an individual's movement patterns can be interrupted, rerouted, or even discontinued as a result of failure to deal with the various tasks confronted at any one of these stages.

## Arousal-seeking Theories

According to *arousal-seeking theories*, the human organism has a constant need for optimal arousal. Behaviors which generate this arousal tend to be learned; those which do not are discarded.

Physiological research has demonstrated the existence of a reticular arousal system (RAS) in the lower brain (12). This system is related to the cortex, which serves to inhibit or counterbalance the RAS. Increasing arousal tends to increase performance up to an optimal level, after which further arousal reduces performance.

Schultz (13) identified a drive, which he called *sensoristasis*, that impels the organism to strive to maintain sensory variation so that an optimal level of arousal is maintained. When behavior results in the optimal level of arousal, the positive effect reduces the drive.

A kindred theory developed by White (14) states that behavior is motivated by a need to demonstrate the ability to control or produce effects on the environment. As individuals interact with the environment and develops a degree of ability or competence, they gain the feeling of efficacy, of being in control. This feeling reinforces the behavior and serves as the motivation to continue attempts to achieve competence. To this theory White gives the name *competence-effectence*.

## Environmental Theories

According to *environmental theories*, the reinforcing and punishing effects of the environment on behavior tend to shape the movement patterns of the individual.

The *classical conditioning* experiments by Pavlov (15) demonstrated the effect of a reward on creating a bond between a stimulus and response. Thorndike (16) added the principles of primacy (first event experienced is retained), recency (newest event experienced is retained), and effect (successful performances tend to be repeated).

Skinner's (17) *operant conditioning* has led to a host of models for the modification of behavior. Simply stated, behavior which is rewarded or reinforced is learned; behavior that is not is eventually extinguished. Various schedules of reinforcement have been developed for controlling behavior.

## THE FIVE BASIC NEEDS

Underlying all these theories, however, seems to be some urge or need, not fully explained by these theories, which the individual is attempting to satisfy. Maslow (18) has proposed a *hierarchy of human needs* ranging from basic physiological needs through self-actualization; not until the lowest set of needs on the hierarchy is satisfied can the next set appear.

Homel and Evaul (19) have identified five dimensions of the human being: physical, emotional, social, intellectual, and spiritual. Every individual needs to grow and mature in each of these dimensions. This need for growth and maturation does not culminate with adolescence, for people continue to grow and mature throughout their lives.

This phenomenon is easily observed in the *physical dimension*, where growth is rapid during the formative years. However, the need for improved functioning never ceases, as evidenced by the number of adults and even senior citizens who take up new hobbies such as golf, yoga, and ceramics. Satisfaction of needs in this dimension requires not only food, clothing, and shelter, but opportunities to learn, practice, and perform new activities.

*Intellectual curiosity* is never quenched. The explorations of the child give way to rap sessions for young people and the urge to travel in adults, the purpose of each being the expansion of knowledge and conquest of the unknown. Not only does one's need for data acquisition continue, but ways of processing these data are also pursued.

The *social needs* of human beings seem insatiable. Parties, dances, singles bars, sports, and outings are just a few examples of the many activities in which people engage in an attempt to quench their thirst for social interaction and acceptance.

One need only observe the spectators at a sporting event, mountain-climbers scaling the face of a cliff, or children precariously balancing themselves on a piece of playground apparatus to see the need for *emotional stimulation* in action. This constant need embraces not only excitement, but the need for love and affection, too. As growth and maturation continue, the need for emotional control and acceptable forms of expression is manifested in conjunction with the need for social acceptance.

A final, and often overlooked, need of people is that of developing some sort of consistency in life—a philosophy, a set of values, attitudes, or beliefs which serve as a guide for decision making and behavior. These *spiritual needs* are satisfied by many activities. As one achieves success, finds a comfortable life-style, or is satisfied with personal behavior and adopts a goal in life, the spiritual dimension matures.

These five kinds of needs provide the motivation for human behavior. In an effort to satisfy these needs, people move: they farm, hunt, work, shop, and build to satisfy their physical needs; they explore, manipulate, travel, and observe in order to learn; they compete, cooperate, join, and participate in order to socialize; they perform for stimulation; they compare, experiment, and test in order to acquire values. All forms of movement can be used to satisfy human needs. Generally, more than one need is met by any given movement. Exercise (a physical need), acceptance (a social need), excitement (an emotional need), achieving an understanding of patterns of play (an intellectual need), and reinforcing attitudes about team work and sportsmanship (a spiritual need) can all result from, say, playing on a basketball team.

Sometimes, because of insufficient or distorted experiences, individuals misinterpret their needs and behave in ways that foster growth and maturation in one dimension at the expense of others. The "dumb athlete" stereotype of yesteryear exemplifies this behavior. Emphasis on growth in athletic prowess at the expense of intellectual, social, and spiritual needs seldom results in a fully satisfied person.

An understanding of these five types of human needs and the importance of balance for total person growth and maturation provides the basis for understanding why people move. Virtually everything people do represents an attempt to fulfill these needs. The importance of the discipline of Human Movement lies in helping the individual select the most efficient and effective form of movement to help meet personal needs.

## PHILOSOPHIES OF MOVEMENT

All theories have important philosophic implications. Endemic to every theory and the satisfaction of a need is a philosophy specific to understanding human behavior. A philosophy is a basic position that is predicated upon one's perception of reality, what one knows, what is valued, how one reasons, and the degree of one's personal sensitivity.

Four great philosophies—idealism, realism, pragmatism, and naturalism—have dominated the philosophic scene. In this chapter we have discussed these and added two others—nationalism and existentialism.

Each philosophy has been clarified and debated according to five perspectives which we have called cornerstones around which an individual philosophy is constructed. Figure 2-1 depicts these cornerstones: (1) questions about reality (metaphysics), (2) knowledge (epistemology), (3) values (axiology), (4) reason (logic), and (5) sensitivity (aesthetics).

Indeed, purists believe that a philosophy is not complete unless it has these five dimensions or perspectives. Be that as it may, heated debate has engaged philosophers for centuries over the respective merits of positions taken by adherents to the four great philosophies and their resultant illustrative behaviors.

### Naturalism

*The laws of nature determine movement.* The naturalists believe in the sanctity of natural biological law and prefer to leave their fate to its dictates. They believe that games, physical activities, and recreative pastimes grossly manipulate the natural environment and are sacrilegious,

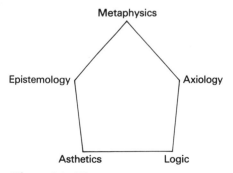

**Figure 2-1.** The cornerstones of philosophy.

even irrelevant. A dislocated knee resulting from playing such unnatural games as soccer or American football would be unpardonable, whereas a similar injury suffered during a rockclimbing expedition is "one of the natural risks in life." Hiking, jogging, swimming, riding, mountainclimbing, and skiing represent legitimate and worthy activities to the naturalist. Beauty is reflected in a radiant sunset and grief in the quick taking of life during a violent winter storm. People should not interfere with biological dictates. Survival is the reward of fitness and superior physical ability. Reality is nature's balance of power, and value lies in the organism's ability to overcome the forces that lead to extinction.

According to this theory, there is no place in the organism's existence for winning or losing, only for surviving. Equally, there is little value in false hierarchies, or in endeavors to equalize individual abilities, or in softness in the face of elemental hardness. Medicine is unnatural. Instead, preventive physiological and psychological measures are employed. Fitness is valued only in that it maintains and helps insure survival. Competition is sound if it insures survival from the elements, other threatening species, or personal indecision.

Naturalists believe in diverse movements provided the movements are in answer to demands from the natural human environment. Their answer to the question of why human beings move is simple. Movement is a biological necessity. Indeed, the naturalist cannot understand sedentary living or the tendency for people to destroy the natural protective mechanisms of the body against the elements and the natural laws. Western man, in particular, is precipitating eventual disaster through such preempting and tampering. Rousseau (28) advocated a socializing environment for the very young which was so free of human manipulation that the evils of current generations would be denied succeeding generations. His classic story, *Emile*, depicted the life of a young boy brought up with the animals of the forest. In it, he illustrated his intense frustration with artificiality and the shortcomings of the human environment. Rousseau wanted the children to "run free" and resented anything which prevented them from so doing. One can tell predominantly naturalistic beings through their choice of movement—the hiker, the adventurer, the swimmer, and the mountain climber.

Stemming from naturalism are two other frequently studied philosophies—realism and pragmatism (experimentalism).

## Realism

*Tangible rewards make movement essential.* The realist, like the naturalist, believes that movement is essential for survival. The realist's concerns, however, are more complicated. Physical appearances, job opportunities, and peer pressures play a greater role in this philosophy. Manipulation of the environment is proper provided that visibility needs and satisfaction of goal-oriented objectives are reached. The realist is strongly influenced by natural law but experiences small discomfort at having to adapt or manipulate the environment to circumstances. The realist, for instance, probably would see nothing wrong in the construction of homes and dwellings or in the maintenance of a 75° F temperature throughout winter. To the realist, comfort is more important than jousting against the earth's capricious climatic structures. The realist, as opposed to the naturalist, favors the use of medicines, for this apparently prolongs life. He would control population, for instance, through prevention of contact, contraception, and abortion rather than rely upon natural selection.

Seeing is believing to the realist. Sensitivity is task-related, and values depend on scientific review and stringent logical analysis. Knowledge is generated through research, especially after multiple replication and confirming measures have been undertaken. Realists tend to be cynical, practical, and incredulous. Some physical-fitness proponents in movement history, C. H. McCloy (20), Frederick Rand Rogers (21), and Thomas Kirk Cureton (22), have urged the profession to return to biological dictates connected primarily with optimal physical functioning. Sometimes realists identify with conservatives and sometimes they encourage radicalism. Their support depends on who is likely to win, since winning and losing are pivotal. Games, strategies, and recreational pursuits which satisfy immediately determined needs are important to the realist only if success is a likely outcome. Rarely does losing satisfy these needs, causing the realist to opt for winning combinations.

The realist moves to survive, to be visible, to obtain comfort, and to protect those loyal to the cause.

## Pragmatism

*Valid research findings are the best determinants for movement (Pragmatism).* Like the naturalist and the realist, the pragmatist sees movement as necessary for survival. The pragmatist's concept of the reasons for movement is based on information gained from the collection and interpretation of data. Accurate interpretation of human needs is determined through movement parameters. If movement for fun and play is found to be more important than movement for biological functioning, then the pragmatist will base curricula on the former. If, however, fun and play are found to be unimportant aspects of physical movement, then the pragmatist will lose interest in these two variables as organizing centers for movement curricula. Any movement which extends, rewards, or enriches life is defensible only insofar as it can be demonstrated. The continuous probing of the pragmatist into questions that were hitherto closed has demonstrated the good sense of the pragmatic approach to movement and living. If data can be provided to show that coming first or winning helps more individuals than it hinders, then the pragmatist will favor competition, especially under handicap conditions. If games and strategies are found to assist in need satisfaction, then they too will receive full endorsement. The pragmatist views as logical whatever makes most sense based on the data available and the understandings gained from empirical research. The pragmatist recognizes individual differences and values varied input. The conception of reality is constantly changing as human beings relentlessly pursue knowledge. Whereas the naturalist is sensitive to biological law and the realist to procedures which will produce results, the pragmatist tends to be more sensitive to the process itself. Sound research design and honest data-collection procedures are more important to the pragmatist than immediate conclusions, especially as these conclusions may change with increased knowledge and more accurate testing. The pragmatist favors any type of human movement which measurably helps human beings develop their potential and meet their needs. Manipulation of the environment is perfectly permissible provided that a balance of natural proceedings is maintained. John Dewey (23), one of the great proponents of pragmatism, represented this balance in the philosophic position referred to as relativism. Dewey believed that a relative position existed somewhere between the extreme polar boundaries of "total freedom" and "total manipulation." This relative position, which was not only discoverable but essential, was the one best suited to the specific environmental needs. Dewey believed that to find solutions to life's problems, pragmatic procedures were necessary through cooperative and meaningful learning based on personal experiences. It is true to say that the predominant philosophy in the United States of America during the twentieth century (with the exception of the sixties) was pragmatism.

The pragmatist moves as science determines. Most of the huge institutions in the United States have been constructed solely on experimental enquiry and the resultant data generated.

## Idealism

*Spiritual considerations are the prime cause for movement (Idealism).* Human movement is frequently spurred on by contingency goals. Although there appear to be tangible reasons for human movement whose validity can be measured, the real reasons that keep an individual active are not always measurable, nor associated with immediate goals, nor predicated upon the demands of biological law. The real reasons may be that indefinable human quest for spiritual satisfaction, for soul enrichment, and for religious peace. Many movements appear motivated by a belief in God or some other ethereal being. These movements defy logic, rational explanation, or empirical justification. What other reasons can be given for such events in history as the slaughter of the first-born child at the altar, the fasting of Mahatma Ghandi, the sacrifice of the Japanese kamikaze pilots, or the conquest of the South Pole or Mount Everest? No rational person would ever move in such a potentially destructive fashion unless there was an urgent motivation often referred to by the idealist as the quest for spiritual satisfaction.

Knowledge to the idealist is infinite, stretching across generations and beyond the boundaries of human perceptions. Logic is subservient to faith, and values tend to be measured in terms of what was attempted rather than what was achieved. To the idealist there are six winners in one foot race if all six have achieved their own best times and have expended their utmost in effort. It had to be an idealist who began the modern Olympic games: " . . . it is not the winning but the taking part. . . ." The idealist tends to be disappointed when people are incapable of abstract reasoning, acute sensitivity to artistic endeavor, or strong patriotism where national ideals are noble and altruistic. It is clear, of course, that all human beings possess a measure of idealism in their personal philosophy. The term—"honor among thieves"—exemplifies this point. Idealists take part in all activities that are supported by spiritual quest. These can range from movements in games and sports to movements in defense and war. The principal determinant of movement for the idealist is not seated in the movement itself, which may be quite irrelevant, but in the spiritual motive and ultimate goal envisaged by the ideal. Plato's theory of ideas or forms was generated from an idealistic base. He looked well beyond points of visibility to a universal, timeless form which existed both inside and outside the realm of human standards and human endeavors. Aphrodite's beauty, for instance, was not peculiar to the Greeks or to that Greek goddess herself. It was merely an example of the universal form of beauty which continues to exist throughout ages. Aphrodite represented beauty to the ancient Greeks as did Helen of Troy, just as Greta Garbo, Elizabeth Taylor, Marilyn Monroe, and Sophia Loren represent beauty to the modern mind. To the idealist, movement is a timeless form which has to be indulged in wherever spiritual dictates are involved. In this sense the idealistic philosophy differs in initiation and strength from the previous three phlosophies.

The twentieth century has seen the growth of two other philosophies which, although existent in other centuries, have become even more meaningful in current society. These philosophies appear to be at extreme ends of a continuum—*nationalism* and *existentialism*.

## Nationalism

*Collective movement serves the best interests of the team or the country. (Nationalism)* The philosophy of nationalism has an intense effect upon the movements of people. In a narrow sense, nationalism has been defined as efforts and loyalties of citizens directed toward the constitutional requirements and public policies of the state. At its extreme, nationalism has required unflagging loyalty, blind or uninformed conformity, and the relegation of individual interests to a low priority compared with matters of national interest. However, nationalism has not remained merely a philosophy binding followers to the dictates of specific political enclaves. We interpret nationalism to be a philosophy that is represented by the existence of teams or groups where people either willingly or unwillingly surrender their individual freedom to a collective or a communal structure. Under this definition, the whole question of teamwork, and team cooperation must be discussed. In the national or team interest, complete individual selection or choice of activities is restricted. Whereas it is true that individuals, initially, may elect to belong to a certain team, once members they are no longer free to do as they please. For instance, when students elect to belong to a college team, they restrict their subsequent activities. Students can elect to follow the dictates of the team or not to continue as members of that team, but these are the only choices that are entirely of their own choosing. In the team situation, their personal interests are subservient to the collective interest of the majority. In this context the nationalistic philosophy is followed at some time or other by every human being.

In the context of the nation, little choice is available on most vital issues. A child is born into a certain nation and is very much at the mercy of that nation's social and political environment. The child usually accepts the socializing product based upon earlier experiences that usually include maintaining citizenship and loyalty to national goals. When such an individual is conscripted into the armed forces, he or she may desert or relinquish citizenship, but this is rare. Most individuals accept the dictates of national constitutional law. Very little choice is available to the individual who must subjugate personal feelings to the will of the majority. An ever-present option for nationalists is the challenge to work

Figure 2-2. From the annals of combat comes a game. *(Courtesy of Boston University Photo Service)*

toward bringing about change from within the system, either through constitutional or group pressure efforts.

To the student of Human Movement, nationalistic philosophy motivates two broad categories of movements: (1) Movements which bring success, which hold high public esteem, and which serve to bind the team closer together. Such movements are heavily rewarded. (2) Movements which are unsuccessful, or which divide, or which produce antibodies. Such movements are denounced and excised from public recognition. Young Americans selected for the Olympic Games team may, for instance, be among the best two or three performers in the world but they are regarded as failures or "let downs" if they fail to win the coveted Gold Medal. Indeed, the United States, the Soviet Union, and the East Germans have skillfully combined to ruin the spirit of the modern Olympic Games through inordinately intense unofficial competition for national kudos. If the competition had remained in the ideal of friendly rivalry, many believers feel that the spirit of the games would have been preserved as an outstanding multinational festival of peace. Unfortunately the three giants, aided by a host of smaller nations, have reduced the Olympic Games to an undignified platform for jingoism, terrorism, and ostentation. Fortunately, there still remain many examples of teamwork which are exemplary. Most of the competitors at the Olympic Games are proud to represent their country and are delighted to be considered members of their respective teams despite the expectations of those whose condemnation or praise is solely dependent upon the athletes' final rankings.

Knowledge to a nationalist is centered around the most good for the most people, as is logic and reality. Values are determined by loyalty, effort, and compliance.

Those individuals who love belonging to teams or playing team games or who prefer company in their movement experiences identify strongly with the philosophy of nationalism and find abrasive individualists or self-oriented individuals sometimes impossible to endure. Many times they cannot understand divisive behavior and are usually supported in this feeling by the bulk of the citizenry. The trend today away from narrow team regulations and mindless rules is changing the concept of team loyalty, and certainly is making conformity more enlightened. A warning note must be sounded, however. Those who claim that the days of the hard-nosed, fist-pounding, bone-rattling coach are over may, unfortunately, be more than a little premature in their forecast.

## Existentialism

*All movement should be initiated by and cater to individual preference (Existentialism).* The existentialist places the individual at the central point in all decision making, claiming that movements are irrelevant and meaningless unless fully endorsed by the individual under consideration.

> . . . . his own ethical reality . . . ought to mean more to him than heaven and earth and all that therein is, more than six thousand years of human history . . . and more than science, thought or luck (24).

An individual may elect to join a team and may elect to surrender some personal freedoms, but the initial choice must be personal. No collective dictates are valid unless the individual elects to obey them.

> Being is near, and yet, since it must be sought after and can never be fully nor finally possessed, it is far off. It is by identifying ourselves and attaching ourselves, and by our full awareness and openness, that we keep close to being (25).

Many have argued that existentialism is the antithesis of nationalism. Their argument is based upon the statement that the individual is more important than the state and that states, in and of themselves, are bogus institutions. The existentialist, however, acknowledges the fact that human beings are social creatures and interdependent for many survival needs, but the existentialist strongly debates any mandatory authority which seizes the power of decision making from the individual.

> The savior and reality of human existence, its perils and triumphs, its bitterness and sweetness, are outside in the street (26).

Perhaps the dichotomous distinction between nationalism and existentialism is too absolute or, at least, premature. Although the existentialist is opposed to blind, nationalistic conformity, he is not opposed to the gathering together of groups of people with common interests and goals, and the performance of the necessary team work in order to accomplish those common goals. In these circumstances, the existentialist supports democratic group decision making and the position that once loyalty is promised, every endeavor should be made to uphold that promise. Therefore, the existentialist tends to favor recreational groups, problem-solving teams, and special-interest groups much more than huge nationwide institutions. In this regard, existentialists are not very far removed from many people who claim a nationalistic philosophy. Indeed, it could be argued that the existentialist may elect to be nationalistic if the need is there.

Many self-centered or selfish people claim adherence to existentialism and seek protection under its self-oriented umbrella; however, there appears to be a subtle difference between the self-development, self-discovery and self-actualization referred to by Maslow, Rogers, and others, and the inconsiderate self-centered, self-serving activities of people who are only interested in themselves.

> To overcome pessimism effectively and, at last to look with the eye of Goethe, full of love and goodwill (27).

This subtle difference is frequently misunderstood by people interpreting the actions of many dissidents in community affairs. Not all protesters, radicals, reformers, or dissidents are self-serving nor is their protest imbedded in disgruntled pique or irresponsible rejection. Many individuals who have elected to stand apart from the common group have done so for the common good. Socrates, Christ, Harvey, Luther, Schweitzer, Churchill, Ghandi, and Franklin are just a few examples. Although some claim that status quo is the sleeping sickness of all productive civilizations, it is equally clear that healthy societies have permitted dissidence and noncompliance. We believe that the child who does not always wish to play a game in an elementary-school gymnasium often represents healthy departure from the status quo and should not be penalized for noncompliance. If we are to believe Sören Kirkegaard, Jean Paul Sartre, and other existential leaders, we must recognize that the child is only

capable of being productive if personal movements are fully understood
and meaningful.

The existentialist tends not to be interested in team pursuits. Personal
freedom is revered, individual needs are the only meaningful reality, and
reasoning must be based on personal fulfillment.

> By the mere fact, indeed, that I am conscious of the motives which
> solicit my action . . . I am condemned to be free (28).

Although common values are shared, the existentialist is prepared to
be disloyal to kin and country where conflict of interest arises. The
existentialist is usually a sensitive person who exhorts others to respect
only what is personally meaningful. Many times personal decisions may
contradict the wishes of the majority. The United States experienced the
strength of existentialist philosophy during the 1960's and early 1970's
resulting from disillusionment with the war in Vietnam and the central
administration. Many movements of an existential origin were visible:
protest marches, desertions, defection from highly institutionalized teams,
and the rejection of many unexplained and traditional training practices.
Traditional values were questioned in what has been called by many the
"second American civil war." Like most revolutions, some good resulted.
Minorities received a better deal. The movement away from looking to
national figures for solutions to problems caused many people to take an
active role and search for more meaningful solutions to health problems,
fitness problems, and lifetime recreational needs. The updating of curricula in schools and colleges to expand opportunities for outdoor education, environmental education, leisure activities, and a more fundamental
look at what is really going on in Human Movement resulted. The essential institutions weathered the crisis, and perhaps a host of new non-
essential common movements replaced those existent prior to the 1960's,
but the judgment of history will most likely treat this generation well.
Certainly a wider variety and a more inclusive model of movement experiences has been made possible by the stimulation of those who follow
existential philosophy.

The existentialist moves according to the recognized and selected
needs of the individual, rejecting the call to arms of the local people on
any grounds other than personal perspective and choice (29).

## HISTORY OF MOVEMENT

Every theory and its underlying philosophic implication is accompanied by a happening or event which gives the theory visibility and valid-

ity. Human Movement cannot be studied in a vacuum. It can only be studied in the perspective of its historical events. Perhaps the reasons human beings move can be classified as physical reasons, curiosity reasons, sociocultural reasons, valuing reasons, and fun and recreational reasons.

## Physical Reasons for Human Movement

### Survival

From the earliest homonids to the struggling citizens of Bangladesh, the quest for survival has dominated human movement (30). Food, defense and protection against the elements have remained pivotal in this quest. Early man fished, gathered, and hunted for his food supply. Although expert use of stone was made, it took centuries for man to evolve from the food-gathering stage to the food-producing stage. Primitive people exist today in isolated geographical areas. The lake villagers in Papua, New Guinea function on similar premises as do the Bushmen of the Kalahari desert, and the aborigines in Australia. For these people, the intake and digestion of food is still dependent upon availability and the consequent conditioned hunger patterns. Prehistoric man needed to fashion weapons to protect his people from animate enemies. As a consequence, bronze and iron implements in the form of axes, flints, and other weapons were fashioned and maintained. Protection from the elements forced prehistoric man to devise clothes from animal skins and build shelters in caves and trees as well as to discover the supplemental warmth supplied by fire. The efforts of prehistoric man in meeting basic survival needs have continued to influence *Homo sapiens* during the course of history. Horses were harnessed for hunting and fighting around 2,000 B.C. The taming and training of this useful transportation medium necessitated specialized and dangerous movement patterns— movements which today continue to fascinate human beings. The Egyptians were convinced that drill and practice in the martial arts was essential for human survival. The Spartans prepared their youth from the first year to be self-dependent, to use but one top garment each year, and to sleep in rough barracks in order to prepare them for the harshness of the elements and human apathy. During the Crusades, English, French, and German knights elected to protect themselves from the enemy by covering themselves with armor, mail, and chains. Ill-advised though this practice was later revealed to be due to a lack of maneuverability, their preparations for survival necessitated the development of entirely new movement patterns. For many centuries human efforts at food production centered around the philosophy of self-sufficiency and subsistence farming. *Manorialism* is the term given to this economic system of the Middle Ages which supported the feudal-istic society and separate village self-sufficiency. Women played little part in earlier human efforts at defense and food gathering. Culturally they were regarded as tools for procreation and early family rearing.

Much of modern man's movement surrounding the supply of food and water is motivated by the desire to replace crude movements with mechanical substitutes. Automatic reapers, harvesters, sowers, and mod-ern factory equipment have dramatically changed the patterns of move-ment for the modern human being. Protection against the elements has undergone similar change. Although the Spartans did not tolerate over-protection, the same thing cannot be said of other generations since that time. The search for better quality protective garments, more permanent domestic shelters, and an easier way to construct those shelters has moti-vated the modern human being to less basic physical movement and more sedentary living. Protection against temperatures has improved as a result of insulatory equipment and greater human understanding of meteorol-ogy. From Cook's three great voyages to the Pacific, through Scott's tragic excursion to the South Pole, to the permanent bases that now settle An-tartica, human beings' survival movement patterns have improved mainly through the realization that skin and bone are insufficient protection. To-day the primitive people of Bangladesh, struggling to survive. are con-stant reminders of the continuing struggle that human beings have to protect the total population from starvation, human vindictiveness, and elemental caprice.

## Work

Both to survive and to secure a place in society, human beings have moved in order to work. That is, they have elected to contract personal services for remuneration through either primary or secondary compensa-tion. Professional work was entirely restricted to the male in earlier cen-turies, but today it is regarded, at least in most Western countries, as the prerogative of all with competitive abilities regardless of sex, creed, race, or political persuasion. In earlier civilizations compensation for work was made by the kings, dictators, or local leaders. The type of work was gen-erally physically oriented such as preparation for war, tilling the land, taming the beasts of burden, or transportation from one area to another. Today the sedentary nature of the work force has caused philosophers to ponder the ultimate wisdom of labor-saving devices. The motor car, the telephone, the typewriter, the air plane, and the computer are the major culprits.

Although in the past all citizens were expected to engage in some work, little individual genius was expected. Mostly the work patterns involved movements predetermined by the leaders and handed down as cultural heritage. Athens in the Golden Age was an exception. Each citizen was expected to make productive, creative contributions. Sparta was also an exception in that every male citizen was expected to be a teacher dedicated to the maintenance of the Spartan system. One of the reasons advanced for the fall of Rome was that during the building stages, hard work held a central place in ethical considerations, but eventually physical labor was delegated to other "inferior" beings.

When the Puritans landed in New England, they brought with them a *work ethic* that has dominated American attitudes to this day. It is only very recently that Americans have begun referring to a new ethic called the *leisure ethic*. This means that many citizens no longer will be required to work in order to meet community needs. Some visionaries foresee the day when only 10 percent of the population will be needed for work tasks. The remainder will embrace new occupations to enrich their local communities. This situation will produce, in contrast to the work ethic, an ethic which will require people to initiate, to develop, and to participate in activities which are spiritually productive and ethically sound but unrelated to rewards generated by financial enterprise. The era of leisure is nearly upon us. Its advent will introduce a host of more sophisticated and farther reaching psychosocial implications. New bartering media, new educational objectives, and revised administrative expertise will accompany the leisure era. It is not hard to see that the effect of the leisure ethic on human movement in the coming era will be of equal strength to the effect of the work ethic demonstrated by the Puritans in their times.

## Curiosity Reasons for Human Movement

One of the principal characteristics evident in the human advance to dominate the earth has been the drive to satisfy a basic curiosity.

Sir Edmund Hilary and Tensing Norkay scaled the summit of Mount Everest, the world's second highest mountain peak. The summit itself is a desolate, wind-swept, gale-strewn, ice-covered rock with impermanent views and exposure hazards. The title "God forsaken" could be applied. Yet these two great men, accompanied by others in support, and preceded by a long list of intrepid adventurers, never hesitated in their quest to conquer Everest. On these slopes men and women have perished, fortunes have been lost, and cruel sacrifices have been made. The mountain had little political or economical advantage and the ultimate rewards certainly were not based on geographical occupation. Why then would so many people move in such an urgent and dangerous fashion? The only sensible explanation from our viewpoint lies in the insatiable quest for discovery, adventure, and the satisfaction of curiosity. Although some historians maintain that necessity is the mother of invention, we propose that this is not always so. Curiosity is its own motive for diverse and disparate movement. When John Uelses began experimenting with the fiberglass pole vault pole at La Salle College in 1959 and 1960, he was experimenting with a tool that was later to revolutionize the sport. Curious to improve the pole's capacity to help him move, Uelses made use of a phenomenon that had been earlier expressed by some users of the bamboo pole and other theorists who were anxious to establish new competitive feats. Dick Fosbury revolutionized the art of high jumping by developing a technique which contravened most of the principles taught and practiced before his time. He adopted a curve approach; he went over backwards head first; he sprinted to the bar; he used a single armed take-off; and he took off from the outside foot. Almost all of these new techniques were later established to be mechanically sound, although one can imagine the derision and comical disregard Fosbury's earlier attempts must have received.

There have been eras in human history characterized by a strong drive to satisfy curiosity, and there have been eras where curiosity or probing criticism of the status quo has been suppressed. The individualism of the Greeks led to a creative age. The gods created by the Greeks were really super humans with the same whims and weaknesses of human beings. It almost seems as though the Greeks were satisfying a curiosity for what human beings might be like if they were not so fragile, impermanent, and restricted by chance. Their gods were pillars of love, fleet-footedness, wisdom, and strength, and their actions very human. Perhaps this fantasy by the Greeks has given us an unfortunate legacy, too, in handing down a dichotomy of body and mind which has continued to hinder our efforts to identify and establish a sound and valid discipline for Human Movement.

The era of the Dark Ages was characterized by such repression of free physical expression that curiosity, dissidence, and scientific enquiry were almost totally repressed. The era of the Renaissance and the Reformation, however, can only be characterized as towering beacons dedicated to the satisfaction of a global curiosity. For instance, universities were born during the Middle Ages, although society was singularly slow in throwing off the mantle of Church and State domination. The many princedoms established after the breakdown of the old Roman Empire so splintered scholastic effort that the world took centuries to redevelop a concerted global curiosity. It was in a handful of tiny Italian princedoms that the cradle of scientific enquiry was regenerated, and the flame of original thought rekindled.

John Locke, the brilliant English political philosopher, was one of the few acceptable free thinkers of his time. He maintained that a child should not be regarded as a little adult, but as a developing, growing, curious being, needing self-discipline and above all the freedom and encouragement to process the data gained through the senses into meaningful and conceptual generalizations. Locke's perceptual theory, later called the "Tabula Rasa Theory," has continued to influence human thinking to this day. Rousseau, the discredited Frenchman, held out against state and parental domination of the child during the earlier growth periods. He insisted that children, allowed to run free, would not develop the vindictiveness or the paranoia of the surrounding adult world. In his efforts to dignify the curiosity processes in the young child, Rousseau showed the strong influence of John Locke.

In current movement theory, efforts have been made to base movement analysis on the curiosity approach. Rudolph Laban and Ruth Morison in the 1950's and 1960's have advocated the teaching of movement through appeals to curiosity. They believe that such questions as "Who Can?", "How can we?", "Can you?", whet the human appetite, producing a deeper and wider ranging pattern of human movement than traditional movement patterns dictated to children by expert elders. The intense research thrust of the twentieth century to validate hypotheses epitomizes human curiosity. An hypothesis is nothing more than a shrewd guess at the likely truth of an undiscovered parameter. The quest to establish the validity of the multitude of hypotheses researched in modern science can be described as monumental, evidence par excellence of the drive in all human beings to satisfy their curiosity. Discovery in movement is motivated likewise.

## Societal and Cultural Reasons for Human Movement

Perhaps we can divide these reasons into five categories:

a. Conformity or nonconformity
b. Prestige and social rank
c. Religious influences
d. Political influences
e. Human and institutional adjustment resulting from changes in technology and material.

### Conformity and Nonconformity

Throughout history human beings have gathered in groups to survive. This has necessitated the development of communicative symbolism, mutual interdependence, systems of governance, and protective regulations. Prehistoric man hunted and lived in packs with precarious survival needs dominating their movement patterns. Today the assembly of human beings into much larger groups called countries coupled with the advance of knowledge has done much to make survival less precarious, but it has not substantially altered the conflict and distrust existing among human beings. A human being is forced either to conform or not to conform to the immediate social environment. An individual may either adjust freely, conform under pressure, or reject the immediate social environment.

Rejection or nonconformity is the harder of the alternatives. Rejection can emanate from illogical hatred or uncontrolled emotions, as was the case when Nazi Germany rejected the Jewish population in the 1930's and 1940's, or it can arise from controlled logical analysis as evidenced by the American rejection of militaristic German gymnastic systems during the 1850's. The effect of intergroup and intragroup rejection nearly always brings some form of vindictive retaliation. Religious leaders were burned as heretics during the Reformation and the lives of many other reformers were threatened during those unsettled years. The Dutch scholar, Erasmus, is a notable example of a humanist refusing to accept the traditional truths embraced and revered from earlier Greek and Roman times. The continual refusal of the British philosopher, Bertrand Russell, to accept the structure of British society during the nineteenth and twentieth centuries resulted in his ostracism from the ruling elite and the reluctance on the part of many British people to accept him as a towering genius. The refusal of some United States athletes to represent their country at the Olympic Games has caused much personal discomfort. Indeed it has become fashionable for college basketball champions to bypass the United States Olympic basketball team in order to hasten the filling of their fiscal coffers.

Most human beings conform to cultural pressures. Many knowingly and without question accept inferior status. They are informed, but rather than change they prefer to retain their original status.

One of the authors held a conversation with a group of South African Olympic athletes just before their country's expulsion from international sport in 1968. Some of the athletes involved expressed disagreement with the national policies that had led to their expulsion, but they maintained a willingness to abide by the decision as they preferred to remain South African citizens. Their desire to maintain national citizenship was unflinching even in the face of fractured goals and aborted dreams.

The Western papers usually make hay of any Soviet athlete who defects to the West during trips abroad. However, since the Russian entry into world sport in 1952, most of their star athletes have elected to return to their country. They have witnessed the degrees of freedom outside Russia and have often been heard to lament the lack of personal freedom within their own country. Although in possession of this privileged information, they have returned.

Sometimes human movement has been motivated by blind acceptance of community norms. The children of Israel expressed such fear of God that their total dependence, as expressed through prophets, led them to obey the Torah and the Talmud with strong moral purity. Whenever they strayed from their religious beliefs and their movements degenerated into heathenistic display, the tragedies that befell them were interpreted as direct punishment from their God. Similar unbending faith and loyalty was expected from the Spartan youths who were conscripted for life, and from the German populace under Adolph Hitler. Erasmus suggested that conformity, based upon ignorance and superstition, was the real enemy of mankind. He advocated and exemplified the critical probing and investigative spirit of the Renaissance.

Most human beings adjust to meet changing needs either within the group or within themselves. As a result of their travels, the early Crusaders introduced new foods and different cooking methods to Western civilization. They underscored the need for money, credit, a form of public banking, and improved measures to reduce the terrible health hazards of their times. The knights found, too, that they had to adjust their personal philosophies as a result of contact with the infidels. Far-reaching adjustments were required after President Theodore Roosevelt issued his famous edict in 1905 to the American football enthusiasts. He directed them to clean up or close up, a directive which resulted in the introduction of the forward pass and restrictions which fundamentally changed the nature of the game. Consistent and continuous changes are made by alert sporting bodies in the hope of keeping their institutions healthy. Individuals have to make personal changes also to adjust to socio-cultural pressures for conformity.

## Prestige and Social Rank

Individual differences have led some people in every generation either to be considered or to consider themselves of greater importance than other individuals. Social ranking, which is discussed more fully in Chapter 7, is an unfortunate fact of life. The rank or position of a person usually determines his value. In closed societies social rank and prestige are determined before birth. The caste system in India, which persists to this day, feudalism in Europe during the Dark Ages, and the patriarchal dynasties of China until 1949 are vivid reminders of the restricting influence that social ranking has upon the average citizen. Efforts to overcome the crippling restraints of social ranking are evident as early as 700 B.C. in Egypt, where successful soldiers from the ranks managed to buy their freedom with the spoils of war or through their heroic deeds in battle. There are similar examples from Greece and Rome but, by and large, the world has had to wait until the nineteenth and twentieth century for a wholesale onslaught against the forces creating inequality. The efforts of the United States in the 1960's–1970's to establish equal rights for all citizens have met with such forceful resistance that change has taken place only in small spurts. Discrimination, prejudice, exclusion, even cruelty have followed in the wake of voluntary efforts to integrate the races. The opposition has been so strong that frustrated reformers and humanitarians have been forced to use the unpopular medium of the courts to press through with needed change.

By contrast, efforts in other countries leave a great deal to be desired. India persists in its rigid caste system. Although the government has made it possible for members of the castes to mingle with each other in such sports as cricket, tennis, and field hockey, only a handful of enlightened athletes have crossed the rigid caste barriers. In spite of the efforts of Mahatma Ghandi and Pandit Nehru, the five major castes are still decided at birth and the lives of all Indians are patterned accordingly. There are the Brahmans (priests and teachers), the Kshatriyas (government men), the Vaisyas (businessmen and farmers), the Sudras (servants) and, of course, the Untouchables. These castes within the Hindu religion predetermine prestige and with it the opportunities for physical activity and expression. The Sikhs (followers of a religious group founded in India in the sixteenth century and distinguished for rejecting idolatry and the Hindu caste system) traditionally have been the great athletes of India. Distinguished by their colorful turbans and flowing beards, the Sikhs have led the world at various times in field hockey, track and field, and cricket. In the past, they have not taken kindly, however, to the intrusion of other faiths into their midst. A person born into prejudice has a permanent millstone around his neck. The nature of the physical activity frequently points to the rank of the participants. Polo is a sport played only by the nobility, the higher ranking on the social scale. Yachting and tennis are only now engaged in by the general ranks of citizenry.

## Religion

Religion exists in some form or another in every tribe on this earth's surface. Its existence provides compelling evidence that spiritual concerns are uppermost in collective human behavior. The ancient Olympic

Games, first recorded in the eighteenth century B.C., initially contained but one athletic event—running once around the stadium or 200 yards. The remainder of the five-day festival was taken up with religious festivity. The evangelizing of the Christian Church, the dissemination of Islam, and the Thirty Years War that plagued post-Reformation Germany give ample illustration of the extent of the universal effect that religion has had upon civilization. Indeed, most sporting festivals were outgrowths either of armed conflict or of religious celebrations. Ceremonial games, dances, and exhibitions were done to either please or displease the gods. These games have led to the founding of myths about heroes and their deeds, establishing ideals which every generation conforms to or rebels against. Religious beliefs have motivated movements to cause rain, to increase fertility, to exorcise demons, and to cure illness. In general, religion has tended to produce conformity of movement such as marching, kneeling, praying, and gesturing, but every so often it encourages radical movements such as fighting or disruptive actions such as Christ's overturning the pharisaical money tables in the temple. Oriental religions produce movements that reflect similar conformity through the martial arts and the special locomotor activities of shuffling or traversing.

The political decisions that ostracized the various religious groups in Europe resulted in widespread colonization of the New World. The Puritans migrated to New England, the Anglicans to Virginia, the Quakers to Pennsylvania, the Huguenots to the Carolinas, and the Dutch Reformed to New York. Spurred by the splintering of the original Holy Roman Empire, a counter reformation took place within the Catholic Church, dating from the Council of Trent. Under the Jesuits, the Catholics also colonized the New World, introducing vigorous physical activity and a plethora of European-oriented movements to the indigenous peoples of the Americas.

The rise of movements associated with chivalric education during the sixteenth, seventeenth, and eighteenth century in Europe, mainly evidenced through courts and religious festivals, has had enormous effect upon the people of the twentieth century. Refusing to accept the tenets of barbarism, the Church divorced itself from what was considered the insane barbaric norms of tent living and nomadic venture, and concerned itself with establishing attitudes of loyalty to God, king, and country. These attitudes fostered respect for women and children, unselfishness and praise, humble courage and enterprise. This unique era was characterized by the bow and curtsy, the grabbing of the hat from the head in the presence of superior individuals, the walking backwards away from important dignitaries whilst still facing them, and the noble gesturing of delicate sophisticated people.

## Politics

For good or evil, national and local politics have continued to influence human movement in incredible fashion. Mass nationalistic movement has characterized dictatorships, whereas existential individualized movement has characterized countries permitting a free political system. The great need for visibility has forced all politicians into advocating and supporting community based movement programs. Most politicians effectively manage to use the sporting institutions to suit their political aspirations. Every President of the United States since William Taft has been on hand to throw out the first ball on opening day of the baseball season. Cuban dictator, Fidel Castro, was sufficiently shrewd to know that strong athletic achievements on the local and national sporting scene would help support his regime. Accordingly he imported plane loads of Russian and Eastern European specialists to upgrade the quality of Cuban sport. Success was reached when the Cuban basketball team defeated the United States basketball team in the Pan American Games in 1971 and Pedro Perez triple jumped to a world record in track and field. Political leaders capitalize on the effect a sporting hero has on small countries. The late Abebe Bikila of Ethiopia, John Aki Bua of Uganda, and the brilliant distance runners headed by Kipchoge Keino of Kenya have made struggling governments highly visible.

Some politicians have used the medium of sport for ignoble reasons, as with Nero in Ancient Rome, and the Organization of African States (OAS), in the expulsion of the Rhodesians from the Olympic Games. Indeed, it has been argued that although politics and sport, especially at the international level, appear to be inseparable, each time a politician or political party uses sport for selfish leverage, humankind is the loser. Not always has the State taken selfish advantage of athletic endeavor. The Greek polis or city state, around 500 B.C. and for some time thereafter, seems to have established a healthy balance between individual and group needs. Although the Greek sportsman was strongly individualistic and was given every opportunity to develop personal qualities, he was constantly mindful of the needs of others in the community. The remarkable development of what the Greeks called the all-round man has continued to serve as a model through the centuries. The polis encouraged the Greek citizen to make his own laws, to serve in the army, to act in community plays, to sculpture, to evaluate the arts, to make music, and to devote time to keeping himself physically fit while still earning a decent living. This versatility has been the dominant model for educators in the twentieth century.

National politics in Germany have strongly influenced the development of movement in that country. Frederick Jahn emphasized gymnastics for nationalistic liberation and national identity (early 1800's). Adolph Spiess preferred formal gymnastics for use in the schools (early 1800's). Koch advocated playgrounds for fun and free play (1800's). Karl Fischer established a strong youth movement (1900–1915), and Carl Diem supported the Turners and sports youth movement to develop skills for nationalistic reasons during reconstruction (1918–1933). Adolf Hitler seized upon the great potential of a highly integrated and emotion charged youth program for indoctrination, toughening, military training, and selective breeding purposes (1933–45). Since the Holocaust, Liselot Diem has emphasized reconstruction through sports and clubs and individualistic body movements for peaceful reasons (1945–present). Physically, the Germans are an enormously talented people, and the forms of movement they have adopted have closely paralleled their political fortunes.

The presence of internal politics inside sporting bodies, teams, and movement families is perhaps even more divisive than the effect of national politics. In general, it is true to say that where groups have maintained either harmony or a balance of political power, they have achieved their goals and have maintained popular appeal.

It would be quite erroneous for us to suggest that only detrimental effects accrue from the use of sport as a political weapon. The sending of an inferior and friendly table tennis team to China by the United States in 1973 opened the way for political discussion at the central government level. Using "ping pong diplomacy," the two major powers introduced their detente intentions to their people through the medium of sport.

## Technology

Human beings have consistently adapted their movement to the demands of technological advance. From the discovery of the spear to the intricate movements necessary to operate a tiny space capsule, human beings have developed and practiced a plethora of specific movements. Much of the movement adaptation has unfortunately been brought about through conflict. The development of movements necessary for self-defense and aggression against others has continued into recent times. Some erstwhile weapons such as cannon shot, javelins, discuses, swords, and arrows are now used for sport instead of destruction. It is interesting to note that where human beings have developed techniques for aggression, sports have assimilated the techniques for peaceful competition. Rifle shooting, parachute jumping, sky diving, and orienteering are all enjoyable peaceful activities which had their origins in recent conflict technology. In sports the influence of technological advance has been revolutionary. The development of the fiberglass pole changed the nature of vaulting techniques as did the introduction of new paddles for canoeing and oars for rowing. Each time important technological discoveries have been made, human beings have demonstrated an ingenious capacity to construct new movements.

## Value Reasons for Human Movement

Throughout history, human beings have placed a high value on movement. Movements which have been revered in some eras and in some lands have been found repulsive in others. Few people today are publicly for bear baiting, cock fighting, or throwing objects at some unfortunate villain locked in a pillory. The modern generation has devised its own form of movement which it values more highly than that of previous generations, and which, in turn, will probably earn the condemnation of future generations. Examples of movements falling in this category might well be karate, the friendly exchanges on the line in America football, boxing, and roller derby. Human beings place a high value on movement if it requires hard work for success. Professional athletes are admired for their skill and respected for their dedication. No athlete could qualify for the ancient Olympic games without training for 10 months prior to participating. The athlete is expected to be in perfect physical shape and of strong mind as well.

This ethic, that of the spoils going to the strong, the good, and the deserving, has preoccupied the value systems of most of the world's religious dynasties. Christianity, Confucianism, Taoism, Buddhism, Islam, and the Ancestral Dynasties (particularly the Ming dynasty of China) have valued the work ethic. They have preached the principle of moderation with a balance between the body and the mind. Disciples denounced Greek professionalism because of its overspecialization which made men slaves to their speciality, their jaws, and their bellies, and which caused overdevelopment of certain parts of their body usually at the expense of the mind. (While most philosophers interpret Plato as a great exponent of body efficiency, some, notably John Fairs, emphasize Plato's denigration of the body) (33). Emanual Kant put forward the body-mind dichotomy in keeping with some of the Greek teachings, but the authors do not accept the existence of this dichotomy, preferring to side with many of the Biblical scholars and John Dewey who assert that the mind and body are indivisible.

The question of values in movement is also closely allied to the question of accreditation to permit movement. In the United States today only trained specialists are permitted to teach movement in reputable institutions. A host of minor accreditations are also evident. Clubs and schools require specialists with experience and a general education. While a complicated system of licensing has grown up, unions and collective bargaining agencies to police those licenses have developed. A person must be a qualified specialist to operate equipment, teach lessons, and coach sporting teams. This has been accompanied by the bureaucratization and humbug of the self-styled expert with relatively worthless "degrees" hiding behind institutions, but in the main, the system of accreditation is a sound mechanism to protect the community from unscrupulous, ill-qualified and single-minded individuals. The values implied in licensing directly correlate with the ethical values of the immediate environment. Not all philosophers have agreed with this accreditation process. John Jacques Rousseau would have been appalled by this structure. "Everything is good as it comes from the hands of the creator; everything degenerates in the hands of man" (31). Rousseau wanted no accreditation at all, he wanted a "hands off" policy with human movement. One has to postulate on the extent to which rigor spasms would set in with the eminent French philosopher wherever he might be over the development of the events sponsored by the NCAA and professional sporting bodies in the United States today.

Of particular interest to the student of Human Movement over the ages has been the phenomenon of what is called psychosomatic illness. The derivation of the word *psychosomatic* stems from two Greek words: *psyche* refers to higher, nonmaterial, immortal realms; *soma* refers to the weaker, real matter. The term implies that people with psychosomatic illnesses are revealing, through apparently unaffected body parts, physical illnesses of the higher realm. This explains why even thorough physical examinations fail to reveal the root cause of some illnesses. Hypochondriacs are accused of psychosomatic illness, frequently without sympathy. The belief in black magic, especially in underdeveloped tribes and peoples, can make psychosomatic illness fatal. The Australian aborigine, for instance, will fade into death if he is cursed through witchcraft by the simple action of having an enemy point a certain type of bone at him. Endeavors by medicos, psychologists, and religious leaders to reverse the effect of the "pointing of the bone" generally have failed. In many parts of the world, including some advanced countries, the existence of psychosomatic illness remains a real problem and general cure is still a mystery.

One cannot leave the discussion of values in Human Movement without referring to the question of aesthetics in sport. The lithe body, the graceful dancer, the agile gymnast, and the limber sprinter have long thrilled competitors and spectators alike. The Greeks idolized the beauty of movement, the Romans respected it, the cultural climate of the Dark Ages feared it, and the Renaissance enthusiasts embraced it. It is true to say that every generation has placed supreme value on excellence and smoothness of movement performance and has gladly thrust its highest rewards in that direction.

## Recreational Reasons for Human Movement

Perhaps the most cogent and compelling reason why humans have moved throughout history is that it produces fun, recreation, adventure, excitement, enjoyment, and good feelings. In the twelfth century, the Pope outlawed jousting tournaments, and in the sixteenth century Queen Elizabeth forbade the playing of "footy ball" (a hybrid form of soccer) on the village greens in England. In 1650, Oliver Cromwell told the people of England that they must stop dancing and other village games. The simple truth is that human beings have defied all attempts through the ages to restrict their pleasure gained from physical activity. Equipment shortages have not been effective either. During World War II as the bombs were falling on London, Britishers, young and old, played soccer or cricket in the underground with rolled up paper for balls and brollies for bats. And in the olden days, it appears they had equal ingenuity. "When the great Fen . . . is frozen . . . some tie bones to their feet and under their heels . . . (and) do slide as swiftly as a bird flyeth in the air, or an arrow out of a cross bow" (32).

It is safe to conclude that perhaps the strongest reason for human movement lies in the direct enjoyment that people derive from participation in the amazingly diverse movement patterns available to them (33).

Any discussion concerning reasons for human movement would be incomplete without at least brief reference to the substance of human movement. What people do either explains or is caused by why they do it. We have chosen a sampling of two typical student days from the perspective of two levels of the maturation process.

## THE STUDENT'S DAY:   A MOVEMENT PLETHORA

The theories, the undergirding needs replete with philosophical and historical context, are still removed from the average student. Why does the average college student move? What does his or her day look like? Is there any difference between the undergraduate and the graduate? Agree or disagree with us if you will—that is your prerogative—but there is no

**Figure 2-3.** Moving for fun. *(Courtesy of Carol Rossvold)*

doubting that the average student demonstrates a plethora of movements each day in the ordinary course of existence.

## Part I   THE UNDERGRADUATE

The harsh "burrring" of the alarm, the end of dreams, the reality of the dawn—the first rays of the sun. First movements are to attend to the alarm—the rising, the relieving, the washing, the brushing, and the dressing. Downstairs and on to the kitchen with its indescribable pleasures—the masticating, the paring, the swallowing, the burping.

Then to class, precariously, for 8 a.m. is alien time to a student. The books feel so heavy. Anita is always smiling; you have to smile back; she seems eager to converse—the talking, the walking, the side-stepping, the laughing. The morning class is boring, deadly dull. The professor is addicted to lecturing, to pacing and pontificating—the listening, the doodling, the leaning, the crossing of legs, the drooping of eyelids, the slumping of posture, the quiet drumming of fingers and occasionally the wry smiling and the mischievous gesturing.

Class is out, the sun is full now and the coffee drinkable. There is time for a quick game of ball with two friends and one stranger—the running, the dodging, the catching, the throwing, the bumping, the calling, the falling, the panting, the sweating, the dunking for baskets, and the leaping for leftovers.

A hasty lunch follows the game. Can't waste precious time sitting and filling—more standing, carrying, bartering, reaching, stirring, ladeling, spreading, forking, munching, laughing, and complaining. Musn't be late for afternoon lectures which are two miles away on the other side of the campus. James has a small vehicle which purports to transport. He has too many clients—the squeezing, the gripping, the swaying, the crunching, the tightening, the peering at fleeting legs and wobbling rumps, and the swapping of secrets. Finally the stopping, the stretching, the jesting, more laughing.

We all like the biology teacher. He is the antithesis of most liberal arts teachers—he is interested in teaching. We enjoy his humor and frequently urge him to cancel busywork assignments, sometimes with success. He enjoys us too—the interacting, the pointing, the questioning, the gesturing, the nodding, the desk thumping, the drawing, the peering through eyeglasses, the subtle lens adjusting, the page flipping, the writing, the hand waving, the bolstering, and the discovering.

The wrestling coach knows we have a party tonight so in Pavlovian spirit he decides to prepare us—the running in place, the pushing, the pulling, the bending, the jumping, the grunting, the grappling, the grabbing, the heaving, the straining, and then the lush warmth of hot soapy water cascading over our gnarled and knotted skins.

More supper but not much to eat because the evening is to be a formal dinner party and we wish to impress. The dressing is not normal, but formal and strained—the brushing, the scraping, the drying, the scenting, the buttoning, the peering, the fingering, the adjusting, the fastening, the smoothing, the straightening, the shrugging, the flicking, and finally the consulting with friends. A short drive to Mary Lou's where nods and hand clasps and assurances of reasonable time series are given; a genuine, final wave to concerned but nice parents. Alone at last—the smiling, the clasping, the brief hugging, the excited chattering, the whistling, the lively conversing, and the enthusing. The dinner dance, as all dinner dances do, goes swimmingly--the pouring, the quaffing, the hearty laughing; then the dancing, the twirling, the romping, the wobbling, the thrusting, the touching, the slowing, the holding, the whispering, the swaying, the tingling, the brushing, the squeezing.

The party is over and the rendezvous with the clock becomes a battle between compliance and defiance, the parting joust is unrequited—the embracing, the grasping, the persuading, the urging, the panting, the shaking, the pressing, but as ever, the withholding, the denying, the apologizing, the accepting, the gallant accepting, and the pressing for future calendar pursuing. And there is just sufficient energy left for the final brushing, disrobing, and dropping with measured breathing and lengthy snorting.

## Part II   THE GRADUATE STUDENT*

Its not quite dawn yet. My lover can't sleep, my baby can't sleep. They are both tossing and turning so guess who else wakes up. The sun isn't even up yet. Mornings are for sleeping but my lover can't sleep. First movements of the day? Something gentle to put my lover to sleep. I sleep again until the sun climbs up. I rise, stretch, tiptoe out, have tea and fruit, tiptoe back, and dress silently in the quiet of the morning. I move like a cat down the hall to the room with the couch, curl up and read existentialism for an hour with yet unfocused eyes. Gosh! This stuff is thick. At last, time to leave. Peek in on my lover. Still sleeping. Good. Start my car. No spark. Heck! Open the hood. Jiggle the carburetor. Now it starts. Off I go. Broom! Broom! Park near the lecture halls and walk briskly to class, breathing deeply. The cold air feels good. Sit and rap with classmates and teachers on existentialism for three hours. Go and buy Rollo May's book. Ask smiling fellow if he owns the busy bookstore since he is so cheerful. The cash register dings. He says, "Why yes. And did you know that it takes less muscles to smile than frown?" I think about that walking out slowly, but in the cold my speed picks up automatically. Back to the car. Back home. My lover is studying. I greet him and go to put some food in the oven. We share the mail and discuss existentialism. We eat and I go off to shower and change for the afternoon classes. A letter has to be written and people drop in to share their experiences. Back in the car, back to school, and up three flights of stairs before I stop to catch my breath. This small inner being glows within. On to the fourth floor students mill around flapping drop and add slips in my face. Please, can I take off my coat? No, this class is closed. Yes, there will be an open session next week. The mats are laid out and we begin. My yoga classes are going well. We are concerned with posture and remedy. I move through kyphosis, lordosis, and scoliosis. The lights go off and the students relax deeply

*Written by a student in answer to the simple question—Why Do You Move? Due to the very personal nature of her communication the student's name has been withheld.

while I walk and talk softly. Lights back on with final instructions for next week. I return home, greet friends, have fruit, and go up to my room. I must read some psychology but I'm so sleepy. In a short while the lights are off. I don't want to move again for a long time.

## References Cited

1. GROOS, K. *The Play of Animals.* Translated by E. L. Baldwin. New York: Appleton, 1898.

2. SPENCER, H. *Principles of Psychology.* 3rd ed. Vol. 2, part 1. New York: Appleton, 1896.

3. TOLEMAN, E. C. *Purposive Behavior in Animals and Men.* New York: Century, 1932. (Reprint ed., New York: Meredith, 1967.)

4. BERKOWITZ, L. "Aggressive Cues in Aggressive Behavior and Hostility Catharsis." *Psychological Review* 71 (1964): 104–22.

5. MALLICK, S. K., and B. R. McCANDLESS. "A Study of Catharsis of Aggression." *Journal of Personality and Social Psychology* 4 (1966): 591–96.

6. FESTINGER, LEON. *A Theory of Cognitive Dissonance.* Stanford, Calif.: Stanford University Press, 1957.

7. ARONSON, ELLIOTT. *The Social Animal.* San Francisco: Freeman, 1972.

8. BERLYNE, D. E. *Conflict, Arousal, and Curiosity.* New York: McGraw-Hill, 1960.

9. MUSSEN, PAUL HENRY; JOHN JANEWAY CONGER; and JEROME KAGAN. *Child Development and Personality.* 3rd ed. New York: Harper & Row, 1969.

10. PIAGET, JEAN. *The Construction of Reality in the Child.* New York: Basic Books, 1954.

11. HAVIGHURST, R. J. *Developmental Tasks and Education.* 3rd ed. New York: David McKay, 1972.

12. DUFFY, E. "The Psychological Significance of the Concept of 'Arousal' or 'Activation,' " *Psychological Review* 64 (1957): 91–96.

13. SCHULTZ, D. D. *Sensory Restriction: Effects on Behavior.* New York: Academic Press, 1965.

14. WHITE, R. W. "Motivation Reconsidered: The Concept of Competence." *Psychological Review* 66, (1959): 297–333.

15. PAVLOV, I. P. *Conditioned Reflexes.* Oxford: Clarendon Press, 1927.

16. THORNDIKE, E. L. *Animal Intelligence.* New York: Macmillan, 1911.

17. SKINNER, B. F. *The Behavior of Organisms.* New York: Appleton-Century-Crofts, 1938.

18. MASLOW, A. H. "Self Adualization and Beyond," in *Challenges of Humanistic Psychology.* J. F. T. Bugental (ed.). New York: McGraw Hill, 1967.

19. HOMEL, STEVEN, and TOM EVAUL. *Understanding Human Behavior—A Needs Approach.* The authors, Temple University, Philadelphia: 1968.

20. McCloy, C. H. "A Return to Fundamentals," Proceedings, The College Physical Education Association, 1941.

21. Rogers, Frederick Rand. *Physical Capacity Test.* New York: Barnes, 1931.

22. Cureton, Thomas Kirk. *Physical Fitness and Dynamic Health.* New York: Dial Press, 1965.

23. Dewey, John. "My Pedagogue Creed," *Classics in Education.* New York: Philosophical Library, 1966.

24. Kierkegaard, Sören. *Unscientific Postscript*, 1846, translated 1941 in *Six Existential Thinkers.* New York: Macmillan, 1952.

25. Blackham, H. J. "On Heidegger's Thoughts on 'Being.'" in *Six Existential Thinkers,* New York: Macmillan, 1952.

26. Blackham, H. J. "On Karl Jaspers," in *Six Existential Thinkers.* New York: Macmillan, 1952

27. Nietzche, Friedrich. "The Will to Power," *Six Existential Thinkers.* New York: Macmillan, 1952.

28. Sartre, Jean-Paul. "L'etre et Le Neant," *Six Existential Thinkers.* New York: Macmillan, 1952.

29. The philosophical section has drawn information from a number of specialized texts, most of them related to human movement.

—Kleinman, Seymour. "Philosophy and Physical Education," in *Physical Education: An Interdisciplinary Approach. Singer* et al (ed.). New York: Macmillan, 1972.

—Felshin, Jan. *More Than Movement: An Introduction to Physical Education.* Philadelphia: Lea and Febiger, 1972.

—Ziegler, Earle F. *Problems in the History and Philosophy of Physical Education and Sport.* Englewood Cliffs, N.J.: Prentice-Hall, 1968.

Blackham, II. J., "On Karl Jaspers," in *Six Existential Thinkers.* New York Harper Torch Books, 1959.

—McIntosh, Peter C. *Sport in Society.* London: C. A. Watts, 1963.

—Hellison, Donald R. *Humanistic Physical Education.* Englewood Cliffs, N.J.: Prentice-Hall, 1973.

—Kroll, Walter P. *Perspectives in Physical Education.* New York: Academic Press, 1971.

—McLuhan, Marshall, and George Leonard. "The Future of Education," *Look,* 31 (February 21, 1967): 23 F.

30. King, C. Harold. *A History of Civilization.* Philadelphia: Charles Scribner's Sons, 1956.

31. Rousseau, Jean Jacques. *Emile, Julie and Other Writings.* R. L. Archer (ed.). New York: Barrow's Educational Series, 1964.

32. Van Dalen, Deobold B., and Bruce L. Bennett. *A World History of Physical Education,* Second Edition. Englewood Cliffs, N.J.: Prentice-Hall, 1971.

33. The historical section has drawn information from many texts, some long gone from human memory. Included are the more recent and important of texts speaking to the history of physical education.

—VAN DALEN, DEOBOLD B. and BRUCE L. BENNETT. *A World History of Physical Education*, 2d ed. Englewood Cliffs, N.J.: Prentice-Hall, 1971.

—HACKENSMITH, C. W. *History of Physical Education.* New York: Harper and Row, 1966.

—GERBER, ELLEN W. *Innovators and Institutions in Physical Education.* Philadelphia: Lea and Febiger, 1971.

## Bibliography

RICE, EMMETT, JOHN L. HUTCHINSON, and MABEL LEE. *A Brief History of Physical Education*, 5th ed. New York: Ronald Press, 1969.

WESTON, ARTHUR. *The Making of American Physical Education.* New York: Appleton Century Crofts, 1962.

## SECTION B

The quality and quantity of Human Movement
affect and are affected by factors within
the individual and the environment.

# 3

## What Enables Human Beings to Move and What Happens to Them Physiologically When They Do?

*Arne Olson*

The basis of all human movement is the body. The structure and function of the human body is remarkable. No artificial machine approaches this natural machine's ability to adapt over time and situation. The first component of the discipline which needs to be mastered is the structure (anatomy) and function (physiology) of the human organism.

## THE SKELETAL SYSTEM

*A human being is composed of muscles, bones, and nerves which are designed to allow the person to move efficiently and effectively.* Human beings are composed primarily of a complex arrangement of approximately 700 muscles, 200 bones, many miles of nerve tissue which serve as a control system, and a "support circulation and digestive system." The muscle-bone-nerve "machine" is the primary factor in movement and forms "simple machines" of the lever type. Joints help facilitate and control movement. A typical arrangement is shown in Figure 3-1. The fuel for the machine is provided by the support systems.

### Composition and Function

*The skeleton, made up of a number of articulating bones of various sizes and shapes, serves to support, protect, and move the body as well as*

49

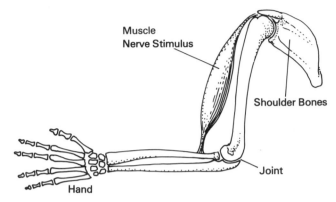

**Figure** 3-1. The      Bone-Muscle      Machine.
1. Nerve stimulus makes muscle shorten.
2. If upper arm is stabilized, the lower arm
rises when the muscle shortens.

*store calcium and manufacture blood cells.* The framework of the human
body is the skeletal system, which consists of approximately 206 different
bones (see Figure 3-2). Bone in adults is about 50 percent water and other
fluids, and 50 percent solids. Approximately one third of the solids are
organic or living matter and two thirds are inorganic or nonliving matter.
If the organic matter and water were removed, the rest of the bone would
crumble easily. However, if the inorganic salts were removed, the bones
would be very flexible. The long bones, for example, could then be tied
in a knot. After one matures, the proportion of water and organic material decreases with age. This is why the bones of older people become
brittle and break easily, and do not heal rapidly following a break.

Bone tissue itself is sparsely permeated with blood vessels, lymph channels, and nerve branches. However, covering the outside of the bones,
except at the articulating surfaces, is a connective tissue called periosteum
which is richly supplied with blood vessels and nerve branches. Most of
the pain associated with bone injuries (bruises or breaks) originates in
this tissue. Muscles attach to the periosteum of the bone. Another function of this connective tissue is the manufacture of bone cells.

Although there are many different types of bones, they can be classified into four categories according to their general shape. First, there are
the long bones found mostly in the arms and legs. Their primary purpose
is support, but they have a hollow center called the medullary canal or
cavity, which contains bone marrow. The function of this marrow is to
manufacture red blood cells. White blood cells and platelets, which are
necessary for clotting, are also produced here. A second type of bone

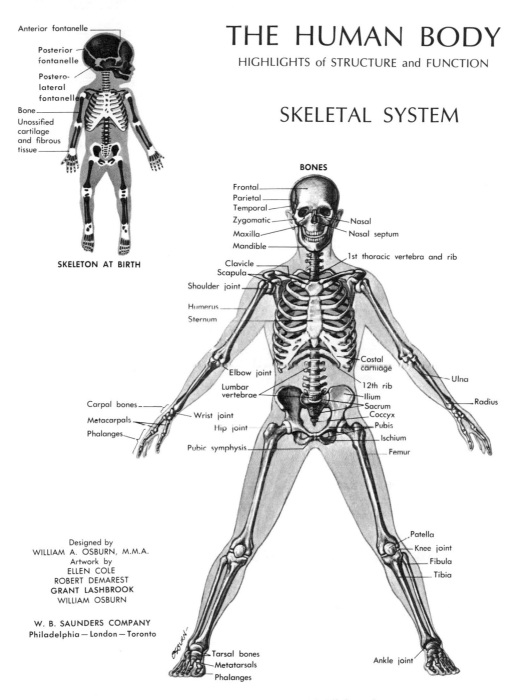

# THE HUMAN BODY
## HIGHLIGHTS of STRUCTURE and FUNCTION

## SKELETAL SYSTEM

**Anterior fontanelle**

**Posterior fontanelle**

**Postero-lateral fontanelle**

**Bone**

**Unossified cartilage and fibrous tissue**

**SKELETON AT BIRTH**

**BONES**

Frontal
Parietal
Temporal
Zygomatic — Nasal
Maxilla — Nasal septum
Mandible
1st thoracic vertebra and rib
Clavicle
Scapula
Shoulder joint
Humerus
Sternum
Costal cartilage
Elbow joint — Ulna
Lumbar vertebrae — 12th rib
Carpal bones — Ilium
Metacarpals — Sacrum — Radius
Phalanges — Coccyx
Wrist joint — Pubis
Hip joint — Ischium
Pubic symphysis — Femur
Patella
Knee joint
Fibula
Tibia

Designed by
WILLIAM A. OSBURN, M.M.A.
Artwork by
ELLEN COLE
ROBERT DEMAREST
**GRANT LASHBROOK**
WILLIAM OSBURN

W. B. SAUNDERS COMPANY
Philadelphia — London — Toronto

Tarsal bones
Metatarsals — Ankle joint
Phalanges

**Figure 3-2.** The Human Body: highlights of structure and function. (From Miller and Burt, *Good Health*. Reprinted by permission of W. B. Saunders Company and the authors.)

**Plate 1**

found in the body is the short bone. This type of bone, located in the hands and feet, is solid throughout and primarily serves to give shape and provide a base for movement in these areas. The third type, the flat bone, primarily serves to protect vital organs of the body. The skull and ribs are examples of this classification. The fourth class is the irregular shaped bones. These bones have different shapes and are each designed for a specific movement or other purpose.

At the point of contact between two or more bones are joints. There are three types of joints in the human body; immovable, slightly movable, and freely movable. Examples of the different types of joints include the immovable sutures of the skull, the slightly movable joints between the vertebrae, and the freely movable ball and socket joint at the shoulder and at the hip.

The structure of the bones and the type of joint limit the motion or specialize the functions of the various parts of the body. For example, the hinge joint at the elbow makes it easy to raise food and drinks to the mouth but requires a complex movement at the shoulder joint in order to throw a ball.

## Growth

*The skeletal system goes through a growth and modification process the same as any other tissues of the body, and is capable of repairing damage.*

### Maturation

*Bones grow by depositing new bone tissue at several sites.*

*An infant's bones are small and are composed of a great deal of cartilage.*

Almost everyone is aware of the "soft spot" in an infant's skull. This is an incomplete formation of the frontal, parietal, and occipital bones. These "soft spots" are actually cartilage and membranous precursor of bone. They permit the skull to be slightly changed in shape during the birth process, and serve as the sites for expansion of the skull as the infant's head grows. The soft spots harden within the first few months, but fusion of the skull bones is incomplete until adult size is reached. The other bones also are mainly cartilage and do not ossify until later. It is possible to injure an infant's bones by picking a baby up by its arms, or by forcing an infant to stand or try to stand too early.

## Ossification

*A person's skeletal age can be determined by the ossification of certain bones.* The growth of the skeleton follows an orderly sequence, with its completion somewhere between ages 18 and 22. An x-ray of the wrist and hand is used to determine a child's skeletal age, since each of the carpals and metacarpals are formed and developed at certain specific ages. The long bones of the body also ossify fully in a regular time pattern. Children can have advanced or retarded skeletal growth relative to their chronological age. When children are growing rapidly at and near puberty it would perhaps be more sound to group children for certain competitive activities by skeletal maturity rather than grade level or body size alone. Girls tend to mature earlier than boys both skeletally and physiologically.

*Children are more susceptible to certain kinds of bone injuries prior to the complete ossification of their long bones.* The wisdom of allowing elementary and junior high school children to participate in such contact sports as football and wrestling has been questioned on the grounds that bone injuries may result in permanent malformation. Even in noncontact activities like baseball, there are possibilities for bone injuries related to the growth areas. A tragic example is the "little league" pitcher who concentrates on throwing hard for long periods in strong twisting actions such as occur in attempting to throw a "curveball." Among such children, stress fractures of the humerus, radius, or ulna are sometimes found, as well as actual separation of the epiphysis at the growth plate. Knowledge about the growth and structure of children's bones should be taken into consideration when planning or conducting such programs. There is no evidence of any sex difference in susceptibility to skeletal injuries of these types. Most are found in males probably because there are more males in these activities.

## Growth Sites and Repair

*There are two primary sites for growth in long bones.*

*Length. Bones increase in length from specialized growth areas called epiphyseal plates.* The epiphyseal plates are located at the junction between the shaft (diaphysis) and ends (epiphysis). Osteoblasts (bone primary cells) are found here in large number, and they increase the length of the bone by adding new tissue and moving the ends of the bone farther apart. Once these growth sites close, the bone may no longer grow in length.

*Diameter. Bones increase in diameter by adding new layers of bone itself just under the periosteum on the outside of the bone itself.* As hard bone is deposited on the outside of the shaft of a long bone, osteoclasts (bone destroying cells) are removing bony deposits on the inside of the shaft so that a central cavity filled with spongy bone and marrow increases in size. Even in adulthood, bones can increase in diameter even though they do not increase in length.

*Bone Injury and Repair. Bones grow and develop in response to the stresses placed upon them.* Bearing heavy loads causes the malformation of certain bony structures to strengthen the areas most subject to the weight. The pull of muscles upon their points of attachment also causes the shaping and strengthening of certain areas.

*When a bone is fractured or injured, bone forming and destroying cells collect at the site and repair the damage.* In the process of healing, bone destroying cells attack the broken ends, "dissolving" some of the damaged portion, and the bone-forming cells reunite the bone. The whole process takes 6 to 8 weeks or often longer depending upon the location and severity of the injury.

Understanding the basic processes of growth and development of the skeletal system will enable teachers or coaches to select activities intelligently for various age groups, appropriate to their skeletal maturity or immaturity. Appropriate activities will neither overstress nor overprotect boys and girls beyond necessity.

## Individual Variations

*Individuals vary with respect to size, strength, and proportions of their skeletal system.*

### Length and Diameter

*Both bone length and bone diameters differ from individual to individual.* The lengths and thicknesses of bones determine an individual's overall frame size. These basic proportions are determined by heredity, with slight modification caused by the state of nutrition, injury, and illness. There is no evidence to indicate that exercise can make a person grow taller or shorter than the normal expectation. Relative length of bones is obvious and easy to observe by comparing height, length of trunk, hands, fingers, and toes. Thickness of bone is often estimated by measuring the circumference of the wrist, knee, or ankle.

## Body Proportion

*Body proportions vary among individuals.* Even though several individuals may be the same height, their proportions may differ greatly. Comparison of arm and leg length, trunk height, hand and foot size, shoulder width, or chest depth reveals a great variety of body proportions related to the skeleton. Some of these proportions show general patterns related to sex, race, or ethnic origin. Females, for instance, tend to have relatively wider hips, narrower shoulders, and shorter limbs than males. Negroes tend to have shorter trunks and longer limbs than Caucasians. Orientals tend to be generally shorter, with relatively shorter limbs than many Western races, and so on down the list. It must be noted, however, that these generalizations are based on "averages." A given individual might or might not fit the racial or sex pattern.

## Effects of Skeletal Variation

*Variations in skeletal structure and proportions can have a profound effect upon the movement capacities of a person.* It is obviously an advantage to be tall if one wants to be a basketball player or wide receiver, however, being tall is just as much a disadvantage to a jockey or gymnast. Certain activities are better for a person with a thick, massive skeleton, while others are favorable to the slight of build. A boxer or basketball player can utilize long arms to advantage, and a high jumper or hurdler is aided by long legs; whereas a weight lifter has to work against less leverage if he has shorter arms and legs. Wide shoulders give a leverage advantage in throwing or striking with the upper extremity. Each activity places specific body demands, giving those with ideal body proportions for that activity an edge over less ideally equipped persons. This is, of course, only a part of the complex set of traits and abilities which enable a person to be successful in a certain activity.

In addition, the general shape of the body is related to performance. A classification of the general body shape has been developed. One's body type is frequently called one's *somatotype*. Each person has some of the characteristics of the three pure somatotypes. Since a seven point rating system of the basic types is commonly used, a 4–4–4 would be classified as a midtype somatotype with each 4 representing a middle rating. The first of the three numbers in this ratio refers to the endomorphy or "ponderousness," with a typical dominant endomorph shape tending to be pear shaped. The middle number refers to mesomorphy or "muscularity" with the typical dominant mesomorph shape tending to be wedge shaped with narrow hips. The third number refers to ectomorphy or "thinness," and the typical dominant ectomorph shape tends to be linear and thin.

In summary, various body types tend to be advantageous or disadvantageous in various sports and other aspects of human movement. "He or she" seems to be made for this or that activity.

## THE MUSCULAR SYSTEM

### Composition and Function

*A muscle is made up of many muscle fibers which in turn are composed of many muscle cells which are the contractile or shortening elements.* The individual cells contain a complex arrangement of protein filaments (actin and myosin) and inactive connective tissue, which is essentially the cell membrane. A schematic representation is shown in Figure 3-3.

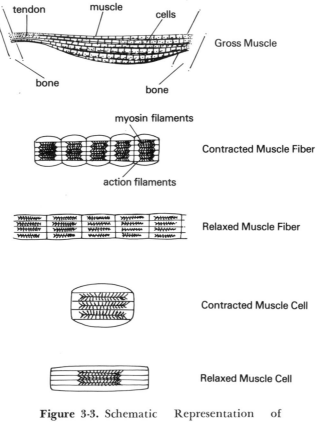

**Figure** 3-3. Schematic    Representation    of Muscle Structure.

*When the muscle is stimulated by the nerve an electro-chemical-physical reaction occurs at the myoneural (muscle nerve) junction.* The "cross bridges" in the individual muscle cell are schematically shown in Figure 3-3. They become very active when the muscle is stimulated and respond with a suction cup-like action as they appear to reach over to the nearby actin filaments and grab and pull toward the middle of the cell. Since the actin filaments being pulled are connected to the ends of the cells by thread-like connections, the two ends of the cells move closer to the middle and hence the overall muscle shortens. As also suggested by Figure 3-3, a shortening of all the cells in the fiber usually occurs as a generalized response of the cells when a nerve stimulates the muscle. This overall shortening results in the pulling on the tendons connecting the entire muscle to the bones at each end. The tendon is noncontractile in nature but has a slight elasticity. The arrangement of the fibers is different for the different muscles, resulting in a strength or range of movement advantage. In general, however, the configuration of muscles of the body is approximately the same for all human beings, but the amount of protein and energy sources present and the specific location of the tendon-bone connection of a bone varies considerably from person to person. This results in individual differences in quantity and quality of movement when the muscles are stimulated. These differences affect muscle size and strength as well as the skill of the movement.

*Nerve impulses which initiate movement originate in the central nervous system or in the muscles themselves.* The stimulus that triggers a muscular contraction is a nerve impulse. For a voluntary muscular movement, this impulse originates in the motor area of the cerebral cortex of the brain. It travels down the spinal cord, out the motor nerve to the junction of the muscle and nerve, called the *motor end plate.* When the nerve impulse arrives at the motor end plate, it stimulates the production of a chemical, acetylcoline. This chemical substance transmits the impulse across the short gap between the nerve ending and the muscle. It is then received by the muscle membrane (sarcolemma) and conducted through the membrane to the contractile substance (the myosin protein) within the cells, stimulating the cross bridges to grasp and pull on the actin filaments, which brings the "Z" lines closer together and consequently shortens the muscle fiber.

A single muscle fiber will contract maximally in response to any stimulus that is strong enough to excite it. This is known as the "all or none" law. The strength of the contraction of an entire muscle depends on the number of fibers contracting at any given time. Therefore, if a large number of fibers are stimulated at any time, the contraction will be stronger than if only a few are activated.

In addition to the impulses that come from the brain, there are impulses that originate within the muscles themselves. These impulses are called *kinesthetic sense impulses.* They allow an individual to have a feeling of a position and movement. In stroking a tennis ball, for example, a person can tell without looking the position of his hands and feet. Within the muscle itself, there is an organ called a *muscle spindle* that lies parallel to the muscle fiber. When the muscle is at normal length, it discharges nerve impulses of a certain frequency. If the muscle is stretched, the frequency of discharges increases proportionately to the amount of the stretch. The frequency with which these impulses are sent to the brain is interpreted as a "feeling of position." Another kinesthetic sense organ that is used by the brain to determine the position of the body is the Golgi tendon organ. This organ is located at the junction of the muscle fibers and the tendon at either end of the muscle in line with the muscle fibers. Golgi tendon organs are stretched both when the muscle is shortened and when it is lengthened, causing them to discharge nervous impulses. A third receptor is located within the joints themselves and is sensitive to the position and rate of movement of the joint. Thus, the brain is able to determine the relative position of body parts by interpreting the frequency of impulses sent by the muscle spindles, the Golgi tendon organs, and the joint receptors of the muscles involved.

A fourth kinesthetic sense organ used for this purpose is the Pacinian corpuscle. This organ transmits impulses when it is compressed or deformed. The Pacinian corpuscles are particularly prevalent in the sole of the foot. Increased pressure on the Pacinian corpuscle helps a person "feel" when he is leaning toward one side or the other.

In sports you try to involve the kinesthetic sense organs so that you will be able to make the right movement automatically without having to "think about" it. The brain is not involved in the stimulus-response action. However, if you think back over a movement (missed shot, bad throw, etc.), sometimes you are able to determine what you did wrong and make a conscious effort to correct it. The reflex movement is exhibited by the skilled performer who has conditioned the movement pattern so that his muscles will respond correctly to a specific stimulus.

In addition to the kinesthetic sense organs, the brain uses the more commonly known senses of sight, touch, and balance (the inner ear) to interpret the position and movements of the body.

*Changes occur as a result of exercise or training which depend on the quantity and quality of movement.* In the actual contractile process, a chemical change occurs to the adenosintriphosphate which is present in the muscle cell. In effect, a part of the molecule (a phosphate) is burned (oxidized) and this reaction gives off energy as well as heat as a waste product of the chemical action. The energy is used in the motion of the cross bridges and heat is dissipated through the body tissues. In an attempt to cool the body and bring it back to an equilibrium, you may sweat if the work is hard or long enough. The evaporation of the sweat results in a cooling effect. Because of the oxidation of the adenosintriphosphate, the potential or available energy stores of the cell is reduced. A person cannot continue to work if the replacement system cannot keep pace. Also, in the oxidation process, oxygen is used in the burning which results in energy release, as a person increases his respiration activity in order to make enough oxygen available. If either the energy supply or the oxygen supply gets too far behind, an exercising person will have to stop or slow his exercise rate because of muscle fatigue. If the exercise is general, the oxygen supply is used up first. If the effort is localized to a small group of muscles, the energy supply fails. This produces a chemical waste product of lactic acid, which may result in local muscle soreness if enough lactate is allowed to build up.

*Muscle soreness results from using muscles at a level and for a length of time at which they are not accustomed (trained) or because of minute injuries to the muscle-tendon junction area.* Occasional muscle soreness may be due to small physical tears that usually occur at the muscle-tendon connection, which is the weakest part of the machine. This soreness is distinguished from the type caused by lactate excess by its longer period of irritation. Another distinguishing feature is new soreness in the same location on another exercise day after apparent recovery, usually without as much effort expended. This soreness is due to the "retearing" of the incompletely healed injured fibers.

## Exercise and Training

*Movement changes body function to produce a training effect. The body goes through a training response and adapts to the new requirements when one exercises regularly.* This is accomplished by depositing or storing readily available sources of energy (such as adenosintriphosphate and phosphocreatine) and increasing the oxygen uptake and carrying capacity of the body. The quantity of glucose, a simple sugar (and a source of adenosintriphosphate, ATP, in the blood or of glycogen, a more complex sugar), with another source of ATP in the muscle cell itself increases with training as does the presence of phosphocreatine (PC). Both ATP and PC can provide a source of energy as the phosphate bond is released. The availability of energy allows a person who has exercised regularly to do more work—at least of the type for which he or she has trained and therefore adapted to. The oxygen carrying capacity of the blood and the greater affinity of the cells for oxygen also are increased as a person trains in ways that require a large oxygen supply. This, again, is an adaptation by a fantastic machine—the human body. This type of training, which is now referred to as aerobic training, results in an improvement of lung functions with hypertrophy of the diaphragm and increased diffusion capacity at the cellular level. The diffusion capacity results from a more efficient exchange in the capillary beds of the muscles and organs required to adapt to the exercise stress. As a by-product of the training process, the blood buffers, which are used to neutralize the lactic acid remaining from the incomplete chemical cycle of energy oxidation, may also increase. This occurs when a person has not yet adapted to an exercise experience or when adequate oxygen cannot be obtained. The blood buffers are not only increased in volume but also apparently become more efficient with regular exercise requiring their action.

*Recent evidence suggests exercise or training responses are quite specific to the type of workout and the specific muscles used.* Intense short-term work of a muscle cell results in gains in local glucose and glycogen storage and an increase in muscle protein filaments. This type of exercise is classified as anaerobic because oxygen is not a limitation factor. Anaerobic training results in an increase in the ATP-PC energy source available and also probably in an increased capability to use the ATP-PC energy source. The most efficient way of increasing this energy source is apparently work wherein the person exercises at an intensity which cannot be maintained for longer than approximately 30 seconds, for example, the sprint interval. The increase in protein results in hypertrophy, which is most efficiently developed through a progressive-heavy resistance overloading type of exercise (i.e. weight training—three sets of exercises with a weight that can only be lifted 6 repetitions maximum).

In order to increase his capability to use lactic acid as a source of energy, the person should work at an intensity that can only be continued for one or two minutes. This type of effort results in a maximum oxygen deficit and consequently a maximum build-up of lactate as a waste product. With training, the human body becomes more efficient in using lactate itself as a source of energy, although it can provide only a part of the required energy since the very nature of the substance is that it is a product of other energy activity.

The oxygen carrying and utilization systems are most efficiently developed through exercise efforts that are of the intensity that they can be continued for an approximate two minute period and are rather "total body" in requirement, such as running or swimming. Undoubtedly, several repeat all-out efforts of this type are needed during the workout in order to cause a training effect. This type of training results in an increase in the number of red blood cells which carry oxygen, diaphragm hypertrophy which helps pull air into more alveoli in the lungs, and possibly an increase in capillary beds in the muscles of the body which are stressed by the effort.

Because a waste product of muscle contraction is heat, some athletes need to dissipate heat efficiently, and a longer term exercise period, say 8–10 minutes maximum is recommended, so that the heat regulatory mechanisms are required to function at near maximum capacity.

In summary then, one's working capacity is affected by the type of exercise as well as the length and intensity of the stress. This fact is the basis for what is called the specificity and adaptation principles of training. The quality of work frequently referred to as skill also improves with repeated efforts because of the increased nerve-muscle-bone synchronization process, which is usually referred to as coordination.

*The results of movement depend upon the kind of movement as well as the length and intensity of the effort.* Externally a person is able to perform physical work or play when moving. In contrast, some movements are used to communicate in a nonverbal manner. Examples of the latter would be to attempt to increase the feeling and understanding of words by using your hands to describe the one that got away or using a dance creation to express "happiness," "sadness," or the "excitement of the movement." You can also perform in sports or games in a manner that brings personal satisfaction or possibly relaxation or change of pace. For many, including people of all ages, this activity provides an important portion of their current life.

Exercise or training of the aerobic type can result in improved physical health. People are able to increase the capillary beds in their heart, for example, through a training program. This increase would be helpful if one of the small arterioles became clogged with a blood clot or other material, since oxygen could still be supplied to the other heart muscle cells through the many adjacent capillary beds from other arterioles. Instead of a large area becoming scar tissue as a result of not being able to function because of the oxygen deficit, a "coronary thrombosis" would result in only a chest pain or angina and a small scar. In contrast, an extended period of convalescence might be required if the coronary collateral (heart circulation itself) was not able to find substitute routes to the area. Insofar as general circulation is improved, the body organs benefit in having their capabilities improved at least as their function depends upon the circulatory system.

## THE SUPPORT CIRCULATORY
## AND RESPIRATORY SYSTEMS

*The support circulatory and digestive systems must function optimally if the individual is to move freely.*

## The Circulatory System

*The circulatory system, consisting of the heart and vascular bed, transports the blood which carries oxygen and nutrients to the active cells and removes the waste products of metabolism.*

### The Vascular System

The major function of the circulatory system is to transport glucose and oxygen to the cells and to remove the waste products of metabolism. The circulatory system has two major components: the vascular system and the blood. The vascular system includes the heart (which pumps the blood), and the vascular bed (arteries, veins, and capillaries).

*The Heart.* The heart is a muscle the size of a clenched adult fist, located slightly to the left of the center of the chest. It is composed of an internal lining, the endocardium, surrounded by the cardiac muscle, which forms the bulk of the heart.

**Figure 3-4.** The heart and lungs give us the data. (*Courtesy of Argus Africa News Service.*)

The heart is divided into right and left sides. The left side contains the oxygenated blood which has just returned from the lungs (ready for distribution throughout the body), and the right side carries the non-oxygenated blood which has returned from the other parts of the body ready for the journey to the lungs. Each side is divided into an atrium and ventricle. Backward flow of blood is prevented by unidirectional valves. The tricuspid valve is located between the right atrium and ventricle and the bicuspid or mitral valve is located between the left atrium and ventricle. Semilunar valves are found at the junction of the heart and the aorta, and of the heart and the pulmonary artery.

The heart rate is controlled by nerves from the autonomic nervous system. Fibers from the parasympathetic system (vagus nerve) slow the heart rate while fibers from the sympathetic system speed up the heart rate. The dominance of vagal or sympathetic nerves is influenced by many factors. Muscular exercise, which requires more oxygen ($O_2$) and greater removal of carbon dioxide ($CO_2$) speeds up the heart rate. High temperature and humid condition also increase the heart rate and keep the rate up for a longer period following exercise. Body position (standing, sitting, lying, etc.) also influences heart rate. Both external factors (such as smoking, certain drugs, and alcohol) and internal factors (such as anxiety or infections) increase the heart rate.

A heart contraction starts in a localized portion of the right atrium called the *sinauricular node*. This site is sometimes called the *pacemaker*. From here, the contraction spreads out over the heart surface and can be studied on the electrocardiogram. When the heart contracts, the blood is forced out of the right and left auricles into the right and left ventricle, respectively. The contraction in the ventricles squeezes the blood from the right ventricle into the pulmonary artery, and from the left ventricle into the aorta. Contraction of the heart muscle is called *systole* and is subdivided into auricular and ventricular systole. The contractions of the ventricular muscle, the closing of the valves, and the blood flow all contribute to the vibrations of the first heart sound heard with a stethoscope. As the contraction force of the ventricle decreases, the blood, under high pressure from the stretched aorta, begins to move backwards. Immediately the semilunar valves snap shut, and the second heart sound is heard. When the heart relaxes following a contraction, blood rushes into the right atrium from the superior and inferior vena cava veins, and from the pulmonary veins into the left atrium. This relaxation is called *diastole* and is also subdivided into atrial and ventricular diastole. In a complete cardiac cycle, the systolic period is followed by a brief rest period and then the cycle begins again.

*The Vascular Bed.* There are three major divisions of the vascular system: the pulmonary (lung), the systemic, and the coronary or heart

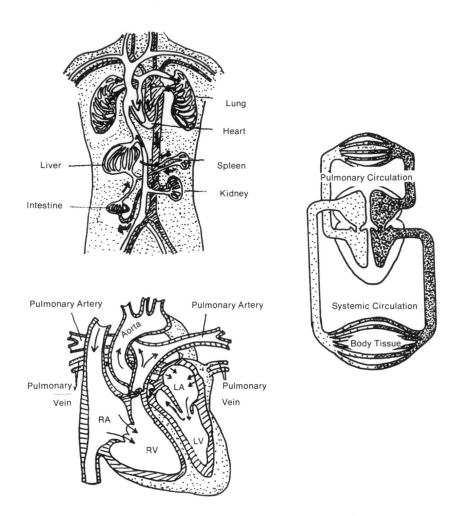

**Figure 3-5.** The Circulatory System.

circulation. Each of these systems has its own arteries, capillaries, and veins. The arteries carry the blood away from the heart. The pressure exerted by the blood against the wall of an artery is called the *blood pressure*, and it is different in all arteries. The usual blood pressure is determined by the pressure of the blood against the wall of the brachial artery just above the elbow. Blood pressure is highest during ventricular systole (systolic pressure) and lowest during the ventricular diastole (diastolic pressure). When blood pressure is reported, the systolic is given first followed by the diastolic pressure.

The arteries contain several layers of elastic tissue and smooth muscles

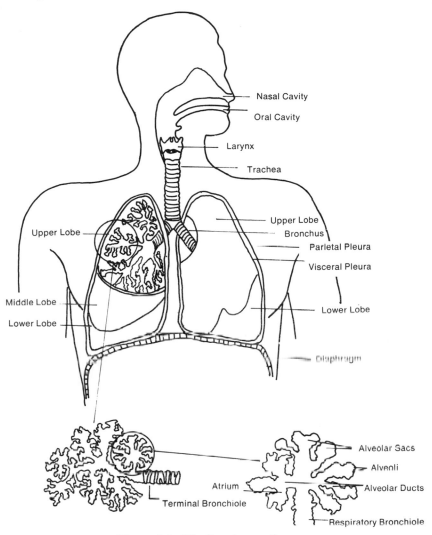

**Figure 3-6.** The Respiratory System.

that prevent rupture. When one ages, vessels are more likely to rupture because the tissue in the arteries loses its elasticity. If this rupture occurs in the brain, it is called a *stroke*. The arteries are occasionally obstructed by clots (thrombi) or other material that may stop the flow of blood. If an obstruction occurs in the coronary portion of the circulatory system, it is called a coronary thrombosis. When this results in nutrition and $O_2$ being cut off from these areas, tissue dies and permanent damage occurs.

The veins carry the blood back to the heart. The construction of veins is less complex than arteries. The walls of the veins are thinner and less elastic. Veins have unidirectional valves that prevent the backward flow of blood. Muscle contractions help squeeze the blood along in the veins. Since the valves allow the blood to go in only one direction, the blood is gradually forced back to the heart. The capillaries connect the arteries and the veins. These are the smallest of the blood vessels and consist of a single layer of endothelium tissue. The exchange of gases and nutrients with the cells and of gases in the lungs occurs through the walls of the capillaries.

### The Blood

The plasma portion of the blood consists mostly of water, which acts as a solvent. The remainder of the plasma, about 10 percent, is composed of dissolved solids and gases (primarily oxygen and carbon dioxide). Nutrients such as glucose, lipids (fats and fatlike substances) and amino acids make up most of the solids in the plasma. Ions of such substances as sodium, potassium, calcium, magnesium, chloride, bicarbonate, and phosphate are present in very small but specific amounts too. When this amount changes, the body makes adjustments to maintain the desired consistency either by storing the excess in other parts of the body or by eliminating it from the body. When the concentration drops below the necessary requirement, the plasma becomes more efficient in extracting these materials from foodstuffs. The plasma also contains the important blood proteins fibrinogen, albumin, and globulin, all of which contribute to blood viscosity and to the osmotic pressure of the blood. Fibrinogen is essential to blood clotting, and gamma globulin provides protection against certain foreign substances. Plasma also carries enzymes, antibodies, and hormones as well as some waste products which are eventually removed by the kidneys.

About 40 to 45 percent of the whole blood consists of solid materials. The cellular portion is almost entirely erythrocytes or red blood cells (4.5 to 5.0 million per cubic millimeter). The red coloring matter or hemoglobin in these cells carries nearly all the oxygen and about half the carbon dioxide transported by the blood. Hemoglobin has the ability to unite readily with oxygen. The resulting compound is called *oxyhemoglobin*. The oxyhemoglobin releases the oxygen near the tissues where it is needed. Then the oxyhemoglobin returns as hemoglobin to the heart and lungs where it recombines with more oxygen in the lungs and again travels to the tissues as oxyhemoglobin. The presence of oxyhemoglobin in the blood makes it a bright red, which is characteristic of arterial blood. When hemoglobin alone is present, a dark red color prevails, which is characteristic of venous blood.

The leukocytes, or white cells, are less numerous (five to nine thousand per cubic millimeter) than the red cells, and their primary function is to fight infection. By taking a "differential" white cell count, doctors can learn of the presence of an infection and its probable causes. They can tell how recently the infection has been contracted or if it has been present for a long time. They can tell if parasites or other foreign substances are involved. The platelets function in blood clotting and are the other solid constituent of whole blood.

## The Respiratory System

*Oxygen, necessary to conduct the metabolic processes of the body, is supplied primarily by the respiratory system.* All body cells metabolize, that is, carry on life processes. In order to do this they need the raw materials of food and oxygen. In the metabolic process, the cells produce waste products that must be removed from the area of the cells. The circulatory system fulfills the transportation needs, but the actual chemical reactions involved are the function of the respiratory system since the prerequisite for most of these reactions is oxygen.

Essentially, the respiratory system has four major purposes: (1) Lung ventilation in which carbon dioxide is exhaled and oxygen inhaled; (2) external respiration which is the exchange of carbon dioxide and oxygen between the lungs and the blood; (3) internal respiration which is the exchange of carbon dioxide and oxygen at the cell membrane; and (4) true respiration which is the actual oxidative process within the cell. Certain structural requirements must be met by the parts of the respiratory system where the processes occur. There must be a membrane thin enough to allow for the passage of gases. This membrane must be kept moist, because a dry membrane is impervious to the diffusion process. This membrane must be vascularized in order to circulate oxygen to the cells which need it and to move the carbon dioxide from the cells to the organs of respiration.

The main organs of respiration include the nose and mouth, the larynx, the trachea, and the lungs. Although air can be taken in either through the nose (nasal breathing) or through the mouth (oral breathing), nasal breathing has several advantages. The hairs at the entrance filter large particles of dirt. Foreign objects which are too small to be trapped by these hairs are trapped by the sticky mucous covering, the nasal epithelium. Nasal air is moistened so it does not dry the rest of the respiratory tract. Nasal air is heated by the larger number of blood vessels close to the nasal passage that raise the temperature of the air to near body temperature.

The air, after passing through the nasal passage, goes into the larynx through a valve-like opening that prevents food and liquid from entering this area. If food does get in, a choking reflex occurs and usually lasts until the food or liquid is removed. The larynx is also the location of the vocal cords. These cords are folds of tissue across the larynx and they vibrate as air passes by them, thus producing sounds. The larynx is continuous with the trachea below, although the trachea is supported by C-shaped cartilages to keep it from collapsing. The trachea divides into the two primary bronchi. These bronchi are also supported by ring-shaped cartilages and divide and subdivide into tubes of smaller diameter called the *bronchioles*. These become smaller alveolar ducts terminating in a small bulb, the alveolar sac. The alveolar sac is pocketed by small alveoli in which the actual exchange of gases takes place. The alveoli are surrounded by small blood vessels, the capillaries, which connect the pulmonary arteries and veins.

The lung tissue itself covers the respiratory tract soon after the trachea splits into the two bronchi. The thoracic cavity, in which the lungs are contained, is an airtight chamber whose volume may be changed by movement of the diaphragm and ribs. Ordinary inspiration occurs when air rushes in to occupy the extra space made available when the floor of the thoracic cage is pulled downward during contraction of the diaphragm (a strong, flat muscle that forms the floor of the thoracic cavity). Expiration is the outward rush of air occurring when the diaphragm contraction ceases and the thoracic cage collapses to its resting volume. The lungs are entirely passive during breathing. They behave as would a thin-walled balloon open to the atmosphere but otherwise enclosed in a partially evacuated space. Atmospheric pressure pushes the lungs closely against the inside wall of the thorax even when they are at rest. Between the outside of the lungs and this wall, a thin layer of fluid lubricates the surfaces, which are subject to continual movement against the inside wall and against one another during breathing. If the thorax is opened to the outside (e.g., an injury or surgery) the lungs will collapse.

The nerve center controlling both the rate and depth of breathing is located in the medulla oblongata of the brain. Because this center is affected by the amount of carbon dioxide in the blood stream, there is a direct relationship between this amount present and the rate and depth of breathing.

The lungs are completely empty at birth. After this, the lungs are never completely empty. The residual air, the amount of air that is left in the alveoli after the most forceful exhalation possible, averages about 1000 cubic centimeters (cc). This residual volume helps keep the small bronchioles and alveoli open. The amount of air normally flowing in and out of the lungs during regular quiet breathing is called *tidal air* and measures approximately 500 cc. Of course, more air can be taken into the lungs. This extra inhaled air, taken in during the most forceful inhalation, is called *complemental air*. It measures about 1600 cc. In similar fashion, more air can be exhaled after a normal exhalation. This air is called *supplemental air* and it, too, totals about 1600 cc. The total amount of air that can be taken into the lungs, which includes the complemental, supplemental, tidal air, and the residual volume, is called the lung capacity. When the residual volume is not included, this volume of air is called the *vital capacity*, which is the amount of air a person can expel from his lungs. The average vital capacity for an adult male is about 4200 cc, and for a female about 3700 cc.

External respiration is the exchange of oxygen and carbon dioxide between the alveolar air and the pulmonary capillaries. The concentration of oxygen in the alveoli is greater than it is in the capillaries, while the concentration of carbon dioxide is greater in the capillaries than it is in the alveoli. The thin squamous epithelium of the alveoli and another thin tissue forming the capillary wall separate the alveolar air from the blood and allow for diffusion. The oxygen and carbon dioxide each pass through the epithelia of the alveoli and the capillary, moving in a direction from the greater to the lesser concentration. The oxygen moves from the alveoli to the capillary and the carbon dioxide moves into the alveoli from the capillary.

Internal respiration takes place in the area of the tissues. The concentration of the oxygen in the blood stream is higher than in the tissue fluid surrounding the cells, while the concentration of carbon dioxide is higher in the tissue fluid than in the blood. The oxygen moves into the tissue fluid and the carbon dioxide moves from the tissue fluid into the blood.

## Circulatory-Respiratory Endurance

*Circulatory-respiratory endurance, which enables one to sustain general body activity for a prolonged time, is limited by the intensity of the activity, one's oxygen debt and one's oxygen intake capacity.* The main function of the circulatory system is to supply the active cells with oxygen and remove the waste products of metabolism, particularly carbon dioxide. The degree to which the circulatory system, in conjunction with the respiratory system, is able to fulfill this function during exercise is called circulatory-respiratory endurance. Stress on the circulatory and respiratory systems is caused by such general body activities as swimming and running, as opposed to such localized muscular efforts as sawing wood or lifting weights.

The ability to sustain physical activity under this type of stress depends on three factors: the amount of oxygen required to perform the activity, the oxygen debt capacity, and the maximum oxygen intake capacity of the individual performing the activity.

There are many factors that influence the amount of oxygen required to perform an activity; the quantity of the activity (walking a mile requires more oxygen than walking a half mile); the speed at which the activity is performed (running a half mile requires more oxygen than walking it); and the load carried (walking a half mile with a 30-pound pack on your back as opposed to just walking it without a pack). In turn, these factors are influenced by other factors such as body weight (heavy people carry a greater load) and skill (a skilled performer makes few wasted movements and therefore performs less activity). The greater the metabolic activity of a muscle, the greater will be the demand for oxygen. If the oxygen requirement for a certain activity can be decreased (e.g., through weight reduction, improved skill, etc.), then the individual will be able to sustain the activity for a longer period of time.

When the oxygen requirement for an activity exceeds the ability of the circulatory-respiratory system to keep up, a deficit-develops. Some of the metabolic processes of muscular activity are anaerobic (can take place without oxygen). Thus, a considerable amount of work can be done before sufficient waste products (carbon dioxide and lactic acid) build up to halt the activity. This build up is called *oxygen debt*. Most likely, you have experienced the symptoms of oxygen debt, better known as physical fatigue, during heavy exercise (breathlessness, muscular pain, dizziness, etc.). After the exercise is stopped, sufficient oxygen must be taken in to enable these waste products to be eliminated. This is why your respiratory and heart rates remain high for a period of time after the activity has been completed. As a result of certain types of endurance training activities, one's tolerance for oxygen debt and the ability to perform more activity are increased.

The final factor, maximum oxygen intake, is generally not limited by the respiratory systems. The increased rate and depth of breathing enables a sufficient amount of oxygen to be taken into the lungs. The ability of the blood to pick up and transport this oxygen to the active cells and remove the waste products of metabolism is the limiting factor in exercise. As a result of endurance training, there are several changes which take place in the structure and functioning of this system that enable it to move more blood at a faster rate, pick up more oxygen, and remove more waste products. These changes include the following:

1. Increase in the size and power of the heart muscles which results in an increase in stroke volume (volume of blood pumped with each ventricular contraction).

2. Increase in the number of capillaries in muscle (both coronary and skeletal) which makes more blood available to these muscles during activity.
3. Increase in the number of capillaries in the lungs making more area available for the exchange of oxygen and carbon dioxide.
4. Increase in the number of red blood cells in circulation enabling more oxygen to be carried to the muscles.

Of all the components of physical fitness, circulatory-respiratory endurance is perhaps the most important. In addition to an increase in the ability to sustain activity, there are many other benefits that result from an improvement of this component. These benefits, which will be discussed in detail later, include the prevention (or at least postponement) of certain degenerative cardiovascular disorders, a quicker recovery from physical stress, and a general feeling of well being.

Circulatory-respiratory endurance may be evaluated in several different ways. Sophisticated laboratory instruments are needed to make some measurement, such as of the actual amount of oxygen used by a person doing a certain activity. Other techniques not requiring extensive equipment can be used to get rather reliable measurements of this component. Placing an individual under a measured amount of stress, such as stepping up and down on a bench, and recording the pulse at the completion of exercise and at some time during the recovery period is one indication of the degree of development of circulatory-respiratory endurance. Another method is to measure one's work output during a given time period, which can be how far one can run or how many times one can step up and down on the bench in a specified amount of time. Persons who have a high degree of circulatory-respiratory endurance can sustain a rapid pace longer than those who do not have this development. The higher the work output, the greater the cardiovascular respiratory endurance.

### Increasing Circulatory-Respiratory Endurance

In order to train the circulatory and respiratory systems, stress must be placed upon them by vigorous exercise using the large muscles of the body. This exercise must be carried on for several minutes, and the heart rate must be elevated well above resting levels. A heart rate of 150 or higher is a rough criterion for the development of sufficient circulatory and respiratory stress. Several types of training may be used.

Anaerobic training requires a maximum amount of activity before oxygen intake becomes a limiting factor. Short bursts of activity at maximum intensity are utilized to accomplish an anaerobic state. In running or swimming, the individual runs or swims as fast as possible for as long as possible. If activity is sustained after approximately 30 seconds, the work is not intense enough. This type of training increases the velocity of ATP resynthesis and glycolytic activity, and promotes an increase in the reserves of phosphocreatine, glycogen, and myoglobin in the tissues.

Aerobic training is designed to increase the oxygen transportation and utilization systems, and it should be of longer duration and less strenuous than anaerobic training. This type of effort heavily taxes the cardio-respiratory and biochemical systems involved. It promotes alveolar hyper-plasia, hypertrophy of the diaphragm, an increase in erythrocytes (red blood cells), a growth of new capillaries, an increase in blood volume, and chemical changes in blood and other body fluids that increase their buffering capacity.

In the final analysis, the ability of the circulatory and respiratory systems to supply oxygen to the working muscles is the limiting factor in sustaining muscular activity. Fatigue of these systems is generally experienced in strenuous activities. The "out of breath" feeling, rapid heart rate, and general weakness are common signs of a lack of circulatory-respiratory endurance. To increase this endurance, any strenuous general body activity, such as running, swimming, or rope jumping, may be used. You must work to the point at which your circulatory-respiratory systems are stressed according to the overload principles in order to improve.

One method of improving circulatory-respiratory endurance is by interval training. This type of training consists of a series of vigorous activity periods interspaced with intervals of reduced activity to permit some recovery to take place. This enables the individual to experience repeated stress in order to adapt to both the physiological and psychological effects of fatigue. As endurance improves several factors may be altered to create the overload necessary to stimulate continued improvement. The length of the recovery interval may be shortened, or the intensity of the activity performed may be increased by requiring a faster pace, an increased number of repetitions, more resistance, or a longer performance. Activities such as running, swimming, and rope jumping are easily adaptable to this type of training. In running, for example, the distance, speed, or number of repetitions of the run may be increased or the time and/or distance of the interval recovery jog decreased as endurance improves. A person training to run a four minute mile may run four quarter miles striving to do each one in 60 seconds. The interval between these runs may be rather long at the beginning, possibly 10 to 15 minutes.

Another endurance training method is known as circuit training. This training program is essentially an all-out obstacle course of exercises. The basic idea is to do the exercises faster each day. This is an overload in terms of effort. For example, a circuit might consist of four stations where one of the following exercises is performed at each station: 10 push-ups,

10 sit-ups, 10 squat thrusts, and 100 repetitions of running in place. The circuit may be run on a time basis or for a certain number of times around the circuit. On a time run you would see how many stations you complete in five minutes. If you were able to get around the circuit four times in 5 minutes you would have completed 40 push-ups, 40 sit-ups, 40 squat thrusts, and 400 repetitions of running in place. Each day you would try to complete more stations. After a period of experimentation, a goal consisting of a number of stations to complete in the time of 5 minutes is set. When the goal is reached, the exercises are made more difficult by each station (e.g. 15 repetitions) and the process begins again.

## Bibliography

ASTRAND, PER OLOF, AND KOARE RODAHL. *Textbook of Work Physiology*. New York: McGraw-Hill Book Company, 1970.

BENDER, JAY A., AND HAROLD KAPLAN. "The Multiple Angle Testing Method for the Evaluation of Muscle Strength," *Journal of Bone and Joint Surgery*, 45A (January 1963): 135–40.

BERGER, RICHARD A. "Comparison Between Resistance Load and Strength Improvement." *Research Quarterly*, 33 (December 1962): 637.

CHAILLEY-BERT, P. LABINGNETTE, AND FALUE-CHEVALIER, "Contributions a l'etude des variations du cholesterol sanguin au coura des activities physiques." Presse Medicale 63 (1955): 415, cited by Henry Montoye, "Summary of Research in the Relationship of Exercise to Heart Disease," *The Journal of Sports Medicine and Physical Fitness*, 2 (March 1962): 38.

CLARKE, DAVID H., AND FRANKLIN M. HENRY. "Neuromotor Specificity and Increased Speed from Strength Development," *Research Quarterly*, 32 (October 1961): 315–325.

COOPER, KENNETH H. *Aerobics*. New York: M. Evans, 1968.

DAWBER, T. R., F. E. MOORE, AND G. V. MANN. "Coronary Heart Disease in the Framingham Study," *American Journal of Public Health*, 47 (Pt. II) (1957): 4.

DE VRIES, HERBERT A. *Physiology of Exercise for Physical Education Athletes*. Dubuque, Iowa: W. C. Brown & Co., 1966.

EVAUL, THOMAS W. "The Effect of All Male, All Female and Coeducational Classes on Skill Development in Badminton," Doctoral Dissertation, Indiana University, 1962.

FALLS, HAROLD B. JR. (ed.), *Exercise Physiology*. New York: Academic Press, 1968.

HENRY, FRANKLIN M. AND LEON SMITH. "Simultaneous vs Separate Bilateral Muscular Contractions in Relation to Neural Overflow Theory and Neuromotor Specificity," *Research Quarterly*, 32 (March 1961): 42–46.

KARPOVITCH, PETER V. *Physiology of Muscular Activity*. Philadelphia: W. B. Saunders, 1965.

KRAUS, HANS, AND WILHELM RAAB. *Hypokinetic Disease.* Springfield, Ill.: Charles C Thomas, 1961.

MATHEWS, DONALD K., RALPH W. STACY, AND GEORGE N. STACY. *Physiology of Muscular Activity and Exercise.* New York: Ronald Press, 1964.

MAYER, JEAN. "The Best Diet is Exercise." The New York Times Magazine. (April 25, 1965).

————, AND FREDERICK STOW. "Exercise and Weight Control: Frequent Misconceptions," *The Journal of the American Dietetic Association.* 29:4:340–43.

————, "Exercise and Weight Control," *Exercise and Fitness.* Chicago: The Athletic Institute, 1960.

MONTOYE, HENRY. "Summary of Research on the Relationship of Exercise to Heart Disease," *The Journal of Sports Medicine and Physical Fitness.* 2 (March 1962): 35–43.

MOREHOUSE, LAURENCE E. AND AUGUSTUS T. MILLER. *Physiology of Exercise.* St. Louis: C. V. Mosby Co., 1967.

SHAW, JOHN H., AND HAROLD J. CORDTS. "Athletic Participation and Academic Performance," *Science and Medicine of Exercise and Sports.* New York: Harper and Brothers, 1960, pp. 620–630.

SPERLING, A. P. "The Relationship Between Personality Adjustment and Achievement in Physical Education Activities," *Research Quarterly.* 13 (October 1963): 351–63.

STEINHAUS, ARTHUR H. *Toward an Understanding of Health and Physical Education.* St. Louis: C. V. Mosby Company, 1963.

STRAUB, WILLIAM F. "Effect of Overload Tracing Procedures Upon Velocity and Accuracy of the Overarm Throw," *Research Quarterly.* 39 (May 1968): 370–79.

TAYLOR, HENRY LONGSTREET. "The Mortality and Morbidity of Coronary Heart Disease of Men in Sedentary and Physically Active Operations," *Exercise and Fitness.* Chicago: The Athletic Institute, 1960.

WHITE, PAUL D. "North American Newspaper Alliance," *Readers Digest.* (September 1959): 69.

# 4

## What Forces Enable Human Beings To Move, and What Happens To Them Mechanically When They Do?

*Barbara Burris*

Every object on Earth, and presumably on any other planet in the universe, whether it is a rocket, a baseball, a bicycle, or a human body, is regulated by certain laws of physics and mechanics. These laws operate regardless of our awareness (or lack of awareness) of them, just as many of the systems of our body function without our understanding how they work or consciously controlling their operation. Knowledge of the principles of mechanics does not automatically guarantee efficient movement, since individual differences in body structure, nerve functioning, and other factors better equip some people for efficient movement than others. However, not understanding these principles and their applications may result in inefficient movement, wasted effort, and sometimes even injury.

For the purpose of this discussion, human movement is divided into two categories: those movements that enable one to maintain stability and those movements that enable one to impart or receive force. The principles governing movement in each of these situations are presented along with some of the fundamental skills illustrating these principles.

## BALANCE AND EQUILIBRIUM

*The way a body moves is affected by its stability and its stability is affected by its movements.* The ability to maintain balance is vital to movement. A lack of balance causes a great deal of awkwardness in learning new activities. Once you learn to adjust your balance while in various positions, you can perform a variety of skills more easily. Some activities demand a position of stability, while others require a position of insta- bility. The wrestler trying to avoid being thrown to the mat seeks stabil- ity, while the sprinter, about to start a race, wants a position of instability so that he can move quickly.

Both while at rest and while in motion, the body constantly is being affected by a variety of forces, both internal and external, which influence its stability. As these forces act on the body, its stability may be altered. Conversely, at any given time, the stability, or lack of it, determines what movements the body can make.

## Gravity

*Gravity exerts a downward force on each object on or near the object.* Every particle of matter in the universe attracts every other particle with a force directly proportional to the product of their masses and inversely proportional to the square of the distance between them. To generations of people who lived before the space age, this *law of gravity* formulated by Newton simply meant "what goes up must come down." Today, how- ever, every college student knows from his reading about space flight that this statement must be modified: What goes up must come down, unless it reaches orbital or escape velocities. We are so accustomed to the effects of gravity here on earth that weightlessness, or zero G, in space flight presents some real problems to orbiting astronauts. Applied to human movement here on Earth, however, it is sufficient to recognize that: (*a*) gravity is constantly acting on every object; (*b*) the force of gravity is always directed toward the center of the Earth; and (*c*) the heavier the object, the greater the gravitational attraction for the earth, and hence the greater the force needed to lift or move the object. Gravitational pull affects the body whether the body is in a standing, sitting, or lying posi- tion. This force pulls the body into or out of alignment, toward the Earth. Gravity influences the path of a thrown ball or a bullet, and the flight of a high jumper or a broad jumper, eventually pulling the object toward the surface of the earth.

*The center of gravity is the point through which gravity acts in its pull toward the center of the Earth.* Every object has a "balance point," that is, a point about which its weight is equally distributed in all direc- tions. This point is called its *center of gravity*. The center of gravity of a round ball (Figure 4-1a) that has uniform density throughout obviously is the exact physical center of the ball. The location of the center of gravity is less obvious in irregularly shaped objects and in objects that are

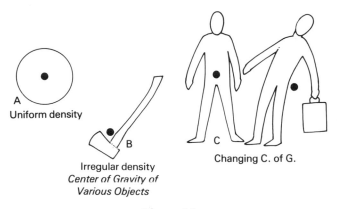

A
Uniform density

B
Irregular density
*Center of Gravity of*
*Various Objects*

C
Changing C. of G.

**Figure 4-1.**

not of uniform density, such as an axe or the human body (see Figure 4-1b), but it can be determined by special weighing methods. The center of gravity of the human body with the arms hanging at the sides is located somewhere in the center of the lower pelvic region. Generally, it is slightly higher for men than for women, although it varies according to body build. The center of gravity in children is much higher than in adults, being located in the umbilical region in the newborn child and gradually progressing downward as the child approaches adulthood. The movement of a body segment, e.g., lifting the arm to the side (Figure 4-1c), or the addition of external weight to the body, e.g., picking up a suitcase (Figure 4-1d), shifts the center of gravity in the direction of the movement or added weight.

*The location of the line of gravity in relation to the base of support determines the stability of the body or object.* Whether a position is one of stability or instability is largely determined by the location of the center of gravity in relation to the base of support for the body. If the line of gravity, which is an imaginary line through the center of gravity to the center of the earth, falls within the base of support, the object will be balanced and will not fall. If, however, the line of gravity falls outside the base of support, the object will not be balanced and will topple. The nearer the line of gravity falls to the center of the base of support, the more stable the object will be.

## Maintaining Stability

*Stability may be maintained or regained by compensating movements which adjust the base of support or the relative position of the body.* There are a number of external forces that can alter the position of the line of gravity. Being pushed, being punched, being hit by a thrown object, or riding in a vehicle that suddenly starts or stops may change the position of the center of gravity and upset balance.

Internal forces originate from within the organism itself. Such internal forces as a shift in a body part, a sudden stop from a run or jump, or a change in the base of support can affect the center of gravity.

Should balance be disrupted by one or more of these forces, a movement can be made to offset or compensate for this force. Listed below are a number of principles that may be used to guide movement in order to maintain stability in a variety of situations.

1. The larger the base of support, the greater the stability, and conversely, the smaller the base of support, the lesser the stability. People can balance much better with the feet spread a reasonable distance apart than with the feet together.

2. An external force acting upon the body to enlarge the base of support in the direction of the force will increase stability. If a person were pushed from the front, it would be necessary for the pushed person to place the feet in a forward stride position to increase stability. Spreading the feet sideward would not help in this situation.

3. Once balance is lost, widening the base of support in the direction of the fall may restore stability. If a person leans too far to the front, back, or side, quickly moving one foot in that direction will establish balance and prevent a fall.

4. Shifting one body part outside the base of support causes the center of gravity of the body to shift toward that part. Carrying an external weight also shifts the center of gravity toward that weight. Another body part may be moved in the opposite direction to counterbalance the weight and move the center of gravity back within the base of support. A suitcase carried in one hand may be balanced by raising the opposite arm, by leaning the whole body away from it, or by carrying another suitcase.

5. A person on a narrow surface where the base is small, such as a fence or balance beam, may improve his balance by raising his arms to shoulder level and adjusting for minor shifts in balance by slightly moving his arms. A tight-rope walker often balances himself in this manner. Raising the arms for balance occurs almost as a reflex whenever balance is precarious.

6. Lowering the center of gravity increases the stability of an object. A file cabinet with the top drawer full and the lower drawers empty is much easier to tip than one with the bottom drawer

full. When the center of gravity is high, as in the first example, the object does not have to be tipped very far to place the center of gravity outside the base of support and make the object topple over. Transferring the load from the upper to lower drawers of the cabinet would increase its stability. In the human body the same effect can be achieved by crouching or bending at the knees to lower the center of gravity.

The principles of balance and equilibrium apply regardless of the position of the body or the type of supporting base. People have learned through practice to maintain balance in most ordinary situations unless something unexpected occurs. An infant just learning to walk, however, must learn to balance his body. Loss of balance results in numerous falls before he masters the relatively simple skills of standing and walking. Whenever he begins to learn a new activity that involves an unaccustomed type of movement, learning to balance in this new situation becomes a necessity. Skating, skiing, surfing, horseback riding, bicycling, boating, dancing, and gymnastics often present new problems in balance. Once one acquires the ability to maintain balance while performing these activities, it is easier to master the remaining skills.

## FORCE AND MOVEMENT

*The application of force to the body itself or to an external object is controlled by certain physical laws.* Balance is a prerequisite of efficient and effective movement. Movement itself is dependent upon other factors: coordinated muscular contraction and using the forces of gravity and momentum in certain situations. These forces can be utilized to cause the body to move itself and external objects. All motion, be it human or otherwise, can be explained by various physical laws.

### Newton's Laws of Motion

#### The Law of Inertia

*Newton's First Law of Motion* states that an object which is at rest will remain at rest, and an object which is in motion will remain in motion at the same speed in a straight line, unless acted upon by a force. This is called the *law of inertia*. It has numerous applications to movement skills. For instance, since an object which is at rest tends to stay at rest, we must exert some sort of push, pull, or other type of force to start a car from a still position and accelerate it to a given cruising speed. This force should be greater than that needed to keep it in motion. Likewise, considerable braking force is needed to overcome the momentum of the car and stop it.

Friction, air resistance, gravity, and other similar factors all tend to modify the tendency of an object to stay in motion, thus making perpetual motion difficult to observe here on earth. However, space science illustrates this condition with every orbiting satellite. Once the object reaches orbital velocity, it continues to travel in its frictionless environment until acted upon by another force.

### The Law of Acceleration

*Newton's Second Law*, the *law of acceleration*, states that when a body is acted upon by a force, its resulting acceleration is proportional to that force and inversely proportional to its mass. This means that more force must be exerted on a heavy object than on a light one to accelerate them both to the same speed. It also means that if the same amount of force is exerted on both a heavy and a light object, the light one will accelerate more rapidly and to a greater velocity than the heavier one. It takes much more strength to put a shot 50 feet than it does to throw a softball the same distance. Likewise, if a softball is thrown with the same force that a shot is thrown, it will accelerate quicker, travel faster, and go farther. Once an object is in motion at a given speed, however, a heavier one has more momentum and will exert a greater force on something it hits than will a light object. This is illustrated in trying to catch a thrown softball or a shot.

### The Law of Action/Reaction

*Newton's Third Law* is *the law of action and reaction*. For every action there is an equal and opposite reaction. That is, when a force is applied upon an object, the object, in essence, pushes back with equal force on the source of original force. When walking, for example, force is applied against the ground by the foot. The ground resists this force and pushes back with an equal opposing force. This counterforce causes the person to move forward. If the object is not sufficiently stable to resist the force acting upon it, it will "give" or absorb some of the force. This is why it is difficult to run fast in soft sand. Since a portion of the original force is dissipated in the movement of the surface, the counterforce is reduced.

## Linear and Rotary Movement

Two types of motion are generally defined in mechanics. *Linear motion* is movement from one place to another in a straight line. *Rotary motion* is movement of an object about a center of rotation. Many types of human movement involve the use of the rotary motion of the legs with the hip joint as the center of rotation to accomplish the linear motion of taking the body from one place to another. An object moving in a circular path has a tendency to move off in a straight line tangent instead of holding its circular path. The force that pushes the object away from its circular path is called *centrifugal* (or perhaps loss of centripetal) *force*. The greater the speed of rotation and the shorter the radius of rotation, the greater the centrifugal force. This explains why a car traveling at a high rate of speed around a sharp curve has a tendency to slide off the curve, while a car traveling at a slower rate of speed around the same curve has less tendency to do so. A discus thrower extends the arm to get greater radius and more release speed, whereas the figure skater narrows the radius in order to spin faster.

*The resulting motion is determined by the amount and direction of the force exerted as well as certain external factors which modify the movement.* Motion results only when a force is applied to an object. Human beings can exert force by using the body musculature, by using the pull of gravity, or by using a machine of some type. Most physical skills involve the use of muscular force, even if the necessary force is only that required to push a button or to start a labor-saving device.

## Muscular Force

*The amount of muscular force which can be developed and used to move the body or an external object depends upon several factors:*

1. More force is available from strong muscles than from weak ones. All muscle groups are not equally strong. The factors affecting the strength of a muscular contraction were presented in Chapter 3. Much greater force can be exerted by the relatively large leg muscles than by the smaller back or arm muscles. Whenever possible, then, the leg muscle rather than the back or arm muscle should be used in performing a heavy task.

2. More force can be developed by using several muscle groups sequentially than by using a single muscle group in isolation. In throwing a ball, for example, the trunk is rotated, the shoulder muscles swing the upper arm forward, the elbow extends, and the wrist snaps as the ball is released. These sequential movements create more force than would result from simply extending the arm or snapping the wrist.

3. The greater the distance over which force is applied, the greater the force that can be developed. This is one reason why a back-

swing is taken in most sports skills which involve imparting force to some object.

4. Muscle groups which are antagonists of those producing the force should interfere as little as possible with the contraction of the agonist. When you lift something by flexing the arm at the elbow, the extensor muscles on the back of the arm should relax so that they do not restrict the pull of the flexor muscles. Unnecessary tension in any activity can cause this interference and inhibit performance.

## Lever Systems

*Internal and external lever systems are utilized by the body to produce movement.* Since actual muscular force is often insufficient, we frequently use machines to supplement our own power. The simplest type of machine is the *lever*. A lever is a rigid bar that revolves about a fixed point called a fulcrum. Levers can be used to gain a *mechanical advantage* so that a small force can be exerted over a fairly great distance to lift or move a heavy object and they can be used to exert a fairly great force over a short distance to move a light object with great speed. Levers are used countless times daily in sports and in performing ordinary movement skills. Internally, the muscles of the body act upon the bones as levers and generally favor speed and range of motion over force. Consequently if greater force is desired, we often resort to the use of external levers to accomplish this.

*A lever has three parts*: (a) a *fulcrum*, about which rotation occurs; (b) a *force arm*, which is that part of the lever between where the force is being applied and the fulcrum; and (c) a *resistance arm*, which is that part of the lever between the resistance and the fulcrum. Levers are divided into first, second, and third classes according to the relative placement of the fulcrum, force, and resistance. (See Figure 4-2).

*Mechanical advantage is gained by the use of levers.* If the force arm is longer than the resistance arm, more force can be exerted on the object to be moved. In doing this, however, the force arm must be moved a greater distance to get the object to move a short distance. The common automobile jack lifts the weight of a car a fraction of an inch (resistance arm) each time the long handle of the jack (force arm) is pumped up and down. In this way a 110 pound person can raise a 3,000 pound car.

If the resistance arm is longer than the force arm, the object can be moved faster and farther. The amount of effort that must be exerted on the force arm, however, must be great in comparison to the load to be moved. The swing of a tennis racket or of a baseball bat illustrates this principle. The end of the racket is traveling much faster than is the hand.

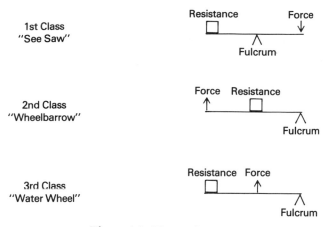

**Figure 4-2.** Types of Levers.

Similarly, more speed is imparted to the end of the racket with the arm fully extended, than with the arm bent, providing the same amount of force is exerted.

### Internal Lever System

*The internal lever system is comprised of muscle, bone, and joint arrangement.* In every human movement, leverage is a critical factor since movement occurs through the action of muscles (force) pulling on a bone (lever) which rotates about a joint (fulcrum) to move the limb, body, or an external object (resistance). A typical example is the movement of the elbow joint, which is accomplished by the shortening of the biceps muscle. The fulcrum in this case is the elbow joint, the lever is the radius and ulna, the force comes from the biceps and acts at its point of attachment, and the resistance is the weight of the arm and hand plus anything held in the hand. Since the resistance arm is obviously much longer than the force arm, the muscle must exert a great amount of force to move the hand, but there is great range of movement and speed possible for a small amount of shortening of the muscle. What class lever is this? This is the most common muscle arrangement which is found in the body (Figure 4-3).

## Application of Force

### Direction and Point of Application

*The direction and point of application of the force are critical in producing movement.* Building up an adequate amount of force does not assure that the movement skill will be performed correctly, or that an

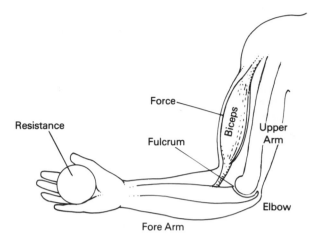

**Figure** 4-3. The human lever (third class).

object you are attempting to move will go where you intend it to go. The direction in which a force is applied and the point on the object to which it is applied are both of great importance.

1. If a force is applied directly through the center of gravity of an object, linear motion will result if the object is free to move. If the object is attached or restricted at one side, rotary motion will result. You must push on the middle of a piano to make it move in a straight path. If one wheel catches on a rug or another obstruction, the piano will rotate around that point even though you are pushing in the middle.

2. If force is applied at a point other than the center of gravity, rotary motion will occur. A push on one end of the piano will cause it to rotate rather than move across the floor.

3. If two forces are exerted simultaneously from slightly different directions, the path of the object will be a diagonal somewhere between the two forces. The exact direction and resultant force on the object will depend on the size of the two forces and the direction in which they are applied. If two people push or pull on a piano, the path it will follow will depend on where the forces are exerted, at what angle each is applied, and how hard each person pushes.

### Initial Impetus and Angle of Projection

*Application of force may be continuous or for only a short period of time. A projectile relies upon initial impetus.* Some movements require

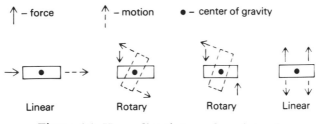

**Figure** 4-4. How direction and point of application of force determine movement.

the continuous application of force in order to maintain motion. However, some objects, including the human body, may be given an initial impetus that causes them to fly through the air as projectiles. An object becomes a projectile when it is thrown or struck. In the case of the human body, a powerful muscular contraction or rebound off of a springing surface such as a diving board or trampoline will project the body into the air. Beside the principles of exerting force already presented, the initial speed and angle at which the object is projected will affect the distance it will travel.

*The path of the projectile is determined by its angle of projection and its initial impetus.* Gravity acts upon the projectile to eventually pull it to the earth. An object projected in a vertical direction will go as high as its momentum will carry it. Since it will not have a horizontal component, it will not travel far horizontally. An object projected near the horizontal cannot attain much distance because gravity will pull it to the earth before it has used all its horizontal force. An angle of 45 degrees is generally the best angle of release for maximum distance. The proper angle for a projectile will be determined by the purpose of the action. The angle will be more vertical if height is desired, as in a high jump. If maximum distance is desired, an angle of about 45 degrees is chosen. A horizontal trajectory may be used if speed and not great distance is the goal, as in an infielder's throw to first base.

## Dissipation of Force

### Friction

*Friction serves to dissipate force which has been exerted on an object.* The force between two surfaces which resists movement of one surface upon the other is called *friction*. Friction is dependent upon the types of surfaces involved and the weight or amount of force pressing the two surfaces together. It is independent of the area involved. Because of inertia it takes more force to counteract the friction between two stationary objects than it takes to maintain motion once two objects are skidding across one another. Rolling friction is much less than sliding friction, therefore it is easier to move a heavy object on wheels than to slide it. Rolling friction is less between hard surfaces than between soft surfaces. This is why low pressure in bicycle tires makes it harder for a person to pedal. In activities such as moving heavy objects, we want to reduce friction to make work easier, while in other situations, such as walking or driving, friction is of utmost importance to the performance of a task. Without the friction of the feet against the ground or the tires against the road, we could not walk or drive, as illustrated by the difficulties caused by icy roads and sidewalks. Since the types of surfaces involved largely determine friction, we can control friction for our own activities. For instance, gym shoes are made with rubber soles so that they will not slip, but the front part of the bowling shoe is made with a relatively slippery surface so that a slide can be taken. Since it is difficult to get traction on a grass surface, cleats are added to football, hockey, baseball, and golf shoes for better footing. But injury can result from too firm a link between the foot and the ground, as when a football player sustains a knee injury when his heel is firmly planted and his leg is hit from the side.

### Air and Water Resistance

The friction of air or water molecules against a moving body tends to retard motion. Resistance in either case is proportional to the surface of the moving object and its speed (or the speed of the air or water moving against it). The texture of the surface moving through the air or water also determines the amount of resistance. A smoother surface reduces air or water resistance. This has given rise to such practices as swimmers shaving their heads and bodies and wearing the so-called "skin suit" of very slippery nylon, and of downhill ski racers wearing slick, skin-tight nylon suits. At championship levels every hundredth of a second counts. Minimizing air or water friction may make the difference between winning and losing.

To reduce resistance, the surface which is moving against the air or water should be as small as possible, and it should be shaped so that the air or water can flow smoothly around it. When diving into the water, we want to decrease the resistance of the body against the water, so the arms are extended overhead and the body is stretched and aligned so that it presents a small, streamlined surface to cut into the water. From this position very little resistance is felt, but if the head is lifted so that a "belly flop" results, the increased water resistance is easily noted.

Sometimes it is desirable to increase the air or water resistance of an object. This is done by broadening the surface and shaping it so that it catches water rather than cuts through the air or water. Sailing a boat and flying an airplane would be impossible without air resistance and force. Likewise, swimming or rowing a boat could not be accomplished without using the resistance of water.

## Momentum

There are three main sources of force available to the body in movement. The first is muscular force. It is available as a result of the contraction of the various muscle groups of the body and is under voluntary control. While this is the most common force used in movement, it is not the only one. Two other forces are constantly present that may be used to advantage or that may cause resistance to muscular effort. The second source is gravity, which is often a resistance, pulling the body and objects with a constant force. Gravity can also be used by the body to start or keep objects in motion. In bowling for instance, gravity helps to accelerate the ball downward and backward as the backswing is begun, and again at the height of the backswing gravity accelerates the ball downward and forward in a perpendicular motion. The third source of effort is momentum, which has been discussed as one of Newton's laws of motion. Once an object is moving, we can use its momentum to keep it moving if it is moving in the desired direction. In the bowling swing, the momentum developed by gravity pulling the ball downward in the backswing helps to carry it upward once it has reached its lowest point. Muscular effort must take over to finish the backswing to the desired height, but momentum makes the task considerably easier. If actions and efforts are timed to take advantage of gravity and momentum, efficient movement is apparent; however, if muscular effort must go against momentum and gravity, the task is more difficult (Figure 4-5).

## Absorption of Force

*Absorbing force involves dissipating it over as great a distance as possible and receiving its impact with as broad a surface as possible.* Many tasks involve absorbing force as well as imparting force. Catching objects and falling and landing from a jump are examples of movements requiring the body to absorb force. If a moving body is stopped suddenly by an external object, the force of impact is great. If the object receiving the force "gives" with the impact, the force is gradually dissipated and the impact is less. The greater the distance over which the force is absorbed, the less will be the impact on the body which receives the force. In catching a ball, for example, the arms should bend as the ball makes contact with the hands. Failure to do this may result in injury or in the

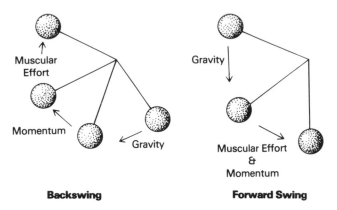

**Figure 4-5.** Utilizing gravity, muscular effort and momentum for movement in bowling.

ball's rebounding off this surface (law of action-reaction).

Another principle of absorbing force is to receive it with as broad a surface as possible. This results in less impact per unit of surface area. In falling, for example, do not stiffen the arm to break the fall. Instead, turn the body to take the force on the broad surface of the back of the shoulder, thighs, or buttocks (the well padded areas!). Relax and roll with the fall to dissipate the force. Techniques of absorbing shock are used in such activities as judo, football, high jumping, tumbling, and modern dance.

The mechanical principles governing the use of force in Human Movement have received considerable attention over the years from physicists and Physical Movement educators, from engineers and coaches, and from equipment salesmen and interested fans.

Today, this area of specialization is referred to as *biomechanics*, which Hay (1) defines as ". . . the science that examines the internal and external forces acting on a human body and the effects produced by these forces."

The advent of the high-speed camera and more reliable electro-organic equipment, along with computer assisted analyses, has precipitated this science into the center of movement study at all levels.

Students are directed to the list of references at the end of the chapter for further, and more specific, application of these forces in human movement.

Reference Cited

1. HAY, JAMES G. *The Biomechanics of Sports Techniques.* Englewood Cliffs, N.J.: Prentice-Hall, 1973.

# Bibliography

BEVAN, RANDALL AND TOM CORSOR. "The Biomechanical Study of Gymnastic Movement," *The Gymnast* (March 1969), p. 30.

BROER, R. *Efficiency of Human Movement.* Philadelphia: W. B. Saunders, 1973.

BUNN, JOHN. *Scientific Principles of Coaching.* Englewood Cliffs, N.J.: Prentice-Hall, 1972.

CARLSOO, S. "A Kinetic Analysis of the Golf Swing." *Journal of Sports, Medicine and Physical Fitness,* 7 (June 1967), pp. 80–81.

COOPER, JOHN M. (ed.). *C.I.C. Symposium on Biomechanics.* Chicago: Athletic Institute, 1971.

COOPER, JOHN AND RUTH CLASSOW. *Kinesiology.* St. Louis: C. V. Mosby, 1972.

DUGGAR, BENJAMIN C. "The Center of Gravity of the Human Body," *Human Factors,* IV (June 1962), 131.

DYSON, GEOFFREY H. G. *The Mechanics of Athletics.* London: University of London Press, 1972.

FROSH, HAROLD M. *An Introduction to Biomechanics.* Springfield, Illinois: Charles C Thomas, 1967.

JENSEN, CLAYNE R., AND GORDON W. SKIELTY. *Applied Kinesiology.* New York: McGraw-Hill, 1970.

KANE, T. R. AND M. P. SCHER. "A Dynamical Explanation of the Falling Cat Phenomenon," *International Journal of Solids and Structures,* V (July 1969), 39–49.

KELLEY, DAVID L. *Kinesiology: Fundamentals of Motor Description.* Englewood Cliffs, N.J.: Prentice-Hall, 1971.

LAUDER, MARJORIE AND PHYLLIS HILL. *Basic Movement.* New York: Ronald Press, 1963.

LONDEREE, BEN R. "Principles of Stability: A Reexamination," *Research Quarterly,* 40 (May 1969), pp. 419–22.

NORTHROP, JOHN W., GENEA LOGAN, AND WAYNE C. McKINNEY. *Invitation to Biomechanic Analysis of Sport.* Dubuque, Iowa: W. C. Brown, 1974.

PLAGENHORF, STANLEY. *Patterns of Human Motion: A Cinematographic Analysis.* Englewood Cliffs, N.J.: Prentice-Hall, 1971.

RASCH, PHILIP J. AND ROGER K. BURKE. *Kinesiology and Applied Anatomy.* Philadelphia: Lea and Febiger, 1972.

WATKINS, DAVID L. "Motion Pictures as an Aid in Correcting Baseball Batting Faults," *Research Quarterly,* 34 (May 1963) 228–33.

WELLS, KATHARINE. *Kinesiology.* Philadelphia: W. B. Saunders, 1971.

WESSEL, JANET. *Movement Fundamentals.* Englewood Cliffs, N.J.: Prentice-Hall, 1965.

# 5

## What Psychological Variables Are Important in an Individual's Movement?

*Leonard Zaichkowsky / Lois Smith*

The study of human behavior falls under the umbrella of the relatively new discipline called *Psychology*. Typically, it involves a wide assortment of phenomena such as learning, intelligence, motivation, and perception. It is also typical for psychologists to study human behavior as it relates to the *cognitive* domain (mental and verbal processes) and to the *affective* domain (feelings). However, there is another domain in human behavior called the *psychomotor* domain (movement) which, until recent years, has received very little study. Although the psychomotor domain is a critical *integrated part* (with the cognitive and affective domains) of man's behavior, much less is known about this domain than about the cognitive or affective domains.

Motor-skill research surfaced during World War II when it was imperative to learn more about man's motor skills. A short while later researchers in the area of physical education began showing a concern for the study of motor skills from a psychological perspective. This emphasis led to scientific publications in the *Research Quarterly, Perceptual and Motor Skills*, and other journals. Textbooks in motor learning began to appear on the scene (21, 69, 81). The formation of the North American Association for the Psychology of Sport and Physical Activity was another indication of a growing concern for the study of the psychomotor domain. The publication of three relatively new journals, *The Journal of Motor Behavior, Medicine and Science in Sports*, and the *Journal of Human Movement Studies* have also provided researchers with a greater opportunity to publish scholarly work dealing with the psychomotor domain.

A number of psychological factors affect human behavior within the psychomotor domain. This chapter provides an overview of some of the more significant phychological concepts involved in motor-skill learning and performance. For more extensive treatment of each concept, the reader is referred to the references cited at the end of the chapter. The first part of the chapter will deal with behavioral change during learning, as well as with those factors influencing skill acquisition. The second part will deal with motivational factors influencing movement, and the third part will discuss how an individual's personality affects and is affected by his movement.

## LEARNING AND MOVEMENT

### Skill Acquisition

*The acquisition of skill affects an individual's movement and is, in turn, affected by individual and environmental variables.* From birth to death, human beings perform skills. In fact, our ability to function independently depends upon our ability to perform a wide variety of skills. In the course of a day, we may walk, serve a tennis ball, drive a car, flip a pancake, play a guitar, or cut a diamond. Although these are diverse human activities, all require muscular movement of the body, all are purposeful, and all are learned. This last point is critical: skills are learned. But, *how* are they learned? Our basic concept doesn't provide much in the way of specific information. However, it does suggest two additional questions. How does the acquisition of skills affect an individual's movement? How do individual and environmental variables affect the acquisition of skills? This section will be concerned with what we know, what we think we know, and what we're pretty sure we don't know regarding the answers to these three questions.

### Behavioral Change

*A variety of behavioral changes occur as an individual acquires various skills.* We will define skill acquisition or learning as a *relatively permanent change in behavior which occurs as the result of prior practice or experience.* At the present time, we cannot observe learning directly. Therefore, we infer that learning has occurred when we observe some change in behavior. However, we cannot state that all changes in behavior are the result of learning. Some changes may be attributed more appropriately to maturation, fatigue, or drugs, for example. Therefore, our definition of learning contains two qualifying statements: these changes must be relatively permanent; and they must result from past experience or practice. What changes in behavior would we expect to observe as individuals learn a skill?

The most obvious answer to this question is that the individual improves performance on the requirements of the skill which is to be learned. This improvement in performance allows us to infer that learning has taken place. Most skills require a specific sequence of movements. Such a sequence is evident in bowling, where the feet, the swinging motion of the arm, and the release of the ball occur in a particular order. Performance of the correct sequence probably is the first observable change in behavior. Most skills require correct timing between movements in the sequence. For example, initial attempts to saw a board may result in jerky movements. The correct sequence is quickly learned—forward, backward, forward, etc. However, learning the correct rhythm requires practice. The fluid or flowing quality of a carpenter's movement is a joy to behold.

As an individual learns the correct sequence and timing of the movements required, other behavioral changes can be observed. The swimmer swims faster (speed). The high jumper jumps higher (distance). The gymnast more closely duplicates a prescribed routine (form). The piano player hits fewer wrong notes (accuracy). The child catches a ball regardless of where it is thrown in relation to the body (adaptability). Speed, distance, form, accuracy, adaptability—these are the changes which we usually measure, since they are typically used as criteria for successful performance. In all cases, the more skilled the individual, the less frequent the mistakes, or the narrower the range within which these mistakes occur (75). As seen from the above examples, sometimes we measure actual changes in *behavior* (i.e. gymnastics). More often, we measure changes in the *consequences of behavior* (the quality of the gymnast's routine). In the latter case, we may *observe* the parallel changes in behavior, but we don't often *measure* them (the gymnast's attitude and self-confidence).

Are these behavioral changes really indicative of learning? When we defined learning, we said that these changes must be relatively permanent and must result from past experience or practice. These are important factors. Many changes in behavior are not the result of learning. For example, a high jumper may improve performance by simply increasing leg power. When there is no accompanying refinement of technique, such improvement should not be attributed to skill learning.

*Behavioral changes, which result from the acquisition of skills, are indicative of changes occurring within the individual.* Our present knowledge and understanding of the internal processes involved in skill learning is far from complete. However, in the final analysis, changes in behavior that we attribute to learning must be the result of changes in the nervous system. Attempts to explain these internal events have led to a variety of physiological and biochemical investigations of learning. Even though these investigations have revealed a number of physiological and biochemical processes that have advanced our understanding of the neural changes occurring when skills are learned, we will not attempt to describe them. Instead, we will merely emphasize that there is a tremendous gap between our ability to observe and measure behavioral changes during learning and our ability to explain these changes in terms of processes taking place at the neural level.

In an effort to bridge this gap, many theories and models of skill acquisition have been developed. After continued research, they are revised. Currently, there is a great deal of research interest in cybernetic and information-processing models and in models combining characteristics of both approaches. In attempting to explain how skills are learned, these models address such issues as the function of feedback, the hierarchical organization of skill, and the role of perceptual, decision-making, and retrieval capacities and limitations. These concepts are employed in describing how the nervous system processes information. Although we will not discuss any of these models in detail, students should realize that many of the following concepts are derived from the cybernetic and information-processing literature. Descriptions of various models with particular application to motor skill acquisition can be found in Fitts and Posner (84), Robb (75), Singer (82), and Stallings (86).

## Learning Environment

*A variety of factors, which are primarily related to the structure of the learning environment, has been shown to influence the acquisition of skills.* There tends to be a great deal of variability in the conditions under which various individuals acquire a particular skill. Take riding a bicycle, for example. Some children initially practice with "training wheels." Others ride along with an adult running along side with one hand on the seat. Still others watch older children riding, then get on a bicycle themselves and go (usually experiencing a series of "spills" as they do). Some children learn to ride on a smooth sidewalk, others on bumpy dirt roads. Some children receive a great deal of "coaching" from a parent; others learn without such instruction. In each of these instances, the structure of the learning environment is different. Is any one condition or set of conditions better than another in terms of the rate or level of skill acquisition?

We will attempt to identify some of the environmental factors influencing skill acquisition and discuss the nature of their influence. Specifically, we will discuss feedback, distribution of practice sessions, size of learning units, mental practice, directing attention, audience effects and coaction effects.

## Environmental Variables in Skill Acquisition

### Feedback

*Motor skills learning is facilitated through the mechanism of feedback. Feedback is necessary for skill acquisition.* In order to acquire a skill, an individual must be able to compare his present behavior or the consequences of his behavior to a standard or goal. Information about behavior is termed *knowledge of performance.* Information about the consequences of behavior is termed *knowledge of results.* Both types of information are considered *feedback.* According to Bourne (11), "feedback is a term which refers to some signal occurring after or at the time of response, providing an indication of the correctness, accuracy, or adequacy of that response." For example, consider a tennis player practicing the serve. After contacting the ball, the server receives immediate visual information regarding the correctness of the serve (whether the ball landed in the service court). This is knowledge of results. In addition, the tennis coach may be observing the practice session and may offer important information regarding the correctness of the technique involved in performing the serve. The coach might say, "Your arm was bent as you contacted the ball." This provides knowledge of performance. Both of these sources provide the individual with feedback which is critical to skill improvement.

If the individual lacked the ability to see the ball land in the proper service court, or if someone did not attempt to correct the server's technique, improvement would not be possible because the server would be unaware of what adjustments to make. Regardless of the skill being practiced, some form of feedback is necessary for improvement to take place.

*Intrinsic and augmented feedback. Feedback provided by an external source facilitates the acquisition of a skill during the intermediate and later stages of learning.* It is common to categorize feedback according to the source of the information. When this information arises as a natural consequence of the movement, it is termed *intrinsic feedback.* In our tennis example, the server received visual information regarding the success of the serve. This is intrinsic feedback. Additional sources of intrinsic feedback would include the feel of stretch in the muscles, the sight of the ball on the toss, and the sound of the racket hitting the ball. Information provided that is not ordinarily present during or after the execution of the skill is termed *augmented feedback*. Again, using our tennis example, the coach provided additional information when he said, "Your arm was bent as you contacted the ball." This information from an external source is augmented feedback. Additional sources of augmented feedback would include information gained by viewing a videotape replay of the serve or by use of mechanical devices to measure the speed of the ball immediately after contact.

During or immediately after the performance of most skills, there is a great deal of intrinsic feedback available to the individual. When this is the case, how valuable is augmented feedback? Bell (6) conducted a study in which subjects practiced badminton long serves under various augmented feedback conditions. She concluded that, where sufficient intrinsic feedback is available, the use of augmented feedback does not further affect the acquisition of skill at the early stages of learning. Beginners evidently cannot use the additional information provided. However, as performance improves, augmented feedback becomes more important. The information provided by an instructor or videotape regarding the correctness of the behavior is more precise than the intrinsic feedback an individual is capable of processing and is needed to further refine the skill. This is particularly true for the skills found in dance, gymnastics, and diving, where the individual may need additional feedback in order to compare his or her present behavior with a particular standard. In these activities, the performer may not be able to identify errors and hence must rely on external sources to provide such information.

*Both internal and external feedback are essential to the acquisition of skill; however, their relative importance changes as performance improves.* Another way of categorizing feedback is by referring to the mode by which information is received. If the information is received by the kinesthetic receptors of the body, the feedback is referred to as *internal* (75). If the feedback is received by those senses receiving external stimuli (eyes, ears, nose), the information is referred to as *external* feedback. When performing a skill such as the tennis serve or golf swing, you are aware of the speed at which you are moving the racket or club without actually looking at it. This sense commonly referred to as *muscle sense* is technically called *kinesthetic sense*. The receptors for kinesthesis are located in the joints of the body. In actuality, unless there is sensory deprivation, we are always receiving kinesthetic feedback. In addition, we receive external feedback regarding the tennis serve from our eyes (visual information telling us whether the ball landed in bounds) and ears (auditory information telling us whether we contacted the ball well). In the golf swing, external feedback tells us whether the ball was hooked, sliced, or missed completely.

There is no doubt that the information provided by internal and external feedback is essential to skill acquisition. However, capitalizing upon internal (kinesthetic) feedback is very difficult during the early stages of learning a skill. Most activities feel awkard to the beginner regardless of whether the sequence and/or timing is correct. Therefore, beginners cannot rely on how the behavior "feels" when making an analysis of the errors made. Instead, they must rely on external feedback. Since all performers have a good idea of what the results of their behavior should be, they can compare this goal with their results. Gagne and Fleishman (37) have given us a good illustration of how the relative importance of internal and external cues (feedback) changes as skills are learned. "In many human motor skills, high levels of proficiency may depend more and more on internal cues as learning continues. The novice golfer checks his grip visually . . . lines up his club head repeatedly. . . . it is only when the internal cues have been dependably sorted out that the golfer can achieve a consistent swing."

One more example might further clarify this concept. In learning to drive with a "stick shift," novices initially must guide their hand visually through the motions. They see their errors and correct them. As they continue to practice, they no longer need to watch their hand, but can now rely on how the movement "feels." Obviously, fewer errors are made, and when they are, internal (kinesthetic) feedback provides information regarding the nature of the error (that's third, not reverse). That internal feedback was always there, but now the driver is capable of interpreting it (the position of the arm really feels different when the car is in third gear as compared to reverse).

*Concurrent and terminal feedback. Delaying terminal feedback can be detrimental to the acquisition of a skill.* The definition of feedback given by Bourne indicated that feedback may be provided at the time of response or after the response. When information is provided during the execution of the behavior, it is referred to as *concurrent feedback.* When information is provided after the behavior has been completed, it is referred to as *terminal feedback.* In our tennis serve example, terminal, intrinsic feedback was available by watching where the ball landed on the court. Terminal, augmented feedback was provided by the coach.

When we practice a skill, we usually perform the skill, receive and process the terminal feedback available, then perform the skill again, attempting to correct the errors committed the first time. What would happen if we didn't receive the terminal feedback for the first attempt until we had made one or more additional attempts at performing the skill? In other words, what are the consequences of delaying terminal feedback? Research investigating this phenomenon has demonstrated that delaying terminal feedback in this way has a detrimental effect on learning and performance (9). In order to be most effective, the terminal feedback for a given serve in tennis must be provided after the completion of that serve. The terminal feedback for a given vault in gymnastics must be provided after the completion of that vault and before the next attempt. In general, the longer the delay, the slower the rate of skill acquisition.

It should be noted that delayed concurrent feedback is even more disruptive. Have you ever tried to talk into a microphone in a large auditorium? You usually hear yourself saying something that you actually said a few seconds before. The concurrent auditory feedback is delayed. Luckily, most skills are not performed under delayed concurrent feedback conditions.

*Constructive feedback. Feedback that is specific, nonredundant, and limited in scope increases the rate and level of skill acquisition.* Besides the delaying of feedback, other feedback conditions affect the learning of skills. Often, the feedback (particularly terminated augmented feedback) is too general. The comment, "That was good!" really doesn't provide any useful information. In order to be helpful, feedback must be specific. In addition, there is no research evidence to indicate that feedback can be *too* specific (77).

Redundant feedback does not improve learning either. When terminal *intrinsic* feedback is available, receiving the same information through terminal *augmented* feedback does not increase the rate or level of skill acquisition. Our tennis coach might say, "You're hitting the ball long." Does this help our beginning tennis player? He already knows that the ball is going out of the service court. What he really needs is information telling him what aspect of his behavior he should change in order to get the results he wants; information such as, "You're tossing the ball behind yourself. Toss it in front, so that you can hit down on the ball."

Closely associated with the quality of feedback is the quantity. If the feedback is of good quality (is specific, nonredundant, and is not delayed), receiving feedback after every attempt will aid skill acquisition. This is particularly true of terminal augmented feedback (8). However, suppose that the coach, after observing a serve, told the server, "This time toss the ball a little higher and in front of you. Transfer your weight to the front foot. Keep your eye on the ball, and make sure you extend that arm." It is quite obvious that this feedback is too much for the individual to retain. Even if the information could be retained, the provision of too much error information may result in "paralysis through analysis." In this situation, the individual may try to analyze and correct so many aspects of the skill that it results in a decrement in performance. In our tennis example, it would be more appropriate to take that aspect of the skill that contributed most to the error in the serve and, through specific limited feedback, attempt to correct it before moving on to the next component. For example, if the ball toss was low, specific feedback might be, "You are tossing the ball just a bit low; this time try to get a little more height on the toss."

## Practice Conditions

*The learning and performance of a motor skill is affected by different practice conditions.* Nothing is more fundamental to the acquisition of a motor skill than practice. As a matter of fact, motor skills are characterized by their almost limitless ability to be improved with practice. Therefore, it is essential that both the teacher or coach and the learner be aware of the various practice factors that affect performance.

*Distributed versus Massed Practice. Although optimum practice distribution varies somewhat with task complexity, distributed practice generally produces better learning and performance than massed practice.* How should I distribute my practice sessions to achieve maximum performance? Should the practice sessions be continuous, that is, with little or no rest? Should the practice sessions be short and interspersed with rest? It is common to refer to the first type of practice schedule as *massed* and to the second type as *distributed* practice. The research literature generally supports the notion that distributed practice sessions produce better learning and performance than do massed practice sessions.

The criteria for mass and distributed practice differ among research studies. As a result, comparisons are sometimes difficult to make. Nevertheless Duncan (30) found that even when the massed practice group had more total practice time than the distributed practice group, their motor performance was not as good as the distributed group. Singer (80) found that a rest interval of 24 hours between basketball shooting drills resulted in better skill acquisition than practice sessions which employed five minute rest periods, or massed practice conditions. In studying the learning of swimming, badminton, and volleyball skills, Niemeyer (66) demonstrated that 30 minutes of practice three times per week produced faster learning that 60 minutes of practice conducted twice a week.

There appear to be two reasons for the relative effectiveness of distributed practice sessions. The most obvious element is fatigue. Continuous practice of a rather difficult skill results in fatigue which hinders further learning. The other element reducing the effectiveness of massed practice is reactive inhibition, which is described by Hull (44). Reactive inhibition refers to a condition that simply predisposes an individual to fail to repeat responses after a succession of trials. Continued practice under conditions of fatigue and reactive inhibition is obviously fruitless.

Rest intervals during a practice session result in "idle" time. An individual can revert to practicing a variety of subskills inherent in the activity. Using our earlier tennis example, it would be reasonable to practice fifteen serves, and then during the "rest" interval, to practice skills which were learned earlier, such as the forehand and backhand volley. After practicing these skills, another round of fifteen serves would be appropriate.

Let us not assume, however, that distributed practice is superior to massed practice under all conditions. Garry (38), for example, states that "massed practice is desirable when peak performance of a well-established skill is required." This situation is commonly exemplified by college and professional football teams. Since there is very little time between scheduled games, teams are forced to use massed practice against the opponents —offense and defense. It is important to note, though, that the skill level of the performers is already high.

Another aspect of massed practice worthy of mention is its relationship to the phenomenon of *reminiscence*. Reminiscence refers to an increase in performance following a period of no practice. Generally we would assume that an extended rest period would lead to some forgetting and hence to a decrement in performance. However, numerous studies have demonstrated an increase in performance in a variety of tasks following rest. These include the pursuit rotor apparatus (2, 46), softball skills (35), and balancing skills (87). The available research tends to indicate that when motor skills are learned under massed conditions, there is more of a reminiscence effect.

In spite of the fact that research studies have used varying lengths of practice times and interpolated rest times, it is safe to conclude that:

1. Distributed practice generally shows superiority over massed practice, particularly on complex skills.
2. Massed practice may be superior to distributed practice if the task is simple or if the skill is already well learned.

*Whole versus part learning. Whether whole or part practice procedures are more effective for learning is dependent upon the nature of the task.* Another important question to ask concerning practice is, "Should I practice the motor skill in its entirety or should I break it down into parts?" Numerous research studies have concentrated on "whole versus part" learning. As was the case with massed and distributed practice, there are problems associated with definition. What constitutes the part and what constitutes the whole? Is the tennis serve a "part" of the "whole" tennis game or is the ball toss prior to the serve the "part"? Therefore *"whole"* could refer to the sport itself (tennis), a skill of that sport (serve), or a part of the subskill (ball toss). For our purposes, *whole* refers to a skill of the sport (tennis serve), and *part* refers to a sub-skill of the skill.

Research has shown that both *whole* and *part* practice procedures can be effective for learning. For example, Shay (79) found that the whole method was most effective for learning a gymnastic skill on the horizontal bar. Niemeyer (66) found the whole method superior for learning to swim and to play volleyball. Barton (5), on the other hand, found that maze learning was most effective under *part* learning conditions. Cross (27) in teaching basketball skills to ninth-grade boys concluded that simpler skills were best taught by the whole method, and the most complex skills by the whole-part method, i.e., learning the skill in total, then going back and practicing the parts.

There are some generalizations that can be made regarding the use of whole or part practice methods. Deese and Hulse (29) state: "Whether or not it is sensible to split some task up into two or more parts depends upon whether or not the interrelations within the task are such that the splitting makes the task structurally simpler or more difficult." This statement is further clarified by Fitts and Posner (34) who state that it may be better to practice the subskills by the part method if the component subskills are relatively discrete or independent of each other. However, it is better to practice the skill as a whole if the subskills involve synchrony among themselves, e.g. a gymnast's routine.

Take, for example, the two verbal lists in Figure 5-1. Which would be the easiest to learn?

Intuitively we can see that List I would be more difficult to learn than List II. If we divide List II into two parts, we see that it has an inherent organization (direction and color) and lends itself to part learning. The strategy to use for learning List I would be the whole method since it does not lend itself to being broken down.

Very similar principles apply to the learning of motor skills. Continuous skills that are fluid in nature, such as the kip in gymnastics and the golf swing, do not lend themselves to a part breakdown and should be learned as a whole. However, complex skills that lend themselves to a part breakdown can be practiced by the part method. That is, the tennis serve can be practiced by first tossing the ball, then combining the toss

| List I | List II |
|--------|---------|
| North | North |
| Yellow | East |
| Red | South |
| South | West |
| West | Red |
| Green | Yellow |
| Blue | Green |
| East | Blue |

Figure 5-1.

with bringing the racket back, and finally combining these two parts with actually making contact with the ball. It is important to note that each part is practiced by itself before it is combined with the earlier learned subskill. This is sometimes referred to as *progressive-part practice* (24).

Since most motor skills are continuous in nature, they should be learned by the *whole* method. When using this technique, however, it is important that the teacher emphasize the *totality* or *wholeness* of the skill. This means that the learner should engage in observing live action of the total skill, or perhaps a film, and should be actively involved in discussing purposes, rules, and strategies.

*Conceptualization.*

> *Mental practice facilitates skill acquisition; however, it is more effective when the learner has experienced prior physical practice.*

Another aspect of practice that contributes to skill acquisition is *mental practice* or *conceptualization.* Some authors refer to this form of practice as sedentary, passive, or covert practice. In essence, mental practice refers to "mentally mimicking" the motor task at hand without actually evoking overt responses. An individual who is mentally practicing usually stands or sits quietly, sometimes with his eyes closed, and pictures himself going through the movement, or he imagines how it "feels" to do so.

Mental practice can be used to learn a skill. It can also be employed effectively in reviewing a skill to be performed or a strategy to be used. For example, a golfer, while waiting to putt, may mentally practice the actual putt. Often, this is followed by overt putting gestures. High jumpers and divers often engage in mental practice while awaiting their turn to perform. Most of us have probably tried this technique when playing chess or checkers ("Let me see . . . if I move there, he'll move there, and I'll move there.") One might say that mental practice is an extension of extreme concentration.

The learner must have had some prior physical practice for mental practice to be valuable. Attempting a giant swing on the high bar or a fancy dive from a three-meter board without a prior physical attempt could end in disaster. Even other skills which are as complex, but not as dangerous, require previous experience as a prerequisite to the effective use of mental practice (19). The studies of Clarke (14), Corbin (18), and Schramm (78) support the concept that prior experience with the skill is essential. However, there are some simple skills that can be learned through mental practice techniques exclusively (72). Numerous other studies on mental practice have been conducted but will not be discussed further in this chapter. Interested readers are referred to Richardson (73, 74) and Corbin (19) for extensive reviews and discussion.

As an illustration of this concept, let's consider the possible uses of mental practice in learning a gymnastics floor-exercise routine. After practicing a number of separate moves, the gymnast might visualize a particular combination. Then she might visualize herself going through the entire routine making sure that each movement flows into the next. Next, she might physically practice the routine. After identifying those movements which give her greatest difficulty, she could mentally practice the way they should "feel" and then go through the routine again—perhaps mentally first. After altering the routine as the result of mental and physical practice, she may perform it at a gymnastics meet. What is she doing just before her event? Why, she's limbering up and mentally practicing, of course!

*Directing Attention. Various instructional techniques aid skill acquisition by directing the learner's attention to relevant cues.* Under typical practice conditions, there are many distractions. The learner, particularly a beginner, may have difficulty concentrating on the task or may not be able to distinguish between relevant and irrelevant cues (feedback). Demonstrations and instructions which point out what the learner should attend to or "look for" during the initial stages of learning may facilitate skill acquisition. As a matter of fact, it appears that the quality of attention is more important to skill acquisition than the amount of time spent practicing. Of course, such instruction is of value only if the individual is motivated to apply it.

During the initial stages of skill acquisition, much of the learner's between-trial effort should be directed toward reviewing and formulating plans to correct previous errors. It is possible that the benefits derived from mental practice are the result of the time and opportunity provided for such endeavors. Thus mental practice, particularly when accompanied by other instructional techniques such as diagrams and demonstrations, may facilitate skill acquisition by directing the learner's attention to relevant cues.

Another instructional technique that aids skill acquisition is the loop film. This is a short (3–4 minute) film that isolates the critical aspects of a specific skill. This technique is of particular value when preceded and followed by physical practice and has been found to be very effective when used in conjunction with mental practice.

After execution of a skill becomes "automatic," the learner should not be instructed to direct his attention toward any particular aspect of the skill while performing. However, he should be encouraged to think about the skill during rest periods. Since less attention is needed for successful performance during this stage, the individual can attend to other things. For example, once dribbling a basketball becomes automatic, the player can attend to cues such as an unguarded teammate cutting in front of the basket. When observing beginners play basketball, we often notice their lack of "ball control." This is understandable since beginning players have to share their attention between performing the skill and picking up important external cues. If you can't remember your first experiences with basketball, just reflect upon your initial attempts at driving a car!

Consider learning a backward roll. If the individual continually rolls over one shoulder, this fact should be emphasized, not the fact that his toes are not pointed. You might be surprised just how much emphasis is placed upon and attention directed toward this aspect by students and instructors.

### Audience and Coaction Effects

*Performance versus Learning. Audiences beneficially affect the performance of a well learned skill, but tend to adversely affect mental skill learning.* Sport or athletic contests are carried out in front of an audience. However, we seldom learn any skills in a situation which is completely devoid of others who might be watching. This audience may consist of a teacher or coach, an employer, parents, judges, or peers.

Although there is much that we don't know about the effect of an audience and the types of individual differences that may modify an audience's effect, physical educators and psychologists have conducted a variety of studies which support our conclusion (see Singer, 1972, for a review of the literature). Most of the current studies are based upon the theoretical and experimental work of Zajonc. According to Zajonc (92), the emission of well-learned responses is aided by the presence of an audience, while the acquisition of new responses is impaired. In other words, the learning of a new skill is negatively affected, while the performance of a well-learned skill is improved. Zajonc, speaking in jest, would advise a student "to study all alone, preferably in an isolated cubicle, and to arrange to take examinations in the company of many other students, on stage, and in the presence of a large audience. The results of his examination would be beyond his wildest expectations, provided, of course, he had learned his material quite thoroughly."

Zajonc's theoretical position has been modified by Cottrell (20). Although not reflected in our conclusion, it has relevance for the study of skill acquisition. Cottrell suggests that an audience affects learning and performance only when the individual anticipates that he or she will be evaluated by the audience members.

The implications of the original conclusion and Cottrell's modification for skill acquisition are quite straightforward. Coaches seem to follow this when they close preseason practice sessions to spectators, and then encourage attendance at the games. In a like manner, gymnasts are advised to incorporate well-learned, lower difficulty skills into optional routines to be performed at a meet. If you have ever taught skill fundamentals to children, you may have heard one exclaim, "I was doing really well until you started watching me!" The child may have been absolutely right!

Therefore, an individual should not learn a skill in the presence of an evaluative audience. However, once the skill is well-learned, the presence of such an audience should improve the performance. How do you know when a skill is "well-learned"? That's simple—does performance deteriorate under the stress of an evaluative audience? If so, the skill is not well-learned.

*Coaction. When individuals practice a skill in the presence of others engaged in the same activity, skill acquisition is impaired unless one learner serves as a model for the other.* Coaction is a term which describes a situation where two or more individuals are engaged in the same activity but don't directly interact with one another. The pregame set shot warm-up drill in basketball is an example of this type of practice situation.

Unfortunately, there is not as much experimental support for this concept as for the concept concerning audience effects. In fact, many of the most impressive studies have been done using animals. The generalizability of these results to human behavior is untested for the most part. As with the previous concept, Zajonc (93) provides the major theoretical position: learning is impaired while the performance of well-learned skills is enhanced. However, as our concept suggests, an exception to this generalization can be found when one learner is free to model or imitate the behavior of another. This is often the case when students wait in line before it is their turn to perform.

After reviewing the literature concerning skill acquisition in a coaction situation, Sage (76) presents the following implications:

> During the learning period the motor-skills instructor may want to isolate students, when possible, while they practice the task that is being learned. However, if the students and the tasks lend themselves to coacting whereby one learner can act as a guide to facilitate learning, improvement in learner rates may be expected.

## Individual Variables in Skill Acquisition

*A variety of variables, which are primarily descriptive of similarities and differences between individuals, has been shown to influence the acquisition of skills.* In the previous section, we discussed some of the environmental variables which influence the acquisition of skills. What would happen if 10 people were selected to practice a skill under the *exact* same conditions? Would they all perform equally well at the end of the practice sessions? Past experience probably tells us that this would not be the case. Intuitively, we know that human beings differ in their ability to learn skills.

No matter how favorable our practice conditions or how long we practice, most of us will never be able to run a four-minute mile. We will never be picked to represent the United States in gymnastics or swimming in the Olympics. We will never break the home-run record of Hank Aaron or be a match for Billy Jean King on the tennis courts. But let's not confine our examples to sport skills. We also differ in the length of time we must practice before learning to drive a car or fly an airplane, and no matter how long we practice, most of us will never be race-car drivers or concert pianists. In this section, we are concerned with those variables which are descriptive of differences and similarities between individuals. Of primary interest is how these variables influence skill acquisition.

Obviously individual variables differ in their degree of influence upon skill acquisition. The fact that some people have blue eyes and others have brown eyes has no bearing on the learning or performance of skills. In fact, the nature of the skill often determines the importance of various individual difference variables. When practicing target shooting in archery, for instance, certain visual-perceptual abilities are required; whereas, in high jumping, visual perception is of less importance, and abilities such as leg power and coordination are of greater consequence.

Perceptual and motor abilities do influence skill acquisition. These abilities and learning in general are in turn influenced by other variables such as age, sex, past experience, motivation, and emotion. Through the following concepts, we will attempt to identify some of the individual variables influencing skill acquistion and to discuss the nature of their influence.

### Perception

*Perception which is made possible by specialized receptors in our body is critical to the acquisition and performance of motor skills.* In the act of reading, people's eyes are focused on the words printed on the page; they may also be hearing a fan in the room, or the ticking of a clock. At the same time, they might be playing with a pen in one hand. Specialized receptors, in this case, eyes, ears, and touch receptors, are receiving *sensations* from the environment. The complex process by which these sensations are organized and interpreted is called *perception*. Indeed, our behavior is very much dependent upon how we perceive the environment around us.

When the word "perception" is used, we think of visual perception. However, even though sight is the dominant sense in most people, it is not the only means of sensory input. As was mentioned earlier, hearing is another form of perception called auditory perception. Other types of perception include: tactile perception (touch), kinesthetic perception (feeling), olfactory perception (smell), and gustatory perception (taste).

If messages from the specialized receptors in the body fail to get to the brain, or if the brain, because of damage, cannot organize and integrate the information, there is likely to be a perceptual deficit. This deficit may have a detrimental effect on motor responses. Specifically, if the eye or its neural network were damaged, we would not be able to perceive clearly (acuity), or perhaps, see depth, hence a complex skill such as the hitting of a baseball pitched at great velocity would be seriously impaired.

When the auditory receptors are not functioning, certain other abilities are restricted. For example, in sprint starting an athlete may lose a split second because he relied on his opponents' start rather than on the sound of the gun. Similarly, hard of hearing football players on offense are at a disadvantage, since they cannot rely maximally on auditory stimuli (signals). Needless to say, many athletes do participate in sports in spite of these handicaps, but they must compensate by relying heavily on other cues or making approximate adjustments. For example, some football players use hearing devices, or if deaf in one ear only, position themselves so that they can hear the quarterback's signals.

Deficits in tactile perception prevent an individual from feeling and interpreting heat, cold, pressure, or pain. These perceptions are critical in providing us with important information for self-preservation. The receptors sensitive to tactile perception are located in the skin and other tissues of the body.

Receptors similar to those involved in tactile perception are responsible for making us aware of our body parts in relation to space. This form of perception is termed *kinesthesis*. Without kinesthetic perception, we would constantly have to look at our feet while we walked because we would not know where they were. When an instructor tells you to "get the feel" of a golf swing, what he is really saying is to use your muscle sense, or kinesthesis.

Failure on the part of the olfactory and gustatory apparatus would undoubtedly deprive a person of the enjoyable smell and taste of food. However, its impact on the performance of motor skills would be minimal.

In complex motor performance, we rely on all of our senses in an *integrated* manner to achieve maximum success. Motor responses in sport cannot exist independently of perceptual processes. The baseball batter uses his vision to perceive the velocity, location, and curving nature of the ball; his ears detect subtle movements of the catcher perhaps cueing location of the pitch; his hands squeeze the bat, providing pressure; he is aware of the location of his arms and bat as he awaits the pitch; at the same time he can (perhaps subconsciously) taste the bubble gum or tobacco he is chewing and perhaps even smell hot dogs in the stands. It should be pointed out that we all differ in our abilities to perceive a moving ball, sense pressure on the baseball bat, and react to the ball. The reasons for these differences are numerous. However, the point is that these individual differences in perception occur and they contribute greatly to individual differences in performance.

### Age

*The learning and performance of motor skills is dependent upon the age of the learner.* Age differences in motor learning and performance are probably obvious to all of us. We are aware of the fact that adolescents can "out perform" elementary-school children who, in turn, have greater capabilities than preschool children. As a child develops, certain behavioral changes occur, partly because of physical maturation and partly because of learning. The present discussion will focus on describing the movement characteristics of a child at various stages throughout development. The stages named here (i.e., neonate, infant, childhood, adolescent, adult) are those typically used by writers in child development.

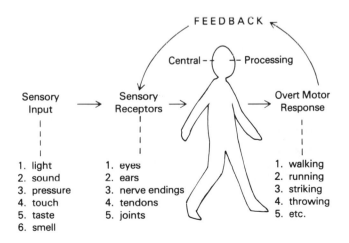

**Figure 5-2.** The perceptual motor system.

*Prenatal. Movement in the form of reflexes occurs during the prenatal stage of development.* The first stage of development is the prenatal stage which begins at conception and ends at birth. During this stage motor behavior occurs in the uterus. Spontaneous movements in the form of mass activity or basic reflexes begin to take place from eight to ten weeks after conception. Reflex movements are involuntary responses of the organism to various forms of external stimulation. Activity generally increases as the fetus develops, until a slowing down occurs as the uteral environment becomes crowded during the last month of pregnancy.

*Neonate. Primitive reflexive or involuntary movement characterize the neonate (one month).* The period of the neonate is traditionally designated as the first month after birth. The newborn is capable of making a variety of responses and adjustments to his new environment. However, most of these responses are reflexive or involuntary. Because of the limited sensory and motor abilities of the neonate, many authorities feel that learning is limited. One of the few studies which demonstrated learning in the neonate is reported by Siqueland and Lipsitt (84). In the study head turning responses were strengthened through reinforcement. Some reflexes which are present during the first month are presented in Figure 5-3.

*Infancy. During infancy (one month to two years) movement progresses from basic reflexes to higher forms of voluntary movement.* As in the neonate, the earliest movements in the infant are largely involuntary. Some of these reflexes, such as the sucking and the pupillary reflex, are essential for survival, however, there are other reflexes that appear to be of little value and that disappear after the first few months of life. Some of these reflexes include: the *Moro reflex* which is a spreading of the arms and legs, followed by a flexing embrace-like movement of the limbs; the *Babinski reflex* which involves a fanning of the toes when the sole of the foot is stimulated; the *Darwinian reflex* which is a prehensile grasp

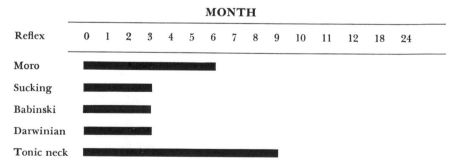

**Figure 5-3.** Appearance, persistence and disappearance of selected reflexive behaviors.

when the palm of the hand is stimulated; and the *Tonic neck reflex* which results in increased muscle tonus in the limbs toward which the head is turned. Although seemingly unimportant, the failure of these reflexes to appear or disappear may be an indication of neurological impairment.

These reflexes serve as a prelude to controlled or voluntary movements; that is, these reflexes are replaced by skilled voluntary movements. A unique aspect of infant development is that the pattern of voluntary neuromuscular control follows in a cephalocaudal direction; that is, infant control over movements develops from the head region to the foot region. Space limitations prevent the presentation of all aspects of infant motor development; however, before upright walking occurs, the infant generally passes through stages of creeping, crawling, standing, and walking. For a comprehensive treatment of infant motor development the reader is referred to Espenschade and Eckert (32) and Cratty (22).

*Childhood. During childhood (three to ten years) children develop and refine fundamental movement patterns.* The childhood years are generally characterized by an increase in body size and changes in body shape. The large, impressive changes exhibited during infancy will not appear again until the adolescent years. However, during the early childhood years marked changes occur in the performance of motor skills. Highly refined, complex skills are difficult for the preschool child, but abilities emerge during school years because of maturation and learning that make such skills possible. Gross motor skills such as running and jumping performed at age three develop into hopping and skipping skills at about age five. The growing child develops fundamental motor skills such as running, jumping, throwing, catching, and kicking which can be applied later in specific situations. Espenschade and Eckert (32) and Cratty (22) are two textbooks which provide a comprehensive description of the motor abilities of children in this age range.

*Adolescence. During adolescence (ten to eighteen years) specific movement skills are maximally refined by many individuals.* According to Buhler and Massarik (12) the adolescent stage is the pivotal point in an individual's development. Adolescents are neither children nor adults. The large bodily changes accompanying adolescence have such strong implications for personality and social and self-concept development that it becomes very difficult to discuss only motor development. Nevertheless, a brief discussion of motor development during adolescence is in order.

In general, research studies have shown performance on most motor tasks to improve until seventeen or eighteen years in boys and until twelve or fourteen in girls before leveling off. For example Keogh (53) showed that in the motor tasks of jumping, running, throwing, footwork, and balance, adolescent boys and girls showed a steady increase in performance. However the girls demonstrated an earlier leveling off or plateauing period.

According to Keogh (53), this early leveling-off period by girls appears to be a result of attitude change. With the advent of society's acceptance of female participation in physical activity, it seems reasonable to expect studies in the future which show boys and girls having similar stages of plateau.

*Adulthood. Adulthood is characterized by a peaking and leveling off on the performance of most motor skills.* The middle years of an individual's life are those in which the individual generally comes to the fullest development in all phases of life activities and plateaus or levels off on most motor tasks. The early adult life features very little upward or downward changes either physically or physiologically (12).

Maximum performance achievement is reached on most motor tasks in the late twenties, providing the individual remains motivated and active in the activity. Important physical processes such as respiratory vital capacity and muscle growth maintain a steady rate until about fifty years.

Predicting optimal age for maximum motor performance is risky to say the least. The interaction of numerous factors such as type of activity, physical maturation, environment, and motivation contributes to large variability in age related performance. A good example is presented by Olympic competitors. Championship swimmers are characterized by being quite young, whereas long-distance runners and weight lifters are generally regarded as being "older."

## Sex

*The performance of a motor task may be dependent upon the sex of the performer. In young children the sex of the child appears to affect certain forms of motor performance.* The question of whether sex differences exist in the performance of motor skills (and, if differences do exist, why) has evoked considerable controversy in recent years? Are they biological, sociological or psychological? The research literature to date does show many sex differences in motor performance. However, it may be that in future years these differences will be eliminated, largely because of a greater exposure of girls to various sports and a change in society's attitudes toward female participation in sports.

As was pointed out in the discussion of age differences, both sexes generally advance in motor performance up to adolescence, at which point the girls tend to level off in performance (12–14 years), while boys continue to improve. Some studies which have demonstrated sex differences, or lack of sex differences, in motor performance will presently be looked at.

Malina (62), relying on his own research data as well as the data of other researchers, states that between the ages of two and six, girls generally excel in tasks of jumping, hopping, rhythm, and balance, while boys generally do better in throwing and catching, as well as in strength and speed tasks. During the elementary-school years, sex differences persist as is demonstrated in the studies of Jenkins (47), Latchaw (59), Keogh (54), and Malina (63). Tasks which have a strong perceptual component to them and require sequential movements generally fail to show sex differences (28, 91). Table 5-1 summarizes a number of studies that analyzed sex differences in motor tasks. For a more comprehensive discussion of sex differences on motor tasks, the reader is encouraged to see Cratty (22) and Espenschade and Eckert (32). Maccoby (61) provides a comprehensive review of sex differences on numerous cognitive and motor tasks.

Existing studies show that girls perform better on tasks that are "fine" motor in nature, for example, writing and threading a needle, whereas boys tend to perform better on tasks that are "gross" motor in nature, for example, jumping and running. In addition, boys tend to reach their peak performance late in their teens, whereas girls level off or decline in performance early in their teens.

*Social Factors. Sex differences in adolescents and adults may be related to social factors.* One could then ask the question, "Why do these sex differences exist?" and "Do these differences persist into adult performance?" Explaining sex differences is not an easy task. However, it does seem reasonable to assume that some differences may be explained by motivational factors created by society. Historically, girls were not expected to perform well in motor tasks, and certainly not in competition against boys. Many fallacies existed regarding training effects. For example, some thought girls might grow moustaches or that they might not be able to bear children if they underwent rigorous physical training. Arguments have been presented which suggest that the leveling off in female performance and the large increase in male performance during early adolescence is due to hormonal changes that favor the male.

Nevertheless, sex differences in performance do, in fact, exist past adolescence. One need not look past the present world records in individual sports. For example, the present world record for the 100 yard dash is 9.1 seconds for males and an even 10 seconds for females. Men are high jumping 7'7½" and women 6'5".

Studies conducted by Dr. Jack Wilmore at the University of California, Davis, over the past few years have added much needed insight

## Table 5-1

### Selected Studies Examining Sex Differences in Motor Performance

| Motor Task | Age | Sex Superiority | Authors |
|---|---|---|---|
| *Agility* | 5–9 | females | Keogh (1965) |
| *Balance* | 7–9 | females | Keogh (1965) |
| dynamic | 7–11 | females | Govatos (1966) |
| static | 6–7 | males | Cratty and Martin (1969) |
| *Ball skills* | | | |
| batting | 6–12 | males | Cratty (1970) |
| catching | 6–12 | none | Williams (1965) |
| kicking | 8–10 | males | Carpenter (1940) |
| | 9–11 | males | Latchaw (1954) |
| rolling | 7–9 | males | Witte (1962) |
| throwing (accuracy) | 6–11 | males | Keogh (1965) |
| (distance) | 6–11 | males | Keogh (1965) |
| | 5–7 | males | Jenkins (1930) |
| | 5–17 | males | Espenschade (1960) |
| | 6–11 | males | Crom and Pronko (1957) |
| | 10–17 | males | Hunsicker and Reiff (1966) |
| *Fine Hand Movement* | 6–10 | females | Connolly (1968) |
| *Hopping* | 6–9 | females | Keogh (1966) |
| *Jumping* | | | |
| Vertical | 8–11 | males | Johnson (1962) |
| | 5–17 | males | Espenschade (1960) |
| St. broad | 6–11 | males | Keogh (1965) |
| | 5–17 | males | Espenschade (1960) |
| *Pursuit Rotor* | 5–8 | none | Davol et al. (1955) |
| | 8 | males | Ammons et al. (1955) |
| *Running Speed* | 6–11 | males | Keogh (1965) |
| | 5–7 | males | Jenkins (1930) |
| | 9–11 | males | Latchaw (1954) |
| | 5–17 | males | Espenschade (1960) |
| *Serial Motor* | 5–9 | none | Zaichkowsky (1974) |
| *Strength* | | | |
| grip | 11–17 | males | Jones (1949) |

regarding female performance. Wilmore's main concern centered on sex related differences in strength, endurance, and body composition. He suggests that female athletes (based on a study using athletes ages 14–22) are capable of improving strength equivalent to males when subjected to weight training. However, girls increase very little in muscle bulk because of hormonal differences. The females, however, use more of their muscle potential. Although men are about twice as strong in the upper body and about 25% stronger in their legs, these differences diminish when the strength scores are related to body weight.

When one looks at endurance differences based on maximum oxygen uptake capabilities, boys and girls have nearly identical values up to the age 10 or 12. Beyond this age untrained males have about a 30% higher value. However, when trained athletes are compared, the difference drops about 12%. Wilmore believes that the lower scores in females are related to their generally sedentary life style, since differences become very small in trained men and women.

The evidence regarding sex differences in motor performance suggests that society may have created some of the differences that do exist. In many tasks, the performance of girls would approximate that of boys if they were provided with the same opportunities for participating, training, and receiving society's approval. Wilmore (89) presents interesting support for this position which is depicted in Figure 5-4. Since 1924, females gradually have been closing the gap in swim time for the 400-meter freestyle. With relatively recent changes in attitudes regarding child-rearing practices, as well as with provisions and encouragement being made for female participation in a variety of activities, it is not inconceivable that this decrease noted above will be present in other activities.

## Motivation

*Motivation contributes to individual differences in the rate and level of skill acquisition.* Psychologists cannot seem to agree on a universal definition of motivation. Some even dispute the need for such a term. Nevertheless, many psychologists have spent their lives developing theories of motivation in attempts to identify the causes of behavior. We will define motivation as a hypothetical cause of goal-directed behavior. Through this concept and those to follow, we will attempt to identify some of the ways in which motivation accounts for similarities and differences between individuals in the rate and level of skill acquisition.

When we speak of motivation and its effect on skill acquisition, we usually think in terms of those factors that motivate individuals to try harder or persist longer. In other words, those factors that keep the individual from simply "going through the motions." These motivation fac-

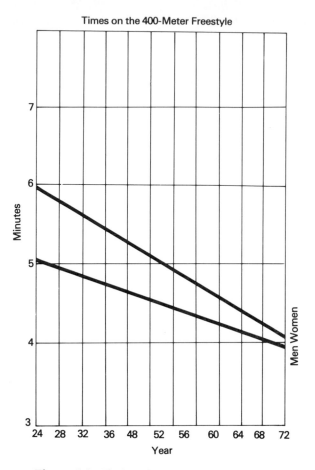

**Figure 5-4.** Closing the gap in swim time for the 400-meter freestyle (Wilmore, 1974).

tors are essential to the acquisition of skill. Sage (76) suggests that "learning without motivation will result in little change in behavior."

Of course, there are many factors that get us into a learning or practice situation in the first place. We will discuss these in a later section of this chapter. But, once we are in a practice situation, how is learning affected by motivation? The illustration which comes to mind is the picture of the young boy all dressed up in his baseball uniform sitting at the piano. One might suspect that this youngster is merely "going through the motions" of learning to play the piano. If we can assume that the boy is disinterested or lacks motivation for playing the piano, we can predict the effect of this disinterest. There will be little change in behavior as practice continues. After a period of time, his parents, having observed this lack of improvement, may decide to discontinue piano lessons. They may conclude that their son lacks the *ability* to learn to play the piano when, in fact, what he lacks is the *motivation* to learn.

Many such examples exist where lack of motivation has slowed the rate of skill acquisition or kept someone from reaching a high level of performance. There can be no doubt that motivation is essential for effective learning and performance.

*Goal-directed Behavior. Motivation facilitates skill acquisition when it leads the individual to set specific, relatively hard goals.* One of the functions of motivation is to direct behavior toward a goal. Motivation also has an arousal function. However, it is its directive function which interests us at this point.

Many things motivate individuals to learn and continually practice skills. For example, the acquisition of skills associated with work may be motivated by money, fear of authority, or satisfaction found in a job well done. The acquisition of sport skills may be seen as a means of receiving praise, approval, or prestige, an outlet for the expression and satisfaction of achievement or aggression needs, or an avenue for becoming a member and affiliate of a particular sports or social group.

There are numerous reasons why an individual might be motivated to learn a skill. It is also probable that individuals who are engaged in learning the same skill may be motivated to do so for very different reasons. Why does one learn to drive a car? Peer pressures, identity-seeking pressures, transportation needs—all are probable reasons which vary among individuals in type and degree.

What is implied in our concept, however, is that regardless of the cause of goal-directed behavior (behavior in this case is practicing a skill), learning is facilitated provided the motivation leads the individual to set specific goals for his future performance. Research in this area, although sparse, is quite convincing. In summarizing a series of studies on the topic, Locke et al. (60) drew several conclusions which have a bearing on our concept. First, it appears that individuals trying to obtain specific, quantitative goals evidence a higher level of task performance than individuals who try to "do their best." Secondly, if an individual sets very easy goals on a task, his performance typically will be lower than if he sets very hard goals.

Goals are often set for the individual by employers, parents, teachers, and/or coaches. How often has this statement been heard, "Stay here and practice until you can make ten out of ten foul shots!"? This is an example of a coach or teacher setting a specific, relatively hard goal for the learner. What motivated the individual to stay and practice? Well, there could be numerous causes (i.e., fear of the coach, desire to achieve the goal, the need for acceptance by peers). The important concept is that if the individual sets and accepts the goal, there should be a faster rate and higher level of skill acquisition than if the individual had been told to do his/her best or try to make three out of ten shots.

It should be emphasized that the mere setting of goals by others will not facilitate skill acquisition. In order for skill acquisition to happen, the individual must accept the goal as reasonable and work toward it. Of course, sometimes individuals set their own goals for future performance. Verbal encouragement, money, praise, criticism, and competition often are used as incentives to motivate behavior, and they may encourage the individual to set goals. All an individual needs in order to do this is an accurate appraisal of how he or she is doing now and perhaps how the performer did on previous attempts (knowledge of results or performance). This phenomenon is called "level of aspiration" and will be discussed in the next concept.

*Level of Aspiration. The setting of unrealistically high or low levels of aspiration can have a negative effect on the acquisition of skills.* One of the most widely accepted definitions of *level of aspiration* is given by Frank (36): " . . . the level of future performance in a familiar task which an individual, knowing his level of past performance in that task, explicitly undertakes to reach." Although there is a variety of ways to determine an individual's level of aspiration, the most common is to ask the person how well he or she *expects* to do the next time. As an illustration, let's consider the trials of a novice skier. On the first three runs down the bumpy slope, this beginner falls six, five, and three times, respectively. On his way back up the slope, he decides that he will attempt to go down at the same speed, but fall only once this time. Our novice has set a goal which he will attempt to reach; he has set a level of aspiration.

Past experience influences level of aspiration. Not only is a measure of past performance needed in order to set an aspiration level, but these levels rise and fall as aspirations are met (success) or not met (failure). Generally, successful performance tends to raise an individual's aspiration; whereas, failure lowers aspirations. It should be noted, however, that the effect of failure on aspiration level is not as consistent as that of success. If the "failure" performance is preceded by a series of "success" performances, it often does not lead to a lowering of an individual's aspiration. Had our skier not succeeded in reaching his level of aspiration for the fourth run, chances are he would not change his aspiration level for the fifth run and that he would still expect to be able to make it down the slope with only one fall. However, a lowering of his aspiration level might be expected to follow repeated failures, such as still falling three or four times during his tenth run.

In addition to past experience, personality variables affect the level of aspiration a person sets. These variables include self-concept, need for achievement, and fear of failure. Individuals who have a high fear of failure tend to set ridiculously high or low goals without regard for their past performance on a particular skill. Low goals insure success, whereas, unattainably high goals may promote the feeling that they have tried hard and that there is nothing "bad" about failing to reach such a high goal. Individuals with low self-concepts, specifically individuals who are insecure or have a past history of "failure" in skill acquisition, may set low goals or may express wide fluctuations in aspiration level in response to success and failure. Atkinson (4), who has done much work in the area of achievement motivation, has found support for the idea that individuals with a high need for achievement set realistic, reasonably high goals. As we know from our last concept, this type of behavior will lead to a higher level of skill acquisition. Thus, an individual's inclination to set specific, relatively hard goals is reflected in his/her level of aspiration. When unrealistic goals are set, either too low or too high, the individual may be protecting him or herself from failure, but the ultimate effect will be a reduction in performance and learning.

*Level of Arousal. Although it is difficult to identify, there does appear to be an optimal level of arousal for the acquisition and performance of skills.* In the last two concepts, we have been discussing the directive function of motivation. Motivation also has an arousal function. As a matter of fact, without the foundation of arousal, the directive function cannot exist. *Arousal* is the energizer of goal-directed behavior. When discussing *arousal level*, we should picture a continuum ranging from excited, alert, and attentive to relaxed, drowsy, light sleep, deep sleep, and coma (71). At any given time, an individual's arousal level lies at some point along this continuum. We will not discuss arousal from its neurophysiological basis except to say that the level of arousal can be described in terms of the degree of neural activity present at any given time. (See Sage, 1971, for a basic treatment of the topic.)

Although there is no universal agreement among motivation theorists, there exists a large body of animal research (and a much smaller group of human research) indicating an optimal level of arousal which contributes to behavioral efficiency. It is further recognized that this optimal level is an intermediate one, lying between the extremes of the continuum (excitement to coma).

How far along this intermediate range the arousal level should be for optimal performance seems to depend upon a number of factors, including how well the skill is learned, how complex the movements are, what the task requirements are with regard to strength, speed, steadiness, and so on. For example, it appears that a lower arousal level facilitates skill acquisition, whereas a higher level is beneficial once the skill is well learned. After reviewing the research relating arousal level to performance, Oxendine (70) set forth the following generalizations:

1. A high level of arousal is essential for optimal performance in gross motor activities involving strength, endurance, and speed.
2. A high level of arousal interferes with performances involving complex skills, fine muscles movements, coordination, steadiness, and general concentration.
3. A slightly-above-average level of arousal is preferable to a normal or subnormal arousal state for all motor tasks.

It appears that when an individual is faced with the performance or acquisition of a skill, he or she should adjust the level of arousal so that it is appropriate to the difficulty of that skill. Not only should the energy aroused be consistent with the demands of that particular task, but it should also be directed or focused on that task. The difficulties which arise in describing *the optimal level of arousal* for a given individual, performing a given skill, under a given set of conditions are far from resolved. However, it is apparent that the energizing effect of arousal upon goal-directed behavior has specific implications for the learning and performance of skills.

### Anxiety

*Anxiety, whether conceived of as a temporary emotional state or personality trait, inhibits the acquisition of skills.* It is appropriate to distinguish between state and trait anxiety. *State anxiety* is conceived of as transitory in nature—fluctuating over time; *trait anxiety* is a relatively stable personality trait (64). Spielberger (86), who has devised a test of both state and trait anxiety, makes the following distinction between the two terms: "Anxiety states are characterized by subjective, consciously perceived feelings of apprehension and tension, accompanied by or associated with activation or arousal of the autonomic nervous system." Spielberger defines trait anxiety as "a motive or acquired behavioral disposition that predisposes an individual to perceive a wide range of objectively nondangerous circumstances as threatening, and to respond to these with state anxiety reactions disproportionate in intensity to the magnitude of the objective danger." The terms *state anxiety* and *stress* could be used synonymously.

What is there in the learning situation that could produce state anxiety or stress? The two tension producers most often encountered are fear of physical harm and fear of failure. In learning or performing a skill, one should seek to avoid feelings of anxiety. However, this is not usually entirely possible. Locke et al. (60) suggest that there are three ways of coping with state anxiety: The individual could leave the situation; the individual could try to overcome it; the individual could compensate for it. Leaving and thereafter avoiding the situation quite obviously inhibits skill acquisition. Locke goes on to suggest that attempts to overcome or compensate for state anxiety might *indirectly* result in improved performance. For example, the young girl learning to twirl the baton might try to ignore the fact that her mother is watching from the kitchen window. The student learning to do tricks on the swinging rings might try to ignore that the person just in front in line fell and will have to have corrective surgery. In these examples, attempts to overcome state anxiety might lead the individuals to concentrate more or try harder, and thus indirectly improve the rate of skill learning. However, since individual reactions to stress are so unpredictable, there is no guarantee that this would be the case. Obviously, there comes a point where increases in state anxiety can no longer be overcome. At this point, performance certainly deteriorates.

Research studies concerned with the effect of trait anxiety on learning and performance have not yielded particularly consistent results. Those studies that required extremely and mildly anxious subjects to learn a complex skill indicate that complex performance is adversely affected by high levels of trait anxiety. As was the case for state anxiety, it may be that the learning and performance of skills by individuals with moderate levels of trait anxiety is *indirectly* facilitated. It may be that they concentrate more upon the skill and try harder. However, the research is equivocal on this matter. For a more extensive review and critique of research concerning state and trait anxiety see Martens (64).

It would be nice if we could avoid getting anxious. We could then continue to do all those things which we do even though they make us anxious or begin to do all those things which we don't do because they might make us anxious. The fact is that we do put ourselves in anxiety-provoking situations—competitive sport is just one example. One of the major reasons people avoid competitive sport is the anxiety manifested through fear of physical harm or fear of failure. Realistically we cannot totally avoid anxiety; we can only try to reduce it. Relaxation training and the relatively new principle of biofeedback training appear to be worthy techniques for reducing state anxiety. Experimental research in this area is currently underway in several laboratories.

It appears that anxiety, be it state or trait, inhibits the acquisition of skill, though the magnitude of its negative effect depends upon the individual's ability to overcome or compensate for it (60).

## Motivation and Movement

*Motivational factors influence the selection, intensity and persistence of an individual's movement.* The concepts derived from learning theories and associated research have added much to our present understanding of how an individual acquires motor responses or skills. The disciplines of Psychology and Human Movement also address themselves to "why" questions. Why do individuals behave the way they do? Why do they choose to participate in one activity over another? Why do they carry on this activity with such vigor? Why do they continue to engage in the activity? All of these questions concern motivation.

We have previously defined motivation as the hypothetical cause of goal-directed behavior. The study of human motivation is concerned primarily with identifying and understanding individual and environmental factors that determine the selection, intensity, and persistence of goal-directed behavior. By studying these determinants identified by motivation theorists, we can hope to further our understanding of the individual and environmental factors which influence purposeful human movement.

Contemporary motivation theories can be grouped into four major approaches. Korman (56) describes these approaches as (1) behavioristic approaches to motivational processes: drive theory, (2) activation-arousal theory, (3) consistency motivation, and (4) cognitive approaches to motivation: the expectancy-value model. Many comprehensive studies in human motivation have followed the cognitive approach. Researchers who adopt this approach are concerned with the feelings and thoughts that accompany an individual's actions. Most of the concepts in this section stem from the theoretical and experimenal framework of expectancy-value theorists. Two of these theorists, Birch and Veroff (10), have identified four determinants of goal-directed behavior: availability, expectancy, incentive, and motive. The first four concepts are derived from their theoretical position. Although expectancy-value theory represents only one approach to the study of motivation, it appears to be particularly relevant to the study of purposeful human movement.

*Individual variables combine with environmental variables to influence purposeful human movement.* The motivational process is a function of both the characteristics of an individual at a given time and the characteristics of the particular environment as perceived by the individual. In order to predict human behavior (which is the ultimate goal of motivation theory), we would have to know all of the variables that might lead an individual to pursue one course of action over another. In addition, we would have to know how these variables interact. It soon becomes obvious that motivation theory has a long way to go before it can be used to predict behavior. However, an introduction to the present state of the expectancy-value model should help us to understand how motivational factors influence human movement.

### Availability

*The quality and quantity of human movement is influenced by availability which, in turn, is influenced by individual and situational variables.* What influences the selection of a particular goal-directed behavior or purposeful human movement? According to our concept one such influence is availability, or "the extent to which a particular stimulus situation makes available a particular course of action" (10). Also, the availability of a particluar response is influenced by certain individual and environmental or situational variables. Suppose a young man were at a club in the company of his friends. The mere fact that he is at a club makes possible certain behaviors. He could dance. He could shoot some pool. He could sit and talk. He could simply watch other people. However, the particular surroundings would not suggest or make available a game of touch football. Often, our physical activity choices are narrowed by environmental factors which limit availability. Lack of access to a body of water bigger than a bathtub keeps many people from learning to swim. And West Texas isn't exactly the place you would go for an invigorating game of field hockey.

The selection of behaviors from which our young man at the club can choose may be limited still further by individual variables, particularly the ability to perform those behaviors made possible by the situation. If he has never learned to play pool or dance, these forms of movement are not available to him unless someone is willing to teach him. Situational and individual variables may interact to limit the availability of movement responses to sitting and talking or watching other people.

Availability is one of the important determinants of purposeful human movement.

### Expectancy

*Past experience influences an individual's expectation that engaging in an activity will lead to a particular goal.* One of the advantages of the expectancy-value model of motivation is the emphasis it places on an individual's thoughts regarding the consequences of a particular action. People participate in physical activity for a wide variety of reasons. These are often expressed as the opportunity to relax, to temporarily forget the trials of the day, to have fun, to be with friends, to lose weight, to gain recognition and status, or to earn money. In other words, people *expect* that engaging in a particular form of movement will lead to a particular consequence. When it does, they may continue to participate; when it doesn't, they may leave that activity for another. For example, individuals previously may have found that when they are tense, playing basketball makes them "feel better" (i.e., relieves muscular tension). The next time they feel tense, they may play basktball (provided such an alternative is available). In other words, consciously or unconsciously, individuals associate the goal of muscular relaxation with the activity of playing basketball.

How does expectancy influence the quality and quantity of human movement? Our basketball players may only expect to feel better if they play a *vigorous* game of basketball. Shooting foul shots may not lead to the goal, while participating in a full court, three-on-three game for an hour is quite a different matter. Through past experiences, they have developed certain expectations which serve to influence the selection and intensity of their movement.

The young man at the club in the previous example may also have certain expectancies which will serve to determine the movement in which he decides to engage. What might be his expectancies?

### Incentive

*Environmental variables influence the incentive value of an activity and its consequences.* Every activity in which an individual engages has certain consequences. If an individual continually participates in or avoids participating in a particular activity when free to do so, then the consequences are said to have positive or negative incentive value, respectively. The consequences of some activities (i.e. studying for a test or running laps) may have both positive and negative incentive values.

How do environmental factors influence the incentive value of an activity and its consequences? Few people would argue that winning has a positive incentive value, whereas losing has a negative incentive value. Let's assume that the individuals in the following three situations expect to win. How does the incentive value of winning vary in these situations? In our first situation, a teenage girl is bowling in a city-wide tournament. In the second, this same girl is bowling with some of her friends. In the third, she is bowling with her date. In which of these situations would the positive incentive value of winning be greatest? Probably in the first (bowling in a city-wide tournament). In which situation might winning have a *negative* incentive value and losing have a positive incentive value? Current cultural norms would probably place winning in the second example, positive, and in the third example, negative. Disagreement with these norms illustrates how individual differences influence incentive values.

If we assume that the incentive value of winning in each of these situations varies, it follows that the quality and quantity of movement also varies. Since the positive incentive for winning is greatest in the first example (bowling in a city-wide tournament), the girl may prefer to bowl in this particular competitive situation. She might concentrate more and, in fact, bowl a better series of games than when she bowls with her friends. In the third example (bowling with a date), variations in quality and quantity may be evident also. If she expects to win and winning has a negative incentive value, she may avoid bowling with her date or she may lower the quality of her game just enough to allow him to win.

The influence of a fourth variable on the quality and quantity of human movement will now be considered. While interacting with the other three variables—availability, expectancy, and incentive—to determine behavior, this fourth variable is primarily responsible for modifying the incentive value of a particular activity.

## Motive

*Individual differences in the strength of a particular motive may modify the incentive value of an activity and its consequences.* The previous concept emphasized the influence of environmental or situational variables on incentive value. We saw that particular consequences of action (winning) may have different incentive values to an individual in various situations. However, incentives alone (or in combination with availability and expectancy) do not determine either whether an individual will engage in a particular activity or the quality and quantity of the activity.

How important is winning? Would people really "rather die" than lose? Do all people feel the same way? Although winning has positive incentive value in most cases, it would seem that individuals differ in the importance they place on winning, just as they differ in the importance they place on social approval, independence, achievement, power, and other consequences of action. When we speak of the strength of the attraction or repulsion to a general class of consequences (i.e., social approval, achievement, etc.), we are referring to the motive for that class. Motives are considered relatively stable human characteristics. As such, a motive acts to modify the incentive value of a particular consequence. For example, performing a double back somersault on the trampoline can have high incentive value, but its ultimate attraction to a particular individual may depend upon the magnitude of the fear of heights, the need to achieve, the need for social approval, or a combination of these motives.

By modifying the incentive value of an activity and its consequence, motives indirectly influence the quality and quantity of movement. For example, in sports, as in other aspects of life, the motive to achieve success and avoid failure acts to increase the positive incentive value of winning. As a consequence, an individual with a high need to achieve may practice longer and harder than an individual with a low achievement need, since winning will have a greater positive incentive value. We would expect that such behaviors on the part of the athlete would subsequently lead to increased performance.

Let's examine another motive—aggression. An individual with a low need for aggression may avoid participating in sports such as football, boxing, and ice hockey where aggressive behavior is rewarded. Instead of playing "regular" football, he may choose to play "touch" or "flag" football. If he does play football, we might expect his performance as middle linebacker to be of a different quality than an individual who has a high aggression motive.

These examples illustrate the ability of motives to modify incentive value, and, thereby, to influence the quality and quantity of movement. Through concepts yet to be introduced, we will take a closer look at some of the specific motives and incentives which influence human movement.

## Fulfillment of Psychological Needs

### Perceived Values of Physical Activity

*The expectation that certain psychological needs can be satisfied through participation in a particular form of physical activity motivates an individual's involvement in that activity.* As we have suggested, individuals differ in their motives for engaging in physical activity. From personal observations and/or introspection, it probably is apparent that an individual's motives for participating in a specific activity may change over time. Generally, however, initial and continued participation is influenced by an individual's *perception* of the values associated with participation. The value associated with physical activity is often the satisfaction of certain psychological needs.*

As the culmination of a series of studies reported in 1968, Kenyon (52) presented six subdomains of physical activity that he identified as representing "the perceived instrumental value of physical activity." These subdomains, their descriptions, and examples of the activities considered to be representative are as follows:

*Note: We have and will continue to use the terms *motives* and *needs* interchangeably.

ion or move-
al, risk seek-
readers are
8) and Har-

two general
ysical activ-
tion, inten-
s clear that
ple, if you
lowing an-
; it's good
tense. All
t motives.
nis as the
play; still
these mo-
behavior.
hange as
up the
roval or
he or she
ion may
ut-off of
ting on
l recog-

en time
alleng-
human
selec-
emer

xperience is characterized by those
ary purpose is to provide a medium
meet new people and to perpetuate
dances, bowling).

ed primarily by its contribution to
health and fitness (calisthenics and
).

suit of vertigo is considered to be those
ding an element of thrill through the
ation, sudden change of direction, or
uations. They involve some risk to the
rticipant usually remaining in control,
high platform, heavy weather sailing,
diving).

ved of as having aesthetic value for the
vities conceived of as possessing beauty or
ies (creative and expressive movements

ived as providing a release of tensions that
rustration through some vicarious means,
rsis (many types of vigorous physical activi-

ceived as an ascetic experience (such as mid-
An attempt to conceive of certain forms of
providing a "competitive" experience did not

ification systems. However, Kenyon's attempt to
upon the perceived intrumental value of physical
ture, help us to identify and better understand the
cipation in physical activity.

there has been little research within the discipline of
t directed towards identifying those motives influenc-
, intensity and persistence of physical activity. Most of
on motives and motivation in physical activity has come
pts to apply principles derived from psychological theory
. In addition, most of the interest has been directed towards
those motives which operate in sports or athletics. Ogilvie and
8) have reported that the needs for love, status, social approval,
and achievement motivate athletic participation. However, re-
the perspective has broadened to encompass physical activity in

general. Among those motives identified are the need for ac
ment, affirmation of self, competition, security, social appro
ing, catharsis, achievement, status, and aggression. Intereste
referred to extensive reviews of the literature by LaChance (
ris (41).

Before examining some of these motives in more detail,
points regarding the nature of motives and involvement in pl
ity need to be made. First, whether we are discussing the sele
sity, or persistence of involvement in physical activity, it seem
there is usually more than one motive operating. For exam
asked someone why they played tennis, you might get the fo
swers from that individual: my wife wanted me to teach he
exercise; I feel in a better mood after playing, it makes me les
of these responses may have their foundation in very differer
Some of them may help explain why the individual selected te
form of physical activity; others, why he or she continues to
others, why the individual plays as often as he/she does. All of
tives may very well be operating at the same time to influence
Second, the motives for participation in a given activity may
involvement continues. For example, an individual may pic
game of golf for recreative reasons. The motives of social ap
catharsis may be operating initially. As the individual improves,
may enter a few local tournaments. Eventually, local competit
not prove challenging, and the golfer may enter and make the
some open tournaments of national caliber. Motives for particip
a team may include achievement, competition, status, and socia
nition.

The fact that more than one motive may be operating at a giv
and that motives may change over time creates interesting and ch
ing problems for the study of motivation and its influence on
movement. This fact appears to have relevance in the study of th
tion, intensity, and persistence of various forms of human mov

## Achievement

*Continued participation in physical activity of a competitive r*
*is often motivated by the need for achievement.* The major charact
of competitive physical activity is that the quality of an individual'
formance is evaluated in terms of some criteria or standard of excell
We often associate this with the terms winning or losing, beating or b
beaten. This implies that one individual is competing against an
or a team against an opposing team and that there can only be one w
ner. However, the achievement motive also operates in circumstance

where an individual competes against a standard (as in Bannister and Landy trying to run under four minutes for the mile) or against a "previous best" (as in the case of a jogger trying to run the Boston Marathon thirty minutes faster than last year). Regardless of which form or combination of forms competitive physical activity takes, participation in this type of physical activity is often motivated by the need for achievement.

Our concept implies that success of some sort is essential if an individual is to be motivated to continue participation in competitive physical activity. Although initial involvement may be motivated by curiosity or the desire to interact with a particular group of people, the desire to achieve success and avoid failure will influence continued participation. It is interesting to note that lack of success is often given by high school girls as the reason why they no longer choose to participate in physical activities.

Earlier, we described a motive as a relatively stable characteristic of an individual. We also commented on the fact that individuals differ in the strength of a particular motive. Individual-difference scores in the achievement motive have been related to a variety of other behaviors. There has been considerable research aimed at discovering the effect of individual performance differences in the motive to achieve. For example, Atkinson (4) found that individuals with a high need for achievement set realistic levels of aspiration. We have seen that the setting of unrealistically high or low levels of aspiration can have a negative effect on the acquisition of skills. Individuals who set very high aspiration levels seem doomed to failure. This continued failure will lead to demotivation and eventual withdrawal from participation. It appears that the strength of the motive to achieve is a very important determinant of continued participation in competitive physical activity. Generally, the research evidence tends to support the conclusion that people with a higher need for achievement learn faster, perform more quickly, and persist under conditions of difficulty (10).

In a previous discussion, we also emphasized the fact that motives are modified by incentive values. What is the incentive value of achievement in physical activity—physical skills in particular? For young children, its value is usually great and positive. In fact, a great deal of parental approval is associated with the mastery of physical skills. However, to assume that the incentive value of achievement is always positive would ignore, for one thing, the social restrictions placed on women. As girls grow older, physical skills required by heavy manual work and certain sports are associated with increasingly strong negative-achievement incentives. For boys, however, the positive incentive value of achievement in physical activity remains particularly strong throughout their school years. Horner (43) has suggested that women in achievement situations must contend with a motive not encountered by men—the motive to avoid success. However, current research indicates that this is changing and may no longer be as important a factor in determining behavior (51).

Generally, it appears that individuals differ in the degree to which they find achievement satisfying. Therefore, they differ in the extent to which they engage in competition with standards of excellence applied to their performance. Since most forms of physical activity contain a degree of competition, it is easy to see why the need for achievement is such an important motivator.

## Affiliation

*The need for affiliation may motivate involvement in physical activities which foster contact with others.* According to Birsch and Veroff (10), individuals are motivated by the need for affiliation when they are attracted to other people for reassurance that they are acceptable. This motive is closely related to Festinger's "drive for self-evaluation" which he describes as the desire "to know . . . precisely what one is and is not capable of doing" (33). Defined in this manner, the need for affiliation is also closely associated with the needs for recognition and social approval.

The needs for affiliation, self-evaluation, recognition, and social approval can all be seen as strong social motives for participation in physical activity. However, it is often difficult to determine whether an individual is participating to fulfill achievement or affiliative needs. In physical activity, social approval is usually based on competence, mastery and/ or achievement. Therefore, the incentive for achievement may be affiliative.

According to Cratty (23), "moderate achievement in certain sports activities frequently enhances the social acceptance of adults." He goes on to state that participation in recreational physical activity is often motivated by the possibility of enhancing one's social acceptability. Activities such as golf, tennis, and bowling appear to have particular appeal for adult males. Observations of a university faculty-staff slow-pitch softball team would seem to substantiate Cratty's position. Members of this team (average age around 30–35 years) seemed more concerned with how a particular play in which they were involved was perceived by their teammates than with the final outcome of the game. In fact, most of the team members were not aware of the score of the game. That this team had what one might politely call a "losing season" supports the numerous research studies which generalize that there is a tendency for affiliative needs to interfere with optimum group effort (21).

The need for affiliation has a particularly strong influence on the selection of the type of physical activity in which an individual chooses to participate. First of all, an individual with a high need for affiliation will be more likely to select a team or dual sport (i.e. volleyball or tennis) over an individual sport (i.e. track and field events or swimming). Secondly, these individuals will tend to select activities which are attractive to those individuals whose acceptance they desire. In our society, some physical activities are more highly approved of than others. Generally, games of skill are more acceptable than games of chance. Moreover, acceptance of certain forms of physical activity is often related to the age and sex of the participant. For example, jumping rope is an acceptable form of physical activity for girls throughout their elementary school years, and certain forms of dance become more acceptable for boys as they reach the upper high-school grades.

Coupled with the positive incentives for affiliation is a negative incentive—fear of rejection. This fear may increase an individual's motivation to participate in a given activity. However, the fear of rejection may be so strong that an individual withdraws from participation. The clumsy child with a high need for affiliation will probably not continue involvement in activities such as Little League baseball or Pee Wee football.

Although difficult to isolate from the need for achievement in games and sports, the need for affiliation does appear to motivate the selection, intensity, and persistence of involvement in physical activity.

### Sensory Stimulation

*Participation in certain psychologically stressful activities may be motivated by the need for sensory stimulation.* This concept is closely linked to Kenyon's subdomain *pursuit of vertigo*. The pursuit of vertigo is seen in those experiences providing an element of thrill but over which the participant maintains control. Skiing, diving from a high platform, heavy weather sailing, mountain climbing, and sky diving were given as examples of activities where the primary incentive might be the pursuit of vertigo. Individuals who constantly pursue such activities are often referred to as risk-seekers, stress-seekers, or stimulation-seekers. Bernard (7) has identified two types of stress—*dys-stress* and *eustress*: the former is unpleasant, perhaps even painful; the latter is pleasant. Discussion will be confined to eustressful activities.

There is increasing evidence that individuals differ in their preference for levels of stimulation (56). Some theorists relate differences to the personality traits of introversion and extroversion. According to Kane (50), the extrovert requires stronger sensory stimulation in order to maintain arousal. In light of this, it is interesting that Klausner (55) found that stress-seekers tend to be extroverted.

The usefulness of a concept related to the satisfaction of a need for sensory stimulation is not confined to explanations of adult participation in "dangerous" sports or such activities as "walking on the moon." It is valuable in understanding certain aspects of the play behavior of children. Slides, swings, see-saws, and self-propelled merry-go-rounds all seem to have elements of risk and thrill which most children enjoy, but to differing degrees. Some children want to go "higher and higher" on swings. The etiquette developed by children for seesawing seems to have taken these individual differences into account, for it is only proper that one should ask a partner whether he wants "bumpsies" (that is when the child at the lower end allows the board to hit the ground, which lifts the child at the higher end momentarily off the seat).

Physical activities vary in the degree to which they provide opportunities for sensory stimulation or the pursuit of vertigo, and individuals differ in the pleasure or satisfaction that they gain from this sensory stimulation. These two statements combine to help explain an individual's involvement or lack of involvement in physical activities as diverse as sliding down a bannister to jumping the Snake River Canyon in a jet-propelled motorcycle.

## The "Feel Better" Phenomenon

*The expectation that participation in vigorous physical activities will produce a "feel better" phenomenon motivates continued involvement in those activities.* It would seem that a discussion of motivation or motives would be incomplete without some reference to the "feel better" phenomenon. People, particularly adults, often attribute their involvement in vigorous physical activity to the fact that they "feel better." A great deal of speculation on the physiological and/or psychological foundation of this phenomenon has not substantially clarified whether it is merely subjective or has some objectively measurable basis.

The literature supports the speculation that vigorous physical activity does have the effect of reducing tension and state anxiety. Thus the "feel better" phenomenon may be an individual's subjective appraisal of this reduction. The phenomenon may also be related to Kenyon's subdomain, labeled *catharsis*, in which physical activity is perceived "as providing a release of tension precipitated by frustration through some vicarious means" (52). Unfortunately, the term *catharsis* is usually associated in sports with the word *aggression*, and there is little support for the theory that participation in physical activity reduces aggression. However, frustration need not lead to aggression or the desire to aggress. When daily frustrations lead to an increase in anxiety and tension, but not aggression, then physical activity may have a cathartic effect. It may be this cathartic effect which leads to the subjective experience of the "feel better" phenomenon. Much more research is needed before an adequate understanding of this phenomenon can be reached.

If our primary motive for participation is to experience the "feel better" phenomenon, what types of activities should we choose? In our concept, we implied that this need is satisfied through *vigorous* physical activity—activity that leads to a mildly fatigued state at least. Weight training, basketball, running, and some dance forms are examples of such activities. Individuals also tend to select activities in which they have a moderate degree of competence or skill ability. The popularity of jogging reflects this fact. Most people feel competent in their ability to run as it is generally a well learned skill.

In this section we have discussed some of the motives and incentives that may motivate an individual's involvement or lack of involvement in physical activity—achievement, affiliation, sensory stimulation, and the "feel better" phenomenon. Motivational factors do influence the selection, intensity, and persistence of human movement. However, it is obvious that much more research is needed before adequate answers to the "why" questions posed in the very beginning of this section can be found.

## PERSONALITY AND MOVEMENT

*An individual's personality affects movement.* As you can see, our concept deals with personality, a term which has many meanings. For example, it is common to hear a person speak of another as having a good personality, a bad personality, or no personality. In this sense, an individual's personality is usually judged by the way he or she interacts with others in social situations. We also refer to personality when we describe the individual as being aggressive, introverted, extroverted, self-confident, or competitive. These are all general descriptions of an individual's surface behavior. In order to really understand personality, we must go beyond the mere description of behavior. Unfortunately, even among personality theorists (personologists), there is no consensus as to the definition of personality. For the purpose of this discussion we will use Allport's (1) definition: "Personality is the dynamic organization within the individual of those psycho-physical systems that determine his characteristic behavior and thought." Allport's definition emphasizes the importance of traits, which are considered to be the outcome of both genetic factors and learning. Many personologists have employed the trait approach to understanding personality. This approach is based on the idea that the key to a person's personality is in knowing his unique pattern of traits. In this context, a trait is "a report of an observed consistency in the acts or behaviors of persons" (42). For example, it has been suggested that athletes possess the following traits: extroverted, tough-minded, self-assertive, self-confident, dominant, and less impulsive (67). You may have noted the similarity between the concept of trait and that of motive. Allport contends that traits *are* motives. Although personologists vary in the number of motivational concepts to which they subscribe, they do see motivation as "the crucial empirical and theoretical problem" (44). Thus, motivation is seen as the key to understanding behavior even among personality theorists.

Our concept suggests that personality factors interact with movement. That an individual's personality affects personal movement suggests that there may be a particular combination of personality traits influencing the selection of specific forms of movement. For example, a person who tends to be extroverted (outgoing, impulsive, uninhibited, sociable) may be prompted to engage in team sports rather than individual sports. Our concept also suggests that a person who has particular traits may be successful in specific activities. Such success would encourage the individual to continue participation. As an illustration, if sky-diving required a high degree of emotional stability (maturity, quiet realism, optimism, self-discipline), we would expect that individuals who continually engage in this activity would be emotionally stable.

The second aspect of our concept has a slightly different interpretation. It states that an individual's personality is affected by his movement. In other words, participation in certain forms of movement may alter or modify an individual's personality. Dance, play, and recreation therapy programs often subscribe to this theory. Children and adults are encouraged to participate in these programs because of the positive influence movement experiences have upon self-concept, mental health, and social adjustment. Similarly, continued participation and success in sport is often viewed as resulting, at least in part, from the development of certain personality traits through involvement in that sport.

Although the concept suggests two possible ways in which personality and movement interact, there is little research evidence at the present time favoring one explanation over the other, nor has a model been developed which combines both approaches. However, it may be that certain personality traits influence the selection of a particular form of movement, whereas modification of certain role-related personality factors may influence continued, successful participation. We can merely speculate. The possibility exists that there is no cause-and-effect relationship between personality and human movement, although this theory is not favored by most professionals within the discipline of Human Movement.

Most of the research that has been conducted concerns itself with personality-trait differences between athletes and nonathletes, individual and team sport athletes, highly and poorly skilled participants, and physically fit and unfit adults. We will not attempt to summarize the literature on these topics for two reasons. First of all, comprehensive summaries can be found in a variety of other sources (15, 17, 41, 57, 65). In fact, Morgan (65) has developed two concepts which succinctly summarize the present status of personality and athletics literature.

1. Athletes from various subgroups differ on a variety of psychological states and traits.

2. High-level performers in athletics are characterized by psychological profiles which generally distinguish them from lower level performers.

The second reason has to do with the general nature of the research conducted up to this time. For the most part, the studies do not originate from a theoretical basis and do not go any further than the examination of personality traits. However, studies are now underway that examine other personality factors with particular emphasis on situational variables and role-related behaviors. As you can see, this approach is very similar to the expectancy-value model of motivation previously discussed. A more thorough understanding of role-related behaviors and traits should greatly enhance our understanding of the relationship between personality and human movement, particularly in sport and athletics.

## References Cited

1. ALLPORT, GORDON W. *Pattern and Growth in Personality.* New York: Holt Rinehart and Winston, 1961.

2. AMMONS, R. B. "Acquisition of Motor Skills: II Rotary Pursuit Performance with Continuous Practice Before and After a Single Rest," *Journal of Experimental Psychology,* 37 (1947) 393–411.

3. AMMONS, R., S. ALPRIN, AND C. AMMONS. "Rotary Pursuit Performance as Related to Sex and Age of Pre-Adult Subjects," *Journal of Experimental Psychology,* 49 (1955) 127–33.

4. ATKINSON, J. W. *An Introduction to Motivation.* Princeton, N.J.: D. Van Nostrand, 1964.

5. BARTON, J. W. "Smaller versus Larger Units in Learning the Maze. *Journal of Experimental Psychology,* 4 (1921) 418–429.

6. BELL, V. L. "Augmented Knowledge of Results and Its Effect upon Acquisition and Retention of a Gross Motor Skill," *Research Quarterly,* 39 (1968) 25–30.

7. BERNARD, J. "The Eudaemonists," in *Why Man Takes Chances*, S. Klausner, ed. Garden City, N.Y.: Anchor Books, Doubleday, 1968.

8. BILODEAU, E. A., AND I. McD. BILODEAU. "Variable Frequency of Knowledge of Results and the Learning of Simple Skill," *Journal of Experimental Psychology*, 55 (1958) 379–385.

9. BILODEAU, I. McD. "Accuracy of a Simple Positioning Response With Variation in the Number of Trials by Which Knowledge of Results is Delayed," *American Journal of Psychology*, 69 (1956) 434–437.

10. BIRCH, DAVID AND JOSEPH VEROFF. *Motivation: A Study of Action*. Belmont, Calif.: Brooks/Cole Publishing Co., 1966.

11. BOURNE, L. E. "Information Feedback: Comments on Professor I. McD. Bilodeau's Paper," in *Acquisition of Skill*, E. A. Bilodeau, ed. New York: Academic Press, 1966, pp. 273–313.

12. BUHLER, C., AND F. MASSARIK. *The Course of Human Life*. New York: Springer-Verlag, 1968.

13. CARPENTER, A. "Tests of Motor Educability for the First Three Grades," *Child Development*, 11 (1940): 293–299.

14. CLARKE, L. V. "Effect of Mental Practice on the Development of a Certain Motor Skill." *Research Quarterly*, 31 (1960) 560–569.

15. COFER, CHARLES N., AND WARREN R. JOHNSON. "Personality Dynamics in Relation to Exercise and Sports," in *Science and Medicine of Exercise and Sports*, Warren R. Johnson, ed. New York: Harper and Row, 1960, pp. 525–59.

16. CONNOLLY, K., K. BROWN, AND E. BASSETT. "Developmental Changes in Some Components of a Motor Skill," *British Journal of Psychology*, 59 (1968) 305–14.

17. COOPER, L., "Athletics, Activity and Personality: A Review of the Literature," *Research Quarterly*, 40 (1969): 17–22.

18. CORBIN, C. B. "Effects of Mental Practice on Skill Development after Controlled Practice," *Research Quarterly*, 38 (1967) 534–538.

19. ———, "Mental Practice," *Ergogenic Aids and Muscular Performance*, W. P. Morgan ed. New York: Academic Press, 1972, pp. 93–118.

20. COTTRELL, N. B. "Social Facilitation," *Experimental Social Psychology*, C. G. McClintock ed. New York: Holt, Rinehart and Winston, 1972.

21. CRATTY, BRYANT J. *Movement Behavior and Motor Learning*, 3rd ed. Philadelphia: Lea and Febiger, 1973.

22. CRATTY, B. J. *Perceptual and Motor Development in Infants and Children*. New York: Macmillan, 1970.

23. ———. *Teaching Motor Skills*. Englewood Cliffs, N.J., Prentice-Hall, 1973a. 1973a.

24. CRATTY, BRYANT J. *Psychology and Physical Activity*. Englewood Cliffs, N.J.: Prentice-Hall, 1968.

25. CRATTY, B. AND M. M. MARTINS, *Perceptual-Motor Efficiency in Children.* Philadelphia: Lea and Febiger, 1969.

26. CRON, G. W. AND PRONKO, N. H. "Development of the Sense of Balance in School Children," *Journal of Education Research*, 51 (1957) 33–37.

27. CROSS, T. J. "A Comparison of the Whole Method, the Minor Game Method, and the Whole-Part Method of Teaching Basketball to Ninth Grade Boys," *Research Quarterly*, 8 (1937): 49–54.

28. DAVOL, S., HASTINGS, M. AND D. KLEIN. "The Effect of Age, Sex and Speed of Rotation on Rotary Pursuit Performance by Young Children," *Perceptual and Motor Skills*, 21 (1965) 351–57.

29. DEESE, J. AND S. HULSE, *The Psychology of Learning.* New York: McGraw-Hill, 1967.

30. DUNCAN, C. P. "The Effect of Unequal Amounts of Practice on Motor Learning Before and After Rest." *Journal of Experimental Psychology*, 42 (1951) 257–264.

31. ESPENSCHADE, ANNA. "Motor Development," *Science and Medicine of Exercise and Sports*, Warren Johnson, ed. New York: Harper and Row, 1960.

32. ESPENSCHADE, ANNA AND H. ECKERT. *Motor Development.* Columbus, Ohio: Charles E. Merrill, 1972.

33. FESTINGER, L. "Motivations Leading to Social Behavior," *Nebraska Symposium on Motivation*, M. R. Jones, ed. Lincoln, Nebraska: University of Nebraska Press, 1954, pp. 191, 219.

34. FITTS, P. M. AND M. I. POSNER. *Human Performance.* Belmont, Calif.: Brooks/Cole Publishing Co., 1967.

35. FOX, M. G. AND E. LAMB. "Improvement During a Non Practice Period in a Selected Physical Education Activity," *Research Quarterly*, 33 (1962) 381–385.

36. FRANK, J. D. "Individual Differences in Certain Aspects of the Level of Aspiration," *American Journal of Psychology*, 47 (1935) 119–128.

37. GAGNÉ, R. M., AND E. A. FLEISHMAN. *Psychology and Human Performance: An Introduction to Psychology.* New York: Holt, Rinehart and Winston, 1959.

38. GARRY, R. *The Psychology of Learning.* Washington, D.C.: The Center for Applied Research in Education, 1963.

39. GOVATES, L. A. "Sex Differences in Children's Motor Performance," *Collected Papers, The Eleventh Inter-Institutional Seminar in Child Development.* Dearborn, Michigan: Michigan Education Department of the Henry Ford Museum and Greenfield Village, 1966, pp. 55–75.

40. HALL, CALVIN S., AND GARDNER LINDZEY. *Theories of Personality*, New York: John Wiley and Sons, 1970.

41. HARRIS, D. V. *Involvement in Sport: A Somatopsychic Rationale for Physical Activity.* Philadelphia: Lea and Febiger, 1973.

42. HERSHEY, GERALD L. AND JAMES O. LUGO. *Living Psychology.* New York: Macmillan, 1970.

43. HORNER, M. S. "Sex Differences in Achievement Motivation and Performance in Competitive and Noncompetitive Situations." Unpublished doctoral dissertation, University of Michigan, 1968.

44. HULL, C. L. *Principles of Behavior*, New York: Appleton-Century-Crofts, 1943.

45. HUNSICKER, P. A. AND G. G. RUFF. "A Survey and Comparison of Youth Fitness 1958–1965," *Journal of Health, Physical Education and Recreation*, Washington: American Alliance for Health, Physical Education and Recreation, 1966.

46. IRION, A. L. "Reminiscence in Pursuit Rotor Learning as a Function of Length of Rest and Amount of Pre-Rest Practice," *Journal of Experimental Psychology*, 1966.

47. JENKINS, L. M. "A Comparative Study of Motor Achievements of Children of Five, Six, and Seven Years of Age," Teachers College. Columbia University, No. 414, (1930).

48. JOHNSON, R. D. "Measurement of Achievement in Fundamental Skills of Elementary School Children," *Research Quarterly*, 33 (1962) 94–103.

49. JONES, H. E. *Motor Performance and Growth*. Berkeley, California: University of California Press, 1949, p. 182.

50. KANE, J. E. "Personality, Arousal and Performance," *International Journal of Sport Psychology*, Vol. 2, No. 1, 1971.

51. KARABENICK, S. "Valence of Success and Failure as a Function of Achievement Motives and Locus of Control," *Journal of Personality and Social Psychology*, 21 (1972) 101–110.

52. KENYON, G. S. "A Conceptual Model for Characterizing Physical Activity," *Research Quarterly*, 39 (1968) 96–105.

53. KEOGH, J. "Development in Fundamental Motor Tasks," *Textbook of Motor Development*, C. B. Corbin, ed. Dubuque, Iowa: W. C. Brown, 1973.

54. ———. *Motor Performance of Elementary School Children*. Los Angeles: University of California, Department of Physical Education, 1965.

55. KLAUSNER, S. Z. "Empirical Analysis of Stress-Seekers," *Why Man Takes Chances*, S Z. Klausner, ed. Garden City, N.Y.: Anchor Books, Doubleday and Company, 1968.

56. KORMAN, ABRAHAM K. *The Psychology of Motivation*, Englewood Cliffs, N.J.: Prentice-Hall, 1974.

57. KROLL, W. "Current Strategies and Problems in Personality Assessment of Athletes," *Psychology of Motor Learning: Proceedings of C.I.C. Symposium on Psychology of Motor Learning*, L. S. Smith, ed. Chicago: The Athletic Institute, 1970.

58. LaCHANCE, R. M. "Principles of Motivation Which Influence Participation in Physical Activity," M. S. Thesis, The Pennsylvania State University, 1972.

59. LATCHAW, M. "Measuring Selected Motor Skills in Fourth, Fifth and Sixth Grades," *Research Quarterly*, 25 (1954) 439–449.

60. LOCKE, E. A., N. CARLLEGE, AND J. KOEPPEL. "Motivational Effects of Knowledge of Results: A Goal-Setting Phenomenon?" *Psychological Bulletin,* 70 (1968) 474–485.

61. MACCOBY, E. (ed.). *The Development of Sex Differences.* Stanford, Calif.: Stanford University Press, 1966.

62. MALINA, R. M. "Environment Factors and Motor Development," *Textbook of Motor Development,* C. C. Corbin, ed. Dubuque, Iowa: William C. Brown Company, 1973.

63. ———, "Growth, Maturation and Performance of Philadelphia Negro and White Elementary School Children," Unpublished Doctoral Dissertation, Philadelphia: University of Pennsylvania, 1968.

64. MARTENS, R. "Trait and State Anxiety," in *Ergogenic Aids and Muscular Performance,* W. P. Morgan, ed. New York: Academic Press, 1972, pp. 35–66.

65. MORGAN, WILLIAM P. "Selected Psychological Considerations in Sport," *Research Quarterly,* 45 (1974) 374–390.

66. NEIMEYER, R. K., "Part Versus Whole Methods and Massed Versus Distributed Practice in the Learning of Selected Large Muscle Activities," *62nd Proceedings of the College Physical Education Association for Men,* Washington: American Alliance for Health, Physical Education and Recreation, 1959, pp. 122–125.

67. OGILVIE, BRUCE C. "What is an Athlete?," *Journal of Health, Physical Education and Recreation,* 38 (1967): 48.

68. ———, AND T. A. TUTKO, "A Psychologist Reviews the Future Contribution of Motivational Research in Track and Field," *Track and Field News,* (September 1, 1963).

69. OXENDINE, J. B. *Psychology of Motor Learning.* New York: Appleton-Century-Crofts, 1968.

70. ———, "Emotional Arousal and Motor Performance," *Quest,* Monograph XIII (1970) 23–32.

71. ———, "Physical Education," *Psychomotor Domain: Movement Behavior,* R. N. Singer, ed. Philadelphia: Lea and Febiger, 1972, pp. 165–92.

72. PHIPPS, S. J. AND C. A. MOREHOUSE. "Effects of Mental Practice on the Acquisition of Motor Skills of Varied Difficulty," *Research Quarterly,* 40 (1969) 773–778.

73. RICHARDSON, A. "Mental Practice: A Review and Discussion—Part I," *Research Quarterly,* 38 (1967a) 97–107.

74. ———, "Mental Practice: A Review and Discussion—Part II," *Research Quarterly,* 38 (1967b) 263–273.

75. ROBB, MARGARET D. *The Dynamics of Motor-Skill Acquisition.* Englewood Cliffs, N.J.: Prentice-Hall, 1972.

76. SAGE, G. H. *Introduction to Motor Behavior: A Neuropsychological Approach.* Reading, Mass.: Addison-Wesley, 1971.

77. SCHMIDT, RICHARD A. *Motor Skills.* New York: Harper and Row, 1975.

78. SCHRAMM, V. "An Investigation of E. MG Responses Obtained During Mental Practice," Madison: University of Wisconsin Press, 1967.

79. SHAY, C. T. "The Progressive-Part Versus the Whole Method of Learning Motor Skills," *Research Quarterly*, 5 (1934) 62–67.

80. SINGER, R. N. "Massed and Distributed Practice Effects on the Acquisition and Retention of a Novel Basketball Skill," *Research Quarterly*, 36 (1965) 68–77.

81. ———, *Motor Learning and Human Performance*. New York: Macmillan, 1968.

82. ———, *Motor Learning and Human Performance* (2nd ed.). New York: Macmillan, 1975.

83. ———, "Social Facilitation," in *Ergogenic Aids and Muscular Performance*, W. P. Morgan ed., New York: Academic Press, 1972, pp. 264–289.

84. SIGUELAND, E. R., AND L. P. LIPPITT. "Conditioned Head-Turning in Newborns," *Journal of Experimental Child Psychology*, 3 (1966): 356–76.

85. SPIELBERGER, C. D. "Theory and Research on Anxiety," *Anxiety and Behavior*, C. D. Spielberger, ed. New York: Academic Press, 1966, pp. 3–22.

86. STALLINGS, L. M. *Motor Skills: Development and Learning*. Dubuque, Iowa: Wm. C. Brown, 1973.

87. STELMACH, G. E. "Efficiency of Motor Learning as a Function of Inter-trial Rest.," *Research Quarterly*, 40 (1969) 198–202.

88. WILLIAMS, H. G. The Development of Selected Aspects of Visual Perception in Infancy and Childhood," Unpublished seminar paper. University of Wisconsin, Madison, 1964.

89. WILMORE, J. "They Told You You Couldn't Compete with Men and You, Like a Fool, Believed Them," *Women Sports*, 1 (1974) 40.

90. WITTE, F. "Relation of Kinesthetic Perception to a Selected Motor Skill for Elementary Children," *Research Quarterly*, 33 (1962) 476–484.

91. ZAICHKOWSKY, L. D. "The Development of Perceptual-Motor Sequencing Ability," *Journal of Motor Behavior*, 6 (1974) 255–261.

92. ZAJONC, R. B. "Social Facilitation," *Science*, 149 (1965) 269–274.

93. ———, *Social Psychology: An Experimental Approach*. Belmont, California: Wadsworth, 1966.

## Selected Readings

ALDERMAN, R. B. *Psychological Behavior in Sport*, Philadelphia: W. B. Saunders, 1974.

BELL, VIRGINIA LEE. *Sensorimotor Learning*, Pacific Palisades, Calif.: Goodyear Publishing Co., 1970.

CRATTY, BRYANT J. *Movement Behavior and Motor Learning*, Philadelphia: Lea and Febiger, 1973.

CRATTY, BRYANT J. *Psychology in Contemporary Sport: Guidelines for Coaches and Athletes*, Englewood Cliffs, N.J.: Prentice-Hall, 1973.

DROWATZKY, JOHN N. *Motor Learning Principles and Practices*, Minneapolis: Burgess Publishing Company, 1975.

FITTS, PAUL M., AND MICHAEL I. POSNER. *Human Performance*, Belmont, Calif.: Brooks/Cole Publishing Co., 1967.

HARRIS, DOROTHY V. *Involvement in Sport: A Somatopsychic Rationale for Physical Activity*, Philadelphia: Lea and Febiger, 1973.

KENYON, GERALD S. (ed.). *Contemporary Psychology of Sport*, Proceedings of the 2nd International Congress of Sport Psychology, Chicago: The Athletic Institute, 1970.

MARTENS, RAINER *Social Psychology and Physical Activity*, New York: Harper and Row, Publishers, 1975.

OXENDINE, JOSEPH B. *Psychology of Motor Learning*, Englewood Cliffs, N.J.: Prentice-Hall, 1968.

ROBB, MARGARET D. *The Dynamics of Motor-Skill Acquisition*, Englewood Cliffs, N.J.: Prentice-Hall, 1972.

RUSHALL, BRENT S., AND DARYL SIEDENTOP. *The Development of Behavior in Sport and Physical Education*, Philadelphia: Lea and Febiger, 1972.

SAGE, GEORGE H. *Introduction to Motor Behavior: A Neuropsychological Approach*, Reading, Mass.: Addison-Wesley Publishing Co., 1971.

SCHMIDT, RICHARD A. *Motor Skills*, New York: Harper and Row, 1975.

SINGER, ROBERT N. *Motor Learning and Human Performance*, New York: Macmillan Publishing Co., 1975.

————. *The Psychomotor Domain: Movement Behavior*. Philadelphia: Lea and Febiger, 1972.

STALLINGS, LORETTA M. *Motor Skills: Development and Learning*, Dubuque, Iowa: Wm. C. Brown, 1973.

WELFORD, A. T. *Fundamentals of Skill*, London: Methuen and Co., 1968.

WHITING, H. T. A. *Acquiring Ball Skill: A Psychological Interpretation*, London: G. Bell and Sons, 1969.

# 6

## What Happens When One Individual's Movement Is Related to Others?

*John Cheffers / Linda Zaichkowsky*

Human beings have been called social animals because we are the products of countless others whose memory we carry in our genes, our history, our culture, and our day-to-day interactions. At the very basis of socialization is human movement, which includes everything from eye contact to total body onslaught. Many factors affect and are affected by man as a social animal: groups, society and culture, social ranking, majorities and minorities, and so on. Such factors are discussed in the present chapter.

### GROUP MOVEMENT*

Human beings spend most of their waking hours moving in groups. A group is not merely two or more individuals in close physical proximity, such as twenty people waiting for a bus; or people with a similar characteristic, such as all bald-headed Americans. A group is characterized by individuals who have mutual responsibilities and similar goals and who are interdependent on one another for the satisfaction of one or more of their needs.

All groups depend on movement in order to function. As the individuals within a group move, the group changes.

*The authors are grateful for the excellent work of Marvin Shaw in identifying many concepts from the literature of groups (1).

## Formation and Development

*The medium of human movement provides meaningful form to symbolic interaction among groups.* Within every group individuals play various roles. On a football team some clear the way (blockers), some carry the ball, some throw and some catch, and some may draw off defenders by faking. In every play, various individuals assume different roles. Some players change their role from one play to the next, one time blocking, another carrying the ball, and still another faking a pass. If individuals fail to carry out their expected roles, the play fails and the group ceases to function in a meaningful way. By accepting and fulfilling a role, each individual interacts with others on the team, with the opposition, and with the spectators. This interaction is a form of communication between individuals. Some interaction may be verbal as when the quarterbacks call the play. Some interaction is symbolic and is solely dependent on movement, as when the quarterback hands the ball off and fakes a run himself.

### The Nature of Group Movement

*Permanent or Temporary Grouping. The nature of the movement within a group determines whether the group is temporary or permanent, primary or secondary.* A young child goes to visit his grandmother and finds to his delight that a family of young children has moved in next door. The child may play with his new friends for that day only, or he may continue to play with them every time he goes to visit his grandmother. The new group is temporary unless the child moves near his new friends. The family is an example of a permanent and primary group. We have many examples of parental movement being passed on to the children. Mozart's father taught him to play the piano. After suffering the effects of class snobbery and having his entry in the world-famous Henley rowing regatta rejected in the 1920's, John B. Kelly carefully and deliberately prepared his own son not only for entry into this famous tournament, but for victory in 1947 and 1949. The senior Kelly, by the very nature of the family structure and the type of predetermined movement, enmeshed his own son in a binding, permanent, and primary group activity. Many athletes seek to join larger groups such as golf clubs, social clubs, and recreational institutions. Their membership is usually dependent upon residence in that geographical area and their continued personal interest in the activities promoted by the club. Secondary groups of temporary status do not have the continuing loyalty and close interpersonal contact that primary groups have. Accordingly, some shrewd coaches or mentors will encourage certain vital members of their teams to not only become close friends, but also to maintain close geographic locations in their personal life. Examples of this close grouping are quarterbacks and runningbacks, pitchers and catchers, tandem bicycle teams, and competitive dance combinations.

*Membership. The nature of the movement indulged in by a group will determine its membership.* People are attracted to groups because groups encourage and promote activities under their auspices that meet the people's needs and interests or appeals to their curiosity. Robust individuals tend to be attracted to contact sports where image reinforcement is more likely, and timid individuals tend to be attracted to physical activities that do not expose them to image-destroying competition. Human beings become lonely and rejected as a result of noncomplementary group membership. In a primary group, the younger son is expected to be another "chip off the old block" or at least as good as his older brother. Where expectations are great and other members of the group are dependent on an individual, the concomitant stresses will determine both the nature and the permanence of that individual's membership. Often harmonious group functioning is facilitated by the pairing of disparate abilities. The legendary friendship between Gayle Sayers and Brian Picolo is one such example. Sayers, the brilliant black running back with obvious professional potential, became a great friend of Brian Picolo, the doomed white substitute player with no professional future. Their disparate physical abilities were unimportant in the formation of an unique friendship. Certainly one conclusion from such an example is that movement has inherent psychosocial parameters more important in group membership than specific ability levels.

*Voluntary or Mandatory Movement. In some groups movement is voluntary, in others mandated, and still others a combination of both.* The movement in groups composed of varied interests tends to be voluntary. Many organizations provide a great variety of movement experiences for their members. Where individuals have a choice of varied activities, their motivation for continuing membership will be high. They may choose their activities by season, such as skiing in the winter or swimming in the summer, or by the current popularity ratings. Members of the armed forces, on the other hand, have little choice in the principal physical activities they are required to undertake. Marching, combat drills, even saluting are mandated in official directives designed for the purpose of regulating mind and body.

Still other groups exist as combinations of voluntary and mandated activities. A young person who wishes to join an ambitious professional organization will find that compulsory conformity to necessary drills is their governing factor. If a young athlete desires to take part in the Olympic games, for instance, he or she can choose the sport, club, event, coach, and technique. But the mechanical and physiological movement principles governing the eventual choice demand binding conformity in movement expression. Under these circumstances, many athletes have been heard to complain that they have become enslaved by the very activity in which they originally sought to participate.

*Size. The size of the group's membership is often determined by its movement levels.* A professional basketball team can only have five members on the court at any one time. This restriction, along with the necessity of having the very best players in combination, restricts that organization to an exclusive membership role. Most educators see the need in college sport, for instance, for the existence of a healthy and all-inclusive intramural program to accompany interscholastic activities. The exclusive nature of the college basketball team denies huge numbers of students the opportunity of taking part in a game which is enjoyable and healthy. Although the intramural programs are sometimes denigrated as unimportant offshoots of interscholastic endeavor, most people see them as pivotal in the cause of promoting physical well-being in general college life.

The factor of exclusivity is sometimes the function of courage and tenacity. Sky diving teams and mountaineering teams are usually small in membership. The nature of the movements indigenous to these activities appeals to relatively small numbers. They are not exclusive in the sense of the movement capabilities required so much as in the courage needed to partake in the movements.

## Socialization and Communication

*The older, more established group members socialize the movement of the younger, more precarious members.* Younger members unfamiliar with group norms quickly tend to learn the rules and regulations of acceptance into group life. There is an initial uncertainty in all group membership that is sufficiently threatening to produce total conformity during the earlier stages. Sometimes a new member will compensate for this initial insecurity by acting brash and disrespectful, but most times new members are quiet, enthusiastic, and highly receptive to socializing activities. An interesting aspect of group membership is that the leader of the group usually most conforms to the norms of the group, and therefore has the most influence in socializing newer group members (2). Often in professional sports, trades have been effected to help the quality of movement of ailing players by helping them to start again or at least to re-examine basic movement principles. It also could be that team co-hesion is resocialized and rendered more effective by this strategy. A recalcitrant, self-made business executive is often helped to resocialize through transfer to another setting. In fact, he may make life-saving ad-justments by the simple transfer from the highly stressful setting of his personal business into a larger more demanding business firm which insists on his taking time to enjoy recreative activity. The wife and mother who, after twenty years of domestic activity, is resocialized into the busi-ness world will usually conform to the new norms quickly and effectively and may enthusiastically embrace an entirely new value structure.

*Group members whose movements are inactive or stagnant rarely en-joy strong social interaction.* Communication through movement is vital if groups are to function in dynamic fashion. This communication is needed both within and among groups. A baseball team will not function effectively unless players in all field positions, including the coaches, are fully aware of the prospective play. Further, a breakdown in the entire structure of the game will take place unless both teams embrace certain norms of social interaction that are necessary for orderly procedures. Many dynamic forms of interaction are taken for granted in competitive situations. If the game is to be effective, both teams must be ready to play at the same time, both must present counteracting abilities (as one-sided games are rarely enjoyed), and both must recognize and conform to agreed upon regulations.

## Cooperation

*Every group appears to value cooperative movement.* Cooperation is promoted and appreciated if it takes more than the effort of one person to accomplish the overall objective (3). Obviously in competitive situa-tions cooperation among team members is necessary and goal achievement depends on the utmost degree of cooperation. Many complicated skills are testimony to this point. Examples from the field of sports are ample, but this point can be illustrated by work tasks as well. The intricate co-operative functioning of a surgical team at the height of a complicated operation and the strong interdependence of air crews during take off and landing clearly underscore the effectiveness of cooperative movement. It may be that groups are in constant competition either with the elements or against other groups, and that the resulting stresses are the real determinants of cooperative effort. Some have even maintained that a symbiotic relationship exists between cooperation and competition. Cer-tainly group harmony and cohesion appear to be greatly enhanced when threatened by alien influences.

*In some cases, cooperation breaks down in the face of conflict.* Perry and Perry (4) make distinction between competition and rivalry. Competition is defined as the striving after goal achievement either individually or through group effort. It can involve effort against the environment or other human beings, but it is characterized by idealistic goal achievements and needs satisfaction. Rivalry, on the other hand, is defined as the need to beat the next person or to triumph over an opponent or group of opponents. This important distinction between competition and rivalry gives significant meaning to the phenomenon of group disintegration in the face of conflict. Any team which feasts upon another's degradation and shame is doomed in turn to internal disharmony and eventual collapse. There is a very different attitude emanating from a group that sets out to win for the sake of achieving its goal (competition) and from a group that is intent on putting the other team down (rivalry). Honest competition can result in mutual respect and dignity to the extent that opposition enriches. Rivalry can result in bitterness, dissention and eventual disintegration. Another variable in the breakdown of group harmony in the face of conflict is coercion. Members who are forced to play roles that are troublesome will often desert that role in times of crisis. Coercion implies unreasonable conformity and rarely stands the test of stiff opposition. Like rats deserting a sinking ship, group members will either defect, undermine, or collapse in stressful situations.

*An encouraging element of most group-movement conflict is seen in the propensity of the majority of members for making peace.* Although one is often cynical about the reasons for fighting in professional sports, it is clear that the majority of uninvolved team members from both sides move quickly to restore peace. Intricate competitive movements among individuals frequently result in loss of temper. Most social groups permit temporary outbursts with minor penalty, but they strongly disapprove of permanent feuding. The small child goes through similar experiences when fighting with peers in the family group. Other brothers and sisters and most parents quickly move to restore order. Justice is dispensed and the incident forgotten. It is in this respect that the authors of this text use the word encouraging. Group members demonstrate a tendency to move to restore order during and after conflict. This is a very definite, positive behavior, and it is present even in groups characterized as predatorial or self-destructive.

## Mobility

*Most groups in modern civilization have permeable walls permitting movement within and without, provided equal exchange takes place.*

The merger of the American Football League and the National Football League took place because the advantages of forming one league outweighed the disadvantages of having two leagues. The knockdown, dragout fight among the various owners was lessened and the drain from the middleman was eliminated. On the other hand, the National Basketball Association and American Basketball Association did not merge harmoniously because the disadvantages for the NBA are greater than the advantages.

Most secondary groups will encourage movement within and among other groups. Primary groups are frequently more rigid in structure and more divisive in nature. The domination of a secondary group by primary group influences, often called *cliques,* is seen in most cases as negative and harmful to group cohesiveness. The tendency for human beings to be drawn into cliques frequently necessitates the establishment of checks and balances. Teachers and coaches are aware of the disastrous side effects of playing favorites. Each member or group of members within a group needs identity, recognition, and reinforcement. To ignore these fundamentals is to toll the bell on total group effectiveness.

## Cultural Grouping and Interaction

*Close contact among group members provides an individual with opportunities to discover yet unidentified movement needs and potentials.* We are all familiar with the story of the young man who joins the track team as a sprinter and finds he is an even better long jumper. Group interaction and the desire for members to promote group achievement through developing their individual potential are clear indications that overall group influence can help the ego development of its members. The young black athlete discovers that not all members of the white race are prejudiced against him or her on the grounds of skin color. The expanded interaction made possible through group interdependence helps the young black to discover educational and social deficiencies in time for appropriate remedy. Most productive members of minority groups have undergone this experience.

*People tend to like each other and imitate each other's movement when there are strong similarities in personality, perception, ethnicity, and attitudinal harmony.* Much progress is being made in breaking down barriers between national and racial groups. But there is little doubt that people congregate and function within their own social and cultural groupings. One only has to look at real estate divisions in major urban areas to appreciate this fact. Further it appears that similar groupings lead to the development of distinct and recognizable movement patterns. These patterns also restrict whole groups of people from attempting to move outside their groupings. American blacks have never distinguished themselves in competitive aquatics, nor have we seen the American black as active in the throwing events of track and field. Few American blacks have participated successfully in distance running, yet blacks have dominated world distance running for the past decade. Preference for organized movement appears to be strongly regulated by the ethnic and racial groupings into which a child is born. The explosion in universal communication techniques and the overwhelming world sympathy for integration is having an effect though. The incredible visibility afforded national and political groups through such institutions as the Olympic Games is bringing hitherto foreign movements into the general public eye. White-water canoeing gained popularity as a result of television coverage at the Munich Olympics in 1972. Perhaps the second half of the twentieth century will receive the praise of history for its role in breaking down racial and ethnic barriers and for popularizing interethnic movement.

## Advertising

*Groups interested in expanding their membership do so by publicizing their more interesting activities and attractive rewards.* The advertising profession has long been aware of the truism that the grass is always greener in the field next door. Such literature is replete with statements advocating physical activities as the panacea for personal and social ills.

> Swim and dance with the singles group this coming Sunday at Buff Water Hotel.
>
> Purchase your new home in the restful country club atmosphere of Bloggs Park—swimming, sauna, golf, and horse riding are available to all.
>
> Vacation at Louis's mountain without pollution and stress—hike, cycle, ride in the summers, and ski in the winters.

Men (7) have tended to "sell" a little harder than women have in the past. However, the women's movement is helping to correct this age-long imbalance (5, 6, 7).

## Successful Group Management

*A group's development is dependent upon consistency of management, loyalty to group goals, and member involvement in decision making.* The modern coach is more concerned with input from the athlete than the coach of bygone eras. He has discovered that loyalty is not necessarily the same as blind conformity to managerial directives, and that a team involved in making important decisions feels less alienated and less insecure than teams who are merely recipients of authoritarian dictates.

Legendary UCLA basketball coach, Johnny Wooden, maintains that he changed his tactics in the 1970's as a result of player influence. He said "you have to listen to an athlete if you expect him to listen to you—that is a fundamental dignity and a right" (A.P. *Framingham Daily News*, Feb. 1975). Consistency of management is important to a group's development; there is a reduction in mistrust and confusion when governance is clear and not confused. The need for managerial consistency is shown in the necessity of protecting athletes against problems caused by their own tendency to become so involved in the complexities of their movement that they neglect other facets of their existence. Many athletes, ranging from school boys who neglect their homework to professional stars who squander fortunes, have benefited from sound advice from managers.

*A group's development is facilitated if its leadership is approved by the members and divisive influences are absent.* Although it is possible for any group to have differential leadership covering a wide range of activities, it is generally felt that singularity of approved leadership in specific group tasks is needed if that group is to make progress. Most of us are familiar with the destructive effect of inner rivalries and bitter jealousies in disintegrating groups. We tend to look toward leaders who have specific abilities and rely upon their judgments to keep the group cohesive, and very few teams who have disregarded this principle have succeeded. Although it may be argued that the highly existential Oakland Athletics winning baseball combination of the early 1970's is an exception, the team is probably the case that proves the rule. In light of their observable game cohesiveness on the field, one has to wonder if their much publicized internal strife was reality or whether it was built up by a sensational press. The important factors of group leadership are covered more fully in Chapter 11.

## The Individual and the Group

### Audiences

*When others are present, the motivation of a performing individual increases.* Triplet's work (8) was first done to show the effect of an audience on the performance of an individual. Recent studies have shown (9, 10, 11) that the performance of an individual is affected by the level of learning the individual brings to the task as well as by the presence of others. Generally speaking, if a task is well learned, the presence of others enhance the performance. When the task is still in the process of being learned, however, the presence of others may decrease the performance. Very few people enjoy naked exposure during the process of learning a competitive task. This is especially true of novice therapists analyzing and teaching movements to handicapped children in the presence of critical parents. It is very difficult for professionals to learn coolness of operation in a threatening environment. This factor is probably the reason for the host of rules and regulations designed to guard the anonymity of most professional diagnoses. Whereas this probably adds to the public mistrust of many professional pursuits, it is understandable and even forgivable in the novice professional. Covert behavior from the experienced professional however, is untenable in any age which seeks to benefit from the scientific analysis of human growth and development.

## Excellence Through Group Effort

*Where the movement of all group members is equally proficient, group compositions tend to be superior to any one individual's composition.* The director of a play is always conscious of the effect that each player has on the audience. An excellent performance results when each actor is carefully trained in the visible movements pursuant to the role. The audience notices when one or two individuals are clearly superior. Effective nonverbal communication contributes to this superiority. In fact, many acting schools today provide intensive training for young actors wishing to learn the movement patterns of widely varying roles. Davis (12) reports that the whole effect is equal to or greater than the sum of its parts, illustrating the integrative action which takes place in a group setting. Successful coaches are aware that strategies are not possible without all players participating fully. The crowd applauds the running back for large yardage gain, but knowledgeable football fans quickly point to the work of the fakers and the blockers as well.

## Group Decision Making

*Productive groups tend to effect more acceptable solutions to problems than do individuals working alone.* A combination of the best ideas of all group members is meaningful and advantageous provided the group is functioning harmoniously. Indeed, it can be argued that a strong sign of a productive group is its capacity to deal with excellent and diverse ideas from individual group members. Each member of a group must realize that constructive suggestions and criticisms are necessary. Baseball players illustrate this point when helping a pitcher decide which pitch to throw two opposing batters. Experience gained in the past, along with decisions on field placement and general expertise in each playing position are just as much a part of that pitch as the speed and flight imparted on the ball by the pitcher. In this sense, the productive baseball team is always a thinking baseball team.

## Group Learning

*Group decisions, especially those involving complicated movement, are usually more time consuming than individual decisions.* When a symphony orchestra functions in an autocratic atmosphere, what concert pieces to play, in what cities, and with what instrumental combinations, can be decided in a single day. When the orchestra is concerned with democratic process, decisions about the year's schedule may take several weeks. The individual players are the best judges of their practice abilities. They usually are aware of troublesome movement combinations in musical scores. Violinists will tell you that some pieces transfer negatively in terms of the fine adjustments needed to produce the best from their instruments. Therefore, it is important that schedule decisions should reflect input from all orchestral members. The greatest orchestras in the world recognize this fact.

Some group decisions tend to be less economical of time and are better implemented when time constraints have been removed. Obviously, the instantaneous action set of a play change at the line of scrimmage is the decision of one person, and has to be so. No self-respecting quarterback would shirk this issue in favor of community sharing that would lead to penalty due to time delay. However, where all group members feel that their thoughts and abilities are appreciated and that due recognition is forthcoming, harmonious and constructive group activity is possible.

*Individuals tend to learn movements more quickly and to a better standard in group settings than they do in isolation.* The norms of the group nearly always determine the rate and quality of group learning. Coaches and teachers in small country towns are eager to expose their champions to better quality competition. This concept is the reason that senior and experienced coaches insist that teams should practice and urge one another along together. It is possible for an individual practicing movements alone to be compounding errors that may go undetected and uncorrected for too long. Bandura and Walters (13) have shown clearly that young children learn quickest through imitation, and we strongly suspect that imitation is a prime learning mechanism in all age groups. An individual learns quickly to imitate common group movements through the multifaceted feedback and the many rewarding reinforcements encountered.

## Group Conformity and Risk-Taking

*Greater synthesis and risk taking is possible when groups can function harmoniously in a critical and analytical atmosphere.* Some researchers have discovered that groups have a tendency to make decisions that are riskier than the suggestions of even the most radical group members (14).

The phenomenon is sometimes known as the *risky shift* phenomenon. Most people can recall instances where groups have made risky decisions to support individual members. This is sometimes called the *safety of the crowd* phenomenon. Teams circumventing laws will tend to be more radical than individual members. Usually punishments handed down to errant teams do not shame individuals, but they may, through the visible notoriety the punishments give the team, even reinforce the illegal behavior. The "safety in a crowd" phenomenon can work against society also. *Psychology Today* has featured at least one article pointing to the lack of helping behavior in our society. Apparently, the larger the group, the greater the tendency becomes for members to assume that someone else has the responsibility for assisting an injured party: people do not feel as personally responsible for others' welfare in large group settings (15). Some explanation of the incredible neglect of people for one another can be ascribed to the fact that large groups tend to disintegrate into aggregates, but this is small comfort to society at large. Incredible stories are told of the insensitivity of people in large crowds. Recently a woman was left unattended and helpless in the wreckage of her car for four days before a passerby's curiosity led to rescue. However, the real tragedy of this story lay in the fact that on the second day the woman called to a passerby who recognized her plight but fled the scene. His pathetic parting words were, "I'm very sorry but I don't want to get involved." His intervention at that time probably would have saved her gangrenous leg from amputation, but the overwhelming suspicion in urban society today took its toll.

A woman was raped in a large railway station in central Philadelphia before a watching, paralyzed crowd awaiting evening transportation during the rush hour. Finally an old man intervened and frightened off the attacker, but he received two serious stab wounds for his efforts. The "safety in a crowd" phenomenon sometimes degenerates into mass paralysis and an unfortunate parade of glib ego defenses. On the brighter side, teams of performers will adopt ungainly poses or humorous postures readily and happily to further the total group effort. The simple actions of most cheer leaders would tend to be dull and unrewarding if performed separately and away from the atmosphere of the game. When brought together as an agonist for fan involvement, however, they are usually very effective.

## Physical Environments

### Territoriality

*Groups tend to assume ownership of certain geographical areas. Ownership intensifies under threats of invasion from outside groups.* The home territory phenomenon is pivotal to all scheduling by professional institutions. Especially at home, groups of spectators tend to gravitate to the same physical locations each week. There is something safe and secure about home. Seemingly mediocre teams and second-rate individuals become forces to be reckoned with, and individuals develop skills seldom seen in alien territory.

Since the dawn of history, human beings have banded together in physical locations around which they have drawn boundary lines, and they have defended these locations even to the point of personal extinction. The intensive nationalism in Europe during the past 400 years has brought tragedy to many, and the persistent refusal of human beings and nations to support world government has clearly illustrated the truth of the central ingredient in this concept. Much of human movement has been structured around territorial defense. Games and skills developed for warfare have been passed onto each generation as a valuable legacy. Today, in the Olympic Games we see javelins, discuses, hammers, and cannon shot hurled for peaceful purposes, although it has not been long since these same implements were the instruments of destruction.

A frequent cause of dissonance and conflict is the tendency for groups to prize ownership of geographical areas. When nations compete peacefully the results can be very enriching. The entire world joined with Ethiopia in saluting the efforts of Abebi Bikela in distance running. The successes of one of a nation's native sons brings great pride and untold positive benefits. However, the political disputes of huge nations during these games invalidates any attempt to ascribe universality of good to world-wide international competitions. Political disputes are readily exemplified in the silly points comparison made between the United States and the Soviet Union every four years at the modern Olympics.

### Personal Space

*The moving individual has a personal space surrounding him/her which is private and inviolable.* The individual experiences this space as a personal right. Although a person will allow others to penetrate it sometimes, the right to determine whether to do so is fundamental. For instance, an intimate family member will be allowed into this area to whisper a secret, to embrace, or to maintain physical contact, whereas a casual business acquaintance would not. The anxiety produced when personal space is violated often leads to conflict. There is the saying that when a person is backed into a corner, he will come out fighting.

Personal space will vary greatly at different times. A tennis player will not serve a ball if spectators are moving. That player may encounter problems when shifting from playing singles to doubles. Many times patients feel uncomfortable at a physical examination, while still others find it impossible to relax during massage. Hall (16) has called the study of this personal space *proxemics.* He maintains that it varies widely across cultures and between nations.

*An individual's personal space increases when he/she feels threatened, destroying group harmony.* An obvious illustration from the field of sport and games is children sulking after having their personal space violated and their own ball taken by an adversary. In adults, we see similar behavior when they resign after suffering personal indignities. We would also like to use a more personal illustration. Movement involving a man and a woman during love making is intricately involved with personal space. Obviously, a rapist invades the victim's personal space, but many a case of unintended rape occurs between partners who are legitimately encouraged to mate. A man who invades his wife's personal space prior to her willing and ready invitation will arouse conflict. This conflict may remain sublimated or it may be displaced, but it certainly has a crucial effect upon the continued interpersonal relationships of the married couple. The woman who overly attaches herself to her husband not infrequently produces feelings of exasperation and eventual rejection. "You don't love me anymore," she will be heard to say. In both cases, their wounded egos are understandable and perhaps their needs for constant physical contact are very real. But persistent invasion of a spouse's personal space surely will lead to marital problems that may later be expressed in an apparently unrelated context.

## Individual Status

*In groups formed with movement as the prime focus, individual status determines the physical position of the group.* Any offensive football team lining up with the quarterback in any other position but immediately behind the center would be most irregular. Basketball games would not seem right if a smaller guard lined up in the center's position for the initial tap from the center jump. The positioning of the best sprinter in any other order but anchor in the sprint relay always raises eyebrows as does the peripheral placement of any acknowledged team leader. In a team setting, an individual's status is determined by physical and social-psychological variables, and it nearly always produces central physical placement. Some quarterbacks line up their offensive team in a circle; others line them up in a straight line. The only action that tends to draw immediate status away from the quarterback is a coach using another player to bring in the strategy. When this happens, group focus is placed upon the coach's deputy. It is not meant to demean the quarterback, but is merely a reflection of the status of the coach in the team hierarchy.

## Cliques

*Constant physical contact will produce interaction which sometimes can lead to the formation of cliques.* Where players are constantly in physical contact, a hierarchy of respect is generated. Some players are respected by all because they are always tough. Others are relatively tough and still others are generally considered to be lacking in toughness. Cliques can be formed among the members of the varying levels of toughness or through the desire of a higher-level competitor to protect a less-respected individual. Physical contact communicates strength or weakness to adversaries. Respect is gained or lost almost instantaneously. The tendency for cliques to form is a function of the precarious and sometimes criticized nature of the heavy contact sports. Cliques result from natural defense mechanisms arising out of apparent needs. They are applauded or condemned according to their degree of social acceptability.

## Sociofugal and Sociopetal Arrangements

*The physical arrangements of lockers, seating, and room configuration will directly affect group activity.* After observing interaction patterns of hospital patients, Osmond (17) called seating arrangements designed to keep people apart *sociofugal*. He called arrangements designed for interaction *sociopetal*.

The arrangement of a locker room with benches in between rows of lockers could be classified as sociofugal. Each row is neatly blocked off from the other by a partition of lockers. Under these circumstances interaction is most likely limited to a smaller group of people than an entire physical education class, or an entire team.

A similar observation can be made of the players on the bench during an athletic contest. They sit side-by-side, limiting interaction except with the player next door. However, when a time out is called, generally they form a circle to increase interaction.

## Centralized and Decentralized Group Structures

*Centralized group structures are more likely to produce singularity of leadership and organizational efficiency than decentralized group structures.* Weber and Blau (18, 19) say beaurocracy is the most efficient organization for the accomplishment of the product oriented goals needed in a basketball team, an Olympic Games team, a ballet, or an institution. Under bureaucratic circumstances, there is a division of labor and a hierarchy or chain of command; evaluation is based on performance merit. It is not difficult, then, to envision a single leader. This is an example of centralized group structuring. By contrast, a recess period at school where a hundred activities can be seen is an example of decentralized group structuring. It is much more difficult to envision a single, strong leader developing in these circumstances. Whenever a teacher disperses the class into smaller groups, the leadership capacity is reduced to the extent that students are thrown into a situation where they need to be trusted to work independently. Some will work hard, others will appear to be working hard, and still others will make no pretensions of working whatsoever. The teacher's leadership is more indirect in these situations. Only well prepared classes can be given large doses of independence with success, especially in the over-protected and far too politicized schools of today.

*Centralized group structures tend to saturate and demoralize human movement more quickly than decentralized structures.* This concept is based on the supposition that closeness of communication, rigid chains of command, and bureaucratic nonsense tend to reduce the individual's feeling of importance to the point of discouraging independent thought and action. Large, centralized teams with singular purpose so saturate individual members with pseudo idealism and "administrivia" that individuals will leave teams just to get a breath of fresh air. Mass claustrophobia seems to be an unfortunate side effect of ponderous institutionalization.

## Personal Environments

### Age

*Physical-participation group socializing tends to increase with chronological age up to a certain point. Then it either stabilizes or falls away.* The group is one of the main vehicles for socializing the child. As children grow to physical maturity, they assume greater responsibilities in the family, the educational system, and in the work world. Initially the child may play with only the mother, but as growth and maturity take place, the child substitutes peer-group activity and occupational ambition for family play. With the approach of the autumn years and the decline in physical abilities, we tend to see the individual revert back to the initial socializing influence—the family.

*Although social interaction becomes more complex with increasing chronological age, there is a peaking effect in the physical aspects of social interaction.* Learning theorists (20, 21) tell us that as a person matures so does his ability to process information. More varied stimuli are processed and organized in strict correlation with past experiences. Differentiations and discriminations become easier and evaluation becomes more complex. The physical abilities show a peaking effect during the twenties and thirties. At this time human beings tend to accomplish a plethora of complicated physical tasks. Highly skilled movements such as tower diving, calisthenics, and putting in golf reach a climax during these important years. Although certain individuals manage to retain complex skills into an advanced age (such as doctors on an operating table and engineers with delicate machinery), most gross motor movements are impaired at this stage. We will know more of people's movement potentials during old age only after the current trend for encouraging play among senior citizens becomes more widespread.

*Group leadership tends to belong to older members.* The tendency for older members to assume leadership in teams is a natural result of their accrued experience and the community's respect for its senior members. In moments of crisis and turbulence, experience prevents hasty judgments. This concept will be discussed more fully in Chapter 11.

*In the very young, conformity of movement patterning tends to be predominant, but as members approach adolescence and maturity, conformity tends to decrease.* This hypothesis arises out of laboratory studies by Constanzo and Shaw (22) and Asch (23). The growth patterns of a child to adolescence show the strong influence of the adult model. A similar pattern can be noticed in the advance of rookies to veteran status. Rookies need to belong so they willingly submit to petty regulations like hair cuts, uniforms, training rules, and street dress codes. To get their opportunity to play regularly, they also tend to perform any task, no matter how menial, for the success of the team. As they mature their needs change. Pride, peer comparisons, and fiscal expectations turn popular heroes into disgruntled veterans. Some evidence is available to support the contention that the personality profiles of many athletes have a tendency to be so conservative and conventional that they will strictly conform to the bitter end (24, 25, 26). This apparent anomaly finds support in the examination of the movement profiles of young business executives who hold their conformity through to final executive status. In spite of these deviations, however, the pattern is fairly consistent; conformity decreases with maturity and the growth of personal independence.

## Sex

*As a whole, women tend to be less assertive and less competitive in groups than men.* The cultural influences in the United States have reduced the significance of women's productiveness to an inferior status. Many studies have shown women to be less assertive, though not necessarily less aggressive, than men. Women have been less dominant in competition based on physical contact where the obvious physical imbalance of men and women plays a major role. Historically, women have not been encouraged to exhibit the type of behaviors that make men successful in athletic competition. With the changing sex roles, however, it is probably safe to assume that women will become more assertive.

### Status and Skills

*In movement-oriented groups, physically superior individuals assume leadership.* Although some teams will elect the most sagacious and respected member to a position of leadership, most teams will elect a leader capable of inspiring personal physical performances. Bill Russell was elected captain and coach of the Boston Celtics because of their sheer respect for him. He was held in awe for his tremendous physical achievements. Defensive football teams will elect the most aggressive player as team leader. In hockey, the position of policeman places a player in a leadership role with or without general membership permission.

*Most groups attach a premium to members who possess special skills.* A prominent American college football coach was heard to proclaim that the annual battle between the two perennial football giants in the midwestern region is usually decided by the kicking game. Statisticians are quick to refer to return yardage, free-throw percentage, goal-tending shut outs, and percentages of double faulting. Every team, whether it be football or mountain climbing, is indebted to special members endowed with rare skills. Their overall contribution in terms of blood, sweat, and tears may be small, but their social acceptability makes them precious to the team effort.

### "People-Oriented" Leadership

*Individuals who are people oriented, rather than idea oriented, tend to enhance the morale and cohesiveness of the group.* Although it is obvious that both people-oriented and idea-oriented leadership are needed, individuals concerned with interpersonal relationships will increase the morale and cohesiveness of the group. The popular television series, "Star Trek," readily exemplifies this fact. Mr. Spock, the monumental and computerized brain, rarely fails to find a solution to the many problems that the space team encounter, but his complete lack of feeling is fully compensated for by the other members of the team who spend most of their time functioning in the affective domain. Fans urge Mr. Spock to have more feelings and to be more human, illustrating vividly the fine human characteristic of applauding and reinforcing group supportive behaviors.

Teachers who show concern for students are rarely likely to abuse, criticize destructively, or absent themselves for long periods of time. In today's schools a strong measure of human caring is the incidence of teacher attendance.

## Social Environment

*Most groups function through a wide variety of individual input based on physical, intellectual, emotional, social, and spiritual dimensions.* While it is true that part of group conflict is caused by the disparity of individual input, it is also true that such variety is the spice of the group's entity. Even in such homogeneous settings as a doubles tennis partnership, important complementary skills are identified. A left-hander and a right-hander playing together as a team will produce withering cross-court forehand drives from all parts of the court. A player who favors the double-handed backhand will sometimes be caught stretching in a singles game, but this player can turn this skill into an asset in a doubles game where he has much less court to cover. In teams composed of heterogeneous abilities, the importance of this concept is clearly evidenced. The quarterback must pass, think quickly, be a leader, and avoid injury at all costs; the lineman must seek out physical contact with lust and zest; the wide receiver must be fast, mobile, deceptive, and have excellent catching hands; the running back must exhibit a combination of the talents of a lineman and a wide receiver. Sometimes specialized input by individuals in the same position is needed. The early seventies saw the rise of the Miami Dolphin football team. This was largely due to the disparate abilities of two of its running backs, especially when teamed together for the same play. Opposition defenses were uncertain whether to cover the center for a bull-like Larry Csonka charge, or the outside for a swerving Mercury Morris sweep. This combination of very different abilities displayed by two men in the same position was immensely successful for the Miami football team.

### Compatibility and Cohesiveness

*Communication is easier among members of highly cohesive and compatible groups than among members of divisive and incompatible groups.* French (27) showed that when dealing with selected learning problems, an organized athletic team had more of an "I" or "we" feeling than an unfamiliar group of undergraduate students. The spirit of friendship prevailing in highly cohesive teams and the harmony between compatible partners allows an integrity of communication to take place. Group cohesiveness is reinforced by good results, and good results more often than not result from a free and accurate interchange of strengths and weaknesses, and a readiness on the part of all to listen to possible solutions.

*High-cohesive groups are more effective, more positively oriented, contain members who are genuinely better satisfied, and exert greater influence over their members than do low-cohesive groups.* Festinger (28) has defined group cohesiveness as "the resultant of the forces acting on the members to remain in the group." We see many examples in the sporting world of highly cohesive college and professional sporting teams that are effective not only on the field but off the field as well. Occasionally we will see an example of a team that is not cohesive off the field, but rarely has there been a team that has been effective and incompatible both on and off the field. The spiritual reinforcement engendered through the high degree of mobility and mutual respect of mountain-climbing teams, sky-diving teams or scuba-diving combinations further exemplifies this concept. Success in college or professional sports may mean first place, but in the case of death-defying team activities, cohesive team work is mandatory. Participants in such activities never fail to report deep interpersonal experiences intertwined with emotional satisfaction.

*Groups composed of members of diverse personality profiles and abilities perform more effectively than groups of similar personality profiles and abilities.* Sometimes petty jealousies and the obvious persisting competition between group members with similar abilities and profiles will destroy the group. Perhaps it is easier for a violin virtuoso to appreciate the movement skills of the piccolo player than to appreciate those of a fellow violinist. The same can be said for any sport that is overstocked with similar team players, or teams who have an abundance of players ready to fill the same position. Certainly conflict tends to be reduced in groups with complementary skills.

### Coeducational Grouping

*Group movement which functions in a coeducational dimension exerts more conforming behaviors upon group members than movement where only one sex is involved.* The presence of the other sex during group movement tends to produce very different behaviors, especially during adolescence. In all young people at certain stages, to impress members of the opposite sex is more important than to impress members of the same sex. This may be accounted for by cultural heritage, but it appears an undeniable phenomenon. Meetings, excursions, debates, even fun activities are that little bit more formal in the coeducational atmosphere. It almost seems as though such group activity is a replica for life itself; nothing is missing. Perhaps the tendency for men to be condescending in games of physical contact explains this phenomenon in part, but in coeducational activities where participation from both sexes is equal (e.g. folk dancing, appropriate racquet sports), the degree of sensitivity and consciousness in upholding the rules is indeed great.

## Status

*High-status group members are permitted more latitude to deviate from group activities than low status members.* This concept is misleading since it is also true that high status group members tend to conform more than low status members. However, this type of norm deviation is observed when high status members challenge the authority of the teacher by making suggestions about class activities that could be conceived as risky. Low status group members often have expectations of such ebullient capacity from leaders within their group, revering such independence. The high status member is expected to further the cause of the group in any way possible and is often permitted unusual norm deviation in the performance of this task.

## Conformity

*Conformity tends to increase with the size of the majority and its unanimity.* The research of Asch (23) gives rise to the formation of this concept. In a classic experiment in 1951 he asked tardy students in a class to rank the length of three lines. He had already briefed the rest of the class to deliberately falsify the rankings. Since the rest of the class gave clear verbal and nonverbal support for the incorrect ranking, in nine out of ten cases the new student, even in the face of obvious error, went along with the majority opinion. Apparently the larger the majority, the more intimidated the subjects became. It seems that isolated individuals will most often pattern their movement behaviors on the model provided for them by the majority. Crowd behavior, which becomes remarkably consistent and authoritative, is an excellent illustration of this concept.

*Conformity generally insures law and order and frees the individual from the divisive activity of splinter groups.* Group members feel safe and order is preserved when most team members are conforming to constitutionality. The rock-like conventions of a large majority provide the strength to protect all group members. Splinter groups desiring change find it difficult to attract individual members who huddle safely under the umbrella of the grand majority.

## Group Norms

*Deviation from group norms is usually punished by other group members.* Group norms provide the common basis for members to know what is expected of them by the group. If a member does not adhere to these expected behaviors, generally some type of group sanctioning is inevitable. This usually involves some type of punishment (29).

The newspapers have carried stories about the benching of certain athletes because they did not adhere to training rules established by the team. In a gymnasium, we see many instances of behavior where some students are not included in the game because of lack of adherence to the rules of the game or to the informal rules of the team members themselves.

## Leadership

*High-powered group members are better liked, have greater influence, are the target of more approval seeking, and are more attractive to the group than low-powered group members.* Whyte (30), when studying a street corner group in Boston, found the above characteristics were easily observed in a group situation. The leader of the group, Doc, had much more power and influence than any other group member. This person was able to give out rewards and mete out punishment as long as the group saw his leadership as legitimate and meeting the needs of the group.

Team captains, particularly if they are selected by teammates, are likely to find themselves in the same position as Doc. They have the "ear of the coach" and are able to effect certain policies and make recommendations about selection, the kinds of strategies used, and the overall congruence of the team. If there is no coach, the leaders still have that power as long as they promote the interests of the group.

## SOCIETY AND CULTURE

### Types of Societies

*Human beings differ in appearance and movement expression as a result of cultural inheritance and societal influences.* Society is a specific term meaning a diverse group with a high degree of self-sufficiency. Examples of societies over the centuries include: *hunting, horticultural, agrarian, industrial,* and *neoleisure.* It is interesting to note that human beings have progressed from societies dependent upon physical activity to a society dependent upon intellectual achievement. The nature of physical activity has changed accordingly. In the hunting society, human beings stalked alongside beasts in a desperate attempt to obtain meat with primitive weapons in desperate situations. The instruments used for survival and the search for food were little better than the defensive weapons (claws, teeth, tusks, fangs, etc.) of the hunted beasts. In the horticultural society, human beings depended upon natural flora and fauna for food. Any person who has climbed a coconut tree and struggled through the process of opening that coconut to get to the precious juices inside knows that heavy physical activity was needed to survive in that society. In agrarian societies, human beings tilled the land with harnessed beasts providing the power. Human beings had to struggle constantly against the vicissitudes of nature. The industrial society concentrated its efforts on freeing human beings from binding and tiresome physical work. The need for alternative leisure activities appeared slowly, but it has grown to the point where many parts of the United States today are neoleisure. A neo-leisure society means that only certain portions of the population are needed to supply the labor force, and that all members can actively choose alternative and interesting ways of occupying their leisure time. Variety of human movement is a central feature, often attracting the leisure devotee to its enticing web.

*Culture is the way of life of the people in any society and is as diverse as that society itself.* Culture is the product of social interaction, it is learned, sometimes it is material and sometimes nonmaterial, and it results from society's attempts to meet the five dimensions of human needs. It is the cumulative effect of ideas, values, goals, and material objects (4).

### Cultural Relativism and Ethnocentrism

*Cultural differences provide an answer to societal differences and in turn an avenue to the resolution of societal problems. Within a culture people behave according to perspectives learned during their socializing processes.* The term *ethnocentrism* describes people who judge another society by the standards of their own society. In contrast, the term *cultural relativism* describes people who endeavor to judge a society by that society's standards. The tolerance required by cultural relativists is nonpartisan, very idealistic, and seen too rarely. We are all familiar with misstatements made by bigots referring to dirtiness of living conditions among desperate minority groups. The bigot is judging (and usually superficially) the activities of another group of people by the standards set in his own society. It is difficult to expect a despotic king to understand the desperate feelings of his penniless, desolate, and downtrodden peasantry. Similar judgments are made by partisan nationalists. Americans frown when they see Italian soccer players embracing or kissing one another after a goal has been scored. The British frown when they see jargonized advertisements dangling from every participle used by American sportscasters. Americans frown when they see the cool reception that certain conservative European countries give their efforts to brighten up athletes' shirts. It is easy to be ethnocentric, and often hurtful. It can lead to intergroup and international conflict. Ethnocentrism is a synonym for excessive patriotism, parochialness, and biased interpretation of international rules. The modern Olympic Games exemplify this unfortunate truth. Ethnocentrism may, when subject to the friendly exchange of national custom, have some redeeming qualities, but unfortunately these qualities recede all too quickly in the face of international competition and the need to discriminate among champions.

Cultural relativism demands much more understanding, especially from individuals seeking to communicate across ethnic or national boundaries. It becomes a rewarding and interesting pasttime to learn and then try to employ movements held sacred over the centuries by other groups. Most Westerners, for example, take a youthful delight in learning to use chop sticks as an eating utensil. A further instance: the Japanese have difficulty pronouncing the letter *l*, which sometimes produces humorous connotations to Westerners. Fortunately most sports people learn quickly to appreciate ethnic and national differences and to adapt to the varying situations without personal discomfort. When athletes are unable to assimilate and adapt to local conditions, their performance invariably suffers and their defense mechanisms are set in motion. The sign of a seasoned veteran in international competition is the ability to attain peak performance regardless of location, specific environment, or petty local interference. Perhaps this is also a sign of maturity.

### Cultural Norms and Subcultures

*Whereas certain movements appear to be universal, cultural differences will produce wide movement variety.* All cultures adopt a form of family structure with some form of marriage. The movements surrounding the conduct of family life are basic. Movements to secure and prepare food are easily recognizable in children's play movements or adults' movements to till the land, market the produce, and reinvest the capital. It appears that certain cultural norms are developed with universal activities like walking, running, throwing, and catching quickly recognized. It appears too, that some movements are allowed under certain circumstances and held to be taboo under others. Movements associated with sexual intercourse are welcomed and fully sanctioned in all cultures among relatively mature and consenting couples. The same movements employed in incestuous situations or in child molestation or between couples where one is unwilling, are universally considered taboo.

There also appears to be a strong leaning in all cultures toward a delicate and intricate form of physical movement associated with the arts and crafts. Indeed, art work becomes an interesting symbol of interaction among many cultures. Certain superstitious movements are universally given meaning through art, and either vehemently worshipped or rejected. It appears, too, that once approval is ascribed to a neighboring culture, universal hospitality takes place; toleration of even the most unusual movements from the other culture occurs.

*Societies develop subcultures of movement which in turn may produce countercultures.* The martial arts, especially judo, originated in the Far East. To the uninformed Westerner, movement subcultures such as judo, kendo, and karate are very similar, but to the Oriental, each of these subcultures means something quite different. One is just a game, another flirts with dangerous instruments, yet another seeks to destroy. Each subculture and its role is sufficiently powerful to stimulate both internally and externally, the development of a counterculture. These countercultures, in time, can sensitize adherents to the point where unity is lost.

## THE INDIVIDUAL IN SOCIETY

*In complex societies such as the United States, people react differently to the same stimulus due to personality differentiation.* Some people see bank thieves as criminals indulging in covetous, antisocial behavior. Others view them as emancipated radicals running to bring the "system" down, while still others see them as hapless products of their environment. Sheldon's theory (31, 32) that body type is closely linked with certain personality traits has infatuated movement specialists for almost half a century. The *ectomorph*—thin, stringent, economical, wiry—plays tennis, studies physiology, lacks generosity, and may be suffering from the "small guy" complex. The endomorph—fat, soft—is weak in decision, easily conformed, jealous but usually generous, addicted to meat, usually lacking in self-image, often apprehensive, tires easily, and is prone to excess. The mesomorph—agile, athletic, good looking—is eminently successful, the protector, the object of infatuation, can be tough, can be generous, a great lover, prestigious to be seen with, and the model around which jealousy, hatred, affinity, and conformity are structured. Obviously, Sheldon realized that the walls between these three categories were thin, and that one attribute could easily slip into another category. But for centuries human beings have stereotyped people according to their body structure. They have distrusted weedy little people and laughed at fat soft people while always urging their young ones to be more like the handsome prince. Sometimes these stereotypes have destroyed human confidence and thoroughly depleted self-image. Fortunately sufficient examples of the "exception" have come to the public eye at least to force people to reconsider, if not abandon, classic assumptions about body types and personality.

## Adjustment

*Human movement, like human nature, is almost unbelievably malleable.* Human beings are called upon to make many adjustments to personal comfort in the course of a life span. Although the odd stubborn individual who refuses to adopt or conform still exists, such individuals tend to be the exceptions that prove the rule. Most human movement represents either adaptation to, or compensation for, the everyday requirements of living and nurturing. Human beings have developed a remarkable capacity to adjust their movement expressions. The introduction of the forward pass into gridiron in 1905 saw an immediate development of very different skills among football players. The decision of the Olympic Committee at the 1912 Olympic Games in Sweden to require all throwers to compete with each hand in separate competition presented few problems to the eager competitors. The adjustment of the kicking rule in 1974 saw immediate expansion of the variety of kicks attempted by punters and field-goal kickers in American football. The changes in the scoring system of traditional tennis brought about by the professional team championships in the United States in 1974 confused no one. The simple fact is that once human beings are forced into a position of adjustment, they do so quickly and effectively, even to such complicated changes as that from the avoirdupois weight system to the decimal.

## Growth and Socialization

*As the individual grows and socializes, body movements symbolize the dramatic change.* It is perfectly normal to expect certain types of movements to emerge at the specific growth periods. We would expect the nine-year-old boy to throw and catch a baseball, to chase lizards, and to abhor clean hands and rosy cheeks. It is equally plausible to see the 15-year-old youth paying more attention to his hair, his clothes, the reactions of the young girls in his class, and his better achievements in the gymnasium. The young woman just married will work twenty hours a day to earn a second income and still perform the many manual duties associated with building a home, raising a family, and attending to her wifely duties. The pattern of expected behavior leads to the development of stereotypes. Many people find it difficult or undesirable to fit their lives into this pattern of behavior. Sometimes this incongruence is subtle (unhappy bride) and at other times, it is overt and visible (the flag-waving radical college student, naked and abusive). Although, in each case, the movements have been stereotyped by the role of expectancy, other confounding movements have been introduced to stimulate the individual's desire not to conform to the stereotype.

*Sometimes people are socialized, then for some reason or another isolated for a sufficiently long period to require a resocialization when the isolation is ended.* The moving French novel *Papillon* with its tragic, extended, brutal, and long-suffering hero imprisoned for most of his life was one illustration of this point. Another vivid example was seen in the return of prisoners of war from North Vietnam during the early stages of 1974. Less dramatic but equally important examples are seen daily. The athlete who prematurely retires and then decides to make a comeback often has to learn new movements or a combination of movements in new surroundings. The adjustments can be sufficiently arduous and unrewarding to abort the comeback attempt. The child who is constantly moved from one school to another, especially after periods of truancy, wrestles with many of the problems inherent in the resocializing process. Two Russian ballet dancers denied the opportunity to migrate to Israel were virtually isolated from their profession at a critical stage in their career. The inactivity was sufficiently extended to terminate the career of one of these great performers. The woman who endeavors to regain movement skills after several pregnancies and extended isolation from her original professional skills frequently expresses dissonance, even to the point of seeking resocialization in an occupation with lesser demands. The resocializing process has serious implications in the rehabilitation of normal and abnormal people.

## Self-Perception

*The individual perceives "self in motion" in relation to society from different perspectives yet with crucial effect.* Cooley (33) saw the individual as seeing self in mirror image. We see ourselves then precisely as others see us. If we are excellent baseball players or mediocre baseball players or atrocious baseball players, we are not deceived provided that others give us accurate feedback and true representation of our exact behaviors. If they don't, we will have another kind of distortion. If Cooley is right, the importance of accurate feedback and the integrity of peer association are crucial. Manipulation from teachers and coaches, and paternalism from parents and friends, can only serve to distort our personal abilities and lead us into deception.

Mead (34) says that we become human only when true interaction takes place between our self-perceptions and our abstract ideas. It resembles the "Camus gap" and the "Hegelian unhappy consciousness," or the distance between our fantasies and our realities. Mead sought to explain self-image as a relation of where we perceived we stood to our abstract ideas about where we stood. It is a difficult concept to understand and one which many behaviorists have abandoned, but in this day and age it appears to be a crucial element in the development of self-image. One of the reasons why elementary school children lose their zest for all kinds of physical activity could well be that as they realize their physical limitations and the futility of romantic goal expectations, their demotivation leads to a depletion of self-image and subsequent ultimate cynicism. Mead goes on to say that a unique human quality is the ability of individuals to assume others' roles, especially through vicarious projection. This is one possible solution to the demotivation problem once the gap between fantasy and reality goals has been realized. Through play, youngsters can satisfy their secret desires for goal achievement. "I will only pretend," is one of the truly precious escape mechanisms open to people. Of course, the danger of this device lies in its excessive use, leading to pathological schizophrenia. The fact remains that when children, and adults too, for that matter, are given time, or indeed encouraged, to play, they are usually motivated and have reasonably high self-images. Could it be that such statements as, "They're not learning anything; they're just playing," "Come inside children—playtime is over—work time begins," and "Jimmy will never get good grades in school; he spends all his time day dreaming," are the real enemies of consummate and sensible growth to enriched self-image. Mead also refers to the individual's tendency to assume the personal element before the social element in human behavior, which could explain the often lamented phenomenon of selfishness in young children. As teachers, we tend to place great premium on cooperation and consideration for others. Notwithstanding the obvious wisdom in this priority, we should at least try and understand that emotional maturity is like physical maturity—a growth problem. Needlessly harsh censure during the early, formative years will undoubtedly have its effect on the development of the child's self-image.

## SOCIAL RANKING

### Stratification

*In all societies, even the very primitive, there have been divisions of members according to some type of stratification system.* Individuals tend to be ranked within a society on a continuum of importance to unimportance. Positions considered the most essential are given the best rewards, with the stratifications persisting because those essential members struggle to keep it this way. Such extensive use is made of expertise, personal ambition, and historical success that a comparative minority usually rules society. In movement-oriented society the skilled athlete earns more money, obtains rewards more frequently, and captures the public eye to such an extent that substratification is perpetuated within that society. It can be said that rewards in society go to the rare, the disinguished, or to the cunning. Most stratifications are artificial, however, representing essential spinoff from the socialization process. An individual who is physically or mentally handicapped is usually pitied and treated differently. In many instances, he or she does not receive the same privileges as "normal" people. Stairs, curbs, and other physical impediments serve as a reminder of this.

The latter half of the twentieth century has experienced a massive attempt by many peoples to right wrongs caused by the social divisions of past centuries. Minorities in the United States have made themselves heard in matters of normal living. In fact, some people claim that we have nearly approached a stage where we are governed by minority ethnic opinion. However, the majority-minority phenomenon is not merely social. It assumes a very different connotation in most ball games, although perhaps some social philosophers will see striking similarities to the game of life. Wherever a team can effect a "two on one" situation, it has a distinct advantage. In the sports of soccer and ice hockey, the penalty of depriving one team of some of its members for periods of time gives the opposition considerable advantage. Indeed it could be said that all successful team-sport strategies endeavor to create the extra person advantage. The scoring of a power-play goal in hockey receives no less recognition as far as the game result is concerned than a goal from the field.

## Minorities

*Majorities and minorities are created when enclaves of people band together and identify in single units.* In order to be successful, groups of people (today ethnically profuse as compared with yesterday) collect in geographically separate areas with the express purpose of being "No. 1," or of protecting lifestyles. Once formed, these groups tend to inbreed and assume ownership rights. Very often the groups are formed along race or ethnic lines but frequent examples of disparate ethnic membership are evident. Children are socialized in these environments to the extent of embracing the various cultural patterns, prejudices, and identities. The play patterns of each ethnic group permanently influence the movement orientation of its youngsters. In this day of mandatory integration, widely differing ethnic groups are expected not merely to coexist but to merge through physical and cultural integration. This integration is not only occurring in the schools, but also in real-estate operations. The son of a wealthy white farmer may well find himself thrown together with a black youth from Harlem to play baseball for a team owned and distributed by a Boston lawyer. The apparent disparate backgrounds count for little in the heat of the pennant race, but they may evoke violent and disruptive interaction when life resumes off the field. The harmony that remains when the last pitch has been hurled and the last shower turned off in the changing rooms tells the real story of majority-minority cohesion. Many players from disparate backgrounds have affected genuine and permanent interpersonal friendships, but the nature of team competition and the current reward system (where a 21–19 victory is the key to re-employment and salary increase) make the social setting of these friendships impermanent. However, some of the common physical features of minorities do gain general acceptance. Such universal features as the sinuous agility of the black, the small, delicate steps of the Chinese, and the rolling gait of the Eastern European have a permanent place in our repertoire of movement experiences. Minorities do become radicalized relatively easily because of feelings of repression and the natural desire to avoid stereotyping: Their distrust is legion.

Although small in number, minorities display great nationalism and incredible perseverance if threatened for survival (Jews in Israel), but once the generations pass and the persecution subsides they tend to proliferate, to become existential, and to identify with diffuse community ideologies and pursuits (Jews in New York). The massacre of thirteen Jews at the 1972 Olympic Games destroyed the team's posture, but the country regained its nationalistic composure. On the other hand, the protest action of two young American black sprinters at the 1968 Olympics resulted in strong censure and further divided an already troubled nation. One unfortunate feature of minority groups is the tendency for infighting, even to the point of acute embarrassment. Warring cliques and inordinate peer pressures can reduce total productivity to disaster levels. By contrast with majorities, whose input is nearly always profuse, minorities can inbreed to the point of total nullification. The United States sets out to protect minority interests. Perhaps this is one of the reasons for the incredible variety of ethnically-inspired movement which exists in this country.

### Social Class, Status, and Power

*Each member of society is classified or ranked on the basis of social class, status or power which has reciprocal effect on movement patterns. Social class refers to the ranked position of each member, based on such* criteria as income, occupation, education, residence, and religion. It is usually determined by lifestyle, reputation, and wealth. Quite naturally, the perspective through which a person judges the status of another person's contributions will tend to reveal social class. Hollingshead (35) considered education and occupation the two most important variables for the ranking of social class.

*Status* is the position of social importance given to individuals or institutions in any society. Obviously, a person may belong to a more prestigious social class through birth or wealth but may not have high status within that class because of personal shortcomings or antisocial habits.

*Power* is the ability of a person or segment of the population to control others in that society. Perry and Perry (4) consider occupation and wealth to be the important factors in status. Wealth and political expertise are the two important variables in the structure of power. These three structures, social class, status, and power, are interrelated. A person in the middle class, for instance, is taught that achievement is important and that social status will increase as a result of good works. You have to practice in order to make a team or to play a musical instrument or to scale a mountain. Studies have shown that the middle-class people are more active in communal affairs with more power and greater visible status than people in the lower class. People in lower classes tend not to socialize their children to the importance of diligence and education (36). Such people are usually poor models to those around them, representing perpetuation of poverty and paucity of achievement. Few of the children from middle-class homes lack food and shelter whereas many children from lower-class homes do. Visibility is another important variable in determining social class. A child from a lower-class neighborhood tends not to have the same opportunity for making important business and sporting contacts as the middle-class child whose parents are often professionally and socially sophisticated.

Status is often reflected through successful movement performance. One sign indicating the city limits in Ohio says, "You are now entering Bowling Green, Ohio, home of Dave Wottle, winner of a gold medal at the twentieth Olympiad." Most individuals actively seek status. Though not as much as in the past, movement-oriented activity gives high status to gifted individuals. Sometimes depredation of status through lack of natural movement ability will cause overcompensation. A familiar example is the clumsy, ignored, and isolated schoolboy who becomes a liberal arts professor and thereafter flunks the "jocks." Status inconsistency occurs where individuals of one status find themselves in another environment. Sometimes they overcompensate by accentuating and defending previous behaviors. They may act common or crude on the one hand, or become affected and artificial on the other. The reverse can also happen. A person may attach himself peripherally but ardently to a status group, although he cannot afford to maintain that lifestyle. Some ambitious young men and women have beggared their families simply to be able to perform menial supporting tasks for the local professional or college teams. This behavior is common among alumni groups. Status also has the persisting effect of locking individuals into stereotyped behaviors, causing dissonance when these predetermined stereotypes are violated. The refusal of major sports stars to sign autographs, appear for charities, or "do something for the kiddies" causes general disillusionment for the population and untold harrassment for the player concerned. After the initial thrill of success, most champions retreat from stereotyped behaviors; it appears that their continuing dissonance in this regard crucially affects their public image.

Movement is a frequent determinant of personal power. The ability levels of the local competitors will command local influence along with wealth and opportunity. Most youngsters receive insufficient introduction to wide-ranging movement activities during their physical-education classes at school to determine their athletic potential accurately. Financial restrictions prevent most young people from entering certain sports— polo, sailing, figure skating, and parachuting. Perhaps the cheaper sports have more seriously tapped community potential and thus have been more truly representative. Basketball, track and field, and boxing are three good examples of inexpensive sports that truly represent the total community. Power has a centralizing effect on big sport, especially in finance. We are accustomed to seeing huge sporting enclaves embodied in institutions that rule with tyrannical power. This same power corrupts in more ways than through the fiscal dimensions. The antics of some professional team owners leave much to be desired. As models to the community of the values implicit in organized sport they are a negative quantity. Devotees of the minor sports can also reign with tyrannical power. Many petty bureaucrats dominate the Olympic sports solely because of their enfranchisement under auspices of the Olympic body. When not shared, power has the unfortunate characteristic of not only corrupting, but also eliminating those who choose not to submit. Whereas authority is a necessary attribute of leadership and is usually legitimate, power is the expression of intent of those in authority. Perhaps nobody has said it better than Erich Fromm.

> To be sure, power over people is an expression of superior strength in a purely material sense. If I have power over another person to kill him, I am "stronger" than he is. But in a psychological sense, the lust for power

is not rooted in strength but in weakness. It is the expression of the inability of the individual self to stand alone and live. It is the desperate attempt to gain secondary strength where genuine strength is lacking (37).

## Social Mobility and Physical Skill

*Social mobility is enhanced if a person possesses superior physical skills.* Social mobility, being able to move up or down in society's stratification system, is looked upon by the lower classes as the way to improve their social standing, status, and power. In closed societies social mobility is slow and beset with discrimination problems. The opening up of baseball to minority players in the late 1940's enabled minority athletes to rise in social acceptability, status, and fiscal power. Although it is true that too much is made of the "rags to riches" syndrome offered to minorities through sport, many young people have achieved their life ambitions solely through the visibility of their movement interests. From Jessie Owens to Mohammed Ali, ambitious young blacks have used sports as a vehicle for success. The second half of the twentieth century has seen Western society move from a socially closed system to a relatively open system. The closed system did have some benefits. There was plenty of security, community idealism was simple, and social interaction was specific for each situation. It is wrong totally to condemn that system, for many fine and decent young people benefited and were appreciated for their efforts. Immortals such as Jessie Owens, Jersey Joe Walcott, and Althea Gibson are three such examples. The distaste which most people have for the closed system, however, forbids its retention and necessitates a much more realistic and sophisticated appraisal of the basic ingredients in social mobility. To treat human beings as inferior is basically inhuman. True talent is often not recognized and individuals' potentials are used against them to keep them under control.

An interesting study by Loy and McElvogue (38) looked at the variable of interaction of team members and their importance or "centrality" to the team. They found that even though blacks held many positions on the team, their roles were generally peripheral in nature. The reluctance of baseball to appoint black managers and of football to employ black quarterbacks supports the findings of this study. In an open society where athletes are free to battle for themselves, they may make mistakes out of ignorance or immaturity as their economic status changes. On the other hand, Bill Russell refused to buy a Cadillac car with his first basketball check, and Moses Malone's first action with his newly earned money was to buy his mother a new home. These two examples break the stereotype of the young sporting great who suddenly finds himself in an elevated economic class and so "blows his stack" on highly visible status symbols.

Berger (39) found that opportunity was the important ingredient in social mobility. Brown (40) found that educational and occupational aspirations of young blacks were not dependent upon sport participation, which is contrary to popular opinion. One possible explanation of Brown's finding could lie in the early maternal domination in the socializing processes of young blacks. Certainly many people in the lower class desire the lifestyles of the middle and upper classes.

Rigid coaches cling to the tenets of the closed society. They shelter and protect their players and make them conform to the rules. They expect each team member to do what is expected in his/her assigned role. Rigid coaches promote "canned security" through adopting a simple decision-making model. They promote the view that upward individual or team mobility is not in its own right a good thing. There is a limit, they say, to the number of quarterbacks, centers, goal keepers and captains any one team can have. They are usually champions of the status quo, perpetrating societal norms. They control, through predetermined criteria (How far should a child be able to kick the ball at 16 years? How fast should a child be able to swim the 100 meters at 8 years?) the direction and quality of each member's development.

Less rigid coaches inform team members of all relevant data and share important decisions with team members. They provide diversified activities to encourage team and individual movement, refrain from perching on thrones in centralized power positions, accept decisions and ideas from all involved, and avoid negative and punitive criticism. It is in their best interests to encourage maximum social mobility. The egalitarian coach is usually philosophical about the problems of an open society. He believes that very few solutions are simple, and that much insecurity attends young athletes who are given decisions to make in threatening circumstances. Nevertheless, the shrewd coach knows that once the game has begun the athletes have to do it alone. Whereas rigid coaches believe they can drill players to react in precise, mechanical fashion, less rigid coaches believe they have to educate players to solve problems by themselves. Certainly one thing is clear—the *educated* athlete will tend to make fewer mistakes in a crisis, be more independent, and take on greater personal responsibilities than the *trained* athlete.

## SOCIETAL CHANGE*

The interaction of the individual with the environment brings about change that may result from either the natural growth processes or unnatural intervention.

*Chapter 15 discusses the important question—How does the discipline change?

*The Explanation of the Causes for Change Varies.* Many theories seek to explain the reasons for change in movement oriented pursuits. Spengler and Toynbee (41, 42) advance a *cyclical* theory, meaning that success runs in cycles. The team recruits well, builds up essential skills, and matures into an outstanding combination of individuals performing skills with harmonious productivity. It becomes successful at accruing status and power. Then little by little it becomes less effective in spite of its widespread acclaim. Former strengths deteriorate as other teams equal and eventually surpass it. The force of this theory is its insistence that no one group or team can retain its secrets or prevent others from learning about them. That special team combination will survive as the natural leader for extended periods (Celtics in professional basketball, India in field hockey, UCLA in college basketball, United States in men's track and field), but eventually opponents will achieve parity.

The *classic functionalists* maintain that although teams come and go, the game remains; whereas units are expendable, the total organism persists. The sport of baseball has seen the Yankees, the Dodgers, the Cardinals, and the Oakland Athletics rise and fall, but the sport of baseball outlives all of its member parts. The classic functionalists' explanation for change is not dependent upon the growth factor, but on the temporary excellence of the various component parts.

The *structural functionalists* believe, as do the Darwinian theorists, that only the strong survive. In the cutthroat world of institutionalized sport, only the fiscally viable operations persist. The ancient Olympic Games (Greece and Rome), jousting (medieval Europe), and the pancratium (ancient Greece) are historic examples of popular institutions which have become extinct. The World Football League and the International Student Games are examples today of institutions that have either lost credibility or are bordering on disintegration and collapse.

According to structural functionalists, the evolution of complex movements from simple movements is inevitable. An ambitious young boy will not be satisfied to continue doing a forward roll on the trampoline. His innate natural ambition will eventually produce a triple-twisting quadruple somersault that, in turn, will survive for only as long as it meets his competitive requirements. Further, perhaps it is true to say that according to this theory, movement does not necessarily have to be refined, but it has to become more complex.

The *cultural lag* theory maintains that the advance of material benefits (television, huge new stadiums, better protection equipment), is incongruent with, indeed not even matched by the advance of spiritual benefits (ideas, values, customs). Cultural-lag theorists maintain that such considerable difference or *lag* exists between the material and spiritual values that extreme dissonance occurs. This dissonance will bring about change. Perhaps this theory explains the many problems associated with vandalism. Most citizens are at a loss to explain antisocial behavior such as graffiti, toilet-wall artistry, the destruction of operating equipment, and the willful theft of necessary equipment from sporting heroes. The desire for material substance is not matched by strong ethical values. The continuing efforts of human beings to close this gap gives possible explanation for the phenomenon of change.

One further theory explaining change is the *diffusion* theory. Cross-pollination results in certain cultures borrowing customs from other cultures. Certainly evidence for diffusion theory is found in many sporting movements today. The existence of the scouting book and the study of game films in football are two such examples of one team learning from other teams. Two innovative American track and field athletes, Dick Fosbury in 1968 and Al Feuerbach in 1972, were never allowed to practice alone. Flocks of coaches, photographers, and track buffs always gathered when Fosbury jumped or Feuerbach pushed his shot. Their unique contributions quickly influenced athletes in other parts of the world.

## Planned and Unplanned Change

*Change may take place through planning or by accident.* Planned change occurs when athletes and coaches formulate new theories or develop new movements, synthesize known data into new combinations, or incorporate one society's movement patterns into another. The shape of the javelin has undergone extensive review over the years as a result of scientific discoveries relative to wind resistance, drag, and vibratory action. Another strong avenue for planned change is the capacity for individuals to incorporate new movements into old techniques. The straddle high jump has experienced interesting re-emphases over its 40 year existence. First there was the bent leg wrap around style, followed by the straight leg rotational technique, the vertical rotation or dive straddle technique, and finally combinations of the movements of all three. The various national emphases—particularly input from East Germany, Russia and the United States—have resulted in many changes in track and field techniques over the years. As each nation produces winning athletes, other nations study and incorporate advanced movements into the performances of their own champions. This action—sometimes called *diffusion*—always results in considerable change.

Unplanned change can be most effective because it usually arises out of immediate necessity and nearly always evokes spontaneous response. As human beings perform, they learn more of their movement potential. The antics of the 1930 gymnasts, for instance, are the subject of polite smiles from modern technicians. Because of planned and unplanned change, the training feats of modern marathoners are incomparable with those of nineteenth-century athletes.

Much advance in sport achievement is due to the constantly changing environment. The wind is never the same from one day to the next. This variable alone is the single most important factor in yachting, skiing, parachuting, and throwing events in track and field. The better an individual learns to "gear up and adapt" the greater the eventual success will be. Spontaneity of reaction is important within a sport (a fumble recovery in football) as well as in specific environments (tacking in sailing).

## CROWD BEHAVIOR

*Crowds tend to gather together in temporary congregation to view activities of common interest and to express support for selected aspects of the activities under review.* Wherever the activities of a group assume widespread movements ranging from an ice follies review to a sombre game of chess, crowds will gather and people will take sides. Individuals who have never previously committed themselves in support of one

**Figure 6-1.** Crowds: collective vicarious behavior. *(Courtesy of Boston University Photo Service)*

faction or another find it virtually impossible to remain impartial throughout the entire process. Some viewers are fiercely partisan to the point of irrational behavior. Others are more sensitive to the vicissitudes of the activity and enjoy the activity without heavy personal commitment to bipartisan factions. Still others take sides because of such external pressures as betting, ethnic membership, or national involvement. The interest expressed in gathering crowds by those with mercenary intent stems from the fact that people gather support, identify with, and become emotionally involved in the activities of others. Crowd behaviors are real.

## Temporary Crowds

*Crowds viewing sporting events are short-lived in structure and expect short lived behavior from the participants involved.* Most sporting events that attract large crowds do so because they evidence rapid social change and competitive activity. The spectators know that they will assemble but for a few hours. A new social environment is created and an atmosphere for quick change is created. Temporary friends are made as spectators happily converse with total strangers for lengthy durations. Social barriers break down as men and women join the gregarious activity in support of one group or another. Instant comedians emerge as the surrounding spectators yearn for entertainment. Exhibitionists scale fences and mingle with players, knowing full well that their escapade will result in temporary censure. Official action from referees and organizers is vocally supported or decried. Vocal expression, frequently accompanied by excessive nonverbal expression, becomes the order of the day. Anxious supporters grasp on to straws of hope as the fortunes of their idols fluctuate. The sounding of the final time piece brings relief or anger, usually with much rationalization. These short-lived social behaviors are intensely motivating and lend themselves to repetition. The exciting nature of short-lived competitive events intrigues most human beings, giving rise to the phenomenon of spectatorism and vicarious sporting involvement.

*Temporary crowds are subject to irrational and compulsive behaviors.* Crowd behavior is not always harmonious. Frequently, antisocial acts are seen as new impetus is introduced. Ownership of the ball, the puck, or territory shifts so quickly that frequent conflicts of values and norms arise as the spectators are moved to feverish excitement. Normally responsible people are torn between support of illegal actions and loyalty to their team. Sudden crises and instant suspicion accompanies all changes in fortune as relaxation of social controls occurs within the comparative safety of the herd environment. Moods and attitudes become contagious and inhibitions recede as inoffensive model neighbors are transformed into yelling, blood-thirsty, vengeful fanatics. Deep frustrations emerge too, as fortunes vacillate. The presence of referees, rival hoodlums, and alien superstars so incites the home fan that he or she is capable of uncharacteristic movement excess. Irrational and compulsive behaviors result which are destructive and inhumane. Individually most participants in mass crowd reactions are disgusted and chagrined when the results of their collective behavior are bared in the hard light of the next day. Mass hysteria remains one of the more serious problems associated with emotional crowd behavior in major sporting activities. Fortunately, few crowds are permitted to run amuck due to preventive action on the part of organizers, security officers and the participants themselves. However, sports which gain prestige and fiscal superiority through persistent appeals to collective hysteria are probably doing the human race as grave an injustice as any dictator or psychopathic leader has managed in the course of human history. Irresponsible rock groups belong in the same category. Public opinion is often swayed unwisely when emotions are aroused and reason is silenced. Fortunately cooler heads seem to prevail at most collective gatherings, but the constant menace of irrational and compulsive behavior remains a challenge to all associated with the business of assembling spectators to view competitive movement.

### The Effects of Overcrowding

*Overcrowded conditions overburden physical and psychosocial relationships to the extent that individuals will behave very differently than they will under conditions of free personal space.* Calhoun's (43) experiments with rats established that very different behaviors occurred when overcrowding took place. We are assuming that this conclusion holds true with human beings as well. This conclusion is supported by Skolnick (44) in his experiments dealing with overcrowded urban dwellers. People tend to become desperate, highly competitive, or easily manipulated under conditions of overcrowding. Human dignity is lost and spiritual values reduced. "Dumb" repetition is encouraged and the models of ambition and social mobility are quickly lost. Crowded conditions in jails, lines, and peak-hour transportation reduce human sensitivity to the point where survival becomes the principal criterion. One only has to see the pushing and shoving, the elbowing and the stomping, to realize that human beings cannot be herded together for long periods of time without severe physical and psychological reprisals. Physical activity is a prime medium for attracting the formation of both temporary and permanent crowds. It behooves us to consider strongly the evils of overcrowding and the possible antisocial side effects when planning spectatorial assembly.

## POLITICAL ACTIVITY

*Politically inspired groups use the medium of games and sports to further their causes and restrict opposition to their cause.* Cheffers (45) has provided primary material on the effect that politically inspired groups can have upon other groups to bring their grievances to world attention. The barring of Rhodesia from the 1968 and 1972 Olympic Games under the flimsiest of possible excuses graphically illustrates the power that majority opinion can have over minority opinion when political causes are at stake. Many countries have used the instigation or threat of boycott to further political causes. Holland withdrew from the 1956 Olympic games in protest of Russia's repression of Hungary. Twenty-four countries threatened boycott of the 1968 Olympic games before the invitation to South Africa was withdrawn. India threatened boycott when it was learned that it was destined to meet the republic of South Africa in 1973 Davis Cup Challenge Round.

World sporting events offer such a unique stage from which local causes can be promulgated, that committed local causes have produced atrocity after atrocity in the full knowledge that world visibility could be gained in no other way. Terrorists from the Black September group so brutally spoiled the Olympics of Munich in 1972 that doubts about the continuance of the Olympic Games received serious airing. The erstwhile idealism of the Games, which contains its own peculiar brand of hypocrisy, has been supplanted by a cynical realism and an indifferent existentialism, both of which threatened to curtail the Games, position as the premier sporting event in the current calender of world movement.

*Internal politics can reduce or enhance the movement in a group.* Internal politics have plagued institutionalized sports as much as external politics. The continuing retention of amateur status by the National Collegiate Athletic Association in the face of wholesale disclosure to the contrary, and the double-dealing associated with maintaining impossible rules and regulations is so reducing the credibility of that institution that wholesale credibility void is rampant and splintering is very likely in the years to come.

## Conclusion

Individuals do not move in a vacuum. The world of human interaction is perhaps the most cogent force in determining the direction of collective human behavior. No one individual moves in unrelated form to those with whom he or she comes in contact. Both the quality and quantity of human movement affect and are affected by the individual and the social environment.

## References Cited

1. SHAW, MARVIN E. *Group Dynamics: The Psychology of Small Group Behavior.* New York: McGraw-Hill Book Co., 1971.

2. HOMANS, GEORGE C. *The Human Group.* New York: Harcourt, Brace Jovanovich, Inc., 1950.

3. DEUTSCH, MORTON. "The Effects of Cooperation and Competition Upon Group Process," in D. Cartwright, and A. Zander (eds.). *Group Dynamics: Research and Theory* (3rd ed.). New York: Harper and Row, 1968, 461–82.

4. PERRY, JOHN AND ERNA PERRY. *The Social Web.* San Francisco: Canfield Press, 1973.

5. GILBERT, B., AND N. WILLIAMSON. "Programmed to be Losers," *Sports Illustrated.* 38 [June 4, 1973 (b)]: 60–71.

6. GILBERT, B. AND N. WILLIAMSON. "Are You Being Two-Faced?" *Sports Illustrated,* 38 [June 4, 1973 (b)]: 45–54.

7. GILBERT, B. AND N. WILLIAMSON. "Sport is Unfair to Women," *Sports Illustrated.* 38 (May 28, 1973): 88–98.

8. TRIPLETT, N. "The Dynamogenic Factors in Pacemaking and Competition," *American Journal of Psychiatry,* 9 (1877): 507–33.

9. ZAJONC, R. B. "Social Facilitation," *Science,* 149, (1965): 269–74.

10. ZAJONC, R. B., AND S. M. SALES. "Social Facilitation of Dominant and Subordinate Responses," *Journal of Experimental Social Psychology,* 2 (1966): 160–68.

11. MARTENS, R. "Effect of An Audience on Learning and Performance of a Complex Motor Skill," *Journal of Experimental Social Psychology,* 12 (1969): 252–60.

12. DAVIS, J. H. *Group Performance.* Reading, Mass.: Addison–Wesley Publishing Co., 1969.

13. BANDURA, W., AND R. WALTERS, *Social Learning and Personality Development.* New York: Holt, Rinehart, and Winston, 1963.

14. DION, K. L., R. S. BARON, AND N. MILLER. "Why Do Groups Make Riskier Decisions than Individuals?" in Leonard Berkowitz, (ed.), *Experimental Social Psychology* (Vol. 5). New York: Academic Press, 1970, 306–377.

15. TAURIS, CAROL. "The Frozen World of the Familiar Stranger: A Conversation With Stanley Milgram," *Psychology Today.* 8 (June 1974): 71–73, 76–80.

16. HALL, EDWARD T. *The Silent Language.* Greenwich, Connecticut: Fawcett Publications, Inc., 1969.

17. OSMOND, H. "Function as the Basis of Psychiatric Ward Design," *Mental Hospitals* (Architectural Supplement), 8 (1957): 23–30.

18. WEBER, M. *The Throng of Social and Economic Organizations*. A. Henderson and T. Parsons, (trans.). New York: Oxford University Press, 1947.

19. BLAU, P. M. *Bureaucracy in Modern Society*. New York: Random House, Inc., 1956.

20. FITTS, P. M., AND M. I. POSNER. *Human Performance*. Belmont, California: Brooks/Cole, 1967.

21. PIAGET, J. *The Origins of Intelligence in Children*. New York: International Universities Press, 1952.

22. CONSTANZO, P. R. AND M. E. SHAW. "Conformity as a Function of Age Level," *Child Development*. 37 (1966): 967–975.

23. ASCH, S. E. "Effects of Group Pressure Upon the Modification and Distribution of Judgment," in H. Guetzkow, (ed.), *Groups, Leadership, and Men*. Pittsburgh: Carnegie Press, 1951, 177–190.

24. SCHENDEL, J. "Psychological Differences Between Athletes and Nonparticipants in Athletics at Three Educational Levels," *Research Quarterly*, 36 (1965): 52–67.

25. KROLL, W. AND P. CRENSHAW. "Multivariate Personality Profile Analysis of Four Athletic Groups," *Contemporary Psychology of Sport*. Chicago: The Athletic Institute, 1970, 97–106.

26. TUTKO, T., AND J. RICHARDS. *Psychology of Coaching*. Boston: Allyn and Bacon, Inc., 1970.

27. FRENCH, J. R. P., JR. "The Disruption and Cohesion of Groups," *Journal of Abnormal and Social Psychology*. 36 (1941): 361–77.

28. FESTINGER, L. "Informal Social Communication," *Psychological Review*. 57 (1950): 271–282.

29. ROETHLISBERGER, F. J. AND W. J. DICKSON. *Management and the Worker*. Cambridge, Mass.: Harvard University Press, 1939.

30. WHYTE, W. F. *Street Corner Society*. Chicago: University of Chicago Press, 1943.

31. SHELDON, W. H., S. S. STEVENS, AND W. B. TUCKER. *Varieties of Human Physique*. New York: Harper and Row, 1940.

32. SHELDON, W. H. *Atlas of Men*. New York: Harper and Row, 1954.

33. COOLEY, C. H. *Human Nature and the Social Order*. New York: Charles Scribner's Sons, 1902. Reprinted by the Free Press: Glencoe, New York, 1956.

34. MEAD, M. H. *Mind, Self, and Society*. Chicago: University of Chicago Press, 1934.

35. HOLLINGSHEAD, A. B. *Two Factor Index of Social Position*. New Haven, Conn.: Mimeographed, 1957.

36. MILLER, H. L. AND R. R. WOOCK, *Social Foundations of Urban Education*. Hinsdale, Illinois: The Dryden Press, Inc., 1970.

37. FROMM, ERICH. *Fear of Freedom*. Broadway House, London: Rutledge and Kegan Paul, Ltd., 1942.

38. LOY, J. W. AND J. F. MCELVOGUE. "Racial Segregation in American Sport," *International Review of Sport Sociology*. 5 (1970): 5–23.

39. BERGER, PETER AND BRIGITTE BERGER. "The Blueing of America," *The New Republic* (April 3, 1971).

40. BROWN, RONALD. "Class, Race and Athletics: A Study of Adolescent Aspiration, Intentions, Interests." Unpublished Doctoral Dissertation, Boston University, 1974.

41. SPENGLER, O. *The Decline of the West*. Charles F. Atkinson (trans.). New York: Alfred A. Knopf, 1939.

42. TOYNBEE, A. J. *A Study of History*. Somervill Abridgement. New York: Oxford University Press, 1946.

43. CALHOUN, J. B. "Population Density and Social Pathology." *Scientific American*. (February 1962).

44. SKOLNICK, P., et al. "The Effects of Population Size and Density on Human Behavior." Paper delivered at Western Psychological Association Meeting, San Francisco, Spring, 1971.

45. CHEFFERS, JOHN. *A Wilderness of Spite or Rhodesia Denied*. New York: Vantage Press, 1972.

# 7

## What Forms Does Human Movement Take?

*John Cheffers* / *Tom Evaul*

Plato (1) developed and articulated a theory of forms. He conceived a form as a permanent, abstract structure or organizing center from which substructures and specific concrete developments could emanate. There was, he maintained, an ideal form of beauty. Beauty was permanent and abstract. Cleopatra reflected beauty, as did Venus de Milo, and Josephine, and Greta Garbo. The natural scent of a floral display reflected beauty as did the brilliance of a sunset and the soft smile of a new mother. The grace of a double-turning gymnast reflected beauty, as did the fluent stroke of the tennis player's forehand and the twirling pirouette of the ballerina. Disparate examples taken from very different models—yes—but all reflecting one universal idea or form: beauty.

Plato's concept of a universal ideal or form introduces the one truly unique aspect of the discipline of Human Movement—its forms. Numerous examples of specific skills are categorized into meaningful conceptual structures. In Bruner's words:

> The curriculum of a subject should be determined by the most fundamental understanding that can be achieved of underlying principles . . . that give structure to that subject (2).

Physical educators have often debated the nature of this structure: "Man manipulates himself and objects in space" is a big idea or concept offered by Ann Jewett (3). This rubric covers such substrata as, mechanical principles, the giving of impetus to external objects, the reception of impetus from external objects, and all of the many movements which exemplify these subconcepts such as catching, trapping, throwing, and kicking. Jewett maintained that every human movement can be placed in a conceptual structure that gives greater meaning to the movement itself and the outcome of its performance (Figure 7–1). If one accepts this viewpoint, the movements of the toiling laborer, the grunting athlete, the breathless dancer, and the dabbing surgeon have important underlying common links. Some of these links are multifaceted fitness requirements, careful work habits, secure self-image, and clear understanding of the mechanical principles involved. The explanation and understanding of human movement is impossible without recognition of such an underlying conceptual structure.

1. *Perceiving:* Awareness of movement positions, postures, patterns, and skills. These awarenesses may be evidenced by motoric acts such as imitating a position or skill; they may be sensory in that the mover feels a posture when the limbs are manipulated; or they may be evidenced cognitively through identification, recognition, or distinction.

2. *Patterning:* Arrangement and use of body parts in successive and harmonious ways to achieve a movement pattern or skill. This level is dependent on recall and performance of a movement previously demonstrated or experienced.

3. *Adapting:* Modification of a patterned movement to meet externally imposed task demands. This would include modification of a particular movement to perform it under different conditions.

4. *Refining:* Acquisition of smooth, efficient control in performing a movement pattern or skill by mastery of spatial and temporal relations. This process deals with the achievement of precision in motor performance and habituation of performance under more complex conditions.

5. *Varying:* Invention or construction of unique or novel options in motor performance. These options are limited to different ways of performing specific movements; they are of an immediate situational nature and lack any predetermined goal or outcome which has been externally imposed on the mover.

6. *Improvising:* Extemporaneous origination or initiation of novel movements or combinations of movements. The processes involved may be stimulated by a situation externally structured, but preplanning on the part of the performer is not usually required.

7. *Composing:* Combination of learned movements into unique

**Figure 7-1.** Human Movement takes many forms. [*Courtesy of: (top and center right) Boston University Photo Service; (center left) Justin Zaichkowsky; (bottom) Argus Africa News Service*]

motor designs or the creation of movements new to the performer. The performer creates his own motor response in terms of his own interpretation of a movement situation.

The challenge presented by the big idea, however, is not based merely in scholarly study. To most people the challenge is transferred to, and tested in, the concrete examples or, if you prefer, the movement skills. For instance, it is entirely functional for a mechanic to master the skills of fastening screws and bolts into vehicles from all positions quickly and effectively. Yet, with each new edition of engines and motor vehicles, the mechanic needs to learn new motor patterns in order to continue to perform this task. Unique skills are constantly being perfected and intricate patterns of participation are constantly surfacing as human beings plunge deeper into the wellspring of their movement potential.

There appear to be two important channels categorizing the forms of movement: The *quantitative channel* which refers to the structure of the types, range, scopes, and categories of movement; and the *qualitative channel* which considers the nature and value inherent in human movement. The former establishes compartments into which movement forms can be placed, while the latter describes differences among movements.

## THE QUANTITATIVE CHANNEL

Many people have endeavored to categorize the scope of human movement. Cheffers' simple classification is dichotomous.

> An individual adapts personal movement to fit in with the environment or changes the environment to suit personal needs and interests.

When people swim, they are adapting their personal movement to the environment, and when they draw lines on the ground to play basketball, football, or soccer, they are adapting the natural environment to suit their movement needs and interests. Under these conditions a track team would be functioning in the former domain during the cross-country season, and the latter domain during the track season. Coaches and teachers have often employed principles from this simple dichotomy to diversify training and vary preparations for important movement tasks.

Some, like Sidel, Biles, Figley and Neuman (15), have endeavored to construct formulae. They represented the fundamental movement skills in equation form.

> 1 (Moving the body through space) + 2 (Moving an object through space) = 3 (Moving the body and an object through space)

$$1 + 2 = 3$$

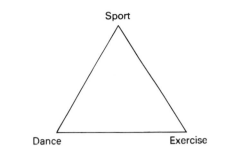

**Figure 7-2.** Jan Felshin (4) talked of a tripartite categorization: sport, dance, and exercise.

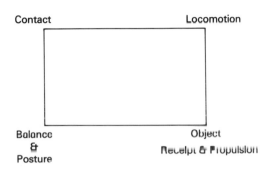

**Figure 7-3.** Godfrey and Kephart (5) had four patterns of motor activities: balance and posture, locomotion, contact, and the receipt and propulsion of objects.

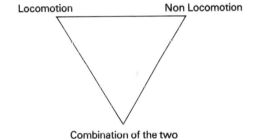

**Figure 7-4.** Hackett and Jensen (6) compartmentalized movement into three forms: locomotor, nonlocomotor, and the inevitable combination of both.

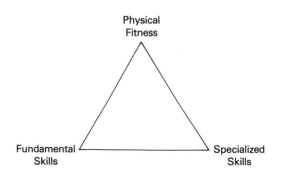

**Figure 7-5.** Kirshner (7) was content with three categories: physical fitness, fundamental skills, and specialized skills.

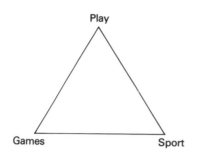

**Figure 7-6.** George Sage (8) offered play, games, and sport for his conceptual umbrella. He considered play to be self-initiated, uninhibited movement activity, games to be competitive forms of play, and sport to be institutionalized and often externally manipulated forms of game.

BASIC (3)                                    COMPLEX (11)

Locomotor                                    Sport
Stabilizing                                  Dance
Manipulative                                 Drama
                                             Aquatics
                                             Play
                                             Work (Labor)
                                             Combat
                                             Music
                                             Oratory
                                             Sex
                                             Crafts

**Figure 7-7.** Evaul (9) talked of basic and complex human movements. He divided basic movements into locomotion, stabilizing, and manipulative, and complex movements into eleven categories: sport, dance, drama, aquatics, play, work (labor), combat, music, oratory, sex, crafts. Gallahue et al (10) developed Evaul's basic movements in this order: stability, locomotion, manipulation.

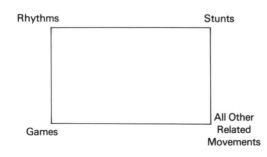

**Figure 7-8.** Gladys Andrews Fleming (11) categorized movement forms into games, rhythms, stunts, and all other related movements.

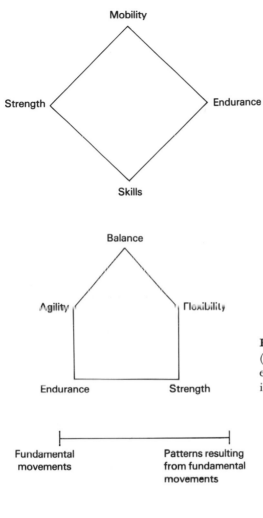

**Figure 7-9.** The English physical educator, A. D. Munrow (12) classified physical activity into four components: mobility, strength, endurance, and skills.

**Figure 7-10.** Muska Mosston (13) had five divisions: agility, endurance, strength, flexibility, and balance.

**Figure 7-11.** Brown and Cassidy (14) saw a dichotomy between fundamental movements and the patterns that human beings weave with these fundamental movements.

Some classifications like those of Cheffers, Sage, Felshin, and Brown and Cassidy have been simple, but others like that of Harrow (16) have been quite complex. She developed a taxonomy of the psychomotor domain. Her concerns were for the taxonomy continuum, levels, definitions, and behavioral activity. Tables 7–1 and 7–2 set out a synopsis of her taxonomy.

Inherent in her work was an ambitious attempt to tease out quantitative aspects of the psychomotor domain similar in developmental param-

**Table 7-1. Summary Outline of Psychomotor
Taxonomy According to Anita J. Harrow (16)**

1.00 Reflex Movements
   1.10 Segmental Reflexes
      1.11 Flexion Reflex
      1.12 Myotatic Reflex
      1.13 Extensor Reflex
      1.14 Crossed Extensor Reactions
   1.20 Intersegmental Reflexes
      1.21 Cooperative Reflex
      1.22 Competitive Reflex
      1.23 Successive Induction
      1.24 Reflex Figure
   1.30 Suprasegmental Reflexes
      1.31 Extensor Rigidity
      1.32 Plasticity Reactions
      1.33 Postural Reflexes
         1.331 Supporting Reactions
         1.332 Shifting Reactions
         1.333 Tonic-Attitudinal
              Reflexes
         1.334 Righting Reaction
         1.335 Grasp Reflex
         1.336 Placing and
              Hopping Reactions
2.00 Basic-Fundamental Movements
   2.10 Locomotor Movements
   2.20 Non-Locomotor Movements
   2.30 Manipulative Movements
      2.31 Prehension
      2.32 Dexterity
3.00 Perceptual Abilities
   3.10 Kinesthetic Discrimination
      3.11 Body Awareness
         3.111 Bilaterality
         3.112 Laterality
         3.113 Sidedness
         3.114 Balance
      3.12 Body Image
      3.13 Body Relationship to
         Surrounding Objects
         in Space
   3.20 Visual Discrimination
      3.21 Visual Acuity
      3.22 Visual Tracking
      3.23 Visual Memory
      3.24 Figure-Ground
         Differentiation
      3.25 Perceptual Consistency

3.30 Auditory Discrimination
   3.31 Auditory Acuity
   3.32 Auditory Tracking
   3.33 Auditory Memory
3.40 Tactile Discrimination
3.50 Coordinated Abilities
   3.51 Eye-Hand Coordination
   3.52 Eye-Foot Coordination
4.00 Physical Abilities
   4.10 Endurance
      4.11 Muscular Endurance
      4.12 Cardiovascular Endurance
   4.20 Strength
   4.30 Flexibility
   4.40 Agility
      4.41 Change Direction
      4.42 Stops and Starts
      4.43 Reaction-Response Time
      4.44 Dexterity
5.00 Skilled Movements
   5.10 Simple Adaptive Skill
      5.11 Beginner
      5.12 Intermediate
      5.13 Advanced
      5.14 Highly Skilled
   5.20 Compound Adaptive Skill
      5.21 Beginner
      5.22 Intermediate
      5.23 Advanced
      5.24 Highly Skilled
   5.30 Complex Adaptive Skill
      5.31 Beginner
      5.32 Intermediate
      5.33 Advanced
      5.34 Highly Skilled
6.00 Non-Discursive Communication
   6.10 Expressive Movement
      6.11 Posture and Carriage
      6.12 Gestures
      6.13 Facial Expression
   6.20 Interpretive Movement
      6.21 Aesthetic Movement
      6.22 Creative Movement

## Table 7-2. Taxonomy for the Psychomotor
## Domain Classification Levels & Subcategories
## by A. J. Harrow

| Taxonomy Continuum | Levels | Definitions | Behavioral Activity |
|---|---|---|---|
| 1.10 Segmental<br>1.20 Inter-segmental<br>1.30 Supra-segmental | 1.00<br>Reflex<br>Movements | Actions elicited without conscious volition in response to some stimuli | Flexion, extension, stretch, postural adjustments |
| 2.10 Loco-motor<br>2.20 Non-Loco-motor<br>2.30 Manipu-lative | 2.00<br>Basic-Fundamental<br>Movements | Required: 1.00 Inherent movement patterns which are formed from a combining of reflex movements, and are the basis for complex skilled movement | 2.10<br>Walking, running, jumping, sliding, hopping, rolling, climbing<br>2.20<br>pushing, pulling, swaying, swinging, stooping, stretching, bending, twisting<br>2.30<br>handling, manipulating, gripping, grasping finger movements |
| 3.10 Kines-thetic Discrim-ination<br>3.20 Visual Discrim-ination<br>3.30 Auditory Discrim-ination<br>3.40 Tactile Discrim-ination<br>3.50 Coordi-nated Abilities | 3.00<br>Perceptual Abilities | Required: 1.00–2.00 Interpretation of stimuli from various modalities providing data for the learner to make adjustments to his environment | The *outcomes* of perceptual abilities are observable in *all purposeful* movement.<br>Examples:<br>Auditory—following verbal instructions.<br>Visual—dodging a moving ball.<br>Kinesthetic—making bodily adjustments in a hand-stand to maintain balance.<br>Tactile—determining texture through touch.<br>Coordinated—jump rope, punting, catching. |

Table 7-2 (con't)

| | | | |
|---|---|---|---|
| 4.10 Endurance | 4.00 Physical Abilities | Functional characteristics of organic vigor which are essential to the development of highly skilled movement | All activities which require strenuous effort for long periods of time—Examples: distance running, distance swimming. |
| 4.20 Strength | | | All activities which require muscular exertion—Examples: weight lifting, wrestling. |
| 4.30 Flexibility | | | All activities which require wide range of motion at hip joints— Examples: touching toes, back bend, ballet exercises. |
| 4.40 Agility | | | All activities which require quick precise movements— Examples: shuttle run, typing, dodgeball. |
| 5.10 Simple Adaptive Skill | 5.00 Skilled Movements | A degree of efficiency when performing complex movement tasks which are based upon inherent movement patterns | All skilled activities which build upon the inherent locomotor and manipulative movement patterns of classification level two. |
| 5.20 Compound Adaptive Skill | | | |
| 5.30 Complex Adaptive Skill | | | These activities are obvious in sports, recreation, dance, and fine arts areas. |
| 6.10 Expressive Movement | 6.00  Non-discursive Communication | Communication through bodily movements ranging from facial expressions through sophisticated choreographies | Body postures, gestures, facial expressions, all efficiently executed skilled dance movements and choreographies. |
| 6.20 Interpretive Movement | | | |

eters to the achievements of Bloom and Krathwhol in the cognitive and affective domains.

While by no means exhaustive, this list of quantitative categorizations of human movement forms gives clear indication that many attempts have been made to structure the scope of human movement.

## THE QUALITATIVE CHANNEL

Some movement exponents have categorized movement without regard to its overall scope. Rudolf Laban (Figure 7–12) (17), the celebrated German exponent of movement exploration working in Great Britain, employed adjectival descriptions of the motions inherent in each movement sequence. He talked of slashing and punching, of gliding and wringing, of dabbing and pressing, of floating and flicking. He further categorized these movements into the conceptual framework of time (fast and slow), space (direct and indirect), and force (strong and light). There is a fourth characteristic of movement called *flow*. It is not a component of the eight basic effort actions, hence, it is not included in Figure 7–12. Exponents of Laban's theory point to the fact that these categorizations can be made of the movements inherent in the entire scope of movement forms.

A host of physicists, chemists, and engineers (Figure 7–13) (18, 19, 20) have also categorized movement forms from a qualitative viewpoint They have been interested in flexion, extension, adduction, abduction, and circumlocution.

They saw chain reactions of movements formed through motor patterns, and they sought the causes, the restrictions, and the better ways to perform each movement. Physicists looked at the mechanics of the movement, chemists were interested in the composition and functioning of the organ that brought that movement about, and engineers were fascinated with the effect of the organ's movement on internal and external objects.

Undaunted by the enormity of her task, Margie R. Hanson (Figure 7–14) (21) endeavored to combine elements of what we have described as quantitative and qualitative channels of movement. She depicted the discipline of Human Movement as a tree nourished by the roots of space, time, force, and flow, and incorporated the fundamental skills of locomotor, nonlocomotor and manipulative movement. Each movement was developed into the sturdy branches of individual sports, gymnastics, aquatics, team sports, dance, and daily living activities. The tree was healthy when the fundamental skills were sound, and the branches were not lopsided.

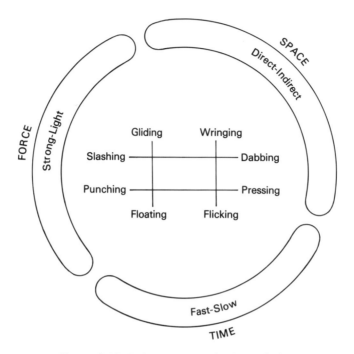

**Figure 7-12.** Laban's categorization of characteristics of movement and basic effort actions.

Movement forms are the visible evidence of the discipline. Some have considered these forms unimportant human endeavors—trivial in the overall patterns of life. They have preferred the mind with all its scholastic emphasis. But most people have identified strongly with some form of excellence in physical expression. These people have invested enormous emotional capital in developing individual potential. Few parents will deny their children the opportunity to realize physical ambitions and few arguments will deter the Olympic hopeful from total and dedicated practice. Entrepreneurs, scholars, mystics, thrill vendors, and sports peo-

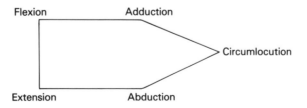

**Figure 7-13.** A typical kinesiological classification.

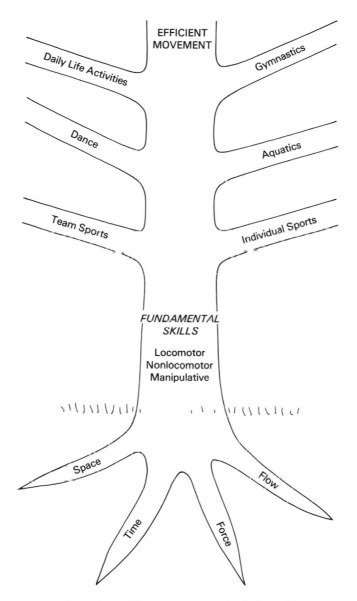

**Figure 7-14.** Hanson's tree depicting the forms of human movement.

ple have joined the average citizen in devoting sizable portions of their daily existence to the conquest of the many movement forms. This fact alone is sufficient rationale for the existence of a discipline called Human Movement.

## References Cited

1. PLATO. *The Republic.* New York: The Modern Library, Random House.
2. BRUNER, JEROME. *The Process of Education.* New York: Vintage Books, 1963.
3. JEWETT, ANN. eds. John E. Nixon and Ann E. Jewett. *An Introduction to Physical Education* (8th ed..), Philadelphia: W. B. Saunders, 1974.
4. FELSHIN, JANET. *More Than Movement.* Philadelphia: Lea and Febiger, 1972.
5. GODFREY, BARBARA B. AND NIHLS KEPHART. *Movement Patterns and Motor Education.* New York: Appleton, Century, Crofts, 1969. Pp. 9–11.
6. HACKETT, LAYNE, AND ROBERT JENSEN. *A Guide to Movement Exploration.* Palo Alto, California: Peek Publications, 1966.
7. KIRSHNER, GLENN. *Physical Education for Elementary School Children* (3rd ed.). Dubuque, Iowa: W. C. Brown and Co., 1974.
8. SAGE, GEORGE H. *Sport and American Society* (2nd ed.). Reading, Mass.: Addison-Wesley Publishing Co., Inc., 1974.
9. EVAUL, TOM. "Where are You Going: What Are You Going to Do?" *Curriculum Improvement in Secondary School Physical Education.* Washington: American Alliance for Health, Physical Education and Recreation, 1971.
10. GALLAHUE, DAVID L., PETER H. WERNER, AND GEORGE C. LUEDKE. *A Conceptual Approach to Moving and Learning.* New York: John Wiley & Sons, Inc., 1972.
11. FLEMING, GLADYS. *Creative Rhythmic Movement for Children.* Englewood Cliffs, N.J.: Prentice-Hall, Inc., 1954.
12. MUNROW, A. D. *Pure and Applied Gymnastics.* London: Edward Arnold (Publishers), Ltd., 1955.
13. MOSSTON, MUSKA. *Developmental Movement.* Columbus, Ohio: Charles E. Merrill, 1966.
14. BROWN, CAMILLE AND ROSALIND CASSIDY. *Theory in Physical Education: A Guide to Program Change.* Philadelphia: Lea and Febiger, 1967.
15. SEIDEL, BILES et al. *Sports Skills: A Conceptual Approach to Meaningful Movement.* Dubuque, Iowa: W. C. Brown and Co., 1975.
16. HARROW, ANITA J. *A Taxonomy of the Psychomotor Domain.* New York: David McKay Co., 1972.
17. LABAN, RUDOLF. *Effort.* London: MacDonald and Evans, Ltd., 1947.
18. HAY, JAMES G. *The Biomechanics of Sports Techniques.* Englewood Cliffs, N.J.: Prentice-Hall, Inc., 1973.
19. DYSON, GEOFFREY. *The Mechanics of Athletics* (2nd ed.). London: University of London Press, 1972.
20. NORTHRIP, JOHN W., GENE A. LOGAN, AND WAYNE C. MCKINNY. *Biomechanic Analysis of Sport.* Dubuque. Iowa: W. C. Brown and Co., 1974.
21. HANSON, MARGIE R. in *Sports Skills: A Conceptual Approach to Meaningful Movement,* ed. Biles Seidel et al. Dubuque, Iowa W. C. Brown and Co., 1975. Pp. 64–65.

# PART III

*Human Movement: Applied*

# 8

*How Do We Help Others by Communicating
Knowledge and Skills in Human Movement?*

*John Cheffers*

Human beings are social animals. They communicate with one another for many reasons. Perhaps the most important communication comes through processes we refer to as teaching, correcting, coaching, giving positive or negative feedback, or giving support and information. Millions of words have been written about teaching. Some educators have suggested that teaching is an entity separate from learning, delving into the many ramifications of developing a theory of instruction. Jerome Bruner (1), B. Othaniel Smith (2), and William James (3) maintained that learning theory, in and of itself, could not explain the phenomenon of teaching. They urged teachers to examine teaching with the goal of developing a theory. This position has led many social scientists and educators to observe teacher behavior both subjectively and objectively. It has brought about the development of systems for describing teacher-student interaction in a wide variety of classrooms. Much of the data collected in this area has potential use for the practicing teacher as well as for the researcher. Educators such as Withall (4), Thelen (5), Taba (6), Tyler (7), Galloway (8) and Bellack (9) have looked at different variables, and they continue to give us a wealth of information about what goes on in the teaching-learning situation. Indeed, over 400 different systems are in existence today (10).

Other educators have been careful to include student learning in the teaching process. They argue that little good is accomplished by teaching unless the learner learns. The entire profession of teaching is there to benefit the student. These educators center their theory around the socialization and the education of the student. Once teaching is divorced from learning, little point is seen for the profession. Modern educators tend to see teaching as much more than lecturing. They tend to see the *process that brings about learning* in a student as a teaching agency (11). (See Figure 8–1.)

A teaching agency is extensive in scope. It can range from a film, to a textbook, to an experience, to a lecture, even to nonintervention altogether. The teacher is seen as any agency which promotes or brings about learning. This admittedly broad, but undeniably accurate, postulation has been supported by David Ausubel (12), Jean Jacques Rousseau (13), Carl Rogers (14), and John Dewey (15). Systems have been developed to incorporate this concept, thus adding to the stockpile of descriptive data gathering on the teaching-learning process (16).

It really doesn't matter which outlook we embrace—whether we view the teacher as one person in a narrow sense, or as an agency in a much broader sense. The fact that human beings teach one another is not in dispute. We coach individuals to better perform skills, we correct those skills where needed, and we admonish or praise the performances of others from all perspectives, and to all ends.

The good football coach is a teacher. He will rarely succeed unless his players are able to learn the skills, the strategies, and the team plays necessary to counter the opposition. Each time a new play is devised or an old play employed, learning takes place. The choreographer of a ballet acts in similar fashion as he or she develops new dances and revises old routines. Two children fishing will teach each other important factors such as the type of bait to use, the place to fish, alternate methods of casting, and how to recognize the fish when it finally arrives. The teaching, coaching, learning spiral continues through life. At the very center of it is movement. Daily, in the lives of most people, new skills are learned, old skills are adapted, and present skills are improved. We help each other continuously.

## THE LEARNING PROCESS

### The Application of Communication Theories

Teaching is one instance of human behavior that involves communication. Teaching involves communication in a special way and it is the task of educators to identify that special way. All communication theories involve a *source*, a *medium*, and a *destination*. The cybernetic model

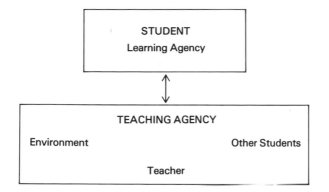

**Figure 8-1.** If learning has occurred, teaching has taken place.

[Taba (6), Suchman (17), Smith (2), Woodruffe (18)] implies that information is encoded at the source, interpreted and developed in the process, and decoded at the destination. If this is true, and research gives us every reason to believe it is, then many teachers are the beneficiaries of knowing and understanding the important elements of communication theories.

Krathwoll (19) has developed a taxonomy of educational objectives in the affective domain. The first parameter developed is known as *attending,* or being aware of what is going on. Without the second parameter, which is referred to as *responding,* little real communication can take place. Communication occurs among people. The mere reception of information does little for the individual other than begin the process. The response enables an interaction to take place which may be conveyed through verbal or nonverbal means, but which, in some form or another, will communicate meaning. Bellack (10) talked of structuring and soliciting as the initiators, and responding and reacting as the next phase. He implied that both these two variables were necessary in teaching if communication is to take place.

Smith's (2) model of classroom discourse is interesting (Figure 8–2).

$P$ means the teacher's perception of pupil's needs, $D$ is the teacher's diagnoses of the pupil's needs, and $R$ is the action taken by the teacher. The second half of this formula refers to the student's perceptions, diagnoses, and reactions to the teacher's behavior. In a very simple, linear fashion, Smith has incorporated the vital aspects of perceptions, decisions, and behaviors that predominate in communication. Gerbner (20), in developing his theory of communication, underscored the perceptions, assumptions, and selection aspects of communication. He added the context of administration, immediate availability of stimulus, effectiveness

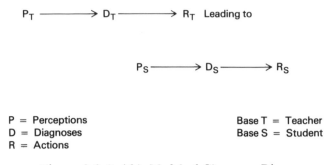

$$P_T \longrightarrow D_T \longrightarrow R_T \text{ Leading to}$$

$$P_S \longrightarrow D_S \longrightarrow R_S$$

P = Perceptions                          Base T = Teacher
D = Diagnoses                            Base S = Student
R = Actions

**Figure 8-2** Smith's Model of Classroom Discourse.

of the channels of the credibility, as well as the contributions of the artist and the scientist. He considered that the scientist tends to verify beliefs, and that the artist, by illuminating the truth, tends to make it believable. Gerbner organized his communications model into a function of administration, credibility through science, and acceptance through art.

Lewis (21) analyzed the communication process as receptiveness, accuracy, mobility, and responsiveness. Communication is "a process by which a person reduces the uncertainty about some state of affairs by the detection of cues which seem to him to be relevant to that state of affairs." By receptiveness he meant the willingness of a person to find out what another person thinks. By accuracy he meant the valid reception of the exact nature and intention of the message. By mobility he meant the capacity of the communicator to be more or less abstract in getting the message across. By responsiveness he meant the communicator's ability to take the audience's reaction into consideration. Lewis believed that possession of these four capabilities is necessary for true communication to take place.

Aronson (22) considered the persuasiveness inherent in the communication process greater when it was designed to appeal to the audience's reason rather than emotions. Further, he thought that the capacity for a communicator to present both sides of an argument increased his credibility. Although in this situation, if a large discrepancy between the communicator's position and the audience's position were present, the communication process would be much more difficult. He was concerned, too, with the order in which opposing views were presented. Aronson postulated that the person first to present the best argument would prevail. However, if a dispute arises between human beings, communication will either be enhanced or depleted by the escalation of defense mechanisms on both sides. Amidon (11) presented an important concept when he referred to the fact that listening skills "are as important as the skills of speaking, reading, and writing. Taking his lead from Ned Flanders, Amidon's insistence upon helping people to listen to one another rather than talk at one another is an important position for it implies that people make decisions too quickly based on too few cues in their communication. Many teachers find unexpected success in their classroom when they adopt a posture of hearing fully what a child has to say before bringing their own value judgments into play.

A common thread runs through all theories of communication with important implications for teaching and learning. For true communication to take place, both sides have to set aside personal prejudices and preconceived biases. Jumping to conclusions or perceiving information through an ethnocentric outlook appears to be the major cause of breakdown in communication. People constantly misperceive. An example of this communications breakdown is frequently seen in the abortive behavior of novice coaches. These coaches frequently interpret player actions out of context. Arriving late for practice, weakness in the face of strong opposition, refusal to obey all of the team's laws, and inability to quickly process strategy symbolisms are inflated by many frustrated coaches into neopersonal attacks, or at least clear indication that the player is not good enough for the team. Teachers, like coaches, make the same mistakes when interpreting the actions of students in the classroom. On the other side of the coin, the alert teacher or coach can gain valuable insights into social situations by quickly assessing and processing student cues. If discovered early, boredom and apathy are curable. When permitted to grow, however, these two variables can thoroughly debilitate the overall class or team effort.

## Teacher Education Programs

Professional preparation begins the first time a child learns a specific skill, and ends when learning is no longer possible. At the college level, it begins with the first skills course in the freshman year and finishes when the student has terminated all contact with the institution.

The thrust of professional preparation today is fast moving from the binding strictures of teacher training into a broader, more diverse, more enterprising, and certainly more appropriate focus. Professional educators are beginning to realize that not all professional programs need to be geared to the preparation of teachers for the public schools. As school systems reach saturation point, the need to develop multiprofessionals is becoming increasingly apparent. Professionals who can stimulate the growth of students into fields identified as recreo-educative and industrio-educative are providing for current needs.

*Teacher trainer* as a term has been replaced by *teacher educator.* In turn, those who educate teachers are being called *professional preparation specialists.* In time they may be called something akin to *teacher development facilitators or resource specialists for learning and development.* The words merely reflect each generation's healthy desire for growth and improvement, and too often they are the cause of disruptive and fruitless inter-generational debate. What is important is that this generation of teacher educators expand its horizons to meet the challenges of today's world—a world which, to understate the obvious, is changing rapidly. Young graduates of programs in Human Movement can expect to find themselves in charge of community facilities that require them to effectively manage a bar, order services and supplies, conduct executive meetings, coach ice or field hockey teams, and develop a curriculum for the middle age members desperately seeking to retain vestiges of physical fitness. Where in past curricula were they prepared for such diverse capacity? Obviously they were not. They had to qualify in a narrow area (business and management, physical education, recreation, public communication), and rely on a canny adaptation of the apprenticeship system for the rest (the good graces of a friend, competitor, or even foe).

The answer to such inadequate preparation is not to further proliferate the multitude of professional preparation areas, but rather to weaken the divisions and encourage individual specialization across disciplines, professions, and facilities. This process is now occurring at many institutions of higher education. The posture of these institutions has been to develop and maintain viable models designed to produce the multiprofessional interdisciplinary educated individual who can readily adapt to the changing job market. One such model was developed at Boston University.

### The Professional Preparation Model at Boston University

Table 8–1 shows the stages through which the students progressed and identifies areas where interdisciplinary and individualized focuses were encouraged. The aim of the curriculum was to provide educational opportunity that gave the student a broad range of techniques and skills within the mainstream, while at the same time maintaining opportunity for specialization to the point of complete departure from the mainstream. In the earlier stages, only a small number of students elected the second route.

The tendency for students to remain in the mainstream was a function of the unidentified job market, the enticing security of the public school systems and the understandable reluctance of parents to influence their children towards new and insecure vocations. As the new directions

## Table 8-1. Synopsis of Professional Preparation at Boston University

| | *Personal Growth in the Arts and Sciences | *Mainstream of Professional Growth and Development | *Specialist Routes in Professional Preparation* |
|---|---|---|---|
| SENIORS | | Professional Semester | Corrective Therapy, Volunteer Agencies |
| JUNIORS | History Philosophy Religion Anthropology Art Music | In-depth, experimental weaning from observation to teaching in university field-based setting for normal and special needs children | or Health Related Areas or |
| SOPHOMORES | Kinesiology Psychology Sociology Physiology Physiology of Exercise | 1. Introduction to and teaching of children with special needs in field setting 2. Observation of children in both field and university settings | Athletic Training and Coaching Outdoor education and Ecology Public Communication and Media or Special Education Management |
| FRESHMEN | English Anatomy Biology Fine Arts | Introduction to and teaching of children in confines of university setting (recreo-educative) | |
| | *Required of all* | *Provided for all* The choice of most | *Highly selective choice* The specialist route may touch upon the Mainstream at any stage or ignore the Mainstream |

*Must have completed:* (3) Humanities, (3) Social Sciences, (3) Physical Sciences

were established, however, increasing numbers traveled the pathways.

Regardless of the route selected by the student, a common denominator of the Boston University model was the component of field experience. It was felt that a good educator needed diversified field experiences throughout professional preparation. Teacher candidates had opportunity to observe and teach programs (K—12) during each of their eight semesters at Boston University. Teaching programs included: peer teaching, one-to-one and small group teaching of normal and handicapped children, and the teaching of inner-city elementary school children. Students did their "formal" student teaching during their senior year at schools of their choice. Supervision for teaching experiences was provided by the Boston University faculty, graduate students, and members of selected schools or agencies who functioned as adjunct faculty. This student-teaching semester is still known at many institutions as the professional semester. It was felt that the professional semester alone was entirely inadequate to prepare a professional.

Non-teaching professional candidates had field experiences in industry, hospitals, political institutions, the performing-arts centers, rehabilitative centers, news offices, and research laboratories.

### Table 8-2. Details of the Professional Preparation Model at Boston University

| | *Mainstream* | *Extensions and Specialist Routes* |
|---|---|---|
| *First Year* | Part 1: Skill and movement exploration courses: during all freshmen skill courses the accent is placed on communication as well as performance.<br>Part 2: Selected Saturday mornings, four each semester. Students prepare to teach small groups of elementary children in the following skills: swimming, movement exploration, gymnastics, track and field, tennis, and skating.<br>　Students are required to prepare the content of each lesson under faculty supervision. | *Special Education.* With retarded, blind, deaf, and physically handicapped.<br><br>*Field Experiences.* With industry, politics, the performing arts, and other institutions.<br><br>*Workshops and Clinics* in Grading, Humanism, Romanticism, Philosophy, Criticism. |
| *Second Year* | Part 1: Full year. One day per week for two hours. Applied section of the course dealing with motor learning and handicapped children. Students prepare and carry out one-on-one teaching with handicapped children at such schools as Perkins, Kennedy, and Fernald schools for special children needs. Their tasks include: | Business administration and management.<br><br>Public communications.<br><br>Athletic training.<br><br>*Outdoor and environmental education:* Participation ranging from Outward Bound experiences to biological excursions. |

Table 8-2 *(con't)*

1. Preparation of
curriculum
2. Learning
communicative skills
3. Preparation for
eventual integration
with other children.

*Part 2:* One semester: 3
sessions per week. The
discipline of Sociology as
it relates to movement.
Conducted by the College
of Liberal Arts. One
theory session followed by
two practical sessions with
600 elementary school
children from inner-city
schools. This program is
conducted at Boston
University by the
Department of Movement
and Health, taught and
planned by faculty and
graduate students.

*Part 3:* Observation of
current school systems:
visits to schools in urban
and suburban settings.

*Part 4:* Seminars in
facilities and management.

Field work in related Liberal Arts areas.

Workshops and clinics in: Applied
educational psychology, classroom
management, moral development,
creativity, social psychology, major
educational theories, measurement and
control.

| *Mainstream* | *Extensions and*<br>*Specialist Routes* |
|---|---|

*Third Year*

*Part 1:* Reassessment and
preparation in techniques
and skills:
a. Intensive participation
in movement and skills.
b. Experience in the
conduct of intramural
activities: refereeing,
organizing, scoring,
development of new
areas, recording, etc.

*Part 2:* Participation in
recreo-educative programs
with underprivileged
children in an urban
community.

Specialized experience in preschool
programs.

Table 8-2 (con't)

*Part 3:* Major preparation for teaching. Twelve credit course entitled Modes and Models of Teaching. Two full days with theory and preparation in the mornings and practical application in the afternoons. Students are taken through a weaning process which begins with individualized contact in group settings. The students adopt a model of "theory into practice," with strong emphasis on experiential learning.

Alternative professional preparation is encouraged where appropriate. It may involve preparation similar to the apprentice system in selected fields or to selected allied fields such as research laboratories, or community based rehabilitative hospitals (Veterans Administration Hospital).

*Part 4:* Elective participation in city programs: leisure services, social agencies, camps, hospitals, municipal recreation departments, ethnic and racially integrated programs.

*Fourth Year*

*Professional semester* One full semester in the field. The student has the choice of any combination of two of the following: elementary school, secondary school, college, hospital, coaching assignments, athletic training, research institutes, preschool agencies, special schools (dance, health, special disabilities, etc.)

Special areas appropriate for the professional semester.

Educational media training and developmental projects.

Overseas and interstate professional apprenticeships and contracts ranging from American military schools abroad, to Peace Corps commitment.

*Graduate*

*Part 1:* Graduate degree courses.
*Part 2:* Clinics and Workshops.
*Part 3:* Cooperation with field settings in the development of new programs, and in identifying new vocational routes.

The faculty at Boston University felt a need to establish constructs that were broader in scope than those traditionally associated with Physical Education, Health Education, and Recreation and Dance. This was readily exemplified by their attempts at naming the new focus. The name, the Department of Human Movement, Health Education, and Leisure Services, was preferred to Health, Physical Education, and Recreation. Later this title was reduced to the Department of Movement, Health, and Leisure. The change in title from the traditional HPER was not capricious, emanating from temporary insanity or pseudo-intellectual activity. It was predicated upon the much broader constructs of the new curriculum. The old title was neither descriptive nor accurate. Movement, Health, and Leisure more accurately approximated the expanded subject area than the traditional nomenclature. The central theme of this text is the construct around which the department was reorganized.

Willgoose (23) has commented upon professional nomenclature across the nation. He noted that states west of the Rockies have been more adventurous than those to the east. The only real test of change in any institution is the quality and quantity of needed programmatic transformation. It is on this basis that professional preparation models everywhere must ultimately be judged. The models must result in better prepared professionals.

The model adopted at Boston University sought primarily a sound mainstream for the majority, and then encouraged planned departure from the mainstream to suit individual students' needs and interests. The model spoke to responsibility, flexibility, variability and compromise.

Professional preparation cannot exist, however, without strong input from the Humanities, Social Sciences, and the Physical Sciences. It is the task of professional schools to initiate and apply knowledge generated in the disciplines.

The construct and courses were as follows:

#### Table 8-3. Construct and Courses for
#### Human Movement

*Man Functions Through Movement*

*Why Man Moves*
> Current Problems in Movement Education
> Purposes in Human Movement

*How Man Moves*
> Biology
> Human Anatomy
> Human Physiology
> Kinesiology
> Physiology of Activity
> Theories in Scientific Conditioning
> Institute on Physical Fitness

Table 8-3  (con't)

*Man Measures and Tempers His Movement*
    Measurement in Human Movement
    Motor Activities for the Handicapped
    Evaluation of Motor Performance
    Advanced Corrective and Adaptive Motor Activities

*Personality, Learning, Development, and Motivation*
*Affect Man's Movement*
    Motor Learning—Theory and Laboratory
    Psychology of Motor Learning and Performance
    Advanced Research Laboratory Techniques in Motor Learning
    Neurological Bases of Motor Learning
    Perceptual-Motor Development

*Man Moves With and Against Other Men*
    Cultural Patterns in Movement
    School and Community Recreation with Practicum
    Sport Theory and Social Systems
    Current Problems in Human Movement

*Human Movement Takes Many Forms*
    Skills and Techniques in Motor Activity
    Techniques and Observation of Motor Activity

*Man Helps Others Function Through Movement*
*Man Teaches and Practices the Teaching of Movement in a Variety of Styles and under a Variety of Stimuli*
    Language Communication
    Modes and Models of Teaching
    Advanced Techniques in Motor Activities
    Student Teaching in Movement Education
    Clinical Observation and Practice
    Observer Systems in Human Movement
    Analysis of Teaching Human Movement
    Program Development in Movement Education
    Movement Education: Early Childhood to Adolescence

*Man Coaches and Corrects Movements Already Encountered*
    Advanced Methods in Coaching
    Advanced Techniques in Aquatics
    Management of Athletics and Physical Education
    Dance in Education
    Movement and Music

*Independent Study and Research*
    Independent Study (Graduate and Undergraduate)
    Seminar in Human Movement and Health Education
    Research Seminar in Human Movement and Health Education
    Advanced Research Seminar in Human Movement and Health Education
    Graduate Level Courses: for full or part time students

**Health Education**

*Man's Movement Is Dependent upon Optimal Health*
    In the Schools

Table 8-3 (con't)

> Foundations of Health Education
> Development of the Health Curriculum
> Health Education in the School and the Community
> Student Teaching in Health Education
> *In the Community*
> Environmental Health Education
> Applied Nutrition
> Health Counseling in Schools and Agencies
> Field Placements in Health Education
> *As Applied to Issues*
> Athletic Training
> Drug Education
> Safety Education
> Sex and Family Living Education
> Drug Abuse
> Adjustment of the Physically Handicapped
> Institute on Cerebral Palsy

*Evaluation of the Model.* All such models are subject to continuing change and evaluation. Their success depends upon several factors: (1) the quality of the professional product, (2) the success of the faculty and students in bringing about productive cooperation among the varying agencies and institutions, (3) a continuing process of evaluation which modifies and refocuses poorer and less productive aspects of the model, (4) formal evaluation procedures which validate the model.

## Helping People Change*

By change we refer to the removal of impediments to the learning process and the encouragement of people to willingly undergo attitudinal, behavioral, and factual reorganization. For instance, a young man may have established the habit of riding his bike from Philadelphia to New York each weekend to visit relatives. Obviously, he has become set in his ways to the extent that other forms of transportation have been ignored. He spends so much time on the bike that he scarcely has time to see his relations in New York, which was his expressed reason for traveling each weekend. His transportation mode is in direct contradiction to his central objective. If he is to achieve his objective more fully, a change in his attitudes, knowledge, and movement patterns has to take place. We are assuming, of course, that his prime motivation is the visitation to his relatives and not the cycle journey through New Jersey's industrial basin.

We might decide to argue our case directly by providing him with

---

*Chapter 15 discusses the important question—How Does the Discipline Change?

a bus or a train ticket. Or we might try an indirect approach by planting the seed of an idea and leaving time for it to germinate within him. In each case, we have contributed to the learning process by helping (or at least providing a mechanism that will help) the person remove an impediment to his learning or bring about change in his lifestyle.

This process is controversial. Many people resent efforts to change their behavior, while still others believe the ethical implications are sufficiently strong to warrant the case for no intervention. Certainly inadequately planned efforts to bring about change will encounter such resistance that the opposite effect takes place—a stiffening of resistance. Change can occur in many ways. Often merely telling or showing alternative methods is sufficient for the mature person to adjust. In many instances Skinner's behavior modification techniques have been employed with success. The thesis of this text, however, is that change brought on by external pressures is too risky. It has been demonstrated that people will change through reward or fear, but the directionality, the permanence, and the reactions are matters of conjecture. Do people really change permanently? And when forced or tricked into changing, do they really fulfill the requirements mandated by the change. Or do they direct hostilities toward new directions? Even contingency management, which simply means that a person is rewarded on the condition that the job is completed, does not fully guarantee permanent internalization. Externally applied pressures will bring about change, but the results cannot be guaranteed, nor can they be fully predicted.

Internally inspired changes tend to be much stronger. When teachers, coaches, and their students picture their behaviors accurately and are motivated to make progress, change is swift and effective. All teachers and coaches should set up an environment that will enable students to analyze in a nonthreatening atmosphere, and to seek out the appropriate change techniques. It is then important that time and support be given for the student to grow in the new directions.

Flanders (24) is one of the vocal proponents of providing a change atmosphere to support pupil initiative and self-direction. He outlined eight objectives of professional self-development that apply to the teacher in the classroom.

1. The competent teacher can identify, describe, and analyze his or her different teaching patterns and use them to develop instructional strategies.
2. The competent teacher can develop and carry out enquiry projects resulting from knowing his or her own teaching patterns.
3. The competent teacher can bring about a balance of pupil initiation and his or her own initiation.

4. The competent teacher can design and use instruments for assessing pupil attitudes and achievements relative to various teaching strategies.

5. The competent teacher can guide students to the discovery of important concepts and how to deal with them.

6. The competent teacher can help peers analyze their teaching behavior.

7. The competent teacher continues to build the underlying theory of his or her own instruction.

8. The competent teacher does not sit on the fence in terms of self-evaluation, or of bringing about change when change is needed.

Flanders, however, expressed frustration at the means by which these objectives could be incorporated into a single, integrated curriculum of professional self-development. He mentioned four excellent techniques for helping the change to occur (*T* groups, microteaching, interaction analysis, simulated skill training) but confessed to knowing little about the intensity of the force needed to bring about change. He despaired at the poor quality of the preservice and educational workshops that fre quently pass as mechanisms for change. He believed there are four major forces operating in the change environment, each leading to and interdependent upon the other.

1. the perceived challenge
2. the required abilities
3. the opportunities
4. self-realization

He believed that teachers and coaches are required to take the initiative in creating the proper environment for change for themselves and others. Critical thinking, self-direction, and willingness to analyze personal behavior must be encouraged. He also acknowledged the deadly effect of habit which locks individuals into predetermined behaviors, and thrives on the lush diet of apathy and laziness. He pointed out the three ways in which research findings have been encouraging:

1. A teacher becomes more responsive to pupil ideas through learning and interpreting personal teaching patterns using interaction analysis.

2. A teacher's behavior becomes more flexible as a result of studying interaction analysis.

3. The attitudes of college students towards teaching become more positive as a result of studying interaction analysis.

Interaction analysis refers to the use of the ten category system developed by Flanders in the early 1950's and widely used today as an instrument for describing teacher and student behavior and their patterns of interaction. Flanders believed that when teachers studied their own behavior patterns, they reacted in the same manner as athletes studying their techniques on videotape and seeing the need for adjustment and change. He found that interaction analysis provided teachers with specific feedback which convinced them of the need to make changes. These research findings are encouraging to the proponents of self-change. Flanders was quick to point out, however, that efforts in self-change were only just beginning and would probably fail more times than they would succeed because of external variables such as job security, administrative pressures, parental resistance to innovation, and the usual run of faddism which so often destroys the credibility of young educators.

We agree with Flanders that individuals can best help others change their behaviors by providing them with an adequate description and commentary only when this commentary is sought and delivered in a nonthreatening atmosphere. The rigid defense mechanisms so much in evidence in our school systems today make change very difficult. In professional sporting circles, change is entirely contingent upon success, which eliminates the sport model as a general instrument for bringing change into the lives of the rank and file. So we are left with the task of helping others to change by convincing them of the need and value inherent in initiating self-change. Pessimism is not entirely in order as many successful models exist today. Teachers who use problem-solving techniques in the classroom and coaches who stimulate an appetite in athletes to dedicate themselves are in sufficient evidence to warrant moderate confidence and continued hope.

## COMMUNICATION IN THE LEARNING PROCESS

*In what ways do we help others communicate knowledges and skills in human beings?* Educators have not neglected this area during the twentieth century. Frequently referred to as "methods," the ways in which we help others to learn have received abundant attention. Bruce Joyce and Marsha Wiel (25, 26) have listed a number of educational approaches to the task of helping people learn. They cite Carl Rogers' nondirective approach, Perl's awareness training, Dewey's group investigation, Hullfish's social enquiry, Taba's inductive reasoning, Piaget's logical reasoning, L. Tyler's psycho-analytic approach, E. Paul Torren's creative reasoning, Skinner's programmed instruction, and Hunt's conceptual systems matching approach. Certainly there have been many efforts directed at exploring appropriate methodology to promote learning. Perhaps there are eight major divisions to the ways we help others learn.

## The Display or "Show and Tell" Method

Many teachers and coaches employ this method. They demonstrate a movement and then tell the students to perform it. If the teachers are incapable of demonstrating themselves, they show a film, a slide, or use a student to demonstrate the movement. This method tends to be effective in simple tasks and is quick and economical to execute, but it leaves a great deal to be desired in the development of independence, self-image, and the skills needed for individual problem solving. Teachers who use this technique to teach difficult or dangerous skills are probably guilty of involving only a handful of their students, and of setting up defense reactions within the majority. The "show and tell" method abounds in our schools, our gymnasiums, and on our playing fields. Certainly it has a place in the educational world, but it does not deserve the central position that it currently holds.

## The "Tell and Test" Method

This method has been the standard model in schools, and it has been tested many times on the playing field. The teacher or coach expounds, instructs, or tells, and then places the students into a situation of assessment. The "tell and test" method is based on the assumption that all students can listen well enough to be able to internalize the parameters under study. The test section of this method is designed to reveal whether the data have been internalized and memorized. Like the "show and tell" method, this mode of communication is effective for simple tasks and for explanations during moments of confusion. The teaching skills necessary are the ability to speak impressively, to use multimedia presentation, and to construct tests that are probing and comprehensive. It is a much more effective method of communication in the cognitive and psychomotor domains than in the affective domain. Virtually no serious socialization takes place and motivation is restricted to the passing of tests. More than any other method of communication, the "tell and test" syndrome is probably responsible for the apathetic attitude toward learning known as "getting by." Where student growth and development is reflected in constant testing, the victim becomes the predator and the predator becomes the victim. We are living in an age of standardized tests, complicated entry formulae, and professional certification based on test results. In such an environment, the danger of the tail wagging the dog is great. Coaches, more than teachers, feel the lash of accountability. Very few athletic coaches have tenure. The fortunes of most are entirely dependent upon the simple "win-lose" statistic at the season's end. The problem of this method lies in the paring of initiative from students and players. "What do we do today coach?" is the type of comment heard from athletes who have been subjected to a continuous barrage of the "tell and test" methodology.

## The "Threaten" Method

This method implies that you perform or pay the consequences of not performing. Readers may be concerned or amused at this term which describes one of the ways in which human beings communicate. Unfortunately this method enjoys near universal implementation. From kindergarten to graduate work, the penalty for not conforming to teacher, administrator, and parental requirements is failure. Unhappily, the rewarding of a person for process and product growth is also part of the "threaten" approach to teaching because it implies that failure has been avoided. Supporters of Edward Thorndike's *Law of Effect* point out that rewards bring repetition and growth, while punishment can bring almost anything ranging from further motivation to full elimination from the program. The fact remains that either overtly or covertly the presence of an authoritarian figure motivates (threatens) against failure.

Many people will object to describing this teaching method by the term "threaten" on the grounds that techniques such as contingency management and reinforcement theory are successful and well intentioned. The thesis expressed here, however, is that whenever a student is confronted with the alternative of getting an A or an F, a pass or a fail, or a check or a cross, the "threaten" method of teaching has prevailed. There can be little doubt that necessity is the mother of invention. Many people have improved their lot under the stimulus of a threatening environment and it might be argued that the very basis of survival in the natural world is founded on the concept of threat. There is no clear evidence, however, that frightened individuals achieve excellence and task fulfillment more effectively than cohesive and happy individuals. Further, defense mechanisms that will reduce and even curtail the learning growing process are a side effect of the "threaten" method. Exponents of the "threaten" method of teaching, who incidentally are very active in the classrooms but impossible to locate at conventions, rest their case on the premise of discipline. They maintain that many children are uncontrollable unless held in check by rewards and punishment. Certainly this method has demonstrated highly visible, surface success, but, unfortunately, it tends to cover the deep wounds that may appear at a later date. We believe that each time a teacher threatens a class, or a coach threatens a team, a barrier is set up, eroding the permanence and strength of the communication. Immediate successes can blind individuals to the long term effect of the threat. Teachers and coaches who avoid this technique tend to have longer tenure, fewer ulcers, and a greater overall effect.

## The "Go Through Others" Method

Mosston (27) referred to this style of teaching as reciprocal. Indeed, it can be a very effective way of communicating. We suggest that when the teacher divides the children into pairs or groups and permits peer teaching to occur, individualization, motivation, and a host of other parameters are faithfully served. The children become much more active in their learning and are given the chance to become responsible for each other's progress. This method also tends to reduce the bald effect of the teacher's direct authority, allowing interpretation and investigation to take part from the students. The use of skilled students or popular class members to assist in the teaching-learning process is a valuable and time-honored technique. In the gymnasium and in the playing arena, peer influence is great regardless of what teaching techniques are being employed. Should teachers and coaches who are not threatened by a sharing of their responsibilities make this phenomenon an asset in the learning process? Sometimes, as expressed in the research reported on the ripple effect (28), some teachers or coaches will convey messages to certain students by clamping down on others. It is argued that the ripple or wave set up when the mentor selects one pupil for censure conveys the message to all others concerned. Certainly this technique can work, but we believe that it is impracticable and implies a number of untenable ethical considerations. First, the use of the innocent victim to confront an adversary is despicable. Second, the ruse frequently does not work. Third, nonverbal communications tend to give the plan away much more easily and quickly than verbal communication, and fourth, the practice implies that the teacher is weak.

The technique of sharing communication with others is generally sound provided sufficient preparation and trust is forthcoming from the principal authorities.

## The Guiding or Leading Method

Teachers and coaches frequently place themselves in the position of "running in front of" their students. Students are usually strongly motivated through this means of communication. The game called "follow the leader" indicates how sports become popular, clothes become fashionable, and people become stars. The population is encouraged to follow and sample the same wares. Under this system leaders can avoid many of the pitfalls of faulty direction and encourage their followers to spend time on appropriate and positive skills. Certainly there is an aura of togetherness about this method of communication. The playing coach, the orchestra leader, the eight-oared stroke, and the team captain are classic examples of teaching and coaching communication through leading or guiding.

Sometimes it is difficult under these circumstances for teachers to see the whole forest when they are surrounded by an immediate circle of overpowering trees. The playing coach may, indeed, miss the overall game strategy of the opposition because he is tied up with the exigencies of the current play, but this method of teaching has more positive than negative aspects. The togetherness, the excitement of sacrifices, and the total involvement tend to give it firm support in the overall assessment of strong teaching and coaching methodologies.

## The Intervening Method

The systems approach based on the cybernetic model falls within the province of this teaching approach (29). This term is used to describe a child-centered learning approach with minimal but essential intervention by the teacher. The student plans the objectives and the activities with help from the teacher. The teacher intervenes only when necessary. Perhaps this situation can be likened to a competitive game on the playing arena. The players are the central actors in the game. Coaches and administrators intervene only where necessary. If the game plan is valid and the players are fulfilling their roles, little intervention is needed from the coaching staff. Indeed, a strong measure of teacher or coach maturity is seen in the appropriateness of the intervention. Repeated interventions imply a rapidly changing game plan, inadequate players, or an overanxious coach. We believe that all students need help at some time or other and that intervention is necessary. The accuracy, manner, and appropriateness of that intervention determines the success level of the teaching. Students are encouraged to show greater independence and contribute more strongly to their learning. The need for teacher authority is reduced.

## The "Pose Problem and Let Discover" Method

Currently enjoying enormous popularity among innovative teachers, this method of communication implies that students are capable of solving their own problems if given the skills and the opportunity so to do. The skill in using this method lies in the original planning, and the way in which the problem is presented. Educational purists believe that such activity on the part of the student is desirable and beneficial. Students are placed in the position of developing self-sufficiency; motivation is presumed to be strong and the shackling constraints of teacher domination are removed. Individualization or group centering are equally encouraged and active student involvement in learning is pivotal. Robert Lentz (30), in developing the Hamilton-Wenham Project in northeastern Massachusetts, has used this teaching technique brilliantly. Through harnessing the adventure tasks of Outward Bound and bringing them within the scope of the average school child, Lentz's staff has achieved an enthusiasm for movement rarely seen on such an universal scale among grade 10 students. The curriculum calls for the solving of a multiplicity of problems posed in the group setting through the medium of ropes, trees, and other natural resources. The students are required to solve the problems in a cooperative, rather than competitive, fashion. The competition is against the task but the resolution involves the cooperation of everybody. This continuing project is living evidence of the value of the nondirective, student-centered, problem-solving approach to teaching. As yet, few examples have been seen in the world of sport although mature and experienced athletes (marathon runners and athletes in the highly specialized events), often experience the same phenomenon in their drive for goal achievement.

## The "Don't Intervene" Method

Over the centuries a select group of educational theorists has continued to offer this alternative to teaching. Their contention is that if left alone, people will solve their personal problems in a nonthreatening and natural way. At one end of the continuum, John Jacques Rousseau (13) wants absolutely no intervention. At the other end, men such as Carl Rogers (14) and Edmund Amidon (11) maintain that nonintervention means the simple decision not to impose one's own value judgments on others. Certainly, Amidon-style nonintervention is the only practical technique of nonintervention that can be used in the schools today.

Most teachers and parents reject the nonintervention method of communication, maintaining that it is a dereliction of our responsibilities as adults and leaders. Children, too, become confused when they encounter a teacher or coach who completely accepts their efforts. The nonintervention technique demands that the student be thoroughly active if his needs are to be met. And perhaps this is expecting too much from the total student population. Table 8–4 outlines these eight ways of teaching

## Table 8-4. Conjecture on Student Growth Parameters

*Methods*                                    *Student Growth Parameters*

| Communicating or Teaching | Motivation | Individual Attention | Group Learning | Independence |
|---|---|---|---|---|
| Show and tell | Maybe | Probably not | Maybe | No |
| Tell and test | Maybe | Only for the test | Maybe | No |
| Threaten | For the wrong reasons | Rarely | Rarely | Rarely |
| Go through Others | Should | Yes | Yes | Can |
| Guide or Lead | Should | Yes | Should | Should |
| Intervene | Should | Yes | Yes | Yes |
| Pose Problem and Let Discover | Should | Yes | Should | Yes |
| Don't Intervene | No— Can't tell | Probably not | Probably not | Yes maybe unstable |

KEY:

MOTIVATION: refers to the arousing effect upon the children. It is assumed that the children's arousal level will be stimulated in different ways by the methodology alone. Naturally, many other factors are also involved in motivation.

INDIVIDUAL ATTENTION: refers to the capacity of the teacher or teaching agency to give each individual child instruction and feedback.

GROUP LEARNING: refers to the capacity of individuals to learn through close interaction with others: to experience the give-and-take of a plural situation; to deal with the many parameters that arise in a group situation—leadership, decision making, conflict, aggression, conformity, and so on.

INDEPENDENCE: refers to the capacity of each child to function with some real degree of self-initiation. In its ultimate form, independ-

## with Selected Teaching Methodologies

*Student Growth Parameters*

| Acquisition of Facts | Involvement of Children | Parental Contribution | Evaluation | Cost |
|---|---|---|---|---|
| Can | No | No | No | Low |
| Yes short term | as victims | No | Yes often surface | Low immediate |
| Yes short term | No | As policemen | Yes often surface | Low immediate |
| Should sometimes distorted | Yes | Maybe | Yes many evaluators | Reasonably High |
| Yes | Yes | Can | Continuous Evaluation | Reasonably High |
| Yes | Yes | Can | Continuous Evaluation | High |
| Yes | Yes | Can | Yes | High |
| Can't tell | Yes | Can | No | No |

ence implies a thorough weaning from paternal and maternal influences.
ACQUISITION OF FACTS: refers to the capacity of each child to show evidence that data or hard information has been memorized.
INVOLVEMENT OF CHILDREN: refers to the amount and quality of effort required of the children themselves during the learning process.
PARENTAL CONTRIBUTION: refers to the amount and quality of parental involvement in their children's education—either at school or at home.
EVALUATION: refers to the capacity of the teaching method to ensure that progress of each student is monitored closely.
COST: refers to the fiscal needs of each methodology in order to carry out its objectives. Interest in some methodologies is a cost effectiveness per child, which insures validity yet which varies greatly from one methodology to another.

and includes comments on their likelihood of success at bringing about student growth.

Although by no means exhaustive in scope, these eight teaching methods, or ways of approaching communication in the teaching-learning process, offer great variety and a wide spectrum of philosophic implication. We suggest that teachers and coaches who employ only one or two of these communicative techniques will suffer eventual apathy from their students and stagnation in their personal endeavors. The discerning teacher can alternate these eight approaches to create an effective teaching style. Another important point relates to the capacity of a teacher to preselect the teaching methodologies best suited to guarantee the desired learning outcomes. The teacher who uses a "show and tell" method for discovering hidden racist tendencies within a group very likely will not succeed. Equally inappropriate would be the teacher who employs the "pose problem and let discover" method for his introductory lessons in tower diving. Surely the 2,500-year span from Socrates to the present has taught us that the ways in which we help people communicate understandings and skills are varied and situation specific.

## COMMUNICATION AIDS IN THE LEARNING PROCESS

### Concept-Centered Curriculum

*With what do we help human beings communicate knowledges and skills?* We help others communicate through the provision of curricula, equipment, texts, field experiences, laws and regulations, and through the setting of group or institutional tone. In schools and in sports, in institutions large and small, and in locations wild or tame, we use a plethora of gadgets and strategies to help individuals communicate. The explosion of knowledge in the twentieth century has necessitated quite radical changes in our approach to curriculum. No longer can the acquisition of little bits of specific knowledge suffice as a modicum of information gathering.

Jerome Bruner (1) and Hilda Taba (6) use the term *concept* to mean the background thought or overall idea underscoring and overriding hundreds of pieces of specific knowledge. Our future curricula will have to be centered around concepts rather than specifics. A boy who smokes for instance, or talks back to his parents, or uses foul language, or wants to quit school to work, is probably trying to prove that he is grown up. The desire to be an adult is the concept and the rebellious behaviors manifest his frustration. The conceptual curriculum and its implications to Human Movement in the latter half of the twentieth century is discussed more fully in Chapter 10.

## Technology

Advanced technology has enabled us to speed up the communication process at a rate never previously enjoyed in human history. First, the wireless or radio eliminated the need for close physical proximity in communication. Whereas the use of semaphore, smoke signals, flares, and jungle tom toms had provided people with relatively crude instruments of communication, the radio changed all that. Boston fans could listen to a baseball game in New York and Americans stationed in Australia could enjoy the Kentucky Derby without agonizing time delays. The development of television, the instant playback mechanism, multidimensional sound, and the laser beam have continued to accelerate the communications revolution. This revolution has greatly improved the ability of the average person to understand complicated movement, and it has broadened his range of movement knowledge. Latest movement fads and "in techniques" such as body gliding are quickly discovered, tried, and either accepted or rejected from the public movement repertoire.

## Cooperative Spirit

We help others move with less tangible items as well. By setting up a tone or spirit of cooperation within a group, we convey a multitude of messages and information. Tone is a word used loosely by teachers in descriptions of classes. But it is often used to convey a special meaning. The tone we refer to is tone in the psychosocial domain similar to muscle tone in the physical domain. When all the fibers of a muscle are relaxed yet firm enough to hold shape, are resting yet instantly ready to activate, and are well formed and healthy, the whole muscle is described as having good tone. Similarly, the "fibers" or forces that hold individuals and groups together in social harmony in work or play are described as having good tone. These forces involve individuals being alert to interpersonal caring, sharing, reflecting, adjusting, and learning.

The spirit of a well-run camping venture illustrates this point. When given the opportunity of moving to another community with new friends, a stimulating curriculum, and no parental restrictions many young people enjoy a closeness and a spirit of personal achievement previously unknown to them. By setting up a similar tone and environment we help others to communicate. Professional coaches have been aware of this valuable asset for years and have run training camps to bring about team cohesion and cooperation. By definition, this tone is needed if hiking groups, mountain climbing teams, symphony orchestras, and commercial enterprises are to achieve their goals. Sometimes the communications are made directly between *A* and *B* and sometimes indirectly through *C*. The important factor remains that interpersonal communication that is devoid of trust and tone will bring about faulty communication, suspicion, and a breakdown in the social effort.

# EVALUATION IN THE LEARNING PROCESS

## Process and Product Measures

Once the communication process has begun, with advance preparation and sincerity of effort from both parties established, we can concentrate on the question of whether or not the respective parties have understood the basic ingredients of the message. Communication has both a product and a process. In other words, it is necessary to know what the message is and how the message is conveyed. Let us take an example. A teacher with a dry sense of humor might say this to a class. "All those children with left legs longer than their right will sit next to all those children who are absent today." The message from a product viewpoint is absurd and to people not used to this teacher's humor, it is confusing, time wasting, misleading, and dishonest. However, the children meet such a communication with laughter, enjoyment, and warmth towards the teacher. Obviously the teacher is a character—one who enjoys joking with the children and probably gives many nonverbal cues to this effect and employs this communicative media to brighten the day. Under these circumstances, the process is much more important than the product.

In another instance, however, if the school caught on fire and the teacher rescued the children by pushing, dragging, or hustling them out of the burning building, the process would become unimportant and the product important. It is impossible to evaluate communication without taking into serious consideration both process and product outcomes. A ruthless coach may trick, badger, or threaten his team into winning a handful of games, but we suggest that his unfeeling tactics will eventually reverse the product effect and defeat both causes. The Italian statesman, Machiavelli, gained notoriety for the principle "the end justifies the means." His concept was entirely centered around the product. Many dictators and petty potentates have adopted similar tactics during the course of human history. It would be erroneous for us to imagine that Machiavellian philosophy is not alive and flourishing today. Many hold the end product to be more important than the means. In far too many circumstances the results of pencil and paper tests, some reputable and some not, are taken as sufficient evidence to alter the lives of young people. Product measures are merely the skeleton of the evaluation corpus. Process measures provide the indication of the body's vitality. Product measures are much easier to construct and take. The game was won or lost, the jumper cleared the bar at seven feet or failed to, the skater made the triple and held or didn't hold balance, the tennis player won two sets to her opponent's one. These are product measures; they are visible and indisputable. Process measures are much less tangible. They require individual judgments and often are open to debate.

Readers are familiar with examples from their own experience in which athletes have performed superbly but have lost the match. Many a gallant effort was made to scale Mt. Everest before Sir Edmund Hilary succeeded in 1954. Although the previous efforts failed to accomplish the product, the data gathered during these unsuccessful attempts were far from futile. Indeed, this data eventually led to the development of successful techniques that aided the conquest of this formidable mountain peak.

Ned Flanders (24) has given the world an outstanding process measure in the Flanders System of Interaction Analysis. This ingenious system captures and measures student and teacher behavior while in session and analyzes it into a series of quantifiable percentages and ratios. This kind of data enables us to look at process parameters in addition to the necessary product parameters and arrive at a sounder and more credible conclusion. Cheffers (16) has adopted the Flanders System to describe nonverbal processes as well.

## Behavioral Objectives

For many years teachers have talked of the need to set up objectives for the teaching-learning act, and measures to help determine whether these objectives are achieved. The stimulus response and systems psychologists have given us important leads in this direction. Through setting up specific behavioral objectives, these psychologists maintain that the evaluation really takes place before the event occurs. They believe a behavioral objective must state the specific student behavior prior to activity. Evaul (31) maintains that a true behavioral objective will contain:

1. The expected behavior.
2. The conditions under which the behavior will take place.
3. The quality of performance of that behavior.

Under these conditions it behooves the evaluator to measure the specifics and to make a data-based decision on whether the teaching or communication has taken place. Prior to the work of people like Mager (32) and Siedentop (33), objectives were too broad and very difficult to measure. There is little doubt, however, that if communication is to take place, the objectives of the sender have to be faithfully perceived by the receiver.

## Self Evaluation

Along with process and product measures and the setting up of a curriculum to achieve specific objectives, the component of self-evaluation is assuming more importance in reputable testing bureaus today. The honest athlete can frequently appraise his/her own effort at least as well if not better than outside evaluators. He knows when he stopped trying, when fear took over, where he made that fatal technical error, and whether he really wanted to win or not. The athlete knows that she delayed on the blocks at the starter's gun, that she missed the turn through desperately lunging at the wall instead of swimming through her lane, that her legs were very tired during the final lap, that she missed two breathing rhythms which caused her to go into increased oxygen debt.

When all the frills are taken away and the defense mechanisms set at rest, the athlete is the best judge of the performance. The same can be said of anyone provided that rationalization does not cloud the evaluation.

## Peer Evaluation

Colleaguial or peer evaluation is an important form of evaluating communication. Peers are in a position to know many things about the overall situation that other generations or outsiders cannot see. Peer evaluation has some problems though. Often peers are either too closely involved or too inexpert to truly evaluate substantive efforts in the communicative effort. A jargon frequently arises between peers that can be unintelligible to outsiders, and that can bias the entire operation. At other times, peer evaluation can be very helpful provided it is free of petty bias and is kept relatively objective. Certainly, it can help bring to the surface important pieces of information that may have been overlooked in other forms of evaluation. We fear that peer evaluations are overrated. They tend either to be too supportive or too divisive. The last thing a running back needs against a tough defensive unit is the knowledge that on Friday he has to give an assessment of his own front four.

### Conclusion

We help others communicate through the application of knowledge gained through research, through teacher education, and through change. We adopt more appropriate methods of communication, while at the same time we establish models for others to improve their communication. There is little doubt that the communicative process is facilitated through conceptualization, the growth of technology, more adequate curricula, and the establishment of a positive. interpersonal tone. In order to be honest in the teaching-coaching procedures, we need to evaluate both process and product outcomes, and to undergo intensive self-evaluation.

Of course, we can help others communicate skill and knowledge in Human Movement. We have to.

## References Cited

1. BRUNER, JEROME S. *Toward a Theory of Instruction.* New York: Teachers College Press, Columbia University, 1966.

2. SMITH, B. OTHANIEL. "Toward a Theory of Teaching," *Theory and Research in Teaching,* Arno A. Bellack, ed. New York: Teachers College Press, Columbia University, 1963.

3. JAMES, WILLIAM. *Talks to Teachers in Psychology and to Students on Some of Life's Ideals.* New York: W. W. Norton 1958

4. WITHALL, JOHN. "The Development of a Technique for the Measurement of Social-Emotional Climate in Classrooms," *Journal of Experimental Education,* 17 (March 1949): 347–361.

5. THELEN, HERBERT A. with Jacob W. Getzels. "A Conceptual Framework for the Study of the Classroom Group as a Social System," *The Dynamics of Instructural Groups, Fifty-ninth Yearbook on Education.* Chicago: University of Chicago Press, 1960.

6. TABA, HILDA (with Freeman F. Elzey). "Teaching Strategies and Thought Processes," *Teachers College Record.* 65 (March 1964): 524–534.

7. TYLER, LOUISE. "The Concept of an Ideal Teacher Student Relationship," *Journal of Educational Research,* 58 (November 1964): 112–117.

8. GALLOWAY, CHARLES M. "Nonverbal Communication in Teaching," *Educational Leadership,* 24 (October 1966): 55–63.

9. BELLACK, ARNO. "The Language of the Classroom," *Teaching: Vantage Points for Study,* Ronald T. Hyman ed. Philadelphia: J. B. Lippincott and Co., 1968.

10. SIMON, ANITA, AND GIL BOYER (eds.). *Mirrors for Behavior.* Philadelphia: Research for Better Schools, 1970.

11. MILLER, ARTHUR G., JOHN T. F. CHEFFERS, AND VIRGINIA WHITCOMB. *Physical Education: Teaching Human Movement in the Elementary Schools.* Englewood Cliffs, New Jersey: Prentice-Hall, Inc., 1974.

12. AUSUBEL, DAVID P. "A Cognitive Structure Theory of School Learning," *Current Research in Interaction,* R. C. Anderson et al., eds. Englewood Cliffs, N.J.: Prentice-Hall, Inc., 1969.

13. ROUSSEAU, JEAN JACQUES, *Emil, Or Concerning Education.* New York: Dutton, 1938, Book 2.

14. Rogers, Carl R. "Significant Learning: In Therapy and in Education," *Educational Leadership*. 16 (January 1959): 232–242.

15. Dewey, John. *The Child and the Curriculum*. Chicago: University of Chicago Press, 1970.

16. Cheffers, John T. F., Edmund Amidon, and Ken D. Rodgers. *Interaction Analysis: An Application to Nonverbal Activity*. Minneapolis, Minnesota: Association for Productive Teaching, 1974.

17. Suchman, J. Richard. "Inquiry Training in the Elementary School," *The Science Teacher*. 27 (November 1960): 42–47.

18. Woodruffe, Asahel. "The Use of Concepts in Teaching and Learning," *Journal of Teacher Education*, XX (March 1964).

19. Krathwoll, David R., Benjamin S. Bloom, and Bertram B. Masia. *Taxonomy of Educational Objectives. Handbook II: Affective Domain*. New York: David McKay Co., 1964.

20. Gerbner, George. "Toward a General Model of Communication," *Audio Visual Communication Review*, IV (Summer 1956): 171–199.

21. Lewis, Wilbert W. "Selected Concepts of Communication as a Basis for Studying Mental Health in the Classroom," *The Journal of Communication*. II (September 1961): 157–162.

22. Aronson, Elliott. *The Social Animal*. San Francisco: W. H. Freeman and Co., 1972.

23. Willgoose, Carl. *The Curriculum in Physical Education* (2nd ed.). Englewood Cliffs, N.J.: Prentice-Hall, Inc., 1974.

24. Flanders, Ned A. *Analyzing Teaching Behavior*. Boston: Addison Wesley, 1970.

25. Joyce, Bruce and Marsha Wiel. *Models of Teaching*. Englewood Cliffs, N.J.: Prentice-Hall, Inc., 1973.

26. Joyce, Bruce. "Curriculum and Humanistic Education: Monolism v Pluralism," from AAHPER Regional Conference for Curriculum Improvement, 1971, Available AAHPER. 1201 16th NW Washington, D.C.

27. Mosston, Muska. *Teaching Physical Education*. Columbus, Ohio: Charles Merrill and Co., 1966.

28. Kounin, Jacob and Paul Lump. "Ripple Effect," *Elementary School Journal*, 59 (3): 158–62.

29. Singer, Robert N., and Dick Walter. *Teaching Physical Education: A Systems Approach*. Boston: Houghton Mifflin Co., 1974.

30. Lentz, Robert. *Project Adventure*. 775 Bay Rd. Hamilton, Mass. 01936.

31. Evaul, Thomas. Behavioral Objectives Program. Paper available from the author, c/o College of HPER, Temple University, Philadelphia, Pa.

32. Mager, Robert F. "Driving Objectives for the High School Curriculum," *N.S.P.I. Journal*. 7 (1968): 1–6.

33. Siedentop, Daryl. *Developing Teaching Skills in Physical Education*. Boston: Houghton Mifflin Co., 1975.

# 9

## How Do We Help Others by Structuring Programs in Human Movement?

*Tom Evaul*

Human movement may be both a means and an end. The development of efficient and effective movement may be an end in itself. One may observe children playing, athletes participating, dancers performing, and joggers running and wonder if the satisfaction of just moving is frequently used as a means of satisfying other personal needs. The achievement of physical fitness and good health, the opportunity to meet and interact with other people, the need for acceptance and prestige, the development of self-confidence and a positive self-image, the need for emotional stimulation such as excitement and joy, curiosity and the need to explore one's environment, a change of pace, recreation, the testing and development of values, the expression of beliefs . . . all of these are needs that may be satisfied through human movement.

In an effort to help people satisfy these needs, individuals, groups, organizations, and institutions structure programs involving various aspects of human movement for specific purposes.

Public, parochial, and private schools provide programs of physical education to help children and youths grow and mature physically, socially, emotionally, intellectually, and spiritually. Intramural and recreation programs supplement instructional classes by providing opportunities for students to use what they have learned. Interscholastic athletic programs for the most talented performers in certain activities provide fulfillment, not only for participants, but for parents who take pride in their offspring's accomplishments, for business executives and political officials who reflect in the achievements of their institutions, and society at large which receives satisfaction through empathy with the contestants.

Both public and private recreation groups use human movement as a way of helping people satisfy their needs. Sports clubs for specific activities such as tennis, golf, swimming, and the like serve as a focus for people not only to participate in the activity, but to socialize, get personal reinforcement, and even conduct business.

Health clubs, clinics, rehabilitation centers, and the like have human movement programs that are designed to help employees achieve both personal and corporate ends. These range from inservice training programs to assist employees who perform tasks requiring motor skills to become more competent in their work to recreational programs that use movement activities in developing morale, improving mental health, and ultimately improving the efficiency and effectiveness of the work force.

Colleges and universities use human movement in a variety of ways for both the general education of the student for life and the professional preparation of teachers, engineers, therapists, physicians, and a host of others who will serve humanity. These programs include instructional classes, intramurals, clubs, recreation, and intercollegiate sports. At the college level is the variety of disciplines and professions other than physical education that include various aspects of the discipline of human movement in their curriculum. Physics, physical therapy, and engineering include the study of the biomechanics of movement. Psychology, special education, and occupational therapy explore movement therapy and perceptual motor development principles and techniques. Acting courses teach stage movement. Dancers study choreography. Sociologists study the phenomenon of sport. Physiologists research the effects of exercise and philosophers ponder the metaphysics of movement. While none of these focus on movement and the whole person, collectively they embrace the entire spectrum of the discipline of movement.

These examples represent only a portion of the vast number of groups that structure and implement human-movement programs to help people meet their needs. These programs range from a formal educational curriculum to a more loosely structured schedule of activities. However, underlying all are certain basic elements that provide structure and organization. These program elements generally include some indication of the goals and objectives for which the program is established, the substance and/or content of the program, the activities of the program in which the participants become involved, and some means of assessing or evaluating the success of the program. Each of these components will be examined in greater detail in the following section with examples drawn from school physical-education curriculum, a cardiac rehabilitation program, and a public recreation program.

## GOALS AND OBJECTIVES

Virtually every program that exists has a set of explicit or implied goals that serves as a guide for that program. Goals indicate the purpose of the program, what the program hopes to achieve, and/or what the participants expect to gain from the program. Goals are usually broad statements and long range in nature rather than specific and immediate. Goals may exist in concrete statements which are available for administrators, implementors, participants, and the public to see, or they may be implied by the policies or activities of the program.

In programs such as a school curriculum, there is either a separate statement of goals or they are included in the philosophy of the curriculum. In a rehabilitation center, the statement may be a part of the corporation charter or the prospectus for patients, while in a public recreation department, the goals may be included in a statement of its missions or a description of its functions. Some programs may have no statement of goals at all but these are implied in the activities of the group or the policies that govern the program.

Whether or not the goals are stated, however, is not the critical point, which is whether or not the goals are actually achieved. Sometimes a statement of goals is very clear, but observation of the program in operation indicates that the stated goals are not the ones being met. Take, for example, big-time intercollegiate athletics. Goals generally stated for these programs emphasize participation, personal development of student-athletes, school spirit, and the like. However, the incidents of recruiting violations, firing of coaches, and other manifestations of the pressures to win communicate a different set of "real" goals.

If meaningful and realistic goals are to be established for a program, several factors must be taken into consideration. The first of these is who should be involved or be influential in the setting of goals? Should participants or clients such as students in a school curriculum, patients in a therapy program, or participants in a recreation program be involved? Should the administrators and implementors (e.g. teachers, therapists, leaders) who have responsibility for conducting the program be involved? Should those who fund the programs or establish policy concerning them be involved; for instance, should business executives, parents, equipment manufacturers, and others who have vested interests be given a voice?

If we believe that those affected by a decision should have some say in the making of the decision, we should find it logical that a number of those groups should have a role in the establishment of program goals. This will vary with the type of program. In the formation of goals for a physical education curiculum, for example, teachers, parents, administrators, school board members, and even students may be included in this process. It may also be desirable to employ outside consultants who can provide professional expertise and unbiased objective judgment to assist the process. A rehabilitation center would certainly involve the controlling board and the administration in the process of goal setting. Professionals who work in the program and representatives of consumer groups may be involved in the process. Depending on the nature of the center, government regulatory agencies and professional accrediting bodies may have an influence also. The goals of a public recreation program may be established by a legislature through some legal document that creates the program, or they may be established by advisory boards or by professional or citizen groups.

Regardless of the program, the major principle in establishing goals is involvement. If those who will eventually fund, create policies, administer, conduct, and participate in the program are involved in setting goals, there is a greater likelihood that they will understand what the program is trying to accomplish and will make a personal commitment to helping achieve the goals.

A second factor in the establishment of goals is the process by which they are established. Here, there are several alternatives, each of which may be viable depending upon the situation. A common method of setting goals is to have a committee suggest, debate, and eventually arrive at a decision as to what the goals should be. The committee may be made up of representatives of those concerned with the program or of those with the authority and power. If the latter is used, some mechanism for their input, such as hearings and testimony, should be a part of the process as well as some means of communicating the goals to all persons and getting their acceptance. Goals that are "laid on" persons who are responsible for conducting a program or who are participating in it run a greater risk of being ignored or subverted if they do not meet the needs of the parties.

We are also concerned with the process for arriving at a decision. One group may favor consensus, another majority rule, and still another may feel that the individual or individuals with ultimate responsibility should make the decision. The important point here is that everyone concerned understands the process and, to the degree possible, concurs with it.

Next we are concerned with those factors external to the organization planning the program. These include the limits imposed by society through law, ethics, and morality; the needs of others not involved in the program who may be impinged upon; resources that can be anticipated for conducting the program; other groups with similar goals and programs; and the need for such a program. These factors must be taken into consideration in developing goals for a program.

Finally we are concerned with the source of the goals for the program. Goals may be derived from existing knowledge and research. They may be based on the needs of participants, on the needs of society; and the needs of leaders or those with power may be another source of goals. For example, during war time, society has a need to develop physically fit youth in preparation for military service. The history of physical education in this country reveals that in both World War I and II, the programs in our schools and colleges were almost totally devoted to this goal. A similar phenomenon is currently extant in the Soviet Union where the leadership is pressing to create a powerful image through international sport. As a result, athletics receives a tremendous emphasis with top performers being totally subsidized by the state. This is evident when the top "amateurs" compete successfully against professionals in the United States in sports such as hockey and tennis. Unfortunately, it is not always the needs of the participants that determine the goals of the programs.

A school physical education curriculum provides an example of one program in human movement for which goals are clearly stated. Physical education curricula traditionally have goals such as the following.

1. To develop motor skills.
2. To develop physical fitness.
3. To develop knowledge about physical activities.
4. To develop desirable social and emotional qualities.

An examination of these goals exemplifies two qualities of goals previously stated. First, they are broad, each one encompassing a wide range of potential outcomes. For example, consider how many motor skills could be encompassed under the first goal. Second, they are long range. The development (and maintenance) of physical fitness, as an example, is a lifelong endeavor, not something to be accomplished during school years and subsequently lost.

These goals do serve several important functions, however. They provide direction for defining more specific and immediate objectives of instruction, which will be discussed later in this chapter. They also give some direction for identifying other areas of the curriculum—the content, learning activities, and evaluation.

An examination of the aforementioned goals typical of so many physical education curricula reveals several things. First, in two of the goals which deal with motor skill and knowledge about activities human movement is an end in itself. Second, in the two which deal with physical fitness and social-emotional development human movement is employed as a means to an end. Reflecting on the basic concept of the discipline of human movement, why people move, it becomes obvious that these traditional goals are rather narrow. They do take into consideration a number of the physical needs aided by human movement, and they consider some of the intellectual, social, and emotional needs. However, they do not utilize the full potential of human movement. For example, movement activities can be used quite successfully to help children develop and reinforce concepts and skills in language arts, mathematics, social studies, and science. Movement activities can be used not only to help people develop social and emotional qualities but to provide opportunities for people to interact, to express their feelings in socially acceptable ways, and to develop new relationships with others around a common interest. Spiritually, human movement can provide a means of clarifying values, testing values in cooperative and competitive situations, and developing attitudes about movement and life in general. These are just a few of the potential goals for the physical education curriculum in schools. Other goals could be included such as:

5. The development of academic concepts and skills.
6. The improvement of human relations.
7. The development of sound values and attitudes.
8. The development of decision-making ability.

These and other goals could be achieved through a sound physical education program. Human movement has much to contribute to the growth and maturation of youngsters if used as a "means" rather than just as an "end."

The goals of a cardiac rehabilitation program, although quite different from a school physical education program, serve the same function of giving direction to the program. The consumers have different needs they wish to satisfy in the program. Those conducting the program have different skills, but their purpose of helping people through movement is the same. Goals for this type of program include:

1. Improved functioning of the cardio-vascular system.
2. Development of a lifestyle compatible with the limitations imposed by one's cardiac condition.

The goals for this kind of program are more limited than those of the school curriculum, but certainly no less important. The major reason for this limitation is the special type of needs that patients in this program have.

Another difference between the two sets of goals is that human movement is not the only focus of the cardiac rehabilitation program. Both goals probably should involve much more than human movement if they are to be achieved.

A public recreation program provides an example of still another set of goals. Here the major function is to get people to participate. What participants gain from the program varies according to individual needs and perceptions. Simply stated, the goals of the recreation program may be:

1. To provide a wide variety of recreational activities for citizens of all ages.
2. To encourage individuals to engage in one or more of these activities.
3. To assure the greatest possible safety to participants.

In contrast to the previous two sets of goals, these are stated for those who are conducting the program rather than for the participants. The leaders will "provide," "encourage," and "assure." However, the goals for participation are implied even in these.

The establishment of goals is but the first step in the formulation of a program. While these statements provide some general direction, they usually lack the specificity to be of significant value in making the program operational. Here, more detailed statements of purpose are required. These are generally referred to as objectives. Unlike goals, objectives can usually be achieved in the immediate future. They may be written in various degrees of specificity ranging from general statements, which may be similar to goals, to very precise statements that identify the desired behavior of participants. A program may contain more than one level of objectives. A school curriculum, for example, may have general overall objectives for the program, more specific goals for grades and/or units within grades, and very precise behavioral objectives for lessons. For any one of the previously mentioned goals of a physical education curriculum, a series of objectives could be designed. For example, the goal "To develop a level of physical fitness" could have a set of general objectives as follows:

1. To improve muscular strength and endurance, cardio-respiratory endurance, and joint flexibility.
2. To be able to evaluate one's level of fitness.
3. To be able to design an individual program.
4. To understand the benefits of physical fitness.

These general statements could, in turn, be translated into specific behavioral objectives describing what students would do to demonstrate their achievement of the objective, under what conditions they would do this, and the standard of performance necessary for success. Such a list of objectives could include the ability to:

1. Execute a military press with a bar bell equal to half of one's body weight.
2. Run a mile and one half in 12 minutes or less.
3. Execute 15 pull ups and 50 sit ups.
4. Touch the toes with knees straight.
5. Demonstrate two tests to evaluate each of the four components of fitness.
6. Develop an exercise program designed to improve each component of fitness and explain the principles of overload and progression utilized in the program.
7. List five benefits that can result from physical fitness.

The above example illustrates how objectives are derived from goals. Since objectives are but an extension of more broadly conceived goals, the process and personnel involved in their creation are quite similar to those involved in goal setting. However, the more technical details of preparing objectives call for a greater involvement of professional personnel.

Objectives for other programs such as the cardio-vascular rehabilitation program and the public recreation program are also viable extensions of the goals. Objectives of the rehabilitation program include:

1. An increase in the capacity to sustain physical activity over a period of time.
2. A reduction in resting pulse rate and blood pressure.
3. The development of the habit of daily planned and controlled exercise.
4. An understanding of the changes that proper exercise, diet, and rehabilitation can cause in the cardio-vascular system.

More specific objectives that will lead to the achievement of the third objective above could be:

1. Prepare a written list of activities to be performed in a daily workout and a quantitative goal (repetitions, time, distance, load, etc.) to be achieved in each activity.
2. Schedule a convenient time and place in your daily regimen to engage in a workout.
3. Participate in the planned workout daily at the time indicated.

For a recreation program, still other objectives may be developed. The goal of providing a wide range of activities for all ages might have as objectives:

1. To survey members of the community to determine recreational interests.
2. To offer instruction in selected activities for all ages.
3. To provide leadership and opportunities for participation in social recreation activities, arts and crafts, sports, and outdoor activities.

These too could be translated into more specific objectives such as the following for the third objective above:

1. To organize social clubs for square dancing, cards, chess, backgammon, and book discussions.
2. To organize leagues in bowling, basketball, softball, and touch football.
3. To provide supplies, equipment and supervision for ceramics, leathercraft, and model building.
4. To organize walking and bicycle trips, picnics, canoe trips, and camping excursions.

Objectives such as these provide concrete statements of purpose which can be used to make the program operational.

## SUBSTANCE

In order to achieve these objectives, one must obtain some substance. In a curriculum, this substance is generally referred to as the content—the knowledge, skills, and attitudes which learners must get in order to achieve the objectives. In a rehabilitation program, the substance would include not only the things a person learns, but the exercises that cause physiological changes in the individual's system. The substance of our hypothetical recreation program includes both the learning and the activities resulting from the achievement of the objectives.

If the objectives have been clearly stated, selecting the substance is a relatively easy task. However, careful consideration needs to be given to the organization of this substantive material to assure that it will help participants achieve the objectives. The center around which the substance is organized is of prime importance. If objectives are to be achieved, the substance must be organized in a manner that will facilitate this.

In curriculum, this concept is known as the organizing center. It is the focus of the content or the approach taken to it. The physical-education curriculum has traditionally been organized around sports and games, dance, and exercise. This approach assumed that learning how to participate in such activities would result in the achievement of such goals as fitness, skill, sportsmanship, and cooperation. A unit in basketball would include instruction in fitness for basketball, basketball skills, sportsmanship in basketball, and teamwork. It would automatically result in the development of self-confidence among participants. The same kinds of content would be included in other units. Collectively, these units should also result in improved fitness, sportsmanship, cooperation, and the like. Unfortunately, history and research have not validated this assumption.

For example, when basketball is used as the organizing center of a unit, the objectives achieved are not always the ones that are stated. Basketball is a game to be won. Because of the high value that much of society places on winning, other objectives tend to take a back seat. If, for example, four of the five players in a game are quite skillful, the fifth player, who needs the experience of handling the ball to develop skill and confidence, may be frozen out by his four teammates who see winning as the important outcome. Although a sly push or verbally riding an opponent may result in an advantage for one individual or team over another, such an action is counter-productive to achieving the objective of sportmanship. Having everyone in the class do the same calisthenics designed to build fitness for basketball may leave some exhausted and sore, while others may not even get the pulse sufficiently elevated to alter their condition at all. This type of standardization does little to teach such fitness concepts as overload and progression—so important in developing a life-long fitness program.

Of course, the organizing center depends on the goals of the curriculum. Organizing centers are quite appropriate if goals are limited to activities as an end in themselves, such as learning the skills, understandings, and values needed to participate in specific activities. However, if movement is viewed as a means to achieving other goals such as fitness, sportsmanship, cooperation and the like, then other organizing centers may be more fruitful. Rather than having units based on specific activities, units focused upon individual objectives are employed with activities that contribute to the objective selected.

A unit on fitness, for example, may draw upon such activities as weight training, calisthenics, jogging, and the like to teach learners about the benefits of fitness, the effects of activity, and the techniques of training. Establishing individual jogging programs and evaluating changes that occur as a result of these programs is much more effective and efficient than playing basketball in meeting objectives dealing with fitness.

Progressive elementary teachers, to cite another example, have developed teaching units around such skills as balancing, locomotion, and ball handling in their movement-education programs. Using big balls, small balls, round balls, oblong balls, heavy balls, and light balls in a variety of activities, they are attempting to help their learners develop a movement repertoire of ball-handling skills that can serve as a basis for learning a host of ball games throughout their lives.

The model of the discipline of Human Movement presented in Chapter 1 can serve as a basis for a variety of organizing centers. Some very relevant and innovative units could be organized around the various purposes for which people move. Units such as "Movements and Health" or "Communicating Through Movement" or even "Ego Satisfaction Through Movement" could produce some exciting learning experiences. What content could be included in each? What sports, dances, exercises, and games could be used?

Parts of the curriculum could be organized around factors affecting or affected by movement. "Body Type and Movement," "How to Learn and Practice Motor Skills," and "Playing Together Effectively" are some unique titles for units involving physical, psychological, and social factors affecting and affected by movement. Such organizing centers can help learners focus on specific factors related to movement so they can become better prepared to use movement as a tool for improving the quality of their lives.

The forms of movement are, of course, the typical organizing centers around which our physical education curricula are organized. Even here, unique units could be developed. "Making Decisions About Movement" could include an examination of the values of various movement forms so that individuals could more intelligently select those they wish to learn or use. Physical educators have done so little in relation to "Movement in Work." This unit could examine various activities such as lifting, climbing, shoveling, and even sitting at a desk.

The development of curricula around these organizing centers requires considerable ingenuity and planning. Isolated efforts around the country have been undertaken with some degree of success. However, if physical education in our schools is going to keep pace with the rapid changes in our society, alternatives have to be created, tried, and evaluated. This is not to say that what we are currently doing is bad, for much of it is useful. However, the full potential of the discipline is not being used because so many of our curricula focus on movement as an end in itself and ignore the other benefits that can result from movement activities. What is needed is more balance in the curriculum. This can be achieved by integrating teaching units focusing on other concepts than sports, games, exercise, and dance.

The substance of a program such as the cardiac rehabilitation program has some similarities with and some differences from the school physical education program. In virtually every program, there is some learning. In this case, the learning may include such concepts as the functioning of the circulatory system under the limitations imposed by the disorder, the effects of exercise, diet, stress, and the like on the system, gradual progression and monitoring of activity, and potential problems to be avoided. In addition to these substantive learnings, there is usually a carefully prescribed exercise program. This exercise program is also a substantive part of the total rehabilitation program for it results in physiological changes in the system.

The recreation program has as its substance both the set of learnings acquired by the participants and the activities engaged in which result in the achievement of the objectives. In the recreational activity of square dancing, for example, one learns to move in time to the music, to execute the various basic movements which callers put together to form the dances, and to follow certain rules of etiquette concerning behavior on the dance floor. Once these learnings have been inculcated, the individual is ready to participate in square dancing itself and enjoy the social, emotional, and physical benefits of it. This activity is a substantive part of the program.

## ACTIVITIES

The third component of a program, the activities, are sometimes difficult to distinguish from the substance. In some cases, they may be identical. Activities are the things a person does in order to acquire the substance. They enable the person to achieve the objectives. In the curriculum, these are generally referred to as learning activities. In learning to shoot archery, a person may watch a demonstration, listen to a lecture, practice skills, get feedback from an instructor or videotape recorder, and perform a variety of other activities. In a unit on cooperation, a person may engage in group activities such as pyramid building and tug-of-war to find out both the need for cooperation and how to cooperate. In a unit on fitness, a person may take various fitness tests, read about overload and progression, establish trial fitness programs, and keep records on changes in order to learn how to establish a personal fitness program.

The important factor is that learning results from the experience of the student. Learning requires an interaction between the learner and his environment. It cannot be passive. A film may be shown, a lecture given, or readings assigned, but if the learner's attention is not focused on the stimulus and if he does not interact with it by raising questions, seeking relationships, and solving problems, learning will not take place. For example, when reading this book, there may have been times when your eyes moved across the words without comprehending. When you finished the page, you realized you knew nothing of what you read. Your mind was not concentrating on the task at hand.

In a class setting, many of the learning activities are designed and conducted by teachers. This task of devising, implementing, and evaluating learning activities is generally referred to as *instruction*. Instruction is distinguished from the previous two (goals and objectives, and content), which are often referred to as the *curriculum*. It is important to design these activities so that the learner is encouraged, even forced, to be actively involved. Human movement, by its very nature, involves learners. Movement activities have been successfully used, for example, to teach reading and mathematics. Relay races that require students to arrange letters into words and modifications of hop-scotch which require them to jump on two numbers and their sum or product involve the learner physically as well as intellectually.

The rehabilitation program, as another example, has many activities, too. Some of these, like the school curriculum, are designed to help participants learn. Thus, to learn about these phenomena students may read programmed instruction materials on diet, view videotapes on coping with stress, or watch their pulse rate on a physiograph as they exercise. The exercise program, which is substantive in itself, also causes a change in the physiology of the body. Students participate in this program as means to an end as well as an end in itself.

The same situation exists in the recreation program. Some activities will be designed to help people learn; others to help them socialize, relax and enjoy themselves—the substantive parts of the program.

## EVALUATION

The final component of a program is evaluation. The purpose of evaluation is to determine the answers to various questions. Such questions include:

1. Are the objectives of the program being met?
2. Are there any positive or negative side effects?
3. What are the strengths of the program and how can it be improved?
4. Is the program worth the time, manpower, and money invested?
5. How is the program perceived by others?

In evaluating a program, it is necessary to design ways to collect pertinent information.

In the curriculum example, there are many ways to do this. Measurement of learners' achievement of the objectives can be accomplished by administering knowledge and skill tests, fitness tests, and attitude tests, and by observing the behavior and performance of learners during activities. The latter technique can often indicate desirable and/or undesirable side effects. Participant, staff and public suggestions, solicited and unsolicited, can reveal strengths and areas for improvement. A cost analysis can be performed and compared to the achievement of the objectives to help determine if the program is worthwhile. A survey of participants, staff, and others concerned with the program can reveal their perceptions of it. These data can be compared with norms, standards, or similar data from other programs in order to provide a basis for answering the aforementioned questions.

The techniques suggested above are also applicable in evaluating a rehabilitation and recreation program. Other techniques, such as physiological and anthropometrical data, changes in habits, and the amount of time needed for rehabilitation may be added for the cardiac program. The recreation program may, in turn, be interested in numbers of participants and frequency of participation, their satisfaction with the program and requests for other activities.

Evaluation is a key component of any program. Without it, there is no basis for making decisions about the continuation or modification of the program. There is no way to determine if participants' needs are being met. It is not possible to certify if participants are accomplishing the objectives. Evaluation requires measurements—tests, observations, questionnaires and other means of gathering data. Measurements, in turn, require interpretation by comparisons with norms, standards, or each other. Only by careful and complete evaluation can the other three components, goals and objectives, substance, and activities be validated.

One of the primary ways that Human Movement is applied is through programs. Programs involving movement have been designed for many purposes including education, development, rehabilitation, and recreation. As our knowledge and skill in Human Movement expands, so will the scope of these programs; new programs will come into existence to meet other needs and old programs will be phased out. The potential of Human Movement has only been tapped on the surface. Much more can be done in using this discipline to meet human needs.

## Bibliography

ALPREN, MORTON, ed. *The Subject: Curriculum Grades K-12*. Columbus, Ohio: Charles Merrill, Inc., 1967.

ASCD. *Balance in the Curriculum*. Washington, 1961.

CHRISTINE, CHARLES T. AND DOROTHY V. CHRISTINE. *Practical Guide to Curriculum and Instruction*. West Nyack, N.Y.: Parker Publishing Co., Inc., 1971.

COHEN, ARTHUR M. *Objectives for College Courses*. Beverly Hills, California: Glencoe Press, 1970.

CONNOR, FORREST AND ELLENA, WILLIAM, eds. *Curriculum Handbook for School Administrators*. Washington: American Association of School Administrators, 1967.

DAVIS, O. L., JR., ed. *Perspectives on Curriculum Development*. Washington: Association for Supervision and Curriculum Development, 1976.

FRAZIER, ALEXANDER, ed., *New Insights and the Curriculum*. Washington, ASCD, 1963.

GOODLAD, JOHN I. *The Changing School Curriculum*. New York: The Fund for the Advancement of Education, 1966.

LEEPER, ROBERT R., ed. *Curriculum Concerns in a Revolutionary Era*. Washington, ASCD, 1971.

MCASHAN, H. H. *The Goals of Approach to Performance Objectives*. Philadelphia: W. B. Saunders Co., 1974.

SHORT, EDMUND L., AND GEORGE D. MARCONNIT, eds., *Contemporary Thoughts on Public School Curriculum*. Dubuque, Iowa: W. C. Brown Co., 1968.

TYLER, RALPH, ROBERT M. GAGHÉ AND MICHAEL SCRIVEN. *Perspectives of Curriculum Evaluations*. Chicago: Rand McNally and Co., 1967.

# 10

## How Do We Help Others by Creating and Manipulating Physical Environments for Human Movement?

*Victor Mancini*

Numerous platform speakers have advocated the worth of manipulating and using the immediate environment to facilitate the learning process. Although people have been part of the total environment, each individual has differed: Continuous personal adjustments have brought about varied environmental modifications. Human beings have a remarkable facility to manipulate and shape an environment to suit their needs and interests. They extened their environments in order to live, to work, and to play.

What is the human environment? Webster has defined the term as ". . . aggregate of all the external conditions and influences affecting the life and development of an organism." In the area of Human Movement, environment has been defined by Rushall and Siedentop (1) as "everything that has an effect on the performer, whether or not that effect is immediate." Organism and environment each influence the other. To the person involved with Human Movement, environment has many aspects other than the physical.

Bigge (2) has presented three incongruent assumptions in regard to human beings and their environment. Bigge felt that environment should be viewed from its physical, social, and psychological aspects. By physical environment, he meant anything surrounding the person, and by social environment he meant the gregarious situation of the person.

These two aspects make up the setting for the psychological environment. The psychological environment was seen to be one's subjective view of "outside" surroundings, different from that of any other who possessed the same social and physical environment.

It is imperative to understand and study the psychological environment as well as the physical and social environment. A teacher may do this by structuring the physical environment in addition to the social and the psychological environments. For example, if we change the physical structure of our house, inside and outside, our old house takes on a new outlook. At one time, banks were designed to project an image of strength and security. This image sometimes backfired since it created a cold, impersonal environment. When banks saw a need to change their image, they presented a warm and friendly physical environment. The structures both inside and outside were changed. Similarly, school, park, and recreational facilities have undergone appropriate change in design.

How do people move in their physical environments? People on land have used their feet to walk, to pedal bikes, to pull carts, to skate; people at sea have adapted to the environment by using boats made of all substances, ships, and submarines; people in the air have used planes, rockets, and spaceships. In order to increase human mobility, various types of footwear and headgear items have been attached to the body. Different occupations have resorted to different articles. The doctor has included a delicate mask, hat, and rubber gloves while the construction worker has used a robust mask, hard hat, and gloves. Each person's environment determines the selection. Dentists, business executives, plumbers, teachers, builders, miners, divers, astronauts, and athletes constitute a growing number of people who need various articles for movement diversity. Today, science has given people artificial or synthetic parts to enable movement. Among these parts are limbs, joints, bony structures, intestines, heart pacemakers, heart valves, and so on.

To facilitate movement, people have developed varied equipment: motor-driven vehicles, elevators, stairs, cybernetics, and satellites. With this technology they have become more creative.

The specific environments through which human beings have chosen to move have included private and public buildings, land, water, dams, mines, and space. The importance of these physical environments is indicated by Oberteuffer and Ulrich (3) ". . . each human is born with a certain genetic potential which may be fully developed within a certain environment, or may not be realized within another type of environment. . . ." Many believe that environment can formulate a potential that was not innate, causing characteristics to be acquired. According to this, it may be possible to develop an athlete by putting the individual into the proper environment, or to structure a personality pattern by placing the individual in an environment which insists upon a specific personality.

An appropriate physical environment can also affect leisure and work. The physical environment is a potential modifier of human behavior. We must accurately predict the behavior of the users of the designed environment. What are these physical characteristics? Environmental factors include the furniture, architectural style, interior decorating, lighting conditions, smells, colors, temperature, additional noises, or music. These physical environmental factors identified by Nelson and Bronson (4) include: 1. meteorological factors such as heat, cold, air pressure, wind, rain; 2. the material such as facilities, equipment, supplies; and 3. the mechanical or spatial factors such as time, space, distance, direction. Brown and Cassidy (5) include force, matter, attitudes of valuing, cultural conditions necessary for healthy growth and development, and the total situation as perceived by an individual.

These factors can and do have direct and indirect effects on the individual. Variations in arrangements of these factors can be influential on the outcome of an interpersonal relationship. For example, Knapp (6) claims that the architecture and the object arrangement in various man-made structures can suggest who shall meet whom, when, where, and perhaps for how long. Variations in arrangements, materials, shapes, or surfaces of objects in the environment can influence the outcome of an interpersonal relationship.

The purpose of this chapter is to classify and emphasize the physical environments in which humans move and to expose future physical educators to different structures, facilities, and equipment that are being used to help create and manipulate movement in the physical environ-

Figure 10-1.

ment. Our role as physical educators in studying Human Movement is to help others to move efficiently, effectively, and expressively! The Human Movement specialist has the responsibility of providing adequate equipment, structures, and facilities to meet the needs, interests, and numbers of people in the program. One of the ways to accomplish this is to become aware of what is available in the field. Most times program offerings depend upon the equipment and facilities available. Movement may be classified around concepts in three areas: (1) the use of the body (what part moves), (2) the use of space (where the part moves), and (3) the quality of the movement (how the part moves).

All professionals have a difficult time in remaining abreast of current equipment, materials, supplies, and facilities available. This chapter is divided into three major dimensions:

1. The equipment people wear or attach to themselves when they move.

2. Equipment people manipulate and use to move.

3. Facilities and structures in which people move.

## EQUIPMENT PEOPLE WEAR
## OR ATTACH TO THEMSELVES

Human beings enter the world naked. Soon they wear or attach apparel to themselves for comfort, for support, for speed, and for protection against injury and against the elements. Suitable dress is worn by people taking part in physical activity, for proper equipment and clothing are an important, even if overlooked, part of any activity program. Apparel needs to fit properly, be appropriate to the activity, be adaptable to change of temperatures, and be safe. The way a person dresses in physical activity has a strong psychological effect on performance. Manufacturers have made materials of contrasting colors, textures, and shapes in order to meet people's movement needs. We remove restrictive outer clothing for better performance in gymnasiums and during warm weather. The materials worn for activity have changed from cotton and wool to lighter, more durable acrylics and even stretched nylon. We wear shorts and tee shirts. We wear heavier-weight gear for warm-ups, lighter weight material for swimming and gymnastics, and protective gear for collision sports.

### Protective Gear

As activities and games became faster and more intense, protective gear developed accordingly: as games demanded more speed, shoes were improved; with the changing of throwing implements catching gloves were revamped. Certain games have demanded more protection. Their needs have been met by improved headgear, face masks, and chest, shoulder, arms, hips, knee, and shin protectors.

At one time, protective gear was bulky, made of heavy and inflexible material. Today's protective gear is light and flexible, yet, paradoxically, it offers the user more protection. The historical development of the football helmet shows this to be true (Figure 10-2). There are cloth headgears for use in tennis, golf, and baseball, rubber headgears for use in swimming, skin diving, and water polo, flexible leather and foam headgears for use in wrestling and boxing, plastic headgears for use in football, lacrosse, ice hockey, cycling, jai-lai, and mountain and rock climbing. The airguard helmet, which is an inflatable headgear fitted to the individual's head shape, is used in football and hockey as an additional safeguard to the plastic headgear. The mesh-covered helmet, used in fencing, performs a similar task. Headgear should protect the head from possible blows, yet allow for full head movement and unhindered all-round vision. It should be well ventilated and of a reasonable weight in order to assist rather than prevent the athlete from performing safely and freely.

## Footwear

Footwear needs to be well constructed and properly fitted. Foot coverings that cause the feet to become excessively hot and footwear with inappropriate surfaces should be discouraged. The soles of shoes aid in proper control and propulsion on courts, gymnasiums, in water, over rocks, and on and through snow.

The flat-soled gear is appropriate in dance, gymnastics, bowling, basketball, tennis, water and land skiing, snow walking, and jogging and distance running. The cleated or spiked shoe is appropriate on dirt, grass, and synthetic turfs. For rock and mountain climbing the rippled sole is used, while the spiked sole is accepted for golf, cricket, track and climbing on ice. The bladed sole is used on ice, and the roller skate is effective on

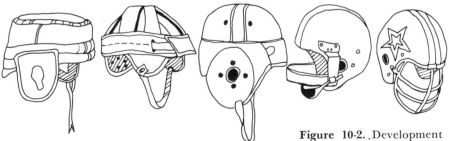

**Figure 10-2.** Development of the football helmet.

**Figure 10-3.** Headgear.

smooth surfaces. Today's manufacturers have developed all-purpose soled shoes for use in a multitude of activities (Figure 10-4).

### Other Protective Gear

Human beings developed eye wear for land, water, and sky. Sometimes eye ware offers protection to the eyes and the bridge of the nose and face. The most commonly worn eye gear are unbreakable glasses and contact lenses, goggles on land and in water, face masks in football, ice hockey, lacrosse, and baseball.

A wide variety of protective gear exists for covering the shoulders, the chest, the arms, the hips, the knees, the shins, the hands, and the groin (Figure 10-5). Both sexes wear these items although some special gear is needed by each sex. The most familiar type is the cup for the male, and the woman's padded belt, for the groin area. The female also has a special bra protector of lightweight, durable plastic allowing for complete freedom, comfort, and protection of the breasts. Rubber teeth guards are mandatory in many contact sports.

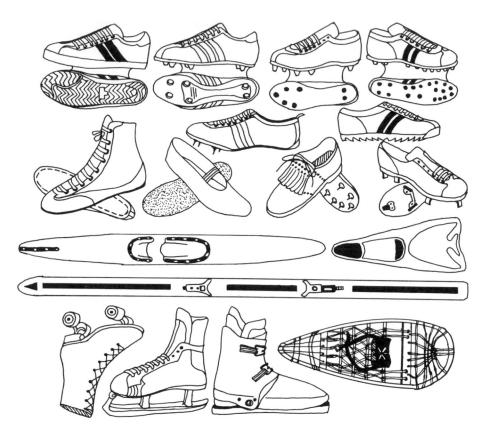

**Figure 10-4.** Footwear.

Gear worn on the hands is used for protection, for grip, and for the certainty of receiving an object. All purpose gloves are used to provide a firm grip in golf, baseball, and racquet sports, to improve grip for archery and gymnastics, to protect in ice hockey, lacrosse, and boxing, to strike in handball, and to catch or receive an object in baseball and softball.

For movement in water, people wear flippers for propulsion, a mask for better viewing, and a snorkle or oxygen mask for breathing. Water-ski belts and vests, life jackets and vests, and the swimming "egg" for the young provide support for people in the water (Figure 10-6).

For climbing over rocks and up mountains, people wear and attach the following for proper support and grip: (1) pack frames and bags to carry the gear, (2) a crash helmet, (3) fingerless mittens or leather gloves, (4) boots with rubber or spiked soles, (5) ropes, belts or harness, karaliners, and slings, and (6) chocks, pitons, hammers, maps and compasses.

To help overload the body, activists in training often wear weighted equipment on the chest, waist, and ankles (Figure 10-7). People also have run in the sand, mud, or surf, wearing weighted shoes or practicing with heavier than normal implements. In summarizing these practices, Katch

**Figure 10-5.** Ice hockey, football, and lacrosse protective gear.

and Cleland (7) state that the weighted devices people use may harm rather than improve athletic performance. They claim the body becomes accustomed to the specific weight during training. When the person removes the weight for the contest, the body has to readjust and possibly suffer a retrogressive effect in running speed, reaction speed, timing, and effective strength. They conclude that there is still much to learn about the effects of weighted practice (Figure 10-8).

Sometimes movement has caused injury. People have worn or attached items to the injured part of the body for support, for preventing further damage, or for rehabilitation. Some of these items are splints, casts, traction and cervical collars, slings, stretchers, instant use packs, tape, resuscitators, mouth-to-mouth rescue devices, artificial limbs, and other first-aid equipment for physical medicine or rehabilitation.

## EQUIPMENT PEOPLE MANIPULATE

### Propelling Equipment

The most common item that is propelled is the ball. Varying in size, shape, and weight, balls are made of different substances, such as hard and

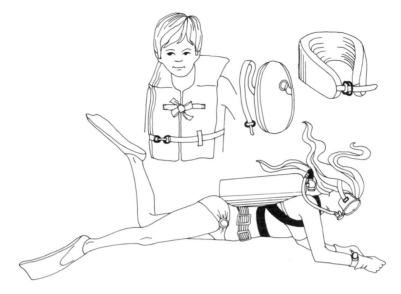

**Figure 10-6.** Gear worn in water.

soft rubber, air-filled leather, yarn, vinyl, plastic with holes, nylon, fleece, sponge foam, paper, wood, and cork-filled canvas. Some balls are made to bounce, and others are not. Balls that no longer hold air can be stuffed with crumpled or shredded paper and covered by either canvas, twine, or tape. Foam, yarn, sponge, supersoft rubber, and plastic whiffle balls are made to be used in limited-area games where safety and action are the main concerns. The fleece ball, a worsted-yarn ball, comes in various

**Figure 10-7.** (*left*). Climbing gear.
**Figure 10-8.** (*right*). Overloading with weighted gear.

sizes. It is a replica of the type of ball used in schoolrooms, gyms, parks, and lawns in the following activities: baseball, badminton, golf, tennis, and softball. The mal-col ball is an all-rubber practice ball developed for indoor use; when it is hit against a wall, it does not rebound equally and only travels half the distance in the outdoors. The Air Ball is a soft foam ball that bounces but is harmless to people, mirrors, and other fragile apparatus. Audible balls are made with bells or other devices inside, allowing the blind to hear sound which aids them in tracking and catching (Figure 10-9).

The bean bag is another type of propelling object used with elementary-age children. The bean bag is inexpensive and has been filled with such material as beans and corn. Children have success in catching the bean bag, for it will conform to whatever body surfaces the person presents and will not rebound against the body like the rubber ball.

Other items that people propel are arrows, darts, discuses, frisbees, hockey pucks, quoits, shots, shuffleboard discs, and shuttlecocks.

## Equipment That Is an Extension of the Individual

Equipment that people use as an extention of their bodies can be categorized as striking, projecting and receiving objects, or as a combination of these. These objects are made of wood, plastic, or aluminum and come in various sizes and shapes. The items most commonly used for *striking* are badminton racquets, paddle racquets, squash racquets, and tennis racquets both regular and shorties—softball bats, baseball and cricket bats, and the polo stick with a sponge foam head. The archery bow, ski poles, and shuffleboard sticks are examples of equipment used in *projection*. Items that are used in *receiving* only are batons, pogo

**Figure 10-9.** Items that people propel.

sticks, and stilts. A *combination* of striking, projecting, and receiving
equipment are the following: Indian clubs, wands, bamboo poles, broom-
sticks, pla-tube, foil, floor, field, and ice hockey sticks, and lacrosse sticks.

Jousters are safe, lightweight equipment used in combat games; and
the bataia bat, like the pillo polo stick, is a harmless pillow soft, club-like
device used for game playing (Figure 10-10).

## Equipment and Apparatus on Which People Move

Equipment and apparatus vary in price range from the very expensive
to the highly economical. Often homemade equipment is inexpensive
and valuable. Under each major heading of equipment and apparatus, a
number of examples have been given for illustrating the equipment or
the sport in which the apparatus is used.

### Commercial

1. *Jumping or vaulting.* boxes, horses, saw horses, tables,
benches, tires, springboards, bent-
boards, boards, minitramps, trampo-
lines, vaulting boxes, planks, hurdles.
(Figure 10-11).

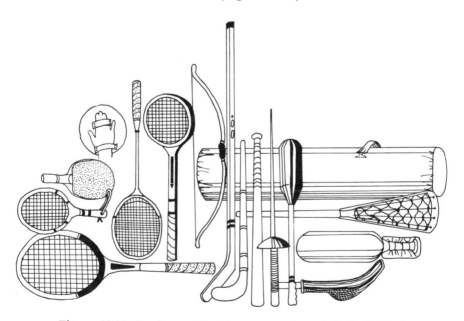

**Figure 10-10.** Equipment that is an extension of the individual.

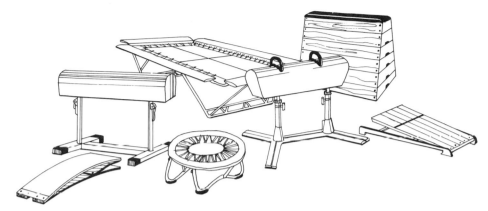

**Figure** 10-11. Jumping and vaulting equipment.

2. *Balance equipment.*  barrels, balance beams (high and low), benches, rocking boards, teeter boards, wooden blocks, rails, etc. (Figure 10-12).

3. *Nets and standards.*  badminton; field, floor and ice hockey; soccer, basketball, water polo, floor, platform, aerial and regular tennis, volleyball, etc.

4. *Mats.*  tumbling, wrestling, safety under and around apparatus for indoors and outdoors, landing mats for pits, etc., exercise, rest, holding, hanging mats for wall protection, mobile mats, all-weather mats, creative block mats, geo-

**Figure** 10-12. Balance equipment.

metric shapes, etc. Mats are usually covered with some form of plastic, rubberized, or canvas material (Figure 10-13).

5. *Climbing and Hanging.*   Jungle gyms, rings, horizontal bars, ladders, still bars, scuffles, peg boards, cargo nets, ropes, Nissen Wall gym, link climber, the stegel, climbing forms, and parallel bars (regular and uneven) have been used for climbing and/or hanging. Ropes have been used in jumping, climbing, fitness, and creative activities. Agility ropes have been arranged in a variety of ways across the gymnasium; creative arithmetic and geometric figures, foot-eye activities using the numbers as pattern obstacles. The rope is also used to line the baseball path for use in softball for the blind. Another example of the use of ropes can be seen in the high rope course illustrated by Jeneid (8) (Figure 10-14).

6. *Water.*   Canoes, boats, kayaks, sailboats, shells, and surfboards.

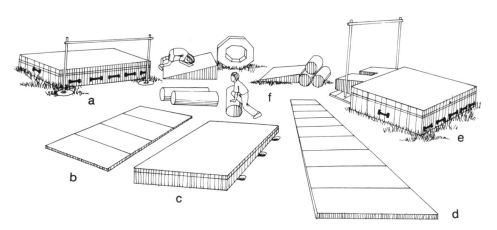

**Figure 10-13.** Mats: a. high jump mat; b. all-purpose mat; c. "box" or landing mat; d. tumbling mat; e. port-a-pit pole vault pit; f. creative foam shapes.

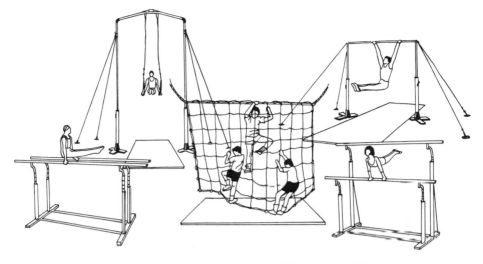

Figure 10-14. Climbing and hanging equipment.

| 7. *Miscellaneous.* | Hoops, scooters, targets, tiles, body image boxes, backboards, parachutes, tumbling sticks, cones, dance equipment. |

## Inexpensive Homemade Equipment

Creativity and innovation will become the answer to many of our school equipment problems. The physical educator should use some imagination and use items that are discarded from society in developing motor skills and directing movement activities. Examples of discarded materials used in physical education are plastic bottle scoops, tin cans, coffee-can targets, lid flying saucers, milk cartons, limmi sticks, paper strips, tubes, tires, hurdles, batons, standards, balance apparatus, chairs, cones flags, barrels, towels, and old coat hangers as paddles.

Cratty (9), Carter (10), Christian (11), Corbin (12), Frederick (13), and Gallahue (14) are a few of the good reference books for the physical educator who needs to make his own equipment.

## Skill Improvement Equipment

There are many teaching devices that aid the physical educator in efficient skill movement. The striking device is one example (Figure 10-15).

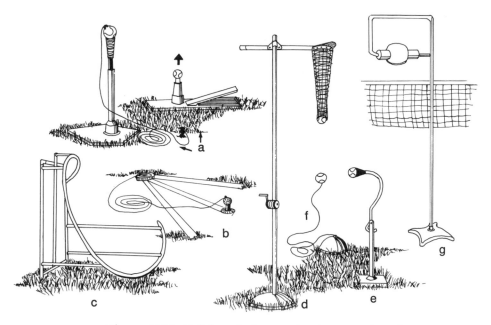

**Figure 10-15.** Striking devices: a. batting tees; b. safe-space golf ball; c. golfer's groove; d. tennis tutor; e. tennis practice tee; f. tennis stroke master; g. volleyball spike-it.

## Striking Devices

The striking devices are batting tees, tennis-stroke developers, tennis practice tees, and tennis trainer, tennis serving devices, tethered rebound balls, tennis trappers to emphasize eye contact, golfer's groove to teach the proper swing, saf-space golf balls, and spike-it volleyball practice devices. They free physical educators so that they may give individual attention while providing the learner with skill development.

## Confining Devices

The confining devices are the golf-driving net, electric golf range that indicates yardage, direction, and degree of slice or hook, football-training net for quarterback drills, passing, kicking, receiving, and centering skills; football practice kicking cages, baseball batting and protective nettings, rebound nets, archery backstop nets for indoor archery, controlled basketball return nets for wheelchair patients, backboards and walls for volleying, football passing devices, and walls for indoor rock climbing (Figures 10-16 and 10-17).

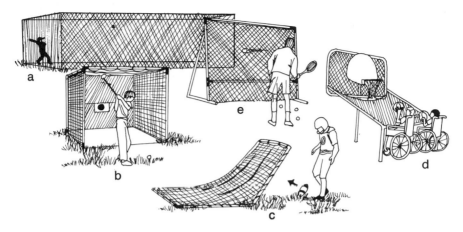

**Figure 10-16.** Confining devices: a. batting cage; b. golf cage; c. football kicking cage; d. basketball return net; e. tennis rebound net.

## Projecting Devices

The projecting devices are Pow-R-Pitch plastic baseball throwing machines with plastic balls and bats, baseball and softball pitching machines that throw curves as well as straight balls, tennis machines, stroke

**Figure 10-17.** Multi-court use of walls. (*Courtesy of J. E. Gregory Co., Spokane, Washington*)

practice machines for badminton, tennis, and volleyball, and football throwing machines (Figure 10-18).

**General Devices**

Hurdle and hurdle adapters, tire resisters for developing driving power, sleds and dummies in football, pacing machines for track and swimming, funnel balls, steel rebound rings that fit inside for developing rebounding and shooting, McCall's rebounders, safety belts in gymnastics, blinders in basketball to prevent the learner from seeing the ball and so develop the ability to dribble the ball by touch, starting blocks in track for indoor and outdoor, bi-handle paddles which are table tennis paddles with two handles for the handicapped, adapted foil for wheelchair patients, adapted archery bows, towel for use in bowling, running ropes as training devices, the Penny's power pullers and running harnesses (Figure 10-19).

## Movement-Measuring Equipment

Timing and space become important in movement when speed and competition are involved. The physical educator then relies upon the stop watch; Acutrack, which is a photofinish camera and electronic timer; cinematography, used to study precise movements of the body and its parts in skill performance; the electromyograph (EMG) which records, analyzes and integrates electrical impulses generated by muscles under contraction or immediately prior to contraction; the Leighton Flexometer and the electrogoniometer, called the "elgon" is used to measure joint flexibility; torqueometer to measure torque at selected joints of the body; reaction performance analyzer; hand dynamometer; cabletensimometer; depth perception apparatus; finger dexterity; biofeedback; electrocardiograph; datagraph; and a spirometer to measure the amount of oxygen used during exercise. The air can be collected by the use of a Douglas bag, and the anthropometric devices.

## Fitness-Developing Equipment

Not many question the importance of physical fitness, but people should question the best approach and equipment to be used to achieve individual physical fitness. The market is saturated with an array of gimmicks, gadgets, and pieces of special equipment to help people become physically fit. Some range in price from $1.00 for a hand-grip strengthener to $1,200.00 for an electric walking device.

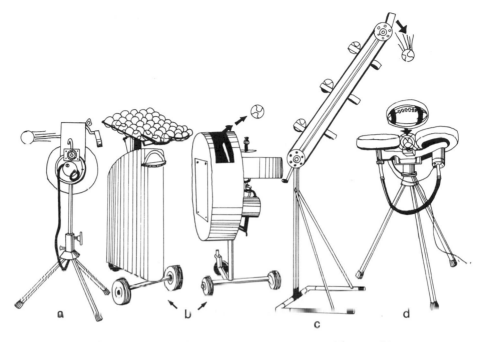

**Figure 10-18.** Projecting devices: a. Jugs pitching machine, b. two tennis pitching machines; c. Johnson set-up machine for badminton, tennis, and volleyball; d. Jugs football passing machine.

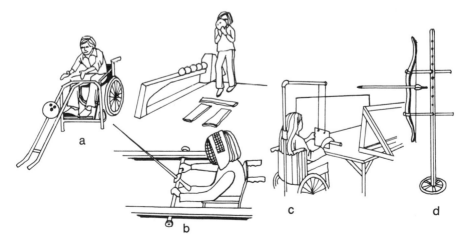

**Figure 10-19.** Adaptive devices: a. bowling; b fencing; c. table tennis; d. archery.

These items include hand-grip strengtheners, rubber and cable tension stretchers, barbells and dumbbells, abdominal boards, chinning bars, exercise wheels, vibrators, bicycle-type exercisers, isometric gadgets, treadmills, roller massage machines, the plug-in, no-work workout devices, and so on.

Johnson (15) claims that careful inspection and experimentation of body mechanics and physiology must be conducted to aid the physical educator in determining the difference between value and fraud. Many companies are doing this and are seeking the assistance of physical educators to conduct such research. We must be cautious of some of the fitness gimmicks, protest the shortcut type of exercise programs, and begin to emphasize research tested concepts in our exercise prescriptions.

Some fitness devices based upon the progressive-resistance exercise principle are the exergenie, the isokinetics machine, the universal machine, and the nautilus machine. The exergenie was one of the first devices to combine the principles of isometrics and isotenics. It is a small exercise device that develops muscle and strength throughout a full range of motion. The amount of resistance or weight from the exergenie is applied by a lever on the handle and can range from an ounce to several hundred pounds. This device can also aid in developing both land and water sports skills by applying resistance while duplicating the exact motion of the sport (Figure 10-20).

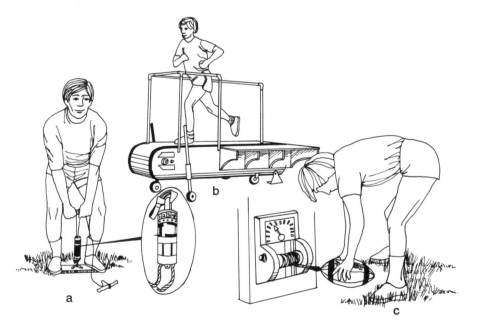

**Figure 10-20.** Equipment to develop physical fitness:
a. exergenie; b. treadmill; c. mini-gym.

Other resistance exercising devices using the principles of isokinetics, both small and large have been manufactured by Mini Gym, Inc., Independence, Missouri. These devices apply the resistance automatically to the amount of force being exerted throughout the full range of motion. Forty such models have been developed for strength and power workouts. The devices are being used in schools and fitness centers.

Small progressive-resistance exercise equipment is being replaced by compact all-purpose weight machines. These machines are safer, provide more exercise stations, and require limited space. Two examples of these progressive resistance exercise machines are the Universal machines by Universal Resilite Company of New York, and the Nautilus machines by Nautilus Sports/Medical Industries of De Land, Florida (Figures 10-21 and 10-22).

Bicycle ergometer-type exercisers that provide training and exercise on a year-round basis regardless of the weather are becoming popular. At one time, such machines were used solely by scientists and researchers

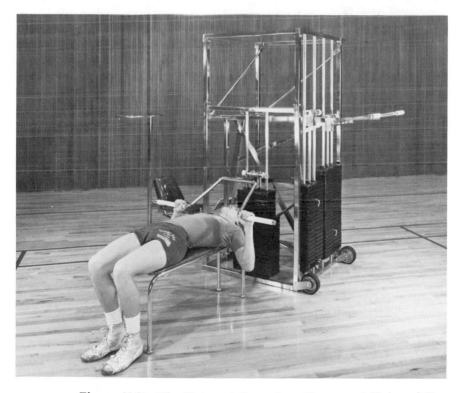

**Figure 10-21.** The Universal Centurion. (*Courtesy of Universal Resilite Company, Hempstead, N.Y.*)

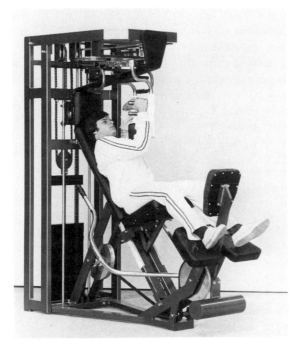

**Figure 10-22.** Nautilus Double Chest Machine. (*Courtesy of Nautilus Sports/Medical Industries, Deland, Florida*)

Treadmill-type machines for walking, jogging, and running are also becoming popular.

## Movement-Clarifying Equipment

Sight and sound have come to play an important role in clarifying movement. For this purpose, human beings have developed a wide range of materials.

### Display Boards

Display boards are such things as bulletin boards, chalkboard, charts, flannel boards, hook and loop boards, magnetic boards, posters, and visuals. Their use has been to give information, to help teach a skill, and to present the rules and strategies of a game. Posters can be mounted on the wall to supplement the lesson or skill. The chalkboard, which is found in every school, gives instant visual illustrations of important points, skills, or game strategies. In the gymnasium, chalkboards are usually portable. Bulletin boards provide visual announcements and lists of team standings. They can be used to emphasize points of the skill unit of instruction. Wall charts can be used to present facts about the program, progression of skill sequence, or routine sequence. The magnetic and flannel boards can be used in situations where space is limited and a portable aid is necessary to teach positions and movements. They also can be used to emphasize strategy and individual player movement as in teaching a dance step by placing the foot print on the boards to represent the dance step pattern.

### Photographs

Pictures can be used to demonstrate a skill. Photographs from a polaroid camera can be used for immediate reinforcement of learning skills. Analysis of the photographs is usually followed by another performance of the skill. Speed-sequence polaroid cameras can film a sequence of the technique, and then the sets of pictures are ready for examination. Cheffers et al. (16) has shown that pictures also can be used to test the expressed attitudes of elementary children toward physical education and to assess their self-concept. [See also Martinek and Zaichkowski (17).] These nonverbal instruments help overcome the lack of verbal ability of elementary children and provide the instructor with information about the children and the program.

### Opaque and Overhead Projectors

The opaque projector reproduces original pictures without damaging the original. For the nonartistic, it allows for tracing of a skill or series of movements. The overhead projector is a reflected projection system by which classes or groups are able to view transparencies in a well-lighted room or gymnasium with the teacher in the front of the class. There are a variety of commercially prepared transparencies available covering all aspects of human movement. With the overhead projector, a teacher is able to emphasize an important aspect of a skill by just pointing to the skill as it is projected on the classroom wall.

### Models

Models and speciments are valuable to the physical education teacher, especially in an anatomy and physiology class. Mannequins and moulages are used to give a realistic appearance to a demonstration on control of bleeding and techniques of bandaging. Bloom (18) explained the effective use of mannequins to simulate the proper anatomical position of swimming strokes. The dolls were plastic or rubber forms and were flexible enough to demonstrate the prescribed positions. Uniformed in mask, fins, snorkel or complete scuba gear, dolls showed the proper wearing of equipment (Figure 10-23).

**Figure 10-23.** Use of a doll in the swimming instruction. (*Courtesy of the Journal of Health, Physical Education, and Recreation*)

### Audio Equipment

The audio equipment used in physical education includes records, record players, tapes, cassettes, and tape recorders. These aids have been used in the performing areas of movement, that is, in gymnastics, dance, swimming, movement education, and calisthenics. They are valuable because of their practicality and ease of operation. They also help create a mood in the gymnasium and aid in putting a routine together.

### Slides and Filmstrips

All aspects of physical education have relied on slides and filmstrips. In dance, they are used widely for showing new skills, and for telling stories of the countries where the dances originated. Slides or filmstrips first show an incorrect skill pattern and then the correct pattern. Audio filmstrips are effective for increasing student interest, clarifying the lesson, and saving time, but still pictures are less effective than motion pictures.

### Loopfilms

Loopfilms are one of the most useful visual equipment aids in physical education. They can be viewed independently by a student or by a group. Cartridges are easy to use and require no threading. The cartridge film loop is one continuous loop that can be played over and over, even by elementary children. Film loops are used to introduce a unit, to aid the classroom teacher in teaching physical education, and to demonstrate the activity.

## Motion Pictures

According to Dowell (19) motion picture films are the most widely used audiovisual technique in physical activity. Motion pictures can be showed in slow motion and used for individual teaching without the presence of the teacher. They can introduce a skill, provide information about a sport, and provide a means to analyze skill performance. The problems with motion pictures have been the cost and the arrangement of the films, and obtaining and operating the projector.

## Television and Videotape

There are two types of television—broadcasting and closed circuit. The problems with using television in physical education have been the cost and selecting the right person to televise. The videotape recorder and camera help us to study movement. Before this, if students wanted to view their own performances, they had a motion picture taken, waited for it to be developed, and then viewed the results several days later. Now the student is able to obtain immediate feedback. With the aid of the instructor or coach, the performer is able to see his or her weak points and immediately work on improvement of the movement. Videotape recorders are portable for use in the gymnasium, pool, and on the athletic field. They have been used to record class proceedings, to analyze skill, to provide immediate feedback for pupils and teachers, to motivate, to give instruction during individual or group work, and as an objective observer system for recording teacher and pupil behaviors (Figure 10-24). [See Miller, Cheffers, and Whitcomb (20).]

## Programmed Materials and Teaching Machines

In programmed instruction, the program takes the place of the teacher. If teaching machines are involved, the machine leads the student through a set of specified behaviors designed and sequenced for the student to behave in a desired way in the future. This instructional approach allows students to work at their own rate and to progress to the next lesson after they have mastered the previous one. These teaching machines help make students more responsible for their own learning progress. This approach has been ideal for teaching the history, rules, and

**Figure 10-24.** Videotapes and film loop projectors.

game strategy of sports—the cognitive domain—but the performance or psychomotor domain needs further development.

These materials, which clarify and analyze movement, are supplements to helping people move and not a replacement for the physical educator. Through the wise use of these teaching aids the physical educator will contribute to the teaching-learning process.

## FACILITIES AND STRUCTURES
## IN WHICH PEOPLE MOVE

When a new physical activity is being planned, the professional is faced with the problem of selecting sites and structure, either natural or constructed. Many times people make the mistake of constructing the facility before they develop the curriculum. [See Straub (21).] This approach limits the program offerings.

Just as traffic patterns in a house can help or restrict movement, our gymnasiums and playgrounds can alter our movement; facilities must support movement not stifle it. Flexibility must be the trend in the structures of tomorrow. Willgoose (22) claims that more teaching stations and large multiuse activity areas are needed. The concept of the box gymnasium, a square space designed around apparatus and two basketball hoops, is dead. Those who advocate getting rid of the "box" feel it locks in students and program offerings.

The time has come to break away from placing the child in a school environment that demands a rigid conformity to inactivity. Ezersky (23) states that corridors can be used as indoor tracks and play areas in the elementary school, and physical education carrels can be put in every room. These carrels can contain various fitness and exercise equipment. He further states that the elimination of the one scheduled gym period would allow time during the day to take advantage of these new school facilities. For many years gymnasiums were built for the gifted to practice and play in, but now we design structures to accommodate as many participants as possible. Browne (24) states that the trends in designing today's physical education complex are varied teaching stations, aquatic facilities, major activity spaces, and synthetic floorings with various spot markings for different sports.

Ezersky and Therbert (25) believe that we must get rid of gymnasiums in big city high schools in order to teach lifetime sports and develop positive attitudes toward fitness, sports, and athletion. They advocate building specialized sports facilities in several locations around the city school. Many different sports activities could be run simultaneously at different sites for all schools. For the overcrowded cities, the sites could range from air rights on top of garages, on railroad tracks, piers, highways, under municipal buildings and complexes, and in vacant lots and areas unsuited for housing or other commercial use.

## New Design Ideas

New approaches to traditional building design and construction have been developed to provide maximum use at minimum cost. Keller's (26) ideas for changing old facilities were removing skylights, replacing gymnasium floors, and restoring old swimming pools with new nonferrous metal pool tanks or on top of the bed of the old pool.

Newer facilities will become larger, more adaptable, more all-purpose, and more mechanical. Motorized rolling bleachers that serve as movable walls; overhead doors on outside walls that can be raised in good weather to include the outdoor areas in the instructional space; pivot walls that serve as storage areas; bulletin boards; projection screens; wall space for games like squash, handball and paddleball, and nets dropped from ceiling to absorb the impact of golf balls, baseballs, and arrows are some of the new innovational designs developed by Kelsey, Kolflat, and Schaefer (27), which they called their "Acre of June" for physical education programs.

# the floor

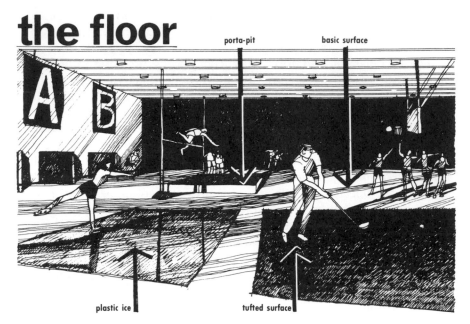

Figure 10-25. "Acre of June."

## Surfaces

Mittelstaedt and Theibert (28) divide surfaces on which people move into four categories: "coverings," which include "coating"; carpeting or matting; grasses, flocks and weaves; and paving and floorings. Outdoor surfaces range from grass, earth, concrete, bituminous, blacktop, and synthetic. The main problem associated with natural grass fields has been excess water resulting from poor drainage. Robey (29) feels that Prescription Athletic Turf (PAT) corrects this problem and the problem of the hard artificial turf. For PAT, 16 inches of sand is used as a base and then instant grass is placed on top. Under the sand is a plastic sheet liner for the placing of small pipes. These pipes attach to a pump that vacuums the water away as it filters through the sand. Water can be added to the turf in a reverse manner. PAT is still being studied by movement specialists who are looking for the perfect surface.

The most common indoor flooring is hardwood or linoleum. These surfaces are being replaced in gymnasiums and fieldhouses by artificial turf. There are many types of artificial surfaces, but the essential ingredient of all is plastic. Artificial coverings include such synthetics as Astro turf, Duna-track, Dynaturf, Elasta turf, Factrac, Firestone, Grasstex, Re-2, Perma-track, Proturf, Reslite, Rub-Kor, tartan, and Uni-turf.

These synthetic substances are the field and floor covering of the future and are already replacing grass and court surfaces. Resiliency, durability, uniformity, longevity, and ease of installation and maintenance are their best features. One advantage, advocates point out, is the polyurethane surfaces which are filled with liquid polyurethane or non-urethane materials like clay. Klumpp (30) feels that these synthetic surfaces aid the person's legs and back. Because of the greater resiliency of these surfaces, people do not tire as easily and the incidence of shin splints is almost nonexistent.

In cities the roofs of all types of buildings are being used for playing areas. These areas are covered with synthetic turf because of its durability, effectiveness, and attractive appearance. Some surfaces, like urethane, have a dual role, providing a playing surface for courts, and a water proofing for the building (Figure 10-26).

Browne (24), Lashbrook (31), and Steitz (32) state that synthetic surfaces increase actual usage time of the field and the number of activities in a program. Grass fields are effectively used only 50 hours per year and many artificial turf fields are used as many as 2,000 hours per year.

**Figure 10-26.** A rooftop facility. (*Courtesy of California Products Corp., Cambridge, Mass.*)

The multipurpose polyturf field installed at Springfield College, Springfield, Mass. shows many and varied uses of synthetic fields. This football field is used for the male and female skill instruction courses, intramurals, the intercollege athletic program, and an NCAA summer sports program. With the addition of lights, the facility is now in constant use from early morning to late at night. During the first academic term after it was installed, it received more use than the old football field had during ten years of use.

Synthetic turfs can be used in a variety of ways as seen at the University of Idaho, whose football field is a one piece portable field which is laid down and can be removed mechanically. With the football field rolled up, the surface goes indoor to its permanent floor markings to provide badminton, basketball, tennis, track, and volleyball.

Although synthetic surfaces have many uses and take hard and diverse wear, there are still many questions that must be answered and many opponents who do not agree with their value to the participant. Those who oppose the synthetic surfaces ask the following questions:

1. What is the life span of these synthetic fields?
2. Will some materials become too hard with long use?
3. What about the injury factor involved in playing on these surfaces?

One should be cautious, keep an open mind, inspect an actual installation, and collect as much data as possible about the synthetic surface before purchasing it.

### Ice and Snow Surfaces

In some areas of the country, outdoor areas are flooded during the winter season and used for ice skating and hockey. Any flat, level area can be turned into an ice-skating rink with the use of canvas and vinyl ice-rink liners. These liners can provide an outdoor skating rink quickly and easily almost anywhere and be ready for use after a short period of freezing weather. The shallowness of the water necessary and the material used in the construction of the rink make this possible.

Iceless ice skating can be done indoors by covering the floor with a slick, thermoplastic material, making a multipurpose flooring. In this way gymnasiums may be changed into combination ice skating-recreation areas, for thermoplastic floorings release lubricants when a skater's blades move across it, thus producing a slippery surface.

Snowless skiing is also possible by using a plastic ski-mat snowtable which allows skiing instruction before snowfall. Plastic snow is a soft

**Figure 10-27.** Plastic ski mat. (*Courtesy of Ithaca College, Ithaca, N.Y.*)

rubberlike material that makes a ski turf that is soft and flexible. This material has the slippery characteristic needed for skiing conditions. Ski instruction can be held on the synthetic snow, indoor or outdoor, in the summer, or in areas that now get little or no snow.

### Water Surfaces

Streams, ponds, lakes, and oceans are natural areas people use to move on, over, and through. Some of the manufactured swimming structures developed for water activities are pools of various sizes and shapes with mechanical devices to alter the depth of the water, pools that are portable and mobile, and facilities for inland water surfing.

There are different sizes and shapes of pools to fit special needs. Some pools have ramps for wheelchairs, and others have hydraulically operated pool lifters that can vary the depth of the water for different activities and different levels of swimming abilities. Money is the main reason for the lack of pools in schools, and communities such as Worcester, Massachusetts and Dallas, Texas now share their swimming facilities with schools. O'Neil (33) reports that fifty-five elementary schools in the Worcester system use a boys' and girls' club to provide swimming instruc-

**Figure 10-28.** The "Big Surf" surfing pool. (*Courtesy of Big Surf, Inc., Tempe, Arizona*)

tion for fourth and fifth grade students. According to Rubinstein (34), in Texas, the Dallas School's Loos Swimming Center, a three-story facility, costs the taxpayer only four cents for each child's swim and nine cents for each child's lesson. In the three years that the center has operated, 10,000 people have taken part in the Dallas program, and it has cut the incidental drowning rate to 26 percent.

Portable pools have been erected on top of the ground, on a floor, and in a vehicle. They have brought increased opportunity for swimming and water-safety instruction to school systems without enough permanent pool facilities. The Miracle's Learner Pool, a complete classroom on wheels, provides instruction in survival swimming.

In Tempe, Arizona, "The Big Surf" surfing pools, complete with landscaping, have been constructed. A summerland pool in Hochioji, Japan and in Decatur, Alabama are examples of inland surfing facilities. A hydraulic system which force pumps millions of gallons of water to a certain level in a reservoir wall produces the waves. Underwater gates are then opened, releasing the water and generating the wave. See [Odenkirr (35) and Runkel (36).] According to Straub (21), waves can be produced at 50 second intervals. These facilities have beaches allowing children gradually to enter the water. They provide for all swimming activities, not just surfing.

## Coverings

The roof is the most common covering of facilities, and its shape has changed from the square and rectangular to the round, semicircular, quadrangular, hexangular, oval, and pentangular. Today, prefabricated subsystems are brought together to erect buildings in months at a considerable reduction in cost.

Indoor tennis courts are completely enclosed, with air conditioning, diffused lighting, and resilient surfaces. These courts provide for year-round, day and night participation.

The translucent membrane roof at Milligan College, Johnson City, Tennessee, is an example of the evolution of the school gymnasium into the open, multiuse, recreational facility. Its roof rolls down in poor weather and opens up in good weather.

The quonset-roofed field house is replacing the gymnasium and has helped to bridge the gap between the spectator sports and the physical education program by opening up a greater range of indoor activities. The field house, with its wide-open spaces, multiuse fixtures, and portable floors and equipment, provides spaces for flexible programs in physical education and recreation. In many cases, the field house is housed in buildings whose main material is fabric.

One of the newest and most promising architectural developments has been the lightweight structure. Some of these are plastic bubbles, geodesic domes, limited shelters, and the tensile membrane structures. Any sport-activity area can be covered with these lightweight structures and even an entire city, as seen in Alaska, can be covered by an air structure (Educational Facilities Laboratories Inc., 1973). The development of structures that can be erected economically and rapidly on available school ground has added a new dimension to the problem of expansion of indoor facilities.

Air structures are large, plastic bubbles that are blown up and supported by continuous air pressure. The air structure has no columns and no restrictions on the type of activity conducted inside it. They are now being used for educational, commercial, and civic purposes. The limiting factor with air structures has been their life expectancy, for the first developed air structures were expected to last only five to seven years. Harold Gores of the Educational Facilities Laboratories stated in an interview with Straub (21) that a new material has been developed that will have a life expectancy of nearly forty years.

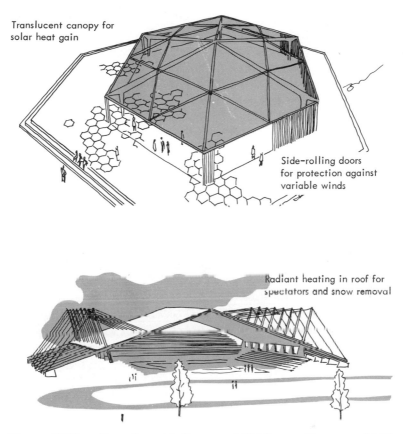

Translucent canopy for solar heat gain

Side-rolling doors for protection against variable winds

Radiant heating in roof for spectators and snow removal

**Figure 10-29.** a. Steve Lacy Air-Supported Fieldhouse (*Courtesy of Milligan College, Milligan, Tenn.*); b. LaVerne College's Tensil-Membrane Student Activities Center; c. Elmira College Geodesic Domes (*Courtesy of Temcor, Torrance, Ca.*); d. the limited shelter.

Other concerns of the air structure have been heat gain and loss, acoustics, aesthetics, and building care problems. On the positive side, repair and maintenance are economical, the price is affordable, the space is enjoyable, the structure is mobile, and the fears of vandalism seem to be unfounded [See Theibert (37)].

The tensil-membrane is another type of lightweight structure that is characterized by supporting or restraining cables which are carried directly to ground anchor points over columns, poles, or masts at stabilization points. The Olympic Stadium in Munich, Germany, is a tensile-membrane structure as is the overnight camping tent with its sharp, center-pointed roofs. The first permanent tensil-membrane structure was constructed at Lawrence College, California [Theibert (37.] This structure can be opened and still have protective floor covering from the roof because it lacks the mechanics of the air lock.

The geodesic dome, made of aluminum tubing bolted together to form a dome, has been constructed for use in schools of all levels. The dome-shaped buildings are less expensive to erect than traditional ones, and they can house any type of sports activity. Various places that have erected geodesic domes are the Ogdensburg Free Academy in New York, Blackfoot High School in Idaho, Clearwater Central Catholic High in Florida, Trinidad High School in Colorado, and Elmira College in New York. It was at Elmira that three geodesic domes were built side by side to house a natatorium, a hockey dome, and a field-house dome for a cost of $26.20 per square foot.

Another lightweight shelter, the limited shelter, provides covered and sheltered space at much less than the cost of the typical gymnasiums and multipurpose rooms. Wagner, Evans, and Novak (38) define limited shelters as any outdoor space that uses natural or manufactured devices for protection against the extremes of the natural elements. These shelters capture and use the desirable elements of our natural environment and create a stimulating backdrop for physical education activities at both the elementary and secondary levels.

Playsheds have been constructed to supplement outdoor elementary physical education programs. Providing protection from inclement weather, they contain roof areas, have either partial or no sides, and cover both hard or grass surfaces.

## Condensed Facilities

Two examples of condensed facilities used for sports activities are Platform Tennis, made by North American Recreation, Platform Tennis Systems Division, Bridgeport, Connecticut, and the "Sportation, the Court for Compact Sports," by Sportation Company, Old Lyme, Connecticut. Both the platform tennis court and the Sportation Court were designed for year-round outdoor use in limited space.

The platform tennis court, sometimes called paddle, is one-fourth the size of a tennis court, and can be placed in a small backyard, on a rooftop, or on badly graded land.

The Sportation, the court for individual and team compact sports, is a 12' × 24' multipurpose recreation enclosure designed to expand and supplement gymnasium, field, and playground programs. Sportation courts are installed singly or in multiple units for outdoor and indoor use on any floor from basement to roof. The "compact sports," which are modifications of games, such as baseball, basketball, golf, handball, hockey, soccer, tennis, squash, and volleyball, may be played in this facility.

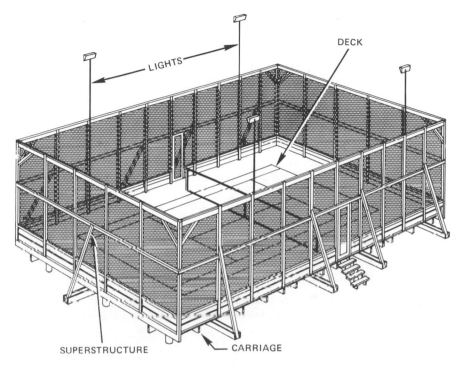

**Figure 10-30.** Platform tennis court. (*Courtesy of North American Recreation, Platform Tennis Systems Division, Bridgeport, Conn.*)

## School-Community Design

The concept of sharing is evident in school-community design in facilities. Many facilities are costly and not used daily; it makes sense to share the school gymnasiums, the fields and the recreation and park areas of the community. In facility-sharing programs, the spirit of neighborhood and community closeness creates a more balanced activity program. Facility sharing is growing in popularity. If both pool their resources, the school need not construct one building or field for its use and the community another building or field for night and weekend recreation use. The taxpayers save not only in the initial cost but in the continual maintenance cost. The economic value is only one benefit of the school-community facility. Generally the quality of life in a community improves as people use the schools' educational and recreational facilities to continue to exercise and participate in various athletic activities. An example of a school-community facility concept is seen in the multipurpose physical education, athletic, and recreation facility of

Juanita High School, Kirkland, Washington. It is a huge, open-concept fieldhouse with an exercise gym, a swimming pool, two sets of locker rooms, and laundry and storage rooms. [See Hulet (39).]

Still another aspect of school-community sharing, the park-school facility, occurs when the school and the city parks are developed as a single unit. When this type of facility is planned, it meets the needs of the indoor and outdoor instructional program as well as the recreation program. This concept of construction of a facility helps in giving the community the maximum facility without duplicating physical and economic efforts. When an area serves both the school and community, a larger facility is needed, but in the long run, if planned properly, it is money wisely spent.

Another concept in school-community sharing is to cooperate with commercial or nonprofit agencies to assure broad participation when school facilities are lacking. In utilizing community facilities outside the school, the physical educator can effectively plan a sequence of experiences in the curriculum that will guarantee exposure to a wide range of activities.

## Playground Facilities

Often playground facilities are attacked for their lack of imagination. Today people are using more creativity in the development of playground areas. Facilities for the use of studying play have been constructed. The University of Illinois, Motor Performance and Play Research Laboratory (MPRRL) developed a center to help study the play and motor learning environments for children. MPRRL is particularly concerned with the gross motor behavior and play of children and with the ecology of play [See Ellis (40)].

Playground facilities have changed to thematic design. Today development of a playground revolves around a theme of interest to children. Weiskopf (41) reports that themes range from the space-age playground with space ships, rockets, and satellites, to the Mississippi River park, complete with riverboat, to a Spanish fort, to culture themes, and to the frontier town.

The "junk" or "scavenger" playground made up of discarded equipment, lumber, ropes, and other scrap material has been an ongoing but questioned adventure. This playground provides many challenges and gives individuals a chance to build and create their own play environment [See Weiskopf (41) and Seker (42)]. This type of playground can be as expensive or as reasonable as the people of the community want it.

Steep grades and contrasts in levels have been another new approach

**Figure 10-31.** Adventure Playground (*Courtesy of the Journal of Health, Physical Education, and Recreation*)

to playground areas. Children are able to hide, to coast down hills, to use rope swings or pulley rides, and to climb along monkey bridges.

## Mobile Facilities

The mobile unit is a facility on wheels used to bring a particular activity to the place best suited to the needs of the people of the community. This approach to movement fulfillment represents a flexible, creative, new solution to the immediate needs of the people. The mobile unit has been used and developed for adapted physical education programs [Flanagan (43)], for lifetime sport activities [Straub (21)], and for general recreational activities [Deihl (44) and Wallach (45)]. These units have been used in a kaleidoscope of ideas: skating programs, warming shelters for skating rinks, exercise areas, craft units, puppeteering, traveling zoos, boxing rings on wheels, archery range, bicycle mobiles, backstops for basketball, instant playground with slides, swings, spring riding animals, climbers, and mobile swimming pools. The swimming unit has been particularly effective in the inner city; a unit can be hooked to a fire hydrant and requires only a few days to set up on any street.

**Figure 10-32.** The Sportsmobile. (*Courtesy of Mr. Clyde Cole, Boycol Corp., Delmar, N.Y.*)

### Natural Outdoor Facilities

The natural outdoor physical environment provides a variety of experiences for all ages with limitless instructional materials at practically no cost. All schools are surrounded by an outdoor laboratory that offers a perennial invitation to teachers searching for ways to motivate reluctant learners [Isenbery in Bucher (46)]. We should provide students with an opportunity to learn through firsthand outdoor experiences. The outdoor education method of learning is not a separate course or specific area of study; it is a method of teaching.

Outdoor education and recreation include a wide variety of activities which fully exploit the natural environment. Man uses mountains, rocks, deserts, prairies, oceans, lakes, forests, slopes, hills, fields, etc., to move. Nature gives natural apparatus and facilities for use in movement. Some of the natural apparatus and facilities that can be used for activity, identified by Smith [see Bucher (46)], are nature trails, trees, bridges, swinging ropes that resemble natural vines, small caves, shallow streams and pools, and fishing ponds.

Orienteering, mountaineering, and backpacking on trails have become popular activities. Orienteering requires people, a terrain, a map, and a compass. A wooded and hilly area is ideal, but a city park or even a densely settled neighborhood may be used. Orienteering can be adapted to such outdoor means of travel as walking, snowshoeing, cross-country skiing, canoeing, and cycling.

**Figure 10-33.** Rope course used in Project Adventure Program. (*Courtesy of Project Adventure, Box 157, Hamilton, Mass.*)

Parks, nature centers, camps, zoos, museums, and wildlife sanctuaries can be used as natural environments for schools and recreational activities. Family fitness and fun centers [Bucher (46)] are popular with families for they include an activity program that all will enjoy. Many forms of entertainment tend to separate the family, but these programs bring the family together. This concept is being endorsed by a year-round family camping and sports activity program in Springfield, Massachusetts, called Camper Wilder. The basic idea is that at least one parent must accompany the child in an activity be it swimming, yoga, tennis, canoeing, macramé, life saving, picnicing, cross-country skiing, or making jam. The family centers, of which Camp Wilder is an example, are quite in tune with nature and serve as places where everyone in the family can relax and enjoy themselves as well as each other.

A Fitness Park, modeled after the roadside park of Switzerland, was developed and opened for public use in the University of Montana Family Housing [Stowe and Burton (47)]. The concept of the Switzerland fitness parks was developed and installed by an insurance company which felt that passing motorists could stop and revitalize their minds and bodies and, in doing so, reduce the number of accidents on the highway. The

Fitness Park constructed by Stowe and Burton (47) consists of a sixth of a mile jogging track and nine exercise stations.

Programs have been developed that help people to know themselves by pitting themselves against nature. Such programs are the Outward Bound, Project Adventure, and Human Environment Institute programs at Boston University. The theme of these programs is growth through group participation. Project Magnet Movement-Athletics, conducted at Boston University, Boston, Massachusetts, is another such program which has tried to facilitate racial integration through movement activities in the gymnasium and the field. A similar program exists at Agassiz Village in Maine. This highly structured, outward-bound type of experience was designed to facilitate interchange among students of different ethnic backgrounds.

We help others move by creating and manipulating the physical environment in a legion of ways. Human curiosity and versatility is testimony to the ingenious equipment and facility forms currently in existence. Selected sources are provided in this chapter's bibliography for the reader to use for further descriptions and practical use of the various equipment, supplies, and facilities.

## References Cited

1. RUSHALL, BRENT S., AND DARYL SIEDENTOP. *The Development and Control of Behavior in Sport and Physical Education*. Philadelphia: Lea & Febiger, 1972.

2. BIGGE, MORRIS L. *Learning Theories for Teachers*. New York: Harper & Row, Publishers, 1964.

3. OBERTENFFER, DELBERT, AND CELESTE ULRICH. *Physical Education: A Textbook of Principles for Professional Students*. 4th ed. New York: Harper & Row, Publishers, 1970.

4. NELSON, N. P., AND ALICE OAKES BRONSON. *Problems in Physical Education*. Englewood Cliffs, New Jersey: Prentice-Hall, Inc., 1965.

5. BROWN, CAMILLE, AND ROSALIND CASSIDY. *Theory in Physical Education: A Guide to Program Change*. Philadelphia: Lea & Febiger, 1963.

6. KNAPP, MARK L. *Nonverbal Communication in Human Interaction*. New York: Holt, Rinehart and Winston, Inc., 1972.

7. KATCH, FRANK I., AND TROY S. CLELAND. "Weighted Practice: Some Theoretical Considerations," *The Physical Educator* 25 (October 1968): 109–111.

8. JENEID, MICHAEL. *Adventuring Outward Bound: A Manual*. Melbourne: Lansdowne Press PTY. Ltd., 1967.

9. CRATTY, BRYANT J. *Intelligence in Action: Physical Activities for Enhancing Intellectual Abilities*. Englewood Cliffs, New Jersey: Prentice-Hall, Inc., 1973.

10. CARTER, GEORGE. "Flag Football Adapted," *Journal of Health, Physical Education, Recreation* 40 (November–December 1969): 56.

11. CHRISTIAN, QUENTIN A. *The Bean Bag Curriculum: A Homemade Approach to Physical Activity for Children.* Wolfe City, Texas: The University Press, 1973.

12. CORBIN, CHARLES B. *Inexpensive Equipment for Games, Play and Physical Activity.* Dubuque, Iowa: Wm. C. Brown Company Publishers, 1972.

13. FREDERICK, JOSEPH. *212 Ideas for Making Low-Cost Physical Education Equipment.* Englewood Cliffs, New Jersey: Prentice-Hall, Inc., 1963.

14. GALLAHUE, DAVID. "Directed Movement Actitvities for Pre-School Children," *The Physical Educator* 30 (May 1973): 70–72.

15. JOHNSON, PERCY B. *et al. Physical Education: A Problem-Solving Approach to Health and Fitness.* New York: Holt, Rinehart and Winston, Inc., 1966.

16. CHEFFERS, JOHN, VICTOR MANCINI, AND LEONARD ZAICHKOWSKY. "The Development of an Attitude Scale Measuring Student Attitudes in Physical Education," *The Physical Educator* 33 (March 1976): 1.

17. MARTINEK, THOMAS, AND LEONARD ZAICHKOWSKY. "The Development and Validation of the Martinek-Zaichkowsky Self-Concept Scale for Children," paper available from the authors, University of North Carolina, Greensboro, N.C. 1976.

18. BLOOM, JOEL A. "A New Model for Aquatic Instruction," *Journal of Physical Education and Recreation* (November–December 1975). p. 67.

19. DOWELL, LINUS J. *Strategies for Teaching Physical Education.* Englewood Cliffs, New Jersey: Prentice Hall, Inc., 1975.

20. MILLER, ARTHUR, JOHN T. F. CHEFFERS, AND VIRGINIA WHITCOMB. *Physical Education: Teaching Human Movement in the Elementary Schools.* 4th ed. Englewood Cliffs, New Jersey: Prentice-Hall, Inc., 1974.

21. STRAUB, WILLIAM F. *The Lifetime Sports-Oriented Physical Education Program.* Englewood Cliffs, N.J.: Prentice-Hall, Inc., 1976.

22. WILLGOOSE, CARL. *Curriculum in Physical Education.* 2nd ed. Englewood Cliffs, N.J.: Prentice-Hall, Inc., 1974.

23. EZERSKY, EUGEN M. "Mini-Gyms and Fitness Courses," *Journal of Health, Physical Education, Recreation* (January 1972): 38–39.

24. BROWNE, ROBERT L. "Multi-Purpose Facilities: More Use per Hour, per Student," *American School & University* (November 1974): pp. 23–27.

25. EZERSKY, EUGEN M., AND P. RICHARD THEIBERT. "City Schools Without Gyms," *Journal of Health, Physical Education, Recreation* 41 (April 1970): 26–29.

26. KELLER, ROY J. "Making the Most of Your Old Facilities," *Journal of Health, Physical Education, Recreation* 42 (June 1971): 26–28.

27. KELSEY, L., F. KOLFLAT, AND R. SCHAEFER. "New Generation Gym," *The Nation's Schools,* 84 (December 1969): 41–56, 60.

28. MITTELSTAEDT, ARTHUR H., AND RICHARD THEIBERT. "Innovative Recreation Surfacings," *Scholastic Coach* 46 (January 1976): 58, 60.

29. ROBEY, MELVIN J. "Pat: Real Grass for Athletic Fields," *Journal of Physical Education and Recreation* 46 (January 1975): 27–28.

30. KLUMPP, ROBERT W. "Synthetic Surfacing," *Scholastic Coach* 43 (January 1974): 62, 64, 76–78.

31. LASHBROOK, LYNN. "Artificial Turf," *Journal of Health, Physical Education, Recreation* 42 (November–December 1971): 28–29.

32. STEITZ, E. "The Synthetic Surface Revolutions," *Scholastic Coach* 39 (January 1970): 100–101.

33. O'NEIL, JOHN J. "Nonschool Facilities for Swimming Instruction," *Journal of Health, Physical Education, Recreation* 39 (September 1968): 88.

34. RUBINSTEIN, MARION. "Facility Design: Dallas Schools; Loos Swimming Center," *Kendall Sports Trail* 29 (November–December 1974): 4–7.

35. ODENKIRK, JAMES E. "Inland Surfing," *Journal of Health, Physical Education, Recreation* 41 (November–December 1970): 26–27.

36. RUNKEL, KENNETH. "Big Surf: Making Waves in Arizona's Ocean," *Journal of Health, Physical Education, Recreation* 44 (November–December 1973): 46.

37. THEIBERT, DICK. "A Re-Evaluation of Air Shelters," *Scholastic Coach* 43 (January 1974): 9, 90.

38. WAGNER, W. G., B. H. EVANS, AND M. A. NOWAK. *Shelter for Physical Education*. Texas: Texas Engineering Experiment Station, Texas A. and M. College, 1961.

39. HULET, RUSS. "A Complex for the Whole Community," *Scholastic Coach* 43 (January 1974): 10–11, 91.

40. ELLIS, M. J. "The University of Illinois Motor Performance and Play Research Laboratory," *Journal of Health, Physical Education, Recreation* 44 (October 1973): 44–47.

41. WEISKOPF, DONALD C. *A Guide to Recreation and Leisure*. Boston: Allyn and Bacon, Inc., 1975.

42. SEKER, JO ANN. "A Scavenger Playground," *Journal of Health, Physical Education, Recreation* 42 (May 1971): 53.

43. FLANAGAN, MICHAEL E. "Expanding Adapted Physical Education Programs on a Statewide Basis," *Journal of Health, Physical Education, Recreation* 40 (May 1969): 52–55.

44. DEIHL, HENRY C. "Mobile Recreation," *Journal of Health, Physical Education, Recreation* 41 (September 1970): 46–47.

45. WALLACH, FRANCES. "Mobility People-to-People Services," *Journal of Health, Physical Education, Recreation* 44 (November–December 1973): 39–40.

46. BUCHER, CHARLES A. *Foundations of Physical Education*. 6th ed. Saint Louis: The C. V. Mosby Company, 1972.

47. STOWE, GARY L., AND JOHN C. BURTON. "A Fitness Park for Adults," *Journal of Physical Education and Recreation* 46 (January 1975): 31.

## Bibliography

ADAMS, RONALD. "Adapted Table Tennis for the Physically Handicapped," *Journal of Health, Physical Education, Recreation* 39 (Nov.–Dec. 1968): 79–80.

ADAMS, RONALD. "Putt-Putt Golf," *Journal of Health, Physical Education, Recreation* 42 (March 1971): 48–50.

American Association for Health, Physical Education, and Recreation, "Products Parade," *Journal of Health, Physical Education, Recreation* 43 (May 1972): 93.

ANDERSON, WILLIAM G. "Videotape Data Bank," *Journal of Physical Education and Recreation* 46 (September 1975): 31–34.

"An Invitation to Visit the Schools and Parks in Dallas." *Journal of Health, Physical Education, Recreation* 36 (February 1965): 36–37.

ARNOLD, CHARLES G., AND ROBERT E. WEAR. "Inner Tube Water Polo," *Journal of Health, Physical Education, Recreation* 41 (February 1970): 85–86.

ARNOLD, W. BRENT, AND WILLIAM B. DECARLO. "XRA: Xerox Recreation Association," *Journal of Health, Physical Education, Recreation* 44 (November–December 1973): 54–55.

ASHTON, DUDLEY, AND CHARLOTTE IREY. *Dance Facilities.* Washington, D.C.: American Association for Health, Physical Education, and Recreation, 1972.

Athletic Institute and the American Alliance for Health, Physical Education, and Recreation. *Planning Facilities for Athletics, Physical Education and Recreation.* Chicago: The Athletic Institute, 1974.

BACON, LUCILLE, HOWARD UMANSKY, AND PHILLIP UMANSKY. "Wheelchair Karate," *Journal of Health, Physical Education, Recreation* 43 (February 1972): 50–53.

BAILEY, DOT. "Elementary School Interest Centers," *Journal of Health, Physical Education, Recreation* 45 (September 1974): 93.

BAILEY, SHERM, AND LLOYD ROWLEY. "A School for Today and Tomorrow," *Journal of Health, Physical Education, Recreation* 40 (September 1969): 31–35.

BAKER, JACK, AND LINDA ARNOLD. "Physical Fitness in a College Course," *Journal of Health, Physical Education, Recreation* 45 (September 1974): 95–96.

BARBER, MARTHA KIPP. "A 'Do-It-Yourself' Indoor-Outdoor Instructional Group," *Journal of Health, Physical Education, Recreation* 41 (September 1970): 67.

BARROW, HAROLD M. *Man and His Movement: Principles of His Physical Education.* Philadelphia: Lea & Febiger, 1971.

BELKA, DAVID. "Improving a Primary Playground," *Journal of Health, Physical Education, Recreation* 44 (January 1973): 72.

BELLARDINE, HARRY E. "101 Ways to Stretch the Subject," *Journal of Health, Physical Education, Recreation* 42 (May 1971): 54–56.

BELLARDINE, HARRY E. "'A Sampling of Activities for the Cargo Net," *Journal of Health, Physical Education, Recreation* 41 (January 1970): 32–33.

BERG, KRIS. "A Functional Approach to Undergraduate Kinesiology," *Journal of Health, Physical Education, Recreation* 46 (September 1975): 43–44.

BERNASCONI, CHARLES E. "Video 'Mini-Lectures' on the Physical Education Program," *Journal of Health, Physical Education, Recreation* 41 (November–December 1970): 80–81.

BERNSTEIN, MICHAEL, JOANNE BERNSTEIN, AND NELSON AVIDON. "Bocci Power!" *Journal of Health, Physical Education, Recreation* 43 (September 1972): 40–41.

BILES, FAY R., ed. *Television: Production and Utilization in Physical Education.* Washington, D.C.: American Association for Health, Physical Education, and Recreation, 1971.

BISCHOFF, DAVID C. "Designed for Participation," *Journal of Health, Physical Education, Recreation* 37 (March 1966): 29–31, 62.

BLIEVERNICHT, DAVID L. "Let's Emphasize the Positive Way to Fitness," *The Physical Educator* 31 (March 1974): 34.

BLEIER, T. J., AND DAVID REAMS. "An Approach to Developing Physical Fitness As an Integral Part of the Physical Education Program," *The Physical Educator* 25 (December 1968): 164–167.

BOCKHOLT, JACK L. "Jungle Time at Westwood School," *Journal of Physical Education and Recreation* 46 (October 1975): 39.

BODLEY, DEAN. "Build an Obstacle Course," *The Physical Educator* 27 (October 1970): 123–24.

BOLT, MARTHA LYNN. "Softball for the Blind Student," *Journal of Health, Physical Education, Recreation* 41 (June 1970): 40.

BOND, GREGORY. "An Adapted Surfing Device," *Journal of Health, Physical Education, Recreation* 46 (September 1975): 57–58.

BOTWIN, LOUIS. "The Media Approach, A Happening in Physical Education," *The Physical Educator* 25 (October 1968): 116–119.

BRESETT, STEPHEN M. "Physical Education in an Inexpensive Classroom," *Journal of Health, Physical Education, Recreation* 42 (May 1971): 54.

"Broad Front." *Journal of Health, Physical Education, Recreation* 38 (November–December 1967): 10–12.

BROWN, RONALD. "Scoop Ball," *Journal of Health, Physical Education, Recreation* 43 (May 1972): 74.

BUCHER, CHARLES A., ed. *Dimensions of Physical Education,* 2d ed. St. Louis: The C. V. Mosby Company, 1974.

BUCHER, CHARLES A., AND MYRA GOLDMAN, eds. *Dimensions of Physical Education.* St. Louis: The C. V. Mosby Company, 1969.

BUDD, BERTEL. "Using Flannel Board and Chalk Board to Teach Square Dance," *Journal of Health, Physical Education, Recreation* 41 (November–December 1970): 78.

BUELL, CHARLES. "Is Vigorous Physical Activity Feasible for Blind Children in Public Schools?" *Journal of Health, Physical Education, Recreation* 40 (February 1969): 97–98.

BUELL, CHARLES. "Physical Education for Visually Handicapped Children," *Journal of Health, Physical Education, Recreation* 42 (April 1971): 63–64.

BULL, FRED T. "Audiovisual Variety for Boys' Classes," *Journal of Health, Physical Education, Recreation* 39 (May 1968): 35.

BURCH, JAY, AND MARCELLA RIDENOUR. "How to make a Good Cargo Net," *The Physical Educator* 32 (March 1975): 17–19.

CABLE, LOUIS A."The Blind 'See' the World of Nature on the Braille Trail," *Journal of Health, Physical Education, Recreation* 43 (January 1972): 85.

CARLSON, RONALD C. "Mini-Lessons and the Videotape Recorder," *The Physical Educator* 31 (May 1974): 102.

CARTER, JOEL W. *How to Make Athletic Equipment.* New York: The Ronald Press Company, 1960.

CASKEY, SHELIA. "Bounce-Jungle Volleyball," *Journal of Health, Physical Education, Recreation* 42 (September 1971): 83.

CELTMEKS, VINCE. "Scoops," *Journal of Health, Physical Education, Recreation* 42 (September 1971): 83–84.

CHALLENGES, CRAIG. "Balance Challenges," *Journal of Physical Education and Recreation* 46 (March 1975): 63–64.

CHAMBERLAIN, JAMES R. "Disney World in an Open Gym," *Journal of Physical Education and Recreation* 46 (May 1975): 43–44.

CHAOSUKO, QUANCHAI, AND DAVID A. FIELD. "TAKRAW Off-Season Sport for Soccer Teams," *The Physical Educator* 26 (March 1969): 41–43.

CHESKA, ALYCE. "Paper Clips Make Inexpensive Team Markers," *Journal of Health, Physical Education, Recreation* 39 (September 1969): 86.

CHEVRETTE, J. M. "Flickerball," *Journal of Physical Education and Recreation* 46 (January 1975): 47–48.

CITRIN, STUART. "Water Baseball," *Journal of Health, Physical Education, Recreation* 45 (March 1974): 83.

CITRON, LESTER. "Tin Cans and Blind Kids," *Journal of Health, Physical Education, Recreation* 42 (April 1971): 64.

COATES, EDWARD. "Modular Design for Activity Spaces in the Physical Education-Intramural Complex," *Journal of Physical Education and Recreation* 46 (April 1975): 30–32.

COFFEY, ROBERT H. "Instructional T-V," *Journal of Health, Physical Education, Recreation* 39 (May 1968): 33.

COLLINS, DON. "Whiffleminton—Game of the Future?" *Journal of Health, Physical Education, Recreation* 42 (February 1971): 61–62.

"Column-Free Membranous Fieldhouse." *Scholastic Coach* 44 (January 1975): 22–23.

COOK, TIFF E. "Crosseball," *Journal of Health, Physical Education, Recreation* 40 (November–December 1969): 54.

CORBIN, DAVID E. "Using Tires in the Physical Education Program," *The Physical Educator* 30 (May 1973): 100–101.

CORBIN, DAVID E., JOHN HANCOCK, AND MRS. BETTY PETTET. "Innovative Equipment for Teaching Tumbling," *The Physical Educator* 28 (December 1971): 287–288.

COSTELLO, JOHN A., AND CARLOS MOLINA. "Videotape for Training Intercollegiate Officials," *Journal of Physical Education and Recreation* 46 (September 1975): 37–38.

CRATTY, BRYANT J. *Learning About Human Behavior Through Active Games.* Englewood Cliffs, New Jersey: Prentice-Hall, Inc., 1975.

CUNNINGHAM, CRAIG. "Balance Challenges," *Journal of Physical Education and Recreation* 46 (March 1975): 63–64.

DARST, PAUL W. "Student Teacher Supervision with Audiovisual Equipment," *Journal of Physical Education and Recreation* 46 (September 1975): 35–36.

DAUER, VICTOR P., AND ROBERT P. PANGRAZI. *Dynamic Physical Education for Elementary School Children,* 5th ed. Minneapolis, Minnesota: Burgess Publishing Company, 1975.

DELMORE, FAYE J., AND GLENN A. GRUBER. "Adapted Table Tennis for Wheelchair Multi-Handicapped Individuals," *Journal of Health, Physical Education, Recreation* 45 (January 1974): 81.

DEL REY, PATRICIA. "Feedback Provided Through Video-Taped Display," *The Physical Educator* 29 (October 1972): 118–119.

DIEM, LISELOTT. "Ideas from Germany—Modern Apparatus for Elementary School Physical Education," *Journal of Health, Physical Education, Recreation* 41 (March 1970): 40–42.

DOHMANN, PAUL. "Water Fistball," *Journal of Health, Physical Education, Recreation* 37 (November–December 1966): 61.

DONNELLY, KEVEN. "Current Trends in Commercial Recreation," *Journal of Health, Physical Education, Recreation* (June 1973): 32–33, 40.

DUDAS, WILLIAM L. "Tire Games for Children," *Journal of Health, Physical Education, Recreation* 36 (March 1965): 61.

EDSON, THOMAS. "Physical Education: A Substitute for Hypersensitivity and Violence," *Journal of Health, Physical Education, Recreation* (September 1969): pp. 79–81.

ELLIS, M. J. "Play, Practice and Research in the 1970s," *Journal of Health, Physical Education, Recreation* 43 (June 1972): 29–31.

ENDRES, RICHARD. "Northern Minnesota Therapeutic Camp," *Journal of Health, Physical Education, Recreation* 42 (May 1971): 75–76.

ETKES, ASHER B. "Therapeutic Playgrounds," *Journal of Health, Physical Education, Recreation* 44 (November–December 1973): 56–57.

FIELD, DAVID A., AND DAVID M. SILVERTONE. "P-E and A-V Join Hands," *The Physical Educator* 19 (October 1962): 101–103.

FLINCHUM, BETTY M. *Motor Development in Early Childhood.* St. Louis: The C. V. Mosby Company, 1975.

FLOYD, WILLIAM A., AND PHILIP K. WILLSON. "Using Videotape in Skeletal System Study," *Journal of Health, Physical Education, Recreation* 41 (April 1970): 81–82.

FLYNN, RICHARD B. "Sequential Planning of Facilities on a Landlocked Campus," *Journal of Physical Education and Recreation* 46 (April 1975): 23–24.

FOSTER, JERRY. "Frisbee Baseball," *Journal of Health, Physical Education, Recreation* 40 (November–December 1969): 50.

FREDERICK, A. BRUCE. "The 'That's It' Response and Audiovisual Instruction in Physical Education," *Journal of Health, Physical Education, Recreation* 44 (April 1973): 30–33.

FREDERICK, JOSEPH. "Ropes for Wheelchairs," *Journal of Health, Physical Education, Recreation* 42 (March 1971): 50.

FREISCHLAG, JERRY, AND RICK McCARTHY. "Community-University Cooperative Physical Education Programming for the Retarded," *The Physical Educator* 32 (March 1975): 11–13.

FROST, REUBEN B. "What Will Physical Education Be Like in 1977?" *Journal of Health, Physical Education, Recreation* 39 (March 1968): 34–35.

FROST, REUBEN B. *Physical Education: Foundations, Practices, Principles.* Reading, Massachusetts: Addison-Wesley Publishing Company, 1975.

FROST, REUBEN B. *Shaping Up to Quality in Physical Education.* Old Saybrook, Connecticut: Physical Education Publications, 1974.

GALLAHUE, DAVID L. *Developmental Play Equipment: For Home and School.* New York: John Wiley & Sons, Inc., 1975.

GALLAHUE, DAVID, AND WILLIAM J. MEADOWS. *Let's Move a Physical Education Program for Elementary School Teachers.* Dubuque, Iowa: Kendall/Hunt Publishing Company, 1974.

GANS, MARVIN. "Providing for Low-Cost, Multiple Use, Community-College Facilities for Physical Activity," *Journal of Physical Education and Recreation* 46 (April 1975): 27–28.

GLASS, HENRY. *Exploring Movements.* Freeport, N.Y.: Educational Activities, 1966.

GOOD, LARRY A., AND JACQUELINN F. OXFORD. "SRS: A Dynamic Tool for Learning," *Journal of Health, Physical Education, Recreation* 45 (April 1974): 53–54.

GORES, HAROLD B. "Community Education: Schoolhouse of the Future," *Journal of Health, Physical Education, Recreation* 45 (April 1974): 53–54.

GRANZA, ANTHONY. "A Measured Approach to Improvement of Play Environments," *Journal of Health, Physical Education, Recreation* 43 (June 1972): 43.

GREENBERG, JERROLD S. "How Videotaping Improves Teaching Behavior," *Journal of Health, Physical Education, Recreation* 44 (March 1973): 35–36.

GRIFFIN, BUDDY, AND EDDIE FRANCIS. *Tug-O-Rope.* By the Authors, Dept. of Physical Education and Athletics, Second Baptist School, Houston, Texas. 1974.

GRIFFIN, FRANK. "Don't Throw Those Bats Away," *The Physical Educator* 19 (May 1962): 59–60.

GROSSE, SUSAN J. "Physically Handicapped Children Use the Stegel," *Journal of Health, Physical Education, Recreation* 43 (June 1972) : 71–72.

GROVE, FRANCES, AND YVONNE WEBER. "Aquatic Therapy: A Real First Step to Rehabilitation," *Journal of Health, Physical Education, Recreation* 41 (October 1971): 65–66.

GROVES, RICHARD, AND DOUGLAS O. WARDELL. "A Videotaped Lecture Series," *The Physical Educator* 31 (May 1974): 97–98.

HACKETT, LAYNE C., AND ROBERT G. JENSON. *A Guide to Movement Exploration.* Palo Alto, California: Peek Publications, 1966.

HANLEY, JOHN B., AND ELDON J. ULLMER. *Educational Media and the Teacher.* Dubuque, Iowa: Wm. C. Brown Company Publishers, 1970.

HANSON, ROBERT F. "Playgrounds Designed for Adventure," *Journal of Health, Physical Education, Recreation* 40 (May 1969): 34–36.

HARTMAN, JOYCE. "Skin Diving is Relevant," *Journal of Health, Physical Education, Recreation* 41 (February 1970): 83–84.

HAVEL, RICHARD C. "An Urban University Builds for Physical Education and Recreation," *Journal of Health, Physical Education, Recreation* 40 (October 1969): 27–31.

HEITZMANN, WILLIAM RAY. "Ecology and Teaching Physical Education," *The Physical Educator* 31 (March 1974): 35.

HELMICK, ROBERT. "Water Polo," *Journal of Health, Physical Education, Recreation* 43 (May 1972): 24–30.

HENDERSON, JOE M. "An Innovation in Higher Education," *The Physical Educator* 25 (December 1968): 150–151.

HENRY, HANS. "Scooter Games," *Journal of Physical Education and Recreation* 46 (October 1975): 42–43.

HERKOWITZ, JACQUELINE. "A Perceptual-Motor Training Program to Improve the Gross Motor Abilities of Preschoolers," *Journal of Health, Physical Education, Recreation* 41 (April 1970): 38–42.

HERMAN, WILLIAM L. "Using Bulletin Boards in Elementary Physical Education," *Journal of Health, Physical Education, Recreation* 40 (September 1969): 53.

HESS, ROLAND. "Floor Hockey," *Journal of Health, Physical Education, Recreation* 45 (September 1974): 67–68.

HICHWA, JOHN S. "The Cargo Net," *Journal of Health, Physical Education, Recreation* 41 (January 1970): 30–32.

HOLYOAK, OWEN J., GEORGE PROTROWSKI, ROBERT E. ALLEN, AND FRANK BRZEY-INSKI. "A Practical Device for Measuring Torque,' *Journal of Health, Physical Education, Recreation* 44 (April 1973): 75–76.

HOFFMAN, JONATHAN. "Are You Ready for Air Structures?" *College Management* 8 (August–September 1973) : 25, 28–29.

HOWARD, SHIRLEY. "The Movement Education Approach to Teaching in English Elementary Schools," *Journal of Health, Physical Education, Recreation* 38 (January 1967): 30–33.

"H. S. GEODESIC DOMES: Efficient, Economical, Exciting," *Scholastic Coach* 45 (January 1976): 22–23, 78.

HUGHES, ERIC. "Video Tapes." *Journal of Health, Physical Education, Recreation* 39 (May 1968): 36.

HUMPHREY, JAMES H. *Child Learning Through Elementary Physical Education.* Dubuque, Iowa: Wm. C. Brown Company Publishers, 1965.

"I Can." *Journal of Health, Physical Education, Recreation* 43 (May 1972): 33.

"Iceless Ice Skating." *Parks and Recreation* (May 1972): pp. 41, 75.

"Idaho's Roll-On Football Field." *Scholastic Coach* 43 (January 1974): 30, 32.

INGRAM, ANNE G. "Children with Impaired Vision Are 'Seeing' through Touch," *Journal of Health, Physical Education, Recreation* 40 (February 1969): 95–97.

JACK, MARTHA. "Cycling," *Journal of Health, Physical Education, Recreation* 43 (June 1972): 20–24.

JACOBSON, STAN. " 'Ideas' Pamphlets," *Journal of Physical Education and Recreation* 46 (January 1975): 57–58.

JENSEN, CLAYNE R. "Designed for a Complete Program," *Journal of Health, Physical Education, Recreation* 39 (September 1968): 27–29.

JENSEN, CLAYNE R. "An Activity Center for both Athletic Events and Cultural Events," *Journal of Physical Education and Recreation* 46 (April 1975) : 28–29.

JENSEN, TERRY. "Creative Ropes," *Journal of Health, Physical Education, Recreation* 42 (May 1971): 56–57.

JEWETT, ANN E. "Would You Believe Public Schools 1975?" *Journal of Health, Physical Education, Recreation* 42 (March 1971): 41–44.

JOHNSON, BARRY L. "A Strike Practice Machine for Badminton, Tennis, and Volleyball," *Journal of Health, Physical Education, Recreation* 44 (November–December 1973): 70–71.

JOHNSON, LEO J. "Parachute Play for Exercise," *Journal of Health, Physical Education, Recreation* 38 (April 1967): 26–27.

JOHNSON, WALTER A. "The Nielsen Tennis Stadium," *Journal of Health, Physical Education, Recreation,* 41 (May, 1970): 36–37.

JOHNSON, WILLIAM P. "Cycling for Fitness at Brookdale," *Journal of Health, Physical Education, Recreation* 45 (September 1974) : 96–97.

JOHNSON, WILLIAM P., AND RICHARD P. KLEVA. "The Community Dimension of College Physical Education," *Journal of Health, Physical Education, Recreation* 44 (April 1973): 40–41.

JOHNSON, WILLIS. "Plastic Traffic Cone," *Journal of Health, Physical Education, Recreation* 36 (May 1965): 70.

JORDAN, BARBARA JEAN. "Teaching Tips for Fins, Snorkle, and Mask," *Journal of Health, Physical Education, Recreation* 43 (September 1972): 87–88.

KAESGEN, NANCY CHISHOLM, AND CHERYL PINCOMBE. "A Junior High Course," *Journal of Health, Physical Education, Recreation* 45 (September 1974): 94–95.

KAHRS, KAROL ANNE. "Cassette Tapes: A Medium for Personal Feedback and Learning," *The Physical Educator* 31 (October 1974) : 159–161.

KEITH, J. ARTHUR. "How Coaches Teach," *The Physical Educator* 24 (December 1967): 162.

KELLER, RUSS. "Elementary School Tumbling Program," *Journal of Health, Physical Education, Recreation* 37 (November–December 1966): 61.

KELLOGG, C. L. "Batting Tee," *Journal of Health, Physical Education, Recreation* 36 (May 1965): 70.

KENNISON, JAMES E. "Saf-Space Golf Ball," *Journal of Health, Physical Education, Recreation* 39 (March 1968): 61.

KRAMER, NOEL. "Quick Ideas," *Journal of Physical Education and Recreation* 46 (October 1975): 40.

KRAUS, RICHARD. *Therapeutic Recreation Service: Principles and Practices.* Philadelphia: W. B. Saunders Company, 1973.

KUGAN, THOMAS F. "A New Safety Device," *Journal of Health, Physical Education, Recreation* 41 (November–December 1970) : 79–80.

LANDERS, BARBARA, AND JAMES W. RAGANS. "Revitalizing a Country-Wide Program," *Journal of Health, Physical Education, Recreation* 42 (September 1971): 38–39.

LAROWE, ESTHER. "Loop Films for Elementary School," *Journal of Health, Physical Education, Recreation* 39 (May 1968): 34, 65.

LAYMAN, RICHARD G. "The Value of Two Man Volleyball," *Journal of Health, Physical Education, Recreation* 41 (November–December 1970): 81.

LEACH, JOHN. "Western Illinois University Shares Facilities and Staff with Inner-City Youngsters," *Journal of Health, Physical Education, Recreation* 41 (March 1970): 34.

LEIGHTON, JACK R. "Simplified Scoring in the Jump-Reach," *Journal of Health, Physical Education, Recreation* 32 (October 1966): 57.

LEIGHTY, JAMES C. "Recreation Break," *Journal of Health, Physical Education, Recreation* 38 (May 1967) : 23–24.

LENTZ, ROBERT R. *Adventure Curriculum: Physical Education.* Hamilton, Massachusetts: Project Adventure, 1974.

LORENZ, FLOYD. "Things You've Always Wanted to Do in Class but Were Afraid to Try," *Journal of Physical Education and Recreation* 46 (June 1975): 38.

LUCK, K. CASH, AND MARGARET NEWMAN. "Physical Education Goes Mod," *Journal of Health, Physical Education, Recreation* 41 (March 1970): 44–45.

MACKEY, RICHARD T. "Sports Skills Lessons on Television," *Journal of Health, Physical Education, Recreation* 39 (May 1968): 31–32, 85.

MACKEY, RICHARD T. "Hula Hoop Golf," *Journal of Health, Physical Education, Recreation* 44 (March 1973): 83–84.

MANN, ALBERT. "Rope," *Journal of Physical Education and Recreation* 46 (October 1975): 39–40.

MARTIN, ROBERT A., AND STANLEY J. HIPWOOD. "Eight Minutes for Fitness," *Journal of Health, Physical Education, Recreation* 36 (November–December 1965) : 63–64.

MASIK, DON. "Innertube Water Polo," *Journal of Health, Physical Education, Recreation* 45 (September 1974): 90.

MATTHEWS, DAVID O. "The University of Illinois Plans an Intramural-Physical Education Building," *Journal of Health, Physical Education, Recreation* 39 (April 1968): 33–36.

MAWSON, L. MARLENE. "The Truth About Saunas," *Journal of Health, Physical Education, Recreation* 45 (June 1974): 22–23.

MAYER, FRANK C, AND JOHN J. GRANT. "Operation Self-Image," *Journal of Health, Physical Education, Recreation* 43 (May 1972): 64–65.

McBRIDE, ROBERT. "Halloween Masks and Perceptual Motor Activities," *Journal of Physical Education and Recreation* 46 (September 1975): 51.

McCARTY, JIM. "Throw and Go Net Ball," *Journal of Health, Physical Education, Recreation* 40 (November–December 1969) : 52–53.

McCLURE, BETSY. "Tenneyball," *Journal of Health, Physical Education, Recreation* 43 (May 1972): 73.

McKINNEY, WAYNE C. "Answers for the Physical Educator," *Journal of Health, Physical Education, Recreation* 43 (May 1972): 49–51.

McNULTY, BARBARA DEVELIN. "The Fashion Predicament for Women Teachers," *Journal of Health, Physical Education, Recreation* 41 (October 1970): 41.

MEAGHER, MARY E. "Balance Board Activities," *Journal of Health, Physical Education, Recreation* 44 (November–December 1973): 71–72.

MEDITCH, CARL. "Physical Educators Plan Facilities," *Journal of Health, Physical Education, Recreation* 45 (January 1974): 32–33.

METZGER, PAUL A., ed. *Elementary School Physical Education Readings.* Dubuque, Iowa: Wm. C. Brown Company Publishers, 1972.

MEYER, LINDA A., AND SHELLEY RUCK. "They Too Can Shoot an Arrow into the Air," *Journal of Health, Physical Education, Recreation* 45 (January 1974) : 79.

MILLAN, ANNE F. "Polaroid-Land Goes to Class," *The Physical Educator* 18 (December 1961): 141.

MILLAN, ANNE. "An Open Gym," *Journal of Health, Physical Education, Recreation* 43 (May 1972): 40.

MILLER, JOHN G. "Biffball," *Journal of Health, Physical Education, Recreation* 36 (March 1965): 60.

MIN, KYUNG H. "Trithlon (Kyuk-Ki-Do)" *Journal of Health, Physical Education, Recreation* 44 (March 1973): 84–85.

MITCHELL, HEIDIE. "Walkie-Talkie Approach to Supervision," *Journal of Health, Physical Education, Recreation* 44 (March 1973): 38–39.

MOOLENIJZER, NICOLAAS J. "Korfball-An International Game of Dutch Origin," *Journal of Health, Physical Education, Recreation* 42 (February 1971): 22–25.

MOORE, JANE B., ALETHA W. BOND AND JANE COBB. "Playgrounds: An Experience Center for Elementary Physical Education," *Journal of Physical Education and Recreation* 46 (January 1975): 21–23.

MORRIS, GORDON. "Background Color: A Limiting Factor," *Journal of Physical Education and Recreation* 46 (June 1975): 8.

MURRAY, J. RALPH. "Huge Sports Complex Has Everything," *American School & University* 46 (June 1974): 24–28.

NAYLOR, JAY H. "Honey and Milk Toast," *Journal of Physical Education and Recreation* 46 (September 1975): 18–19.

NEWMAN, JUNY. "Swimming for the Spina Bifida," *Journal of Health, Physical Education, Recreation* 41 (October 1970): 67–68.

NIXON, JOHN E., AND ANN E. JEWETT. *An Introduction to Physical Education.* 8th ed. Philadelphia: W. B. Saunders Company, 1974.

O'DONNELL, CORNELIUS R. "Carry Over Physical Education in Elementary School," *Journal of Health, Physical Education, Recreation* 44 (January 1973): 69–71.

OLIVER, JAMES N. "Blindness and the Child's Sequence of Development," *Journal of Health, Physical Education, Recreation* 41 (June 1970): 37–39.

OLSON, GARETH. "Creative Guidelines for Using Multi-Purpose Sports Facilities," *Journal of Physical Education and Recreation* 46 (April 1975): 33–34.

O'SHEA, JOHN PATRICK. "Mountaineering Survival," *Journal of Health, Physical Education, Recreation* 43 (May 1972): 36–39.

PALMER, LES. "Don't Throw in the Towel—Use It," *The Physical Educator* 29 (March 1972): 45–46.

PARKER, MARTHA T. "Field Too Wet for Field Hockey?" *Journal of Health, Physical Education, Recreation* 42 (February 1971): 62–63.

PASTOR, GEORGE. "Student-Designed," *Journal of Health, Education, Recreation* 42 (September 1971): 30–31.

PEAKE, LES "Tchouk-Ball for the Middle School Years," *Journal of Health, Physical Education, Recreation* 44 (March 1973): 83.

PEARLMAN, STUART. "Plastic Baseball Throwing Machine," *Journal of Health, Physical Education, Recreation* 41 (November-December 1970): 76–78.

PEASE, DEAN A., AND DARRELL CRASE. "Commitment to Change," *Journal of Health, Physical Education, Recreation* 44 (April 1973): 34–37.

PEERY, ANN JOHNETTE. "Teaching Circus," *Journal of Health, Physical Education, Recreation* 41 (October 1970): 36–40.

PENNINGTON, G. "Equipment Which Should Be Found in Every Gymnasium," *The Physical Educator* 22 (December 1966): 173–174.

PETTIT, MILTON H. "Physical Education for Orthopedically Handicapped Children," *Journal of Health, Physical Education, Recreation* 42 (February 1971): 75–78.

*Physical Activities for the Mentally Retarded: Ideas for Instruction.* AAHPER. Washington, D.C.: NEA Publications-Sales, 1968.

"Physical Efficiency Laboratory at University of Guelph," *Journal of Health Physical Education, Recreation* 40 (February 1969): 106.

*Physical Recreation Facilities.* New York: Educational Facilities Laboratories, 1973.

PITCHER, LYNN. "Tumbling Made Easy on the Tube," *Journal of Health, Physical Education, Recreation* 36 (May 1965): 72.

PISCOPO, JOHN. "Videotape Laboratory: A Programmed Instructional Sequence," *Journal of Health, Physical Education, Recreation* 44 (March 1973): 32–35.

PISCOPO, JOHN, AND STEPHANIE BENNETT. "Television Appied to the Study of Human Motor Performance," *The Physical Educator* 30 (March 1973): 35–37.

"Plastic Snow." *Parks and Recreation* (May 1972): 41.

POINDEXTER, HOLLY B. W. "Motor Development and Performance of Emotionally Disturbed Children," *Journal of Health, Physical Education, Recreation* 40 (June 1969): 69–71.

POND, PAT, "Elementary School Cycling," *Journal of Health, Physical Education, Recreation* 45 (September 1974): 93–94.

PORTER, CHARLES MACK. "Boardless Basketball," *Journal of Health, Physical Education, Recreation* 40 (November–December 1969): 53.

PUCKETT, JOHN. "Two Promising Innovations in Physical Education Facilities," *Journal of Health, Physical Education, Recreation* 43 (January, 1972): 40.

RANKIN, KELLY. "Make Use of Blacktops and Sidewalks," *Journal of Health, Physical Education, Recreation* 41 (October 1970): 60–61.

RASMUS, CAROLYN. "The Creative Playground," *Journal of Health, Physical Education, Recreation* 40 (January 1969): 40.

REID, JUDITH SHOTWELL. "A High School Cycling Program," *Journal of Health, Physical Education, Recreation* 44 (November–December 1973): 13–14.

REID, J. GAVIN. "Muscles in Action: Use of Videotape and Electromyography," *Journal of Health, Physical Education, Recreation* 42 (September 1971): 61–62.

RESICK, MATTHEW C., AND CARL E. ERICKSON. *Intercollegiate and Interscholastic Athletics for Men and Women.* Reading, Massachusetts: Addison-Wesley Publishing Company, 1975.

RIDENOUR, MARCELLA V. "Playgrounds: Equipment from Recycled Materials," *Journal of Health, Physical Education, and Recreation* 46 (January 1975): 24–25.

ROBERTS, FRANK. "Rollerboard Hockey," *Journal of Health, Physical Education, Recreation* 40 (November–December 1969): 51.

ROURKE, R. J. "A Share of Summer Fun," *Journal of Health, Physical Education, Recreation* 42 (May 1971): 71–72.

RUPNOW, ALLAN A. "Ladders in Elementary Physical Education," *Journal of Health, Physical Education, Recreation* 42 (May 1971): 57.

SALLIN, CRAIG. "Team Handball," *Journal of Health, Physical Education, Recreation* 41 (March 1970): 46–47.

SCARNATI, RICHARD ALFRED. "Special Olympics," *Journal of Health, Physical Education, Recreation* 43 (February 1972): 49–50.

SCHROEDER, CHARLES ROY. "A New Look at Boxing for Physical Education," *The Physical Educator* 31 (May 1974): 103–105.

SCHUMACHER, JAMES. "Homemade Games and Equipment," *Journal of Physical Education and Recreation* 46 (October 1975): 40–42.

SCHURR, EVELYN L. *Movement Experiences for Children: A Humanistic Approach to Elementary School Physical Education.* 2d ed. Englewood Cliffs, New Jersey: Prentice-Hall, Inc., 1975.

SCOTT, ROBERT S., AND WILLIAM B. MEISER. "Portable Climbing Apparatus," *Journal of Health, Physical Education, Recreation* 44 (March 1973): 61.

SEIDEL, BEVERLY L., AND MATTHEW C. RESICK. *Physical Education: An Overview.* Reading, Massachusetts: Addison-Wesley Publishing Company, 1972.

SHARMAN, JAMES E. "A Physical Education Plant Concept to Provide Greater Flexibility at Minimum Cost," *Journal of Physical Education and Recreation* 46 (April 1975): 25–26.

SCHRADER, ROBERT D. "Individualized Approach to Learning," *Journal of Health, Physical Education, Recreation* 42 (September 1971): 33–36.

SIEDENTOP, DARYL. *Physical Education: Introductory Analysis.* Dubuque, Iowa: Wm. C. Brown Company Publishers, 1972.

SLAUGHTER, C. H., AND ROBERT IRVING. "Physical Fitness for 72¢," *The Physical Educator* 22 (October 1965): 115–116.

SLAUGHTER, MARY. "Racquet Ball," *Journal of Health, Physical Education, Recreation* 45 (September 1974): 66.

SMATHERS, KEENE, AND LESTER VAN GILDER. "Experiences for Future Teachers," *Journal of Health, Physical Education, Recreation* 45 (May 1974): 77–78.

SMITH, LARRY. "Three Team Volleyball," *Journal of Health, Physical Education, Recreation* 42 (February 1971): 59.

SMITH, CHARLES D., AND SAMUEL PRATHER. "Group Problem Solving," *Journal of Physical Education and Recreation* 46 (September 1975): 20–21.

SNYDER, DENNIS R. "There's Always Another Way!" *Journal of Health, Physical Education, Recreation* 42 (May 1971): 57.

SOL, NEIL, AND LINDA ZWIREN. "Fencing for Quadraplegics," *Journal of Health, Physical Education, Recreation* 45 (January 1974): 79–81.

"South Adams Double Decked Gym Plant." *Scholastic Coach* 44 (January 1975): 18–19.

SQUIRES, RICHARD C. "Platform Tennis," *Journal of Health, Physical Education, Recreation* 44 (March 1973): 85.

STANLEY, PHILIP L. "Implementing Off-Campus Activities," *Journal of Health, Physical Education, Recreation* 45 (June 1974): 16–18.

STEVENSON, MICHAEL J. "Ringette," *Journal of Health, Physical Education, Recreation* 45 (September 1974): 66.

STONE, HARRIET FORKEY. "The Case Against Sneakers," *Journal of Health, Physical Education, Recreation* 42 (May 1971): 26.

STONE, WILLIAM J., AND VICTOR A. BUCCOLA. "A Cycling Program for Senior Citizens," *Journal of Health, Physical Education, Recreation* 45 (September 1974): 97–98.

TANNER, PATRICIA. "Film Loops for Elementary School Physical Education," *Journal of Health, Physical Education, Recreation* 41 (June 1970) : 51–52.

"The Elmira Story: Three Geodesic Domes and a Natatorium." *Scholastic Coach* 44 (January 1975): 21–22, 80.

THEIBERT, DICK. "Instant Fieldhouse Answer to Title IX," *Scholastic Coach* 43 (June 1974): 40.

THEIBERT, DICK. "Coming On (and Going Up) Fast!" *Scholastic Coach* 43 (January 1974): 14–15, 98–99.

THOMAS, JERRY R., AND DOYICE J. COTTON. "Are Elementary School Rhythms Dying in the South?" *The Physical Educator* 28 (December 1971): 214–217.

THOMPSON, BOB. "Intramural Game of the Week Televised," *Journal of Health, Physical Education, Recreation* 45 (May 1974) : 67–68.

TOMAN, THOMAS G. "New Equipment Features Horizontal Ropes," *Journal of Health, Physical Education, Recreation* 44 (March 1973): 61.

TREMONTI, JOSEPH B., AND MURIEL REINGRUBER. "Kankakee State Hospital Summer Camping Program," *Journal of Health, Physical Education, Recreation* 43 (May 1972): 77–78.

TRERMAN, RICHARD. "Climbing Poles in Physical Education Programs," *Journal of Health, Physical Education, Recreation* 42 (February 1971): 60–61.

VANNIER, MARY HELEN, MILDRED FOSTER, AND DAVID L. GALLAHUE. *Teaching Physical Education in Elementary Schools,* 5th ed. Philadelphia: W. B. Saunders Company, 1971.

VANNIER, MARY HELEN et al. *Teaching Physical Education in Secondary Schools.* 4th ed. Philadelphia: W. B. Saunders Company, 1975.

WAGNER, PAT. "Stretching Your Way to Fitness," *Journal of Physical Education and Recreation* 46 (March 1975): 65.

WASEM, JIM. "Indoor Speedball," *Journal of Health, Physical Education, Recreation* 43 (May 1972): 73–74.

WATTS, JOAN, AND DAVID WIENER. "Learning in the Gymnasium," *Journal of Physical Education and Recreation* 46 (March 1975) : 64–65.

WEBB, WELLINGTON. "Physical Education Classes for the Emotionally Disturbed Child," *Journal of Health, Physical Education, Recreation* 42 (May 1972): 79–81.

WEBER, JOHN D. "Motivational Wizard," *Journal of Health, Physical Education, Recreation* 44 (April 1973): 50–54.

WEISS, STEVEN A. "Wall-Ball," *Journal of Health, Physical Education, Recreation* 39 (September 1968): 86–87.

WEINER, GEORGE. "Self-Testing Circuits for Primary Grades," *Journal of Health, Physical Education, Recreation* 37 (November–December 1966): 61–62.

WEINER, PETER. "Physical Education During the Pre-School Years," *The Physical Educator* 29 (December 1972): 180–183.

WEINER, PETER H., AND RICHARD A. SIMMONS. *Do It Yourself: Creative Movement with Innovative Physical Education Equipment.* Dubuque, Iowa: Kendall/Hunt Publishing Company, 1973.

WHITLOW, GARRY. "Elementary Circuit Training," *Journal of Health, Physical Education, Recreation* 39 (May 1968) : 26–27.

"Why Won't the Bubble Burst?" *College Management* 8 (September 1973): 28–29.

WICKSTROM, RALPH L. "Le Beanbag, Tres Bien," *The Physical Educator* 29 (December 1972): 209–211.

WILLIAMSON, BOB. "Hidden Treasure in Your Refrigerator," *Journal of Health, Physical Education, Recreation* 41 (September 1970): 77–79.

WILSON, PHILIP K. "Bell Ball," *Journal of Health, Physical Education, Recreation* 40 (November–December 1969): 52.

WIRTANEN, WILLIAM. "Course for First Aid Instructors," *Journal of Health, Physical Education, Recreation* 42 (March 1971) : 71.

"W. I. U.'s Dream P. E. Facility for Women," *Scholastic Coach* 46 (January 1976): 24–25.

WOLVEN, BARRY. "Homemade Scoop Ball," *Journal of Health, Physical Education, Recreation* 42 (February 1971): 59–60.

WRIGHT, BETTY. "The Wedde Handiswimmers," *Journal of Health, Physical Education, Recreation* 41 (October 1970): 69–70.

WRIGHT, KATHRYN, AND JOY WALKER. "Rainy Day Golf," *Journal of Health, Physical Education, Recreation* 40 (November–December 1969): 83.

YARBER, WILLIAM L. "High School Health Students Conduct Elementary Bicycle Safety Rodeo," *Journal of Health, Physical Education, Recreation* 41 (September 1970): 32.

XANTHOS, PAUL. "Instructional Aids," *Journal of Health, Physical Education, Recreation* 45 (May 1974) : 38–39.

ZEZULA, PATRICIA. "Cycling and Camping in Florida," *Journal of Health, Physical Education, Recreation* 45 (September 1974): 95.

# 11

## How Do We Help Others by Providing Leadership and Developing Organizations for Human Movement?

*Linda Zaichkowsky*

In all professions, especially teaching, one of the main considerations is helping others—whether it be by guiding children toward adulthood, teaching basic skills, or helping others to achieve their own potential. When the educational concern deals with the movement phenomena, the goals are the same only the medium is different.

People involved in teaching Human Movement need to be able to provide leadership, not only to their students, but to peers, administrators, and community residents. This means that knowledge of leadership is an important consideration in the preparation of those people who teach Human Movement.

## THE PROCESS OF LEADERSHIP

The process of leadership can be thought of as an influence relationship among group members. It involves the leader, the followers (members of the group) and the situations (group goals) [Hollander (1).] The leader is the group member who exercises the most influence over the group or the person who influences more than is influenced. Some authors feels that the legitimate process of leadership is applicable only when it is voluntarily accepted and when the goal is shared by all group members [Gibb (2).] This would exclude the teacher-pupil or officer-enlisted personnel relationship in which the direction of the group is generally determined by the "person in charge" who is appointed rather than selected by the group. Regardless of whether this distinction of leadership is semantic or real, for our purposes we will assume that a teacher can be a leader even though teachers are placed "in charge" by an outside authority (i.e., community, school board, principal).

## Leadership Behavior

*Leader behaviors are central to the concept of leadership.* The work of Hemphill and Coons (3) and other researchers (4, 5) broke down the process of leadership into various factors contributing to the effective functioning of the group; i.e., the accomplishment of the goal or task of the group and factors concerned with group morale. A more complete explanation of this research is presented by Halpin (6).

Historically, two factors were recognized as basic for effective leadership. These were called "Consideration" and "Initiating Structure." The person who is high in consideration is concerned with the social-emotional climate of the group or the personal processes that are occurring within the group (morale). The person who is high in initiating structure is generally concerned with achieving the group goals by maintaining positions and functions and setting up procedures that assure that tasks are accomplished. This person is assumed to have the physical or intellectual capacity to accomplish the task of the group. Belcher (7) refers to these two basic leadership functions as process oriented and task oriented.

In many large groups, particularly complex organizations, these two functions (consideration and initiating structure or process and task orientation) may be carried out by two different people. For instance, a large school district may have a performance (goal) minded superintendent, and various principals in the organization who maintain the necessary personal relationship with teachers. In a classroom situation these two functions are commonly assumed by one person, the teacher. This means that an effective teacher should be concerned not only with the accomplishment of certain goals but also with understanding the difficulties students have in realizing those goals.

## Leadership Functions

*The leader performs various functions for the group.* Some of the details with which a leader needs to be concerned are establishing or facilitating the goals of the group, establishing structure and organization for the group to accomplish goals, providing resources so that the goals may be accomplished, and determining future directions for the group. Let us take a specific situation and determine how a leader might perform these functions.

Let us assume that there is a coeducational physical education class of 30 ninth-grade students who are involved in a unit on volleyball. In this group there is a range of abilities from very good to mediocre to poor. How should a teacher deal with this situation?

One of the first functions of the leader (teacher) is to facilitate the group process. Whatever the goal(s) of the group, whether established by the teacher without student input or by teacher-student decision making, the person in charge should help the group accomplish the goal(s). In this particular situation the teacher should establish what the students would like to accomplish and combine these wishes with his or her professional knowledge of the essential aspects of volleyball. This should result in a determination of what should have been learned at the conclusion of the unit on volleyball. In this case the ultimate goal might be learning the necessary skills of volleyball so that the students would be able to compete in a tournament.

The teacher needs to provide some type of structure for the students to learn the game. After deciding what skills need to be taught, the teacher must establish some type of procedure for instruction.

The leader must provide the sequence of instruction for the requisite skills, organize the class into appropriate proficiency groups to facilitate learning, and display the necessary expertise in teaching the skills. These are only a few of the tasks that need to be taken care of to provide some type of structure or organization in order to facilitate the goal of the group (learning to play volleyball).

Even after the above decisions have been made, a unit will not be successful unless the teacher is able to motivate the students. As teachers, we attempt to structure learning situations that will convert extrinsic (external) motivation into intrinsic (internal) motivation. This means that participation in physical activity becomes rewarding in and of itself. Can we make learning drills interesting and exciting? Should modified games be introduced when only some of the basic skills have been learned? In other words, the teacher must use varied techniques to keep pupil motivation high.

The leader must also be able to provide the necessary resources so that the basic skills of volleyball can be mastered. Are there enough volleyballs? Is there adequate room in the gymnasium so that areas can be established to insure that all students are active? Are loop films or books desirable and if so are they readily accessible to the students? Teachers have to have adequate material available to promote skill acquisition.

After the teacher has created the proper learning environment and the immediate goals have been realized, there is a need to determine and set future directions. So the process starts again of determining goals and assisting in their consummation. Should another activity be learned? Should a higher level of skill be acquired? The leader is in a position to make these determinations and to help the group establish new goals or follow the goals which the teacher has already determined.

The teacher continues to lead not only because he or she is "in charge," but because the immediate goals of the group have been accomplished. The teacher has also established a good social-emotional climate in the class, an essential leadership activity. This climate enhances motivation and fosters positive attitudes which in turn can positively affect the morale of the group.

## Approaches to Leadership

*Leaders perform their functions differently.* There have been three basic approaches to the study of leaders and leadership. They have been evolutionary in nature. As the research techniques have become more sophisticated one approach has been substituted for a different one.

The first idea was that one could determine what a good leader was by the traits that leaders possessed. Researchers observed the leader in action and tried to make statements as to what characteristics or traits were common to all or most leaders. Such traits as height, weight, appearance, intelligence, and self-confidence were commonly assumed to be necessary characteristics for effective leadership. Stogdill (18) and Mann (20) concluded that intelligence was the one factor that had the highest relationship to leadership, although the relationship was not a very strong one. However, this line of inquiry did not find consistent traits that were exhibited by all leaders.

Then came the "situational approach." The basic premise was that the type of environment or situation that a group was in resulted in certain people becoming leaders. Change the situation and the leader might also change. In Human Movement we find that often people involved in the teaching and/or coaching of physical education are good leaders; however, when they assume positions of administrative responsibility outside the field they may become ineffective. The condition under which certain leadership techniques were effective (dealing with students) may no longer hold true (dealing with teachers and parents).

As research continued it was determined that the important element of group interaction had not been adequately taken into account. How does the relationship between all group members affect the leadership conditions and what effect do the relations between the leader and other group members have on the group? [Interested readers should see Whyte (8).]

In their classic study in 1939, Lewin, Lippitt, and White (9) looked at the "social climates" of groups. [Also see (10) and (11).] In a series of experiments they determined the effect of a democratic, autocratic, and laissez-faire leader upon group process. Each leader performed under all three social climates. The autocratic leader made all policy decisions, dictated the task, and assigned tasks and coworkers.

The democratic leader encouraged group discussion and decision making, outlined general steps to goals, and allowed free choice of coworkers. The laissez-faire leader allowed complete freedom for decision making, supplied materials, answered questions when asked, and did not participate in the group task.

The major conclusions reached by the investigators in regard to group process were:

1. Poorer quality and quantity of work was performed in the laissez-faire situations and the activities of the group were play oriented.

2. The tasks were performed adequately in the democratic situation, the work motivation was strong, and the group appeared to be more friendly and cohesive. Creativity was also fostered in the democratic group.

3. The greatest amount of work was produced in the autocratic situation, but some hostility and aggression by group members toward others also was created. Additionally, the group was dependent upon the leader.

Further research has supported the findings of these initial Iowa studies (12, 13), indicating that in a society a leader who uses the democratic style of leadership is more likely to keep morale high (group more friendly) as well as accomplish the task. The practical application of this style of leadership or teaching is clearly evident in the work of Mosston (14), Mancini, and Martinek (see Chap. 13).

## Leader-Follower Interactions

*Leaders lead and followers follow.* There are various relationships between leaders and followers. If a group views the leader as an appointed one (a position derived from a higher authority in the hierarchical structure), the power and authority of the leader are mandated by the organizational structure. A teacher placed in a position of authority (appointed) and viewed as the group leader by the students is perceived as having this power and is thereby able to exert influence over the class [see Raven

(15)]. According to Horwitz (16), the use of this power is considered legitimate by the students and does not arouse hostility as long as it does not violate the students' expectations of the teacher's role. Therefore, a group will be influenced by the teacher as long as the teacher stays within the role definition of a "teacher."

A coach is also viewed as an appointed leader, but the relationship between a "coach" and the team is somewhat different. The members of the groups more or less choose to be there voluntarily (the pressures to achieve social status through athletics notwithstanding [see Coleman (17)]. It is easier to establish a close personal relationship with the coach (head coach or the assistants) than with the teacher because of the cohesiveness of the group (team spirit). This relationship is established because the coach is trying to put together the basic skills for the proper execution of a sport and still maintain a personal concern for his players. An example of this type of behavior was exhibited by John Wooden, the former basketball coach for the UCLA Bruins [see Stogdill (18)]. The leader in this instance was in complete charge and insisted upon task success (practice and game situations) but was personally concerned about the players and their problems.

The relationships between an administrator and his staff is different still. In this situation a leader is working with peers. In order to be effective leaders, administrators must use the expertise of teachers to assist in the decision-making process. They consult with teachers, rely on their expertise, and determine policy. In addition, they are evaluated on the basis of their ability to adequately utilize the information available to them.

## Inadequate Leadership

*Lack of leadership will affect group functioning.* A group may splinter if it has poor or unpopular leadership that is unable to effectuate the goals of the group. One part of the group may form a different association to satisfy its needs. An example of this type of splintering occurred during the Reformation with the rise of Protestantism due to disenchantment with certain aspects of Catholicism.

A consequence of no leadership is extinction—a group or organization ceases to function because it no longer has a necessary function or a leader who can take charge. A radical group whose leader dies may go out of business because this person was the driving force behind the group. The cause the group has been fighting for has a tendency to disappear when the leader is changed.

A further consequence of inadequate leadership is stagnation or loss of productivity. When a group is unable to accomplish its goals but continues to exist, motivation to perform the tasks will decrease, and the product of that group declines. An athletic team with a high loss record and the inability to reach its goal of winning is an example: team members become frustrated. If the coach is unable to make any constructive changes, the team will continue its downward path and even perform worse. The team that fails to make progress will probably see its output, in terms of victories, decline.

A group faced with inadequate leadership probably should make a change in order to preserve the functioning of the group. This can be done in an orderly or disorderly fashion. A president of a country which is based on democratic principles can be replaced through the orderly governmental process of elections. A president can also be removed in a disorderly fashion (an assassination, a coup, or a revolution are examples), which will certainly result in change, perhaps even in chaos. In civilized societies, it is desirable to provide some process or system that allows for orderly change in leadership.

## Application of Leadership Theory

*Teachers and administrators in the field of human movement apply leadership theory.* As a result of the exploration by researchers of leadership and leadership behavior, we find that the trait and situational approach for studying leaders is no longer effective. The researchers are now investigating leader-follower behaviors of the group (interaction) and the leader behavior exhibited in groups. This approach requires that leadership be viewed as a multidimensional process involving the leader, the followers, and their behaviors in relation to one another.

A teacher is able to exert influence over the students in the classroom. However, in order to be an effective leader, the teacher must be able to set up adequate procedures and processes for the completion of objectives concerning the acquisition of knowledge and the development of each student's potential while complying with the policies and procedures established by the employing institution. In addition, the teacher should be a warm and empathetic person.

This relationship of task accomplishment and concern with the morale of the group is shown through the following model. The model illustrates relationships on two different levels.

| *Principal* | *Department head* | *Views effectiveness of leader as task accomplishment* |
|---|---|---|
| department head | teachers | appointed leader |
| teachers | students | views effectiveness of leader as showing consideration |

Regardless of how one applies the information about leadership and behavior, *"effective* leadership can be viewed as an influence process in which the leader achieves willing group support in the attainment of group goals" (1).

## THE DEVELOPMENT OF ORGANIZATIONS

*Organizations or structures evolve to serve large numbers of people.* When the automobile was first introduced, it was often manufactured by one person or a very small group of people. Although the process was slow there was no need for rapid production at that time. However, as the car became increasingly popular and important to the economic structure of the country, it became necessary for manufacturers to become more proficient at producing their product. Thus the assembly line came into being and specific guidelines for production were established. The bureaucratic structure was necessary in order to increase efficiency and to serve the needs of a large number of people.

Organizations evolved in the teaching profession in a similar fashion. The need for more teachers increased the need for more "plants" to "manufacture" teachers. More and more colleges became involved in the business of producing (educating) people to become teachers. By increasing production plants the supply of teachers was increased.

Today, as the demand for teachers decreases, the need for teachers' colleges decreases. Some of these schools are either going out of the business of professional preparation, or are "retooling" to put students through a program that does not necessarily lead to teaching at the end of four years. People concerned with human movement are now educating students in areas dealing with sport communication, the media, and so on. Whatever the demands of the society, some type of organization or structure is always assembled to create the supply.

### Organizational Functions

*The functions of organizations are varied and diverse.* Organizations exist for reasons other than the manufacture of goods. People concerned about their profession form groups to handle and disseminate information in order to improve the final product. A very potent function of any organization is to allow opportunities for the exchange of ideas. This can be accomplished through professional journals and publications or through person-to-person contact at meetings.

There are local, state, district, and national organizations that serve the interests of specific groups of people (movement educationists, for example). There are annual meetings (conventions) held that promote the exchange of ideas through informal discussions among conventioners and seminars organized to deal with relevant topics. Professional organizations also provide a place for the more formal presentation of research reports and theoretical constructs.

Commercial displays at conventions provide a chance to view the latest materials, such as textbooks, uniforms, and equipment. Conventions also provide an employment marketplace. Employers and employees can interview each other at the job placement center. New positions are listed, resumes exchanged, and initial interviews arranged.

People also belong to organizations to increase their power. People need power in order to achieve desired ends. A power base can be established through sheer size. The labor unions have power because they represent a large number of people. Teachers have also shown their power through the use of unions and strikes to achieve desired goals. Until the early 1960's, it was not considered "professional" to join a union—let alone go out on strike. Teachers have, however, come to see the advantages of collective bargaining, not only to achieve better monetary packages, but also to achieve educational goals such as smaller class size, innovation, and so on.

In conjunction with gaining power from the group, an individual can derive prestige from joining and serving an organization. For instance, election to the Academy of Physical Education, a very select group, enhances a person's prestige. Holding an elected office in a professional organization also is advantageous. Serving others and doing a good job raises the visibility and credibility of an individual in his/her profession.

Another important function of an organization, particularly in the teaching profession, is providing opportunities for professional growth. These opportunities are available through attendance at conventions and conferences. Workshops are also offered by various organizations to meet the particular needs of their constituency. Some organizations serve as clearing houses for information. They compile data on research that has been completed, compile bibliographies, and perform many other services to meet the demand for knowledge about one's chosen profession.

## Human Movement Organizations

*Organizations exist which are concerned with the discipline as well as the application of human movement.* There are many organizations concerned with the discipline of Human Movement; however, because of their large number, only several will be mentioned.

The most prominent organization is the American Alliance for Health, Physical Education, and Recreation (AAHPER), which is concerned with promoting the interests of persons involved in the fields of health, physical education and/or recreation. This organization holds an annual convention at which papers are presented that reflect the most current information in the field. It also sponsors and supports various types of workshops which are of interest to the membership. These workshops are held throughout the country to allow easy access for a large number of people.

The national association serves the interests of all its members, which are quite diverse. There are also districts based on geographical areas of the country that are representative of the needs and interests of their membership. In addition, each state has an association that is concerned with the dissemination of information to its members. The district and state organizations also have annual conventions designed to give individual members a chance to keep current in their field. The Canadian Association for Health, Physical Education, and Recreation (CAHPER) was formed to meet the needs of those people concerned with these professions in Canada. This national organization also holds an annual convention, has an association in each province, and publishes a bimonthly journal that contains articles related to the interests of its members (*CAHPER Journal*).

Periodicals that mainly deal with the discipline of Human Movement are available through membership in professional organizations. Two major periodicals of interest to movement educators are published by AAHPER. One, published monthly, is the *Journal of Physical Education and Recreation* (JOPER). This journal contains articles that are practical in nature and deal with information that can be applied in the teaching situation.

The second publication is the *Research Quarterly*, which is published four times per year. The articles in this journal contain reports of research that has been done in the not too distant past. Generally the articles are concerned with specific subareas of Human Movement such as Physiology of Exercise, Motor Learning, Biomechanics, and History and Philosophy.

Several other organizations and the journals that they publish are listed below:

| NAPECW | National Association of Physical Education for College Women | *Quest* |
|--------|-------------------------------------------------------------|---------|
| NCPEAM | National College Physical Education Association for Men | *Quest* (with NAPECW) *Proceedings* of the association |
| ACSM | American College of Sports Medicine | *Science and Medicine in Sports* |

ISSP          International Society of Sport Psychology          *International*
                                                                  *Journal of Sport*
                                                                  *Psychology*

The NAPECW and NCPEAM were both established to meet the needs of persons involved on the collegiate level in the area of Physical Education. The ACSM was established by physicians, physical educators, and exercise physiologists to encourage the investigation of the relationship between exercise and sport or physical activity. The ISSP was established to meet the needs of those people who were interested in the area of Sport Psychology.

There are, of course, other organizations dealing with the other sub-areas of Physical Education. The above list is representative of only a few of those specialized organizations concerned and interested in the area of Human Movement. The literature of the profession is diverse and teachers are encouraged to read as many publications as possible in order to increase their own knowledge and teaching effectiveness.

Organizations also exist that deal with the conduct of intercollegiate and interscholastic athletics. The National Collegiate Athletic Association (NCAA) is the governing body of men's athletics at the collegiate level. This body establishes and enforces rules and regulations which attempt to maintain fair competition amongst different institutions. The association also conducts tournaments at the conclusion of the respective seasons (football being an exception) to determine which school has the best team in a particular sport.

The Association for Intercollegiate Athletics for Women (AIAW) is the governing body for women's athletics at the collegiate level. This organization has established procedures and guidelines that are to be followed by member institutions in the conduct of competitive athletics. Although this organization is not as large and powerful as the men's association it holds national tournaments in many sports some of which are swimming, volleyball, basketball, and field hockey.

Interscholastic competition is controlled by the State Athletic Associations. The guidelines they follow are the standards for interscholastic competition that have been suggested by those associations of AAHPER concerned with the safety of the participants and the control of sporting competition. These organizations are the National Association for Girls and Women in Sport (NAGWS) and the National Association for Sport and Physical Activity (NASPA).

## Conclusion

*Information needs application.* The material presented in this chapter is not important unless those who read it use it in their own unique situation—in that special environment where a person is concerned with trying to improve the human movement of others. As educators, we must be concerned with the manner in which we provide leadership for the students in classes, our fellow workers, administrators, and/or the people in the community as well as with the development of virile organizations.

## References Cited

1. HOLLANDER, EDWIN P. *Principles and Methods of Social Psychology.* New York: Oxford University Press, 1971.

2. GIBB, CECIL A. "Leadership" in Gardner Lindzey and Elliot Aronson (eds). *The Handbook of Social Psychology,* 2nd ed. Vol. IV. Reading, Mass.: Addison-Wesley Publishing Company, 1969, 205–282.

3. HEMPHILL, JOHN E. AND ALVIN E. COONS. *Leader Behavior Description.* Columbus, Ohio: Personal Research Board, The Ohio State University, 1950.

4. HALPIN, ANDREW W. *The Leadership Behavior of School Superintendents.* Chicago: Midwest Administration Center, The University of Chicago, 1959.

5. HALPIN, ANDREW W. AND B. J. WINER. *The Leadership Behavior of the Airplane Commander.* Columbus: Research Foundations, The Ohio State University, 1952.

6. HALPIN, ANDREW W. *Theory and Research in Administration.* New York: Macmillan Company, 1966.

7. BELCHER, DUANE M. *Giving Psychology Away.* San Francisco: Canfield Press, 1973.

8. WHYTE, W. F. *Street Corner Society.* Chicago: University of Chicago Press, 1943.

9. LEWIN, K., LIPPITT, R., AND R. K. WHITE. "Patterns of Aggressive Behavior in Experimentally Created Social Climates," *Journal of Social Psychology.* 10 (1939): 271–99.

10. LIPPITT, R. "An Experimental Study of the Affect of Democratic and Authoritarian Group Atmospheres," *University of Iowa Studies in Child Welfare,* 16 (1940): 43–195.

11. WHITE, R. AND R. LIPPITT. "Leader Behavior and Member Reaction in Three 'Social Climates'," D. Cartwright and A. Zander (eds.), *Group Dynamics,* 3rd ed. New York: Harper and Row, Publishers, 1968, pp. 318–35.

12. LIKERT, R. *New Patterns of Management.* New York: McGraw-Hill Book Co., 1961.

13. SELVIN, H. C. *The Effects of Leadership.* New York: Free Press, 1960.

14. MOSSTON, M. *Teaching Physical Education.* Columbus, Ohio: Charles E. Merrill Publishing Company, 1966.

15. RAVEN, B. H. AND J. R. P. FRENCH, JR. "Group Support, Legitimate Power, and Social Influence," *Journal of Personality,* 26 (1958): 400–408.

16. Horwitz, M. "Hostility and Its Management in Classroom Groups" in W. W. Charters, Jr. and N. L. Gage (eds.), *Readings in the Social Psychology of Education.* Boston: Allyn and Bacon, 1963, 196–211.

17. Coleman, James S. *The Adolescent Society.* New York: The Free Press, 1961.

18. Stogdill, R. M. "Personal Factors Associated With Leadership." *Journal of Psychology,* 25 (1948): 35–71.

19. Tharp, R. G., and R. Gallimore. "What a Coach Can Teach a Teacher," *Psychology Today,* 9 (January 1976): 74–78.

20. Mann, R. D. "A Review of Relationships Between Personality and Performance in Small Groups," *Psychological Bulletin,* 56 (1959): 241–70.

# 12

## How Do We Help Others by Providing Models of Human Movement?

*John Cheffers / Leonard Zaichkowsky*

Human beings provide their young with models of human movement that may be viewed, emulated, or participated in. Models refer to structures that are relatively complete, visible, and influential. These models vary with sex and age levels. In young children most models of human movement are stimulating, interesting, and compelling. There appears to be an age of "sorting out" or becoming disillusioned where the child begins to realize that these models are bipolar—that is, they are exclusive or inclusive. We believe this age group ranges from 11 to 16 years, which corresponds with the youngster's experiences in high school. Much of the bitterness or the joy we feel in adulthood stems from this age period where the gap between what a child would like to do and what he or she believes him or herself capable of is more precisely determined.

It should be pointed out that children begin modeling behavior at a very young age. The earliest power figures in their environment are their parents. Later on other individuals such as peers, relatives, teachers and star athletes serve as their model. Not only is a Billy Jean King, a Joe Namath, or a Reggie Jackson a model for young children, but they serve in this capacity for adolescents and even adults. Their behavior is imitated not only on the playing field but off the playing field as well.

There are perhaps four distinct types of models:

1. *Closed models.* Closed models cannot be joined randomly, existing completely out of the range of the majority of individuals.

314

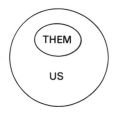

**Figure 12-1.** A closed model.

2. *Open models.* Open models are designed for participation by everyone no matter how important or insignificant that person perceives self to be.

**Figure 12-2.** An open model.

3. *Progressive/Regressive models.* Progressive models are open to those with ambition to proceed through the various experiences leading to the ultimate goal. Each new challenge represents new experiences and new motivations accompanied by the recognition of the need to acquire new skills. When these skills are achieved, the individual moves to the next stage. The progressive model offers human beings the chance to discover originally undreamed of personal potentials and achievements.

Regressive models represent the antithesis of the progressive model. An individual regresses from one step to another as in the case of the veteran performer who slips from invincibility.

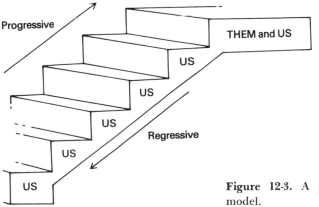

**Figure 12-3.** A progressive/regressive model.

4. *Fantasy/Reality Gap Models.* As the name implies fantasy/reality gap models represent the distance or gap between achievements and experiences about which a person fantasizes or dreams, and accomplishments about which an individual thinks are real or possible.

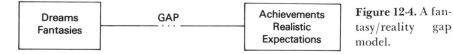

**Figure 12-4.** A fantasy/reality gap model.

Although it is possible for human beings to view and experience all four models during a life span, individuals tend to be drawn toward some models more than others. The phenomenon of spectatorship necessitated by the very nature of the closed model, for instance, has had enormous influence on mass human behavior during the twentieth century. The discovery process, inherent in the progressive model, has been praised by numerous educators, but all too frequently it proves too expensive. Open models tend to fade at adulthood, which has led leisure educators to emphasize adult play. Psychiatrists point to the very real danger of unwittingly encouraging schizophrenic behavior by masking the gap between what an individual fantasizes and what he knows to be real. Certainly, people dream and experience great pleasure through vicarious participation with heroes, but the fact remains that vicarious participation cannot take the place of active participation.

As we discuss the characteristics of each of these models and their effect upon the human environment, it becomes clear that a balance between all four is necessary if human beings are to enjoy optimal life-spanning movement.

## CLOSED MODELS

Perhaps we can divide the categories of models classified as *closed* into four broad headings.

1. Groups whose membership depends upon rare skills developed over lengthy time periods.
2. Groups formed by secondary association, especially with the criterion of birth or wealth.
3. Groups functioning with discrimination as their basal criteria.
4. Groups whose performances take place prior to specific recognition and in distant lands.

## Rare Skills Groups

*Groups whose membership depends upon rare skills developed over lengthy time periods.* The exclusivity of these groups and their competitive involvement proves very attractive to the populace. Although it is possible to have direct contact with such groups, they cannot be joined without considerable sacrifice, personal ability, and good fortune. The glittering array of professional teams which yearly saturate the American sports scene testifies amply to this point. Although membership is frequently impermanent, with heroes coming and going, the model of the professional sporting team continues to enthrall the public (Figure 12-5). It seems to make little difference whether individuals are in favor of the team's activities or strongly opposed to them, the model remains intact. For years the second Sunday in January has assumed great importance. It is known as Super Bowl Day, and this day directly affects the majority of Americans at home and abroad. For those fortunate enough to obtain entry tickets, secured at exorbitant prices, the game consumes every minute of the day. For the other interested millions, three hours of television time becomes mandatory. Those who are disinterested have difficulty es-

**Figure 12-5.** A closed model. (*Courtesy of Boston University Photo Service*)

caping the activity and fanfare of this special day. Considerable sums of money are invested legally and illegally in the game, with the result directly affecting the health and fortunes of an alarming number of people. Added to this is the usual parade of slogans such as "we're number one," "coming second is like kissing your sister," or "competition builds character." Pursuant to such philosophic outbursts is an array of peripheral activity: dancing girls, jazz bands, marching trumpeters, flag wavers, comics, and occasional intruders all get into the act. National anthems are played and a festival spirit is promoted. To most people this is an important day, but nevertheless a day in which they are reduced to vicarious participation. It is a model of entertainment which places the structure of professional football high in the hierarchy of public affairs. The principal actors are given instant status and, if successful, their names are enshrined in history. It is probably true to say that the country stands still on Super Bowl Sunday. And although many social critics have condemned certain aspects of this gala festival, it continues to increase in importance, in priority, and in fiscal strength each year. Most citizens view this closed model benignly, resigning themselves to spectator status. In a sense, however, it is a reminder of their shortcomings, and the enormous influence that professional football has in socializing individuals to a kind of mass conformity. Many people handle this adaptation of independence with ease, and they should not be condemned for there is nothing inherently wrong in spectating. Curiosity for viewing others' movements seems a natural phenomenon and can be very enriching. Perhaps the real danger in closed models lies in spectatorship becoming the sole outlet for physical expression.

To a lesser extent high school and college teams contain the same exclusivity element. As the child approaches adolescence, the opportunities for diverse movement participation diminish. They converge into exclusive models because of the reduction in community teams, the growing insistence upon national standards, and the failure of parents and teachers to educate children to value lifelong movements over glamorous young people's pastimes. Perhaps this convergence, more than any other single factor, contributes to the unfortunate epidemic of nonparticipation that afflicts the Western world in the twentieth century.

Other closed models spring to mind. Performing troops such as the Ice Follies, Shakespearean players, symphony orchestras, and other entertainment groups have exclusive membership. At times, a person who is feeling uninhibited will try to break into this group. After several effervescing glasses of good cheer, Mr. Jones may join the band to give the drummer, the vocalist, or the trombone player a helping hand. This spontaneous intervention is usually treated humorously. However, Mr.

Jones's action is an interesting example of an outsider's attempt at breaking public norms of participation in closed groups—especially groups whose existence is dependent upon skills far in advance of anything neighbor Jones may possess.

## Secondary Association Groups

### Birth

*Groups are formed by secondary association, especially with the criterion of birth or wealth.* The settlement of the new world, very much the offshoot of the internal revolutions in Europe over three centuries, provided an avenue through which the exclusive model of birth privilege could be circumvented. In recent history, one of the true examples of the rigid closed model is the aristocracy. Although less important today, privileged birth still commands an incredibly large portion of power on the world's stage. The coronation of a British Queen or the marriage of royalty is always accompanied by exclusivity of invitation and rigid social ranking. Even the movements of royalty are mandated by parameters associated with rank. Citizens of the British Commonwealth have never seen Queen Elizabeth jump out of her royal carriage and embrace an old friend in the crowd nor for that matter have they ever seen her wave vigorously. A fascinating point of royal protocol is seen in the behavior of Winston Churchill and George VI in 1945. Churchill was respected and applauded for giving his famous V signal while at King George's side, but George VI never attempted to emulate this convincing, impelling, and highly appropriate nonverbal communication. The public movements of the closed model represented by royalty are very different from the public movements of other famous people. And the expectations are such that if royalty abandons its inherited dignity, controversy immediately ensues. Some of the antics of Queen Elizabeth's consort, the Duke of Edinburgh, have raised eyebrows because they are out of keeping with the expected behaviors of those in the closed model of royalty.

Although birth is not so evident as an exclusive model in the United States, nevertheless it exists. There is a closed society which exists in Philadelphia, New York, Rhode Island, and Boston that excludes those of inferior birth. The movements or activities of these people are restricted to such sports as polo, yachting, and within further enclosed boundaries, skiing, aquatics, the hunt, and auto racing. With a few exceptions, these activities do not readily lend themselves to modeling by others than those within the closed system.

**Wealth**

Wealth, although not as exclusive as birth, forms another secondary characteristic evidenced in the closed model. Certain communal activities are impossible without financial backing. Yachting, auto racing, and equestrian endeavors are obvious examples, but less obvious are figure skating, ballroom dancing, and participating in a band. These activities also tend toward the closed model, on account of money as well as innate physical abilities. The system of sponsorship is probably as important today as it was during the eighteenth century, where every petty potentate maintained a model of paternalistic skill promotion. Again the majority of young people fail to identify with or model the behavior of those termed wealthy, because the wealthy fail to engage in activities which the majority of young people deem important.

## Discriminatory Groups

*Some groups function with discrimination as their basal criterion.* Closed models of human movement are exemplified through a wide variety of groups. Competitions conducted within age groups are exclusive. Attempts by individuals to violate such regulations are universally denigrated. Women's competition and men's competition are equally discriminatory. There have been isolated examples of men dressing as women to take part in sporting events. This, of course, is universally taboo. There are closed models within closed models, too, as seen in the novice championships conducted by golf clubs, which are further restricted to the female members.

Less acceptable are the closed models designated on such discriminatory grounds as race or ethnicity. The decision of South Africa to partition her country into racial groups and segregate sporting activity even to the point of residential exclusivity angered the watching world. The world group reacted by banning South Africa's athletes from participation in many world festivals. Today, through the efforts of a few courageous individuals, Gary Player in golf, Paul Nash in track and field, and Johannis Botha in the Olympic Federation, South African teams are not closed models and perhaps should be readmitted to world sporting competitions.

## Past-Performance Groups

*Groups whose performances take place prior to specific recognition and in distant lands may be called past-performance groups.* One classic example of a closed model with enormous power in communication is the media. Newspapers, television programs, periodicals, news letters, and published sets of regulations are examples of closed models. They function as such because the performances have either already taken place or are occurring at such great distance that we have no say in the functioning of that model. Events which have happened in the past represent a closed model of communication to human beings. We cannot turn back the clock in time, we cannot retract the spoken word, and we cannot undo wrongs that have been done. Many human activities represent attempts to refocus, redirect, or correct the results of movements that have been perpetrated, and which are now regretted. Playing "catch up ball" or "making up" to people are common pursuits resulting from closed models of human movement and the various effects they have had upon society and the individual.

Human beings are interested in past events, many times trying to emulate skills and performances preserved for current study. However, teachers and coaches usually find that film or printed accounts of past movements are less effective than live viewing or communication models that permit instant practice with accompanying reinforcement. Perhaps the closed model perspective gives us insight into the reasons why media presentations based on past performances are proving disappointing in the teaching-learning process.

## OPEN MODELS

We can divide the categories of open models into four broad headings:

1. The family.
2. School and community recreational groups.
3. Groups seeking expansion of membership.
4. The end of openness, or "the chop."

### The Family

Parents serve as very powerful models for their children, however, they lose their effectiveness as models if they fail to communicate with their children. The most common characteristic of family groupings is the capacity of involvement all members have in play or work regardless of chronological age. Many commercial enterprises are family-centered and many sporting groups are brother, sister, or father combinations. The seemingly ageless United States golfer, Sam Snead, has carefully guided his talented nephew, J. C. Snead, to equal prominence in professional golf today. Bobby and Al Unser, although rivals in auto racing, are brothers and close friends. In 1952 the famous Zatopeks, Emil who won three gold medals, and his wife, Dana, who won one gold medal, completed a unique sweep at the Helsinki Olympics. Championship standards aside, the family sets out to include all members in friendly communal effort. Such familiar sights as families or collections of families playing volleyball on beaches, football in parks, or tag on rinks illustrates the excellent use made of family-oriented movement for the socialization of coordinated bodies, values, attitudes, and loyalties.

Occasionally families will be in conflict. Rivalry in movement capabilities can bring this about. Shakespeare, in his immortal *Romeo and Juliet*, illustrates the deadly and unerring effectiveness to which feuding families can gravitate. The intense rivalry between the Montague and Capulet families eventually destroyed the very lifeblood of both families, bringing degradation, shame, and despair. Under certain circumstances the nature of the open group in welcoming all under its umbrella can, through its group loyalty, accentuate bitterness and disruption to the point of total destruction.

Families are expected to be open models that give warmth and support not encountered in more scattered groups. Families with only one child or with all boys or all girls sometimes suffer from imbalance. Children who grow up brotherless or sisterless are deprived of making the

**Figure 12-6.** An open model. (*Courtesy of Jim Schaadt, Human Environment Institute, Boston University*)

necessary adjustments necessitated by composite behavior. A frequent behavior of unbalanced families is to encourage openness and gregariousness with neighbors and friends. Sometimes, of course, the opposite occurs and children are closeted away to avoid pollution with the common breed. Such actions by parents are criminal. There is abundant research evidence condemning isolation and repression in young children. By contrast, scientific evidence extols the need for young people to experience the warmth and togetherness that open groups tend to give.

Sometimes the openness of the family model can have unfortunate consequences. Where leadership is lacking or neglect is evident, the more immature members are roused to action or subjugated into stagnation. Physical or psychosocial excesses by parents can have a disastrous effect on the family group. Many social critics today consider the departure of the modern family, one of the genuine open models, from a stable and supportive base to be the single most important factor promulgating insecurity, paranoia, and alienation.

## School and Community Recreative Groups

The young child is encouraged to join Little League or Pop Warner football or skating clubs or dance groups. The important variable should be, and is in many cases, universal participation. The joining of such groups existing in the rubric of the open model is motivating and meaningful to the young child. At school the existence of a strong intramural program, where all children are encouraged to participate, can be similarly motivating. Each time a community sets up an important movement facility it is, in effect, establishing an open model around which the community can function effectively. Swimming pools, playing fields, parks, and skating arenas are all positive examples of open models showing community interest.

One significant feature of an open model set up by school and community recreative groups is the reduction in need for idols or heroes. The participant—that is, each citizen—becomes his own hero. The challenge of accomplishment falls back on the individual battling against personal standards, or at least against a peer of comparable quality. The outcome of such endeavors is likely to be continued participation. The adult leaders of these groups become important models for the youngsters. It is most important that the individuals filling these roles demonstrate those attributes that children look for in an ideal model. These attributes include physical power and expertise [see McCandless *et al.* (1)]. The leader must demonstrate the capacity to control the immediate environment as well as knowledge and good judgment.

## Expanding Groups

Groups seeking to expand their membership establish open models. The street gang does not rest until all members in the street are at least sympathetic to the gang's causes. Public golf clubs, commercial enterprises, public charities and nonethnic enclaves are anxious to expand their memberships and to involve all members in active support of group goals. Many human beings appreciate such open models, accounting for the multiplicity of community enterprises and the large numbers enrolled in them.

The less savory side of open membership can be seen in the multitude of humbug television clubs, commercial sell clubs, stacked TV quizzes, and the "mush" of soap operas or fan clubs.

## The End of Openness or "The Chop"

As the individual approaches adulthood most open models either disappear or change. Sometimes this happens subtly and sometimes with unfortunate public connotations. Certainly the "chop" is applied to many young people who are now forced to adapt to totally different environmental expectations: Some remain stunned at the differences in their life styles. Most American communities provide wide and varied opportunities for their children to belong to an interest group. However, fewer opportunities exist for the adult. It could well be that this is the significant reason for the paucity of adult play and the resultant demotivation seen so clearly as children progress through school. Social researchers, conscious of this point, are strongly in support of sports being maintained at all age levels. They correctly infer that where a diversity of open movement models is available to the public, the opportunity at least exists for all citizens to lead constructive, rewarding lives.

## PROGRESSIVE-REGRESSIVE MODELS

### The Progressive Model

The making of a champion is an example of the progressive model which opens up new experiences and new motivations as the goals of each progressionary stage are reached. The word champion refers not only to those individuals who achieve fame and notoriety, but to all citizens who develop their talents to their ultimate potential. The important parameters are the discovery points around which an individual makes directional decisions on future performances. Even champions rarely make the giant leap from immaturity to ultimate achievement in one step. Most undergo growth periods, discovery periods, skill-building periods, and periods of testing before their ultimate potential is realized.

Certain interim decisions can have a crucial effect upon the Olympic champion's future health or happiness. "Can I stay in school and skate the necessary daily ten hours needed to make the Olympic team?" "Can I date regularly and participate in the activities of my peers and still fit in the mileage necessary to run an Olympic marathon?" "Can I heave the shot put, discus, or javelin sufficient distances to make my country's Olympic team without taking anabolic steroids?" "Can I, a young mother, devote sufficient time to my family and still chase the necessary preliminary competitions around the countryside to win the coveted Olympic berth?"

Very few athletes initially realize the full personal implications surrounding the careers on which they are about to embark. Important decisions have to be made at crucial points in the progression. Many people drop out because they refuse to become enslaved to the rigors of international competition. Sometimes ethical considerations such as drugs, sex, or authority issues cause young athletes to drop out. Additionally, the progressive model moves from a posture of open to closed as it progresses, and fundamental changes in life styles are frequently necessary. Friends and local environments pervasive at the beginning of the experience are oftentimes forgotten and replaced by the time the athlete has progressed to international prominence. Alienation and accusations, ranging from snobbery to cruelty, are frequent outcomes for the budding champion. The build-up and the consequent growth, coupled with timely opportunities, can make the young athlete insensitive to warning signals or friendly advice. Certainly this model is all-pervasive to the ambitious youngster, and continues in life as exemplified through goal-oriented executives, officials, and coaches.

Perhaps we can say that the progressive model is the only sensible model offering appropriate reinforcement and adjustment, time for maturation processes to take place, and time for the necessary adjustments to be made for any individual to become a champion.

## The Regressive Model

In reverse order to the progressive model, the regressive model can point to the reduction or debasement of humanity. It is this process which sees the normalizing of hitherto unthinkable habits take place through successive stages. Most human beings are familiar with the tragic case of the athlete who succumbs to alcoholism through a succession of deprivations which gather more serious and often unrecognized psychosocial connotations as each stage is reached. Similar degrading sequences can be seen in drug addiction, sexual excesses, and criminal activity. Children are not born addicts or criminals. But many are born with certain characteristics that can lead to degradation if they are not controlled and if certain experiences are presented. The authors do not support the fatalistic contention offered by some scientists that children are born and will become social outcasts as a result of heredity. We firmly believe that the environmental influences are by far the most important influences. One of the unfortunate characteristics of the alcoholic environment, the drug culture, and the criminal community is an openness or readiness to accept any individual willing to travel that road. Regression, however, can be retarded at any one of the stages in the total act.

Experiences based upon uninhibited and communal movement are only effective if accompanied by strong ethical and genuine helping characteristics. Sports, for instance, do not necessarily build character. Sports can build character and are a prime medium through which character can be constructed and healthy, happy life styles produced, but the essential ingredients of humanity—caring, sharing, and mutual appreciation of universal effort—have to be present. Indeed sport can be a model of destruction and disintegration. The tragedy of the young sport participant becoming mesmerized by peripheral antisocial happenings and falling prey to their many pitfalls is all too readily exemplified. We hope that as these problems are more generally understood, community leaders will stop making universal statements about the value of sports and physical education, and will support more deeply the essential ingredients within physical activity that account for genuine growth of human understanding and sociability.

## FANTASY-REALITY GAP MODELS

This model can be subdivided into two categories:

1. Functional model—where individuals come to realize that they can close the gap if they wish.

2. Structural model—where fate and/or physical and psychosocial capabilities are the sole determinants of gap reduction.

### Functional Model

We have called this model *functional* because the gap is a function of the *supposed* differences between what a person thinks is possible and what he or she is actually able to achieve, rather than the *actual* differences.

There are those individuals who have high levels of aspirations and others who have low levels of aspiration. Having high aspirations does not necessarily mean achievement. On the other hand, athletes such as Mark Spitz who have a high level of aspiration succeed very well. Generally those individuals who have low levels of aspiration will not achieve what they are capable of.

Psychoanalysts tell us that all human beings experience their cherished goals through dreams. Their hopes, aspirations and desires are identified through unintentional dreams expressed in sleep and intentional dreams sometimes referred to as day dreaming. We do not need to be told that many individuals are cynical about their capacity to achieve their inner goals and dreams. There is a measurable gap between their aspirations and their perceptions-achievement potential. Many encouraging models are presented to individuals through films, stories, poems, plays and sporting accomplishments. Biographies of great people are usually accompanied by stories of how their original ambitions were brought to fruition, and often these are exaggerated. There seems to be a defantasizing adjustment, however, with most people when they view screen idols and compare them with their own mundane existences. There is something unreal about the glamorous performances of successful people. It is possible that the portrayal of heroic achievements in the media has a reverse effect, convincing the common man of his comparative shortcomings and anchoring him well short of his full potential.

Coaches, directors, teachers, and peers are never more active than when trying to convince an individual that his or her capacity to achieve is richer than suspected. Sometimes this activity is called "lifting the morale" or "pep talking" or "getting the team psyched." Many times apparently mediocre groups have risen well above expected levels to attain undreamed of achievements through such mentor activity. Each time this happens the fantasy-reality gap is closed and anticipation and hope become principal ingredients in the world of competitive movement.

Teachers, through their grading practices in schools, can help or hinder the youngster to reduce the gap. If grading is used to eliminate, to discriminate, to rank, or to punish, the young person is likely to experience an increase in the fantasy-reality gap. Under these circumstances only those who are rewarded with excellent grades are encouraged to reduce the gap. Others receive reinforcement that they are stupid, inadequate, untalented, and low achievers. Where the teacher uses grades as a system of rewards for effort, improvement, stimulation, and healthy competition, the students are more likely to begin reducing the gap. The use of grades in this manner can greatly affect the child's self-concept. Students can be paralyzed through punitive analysis and can be motivated to much greater achievement through encouraging evaluation. Many discipline-oriented teachers today view grading as an elimination procedure designed to encourage the select few towards attaining excellence. At some stage or other, most students have been exposed to this model. We maintain that this model has legitimacy only if convergence to selectivity is required, such as selecting the fittest and most suitable astronaut to fly to the moon. We do not believe that this is a general education model designed to help all citizens close their fantasy-reality gaps. Individual differences will and should emerge as a result of life's challenges and life's opportunities, rather than as a discriminatory function of some mentor eliminating children from general performance long before the maturation process has taken place.

## Structural Model

The structural model is concerned with the fantasy-reality gap that occurs through physical or psychosocial differences in ability levels. There can be no denying that individual abilities differ. There is much truth to the statement that you cannot make a "silk purse out of a sow's ear" or "you can't win the Kentucky Derby with a jackass." Some individuals aspire to levels well beyond their capabilities. This can result in disastrous psychopathological problems. The nonproductive boaster and the pathetic defeatist tend to be products of this model. Important methodological lessons, however, can be learned from such people. Children of famous parents or relatives of gifted individuals find themselves in the odious position of being compared to their more illustrious relatives. For example in the sport of hockey, Henri Richard was always identified with his famous older brother, Maurice "Rocket" Richard. When the younger Richard failed to be as productive as his older brother, he was dubbed a failure by many fans. Similarly, the two hockey playing sons of Gordie Howe must endure a great deal of pressure in order to live up to their father's image. We propose that many inferiority complexes result from public expectations which extend rather than diminish the fantasy-reality gap of the individuals involved.

Teachers who use grades to remind students of their shortcomings through comparison with more talented students in the immediate environment are contributing to the inflation of this gap. Perhaps this is the most cogent argument in favor of using grades that stimulate personal achievements and personal potential achievement rather than focus on comparisons among students. It doesn't make much sense to tell an "idiot" that he is an "idiot." It probably makes more sense to help an idiot achieve movements of illumination, and perhaps discover that he is not so idiotic as originally presumed.

## Conclusion

Every human being is the product of personal behaviors and imitative behaviors modelled from institutions or people encountered in life experiences. Before we can expect individuals to behave differently, we have to provide different models for them to emulate and with which to identify. Tantrums on the tennis court and crack-back blocking on the football field are examples of models which help shape the community's behavior negatively. Fortunately for humankind there are sufficient positive models to keep the cart from tipping over. We trust that communal vigilance will remain, and that public models will continue to offer productivity and warmth as essential parameters productive to human behavior.

## References Cited

1. McCandless, B. R., C. B. Bilous, and H. L. Bennett. "Peer Popularity and Dependence on Adults in Preschool Age Socialization," *Child Development*, 1961. Pp. 32, 511.

# 13

*How Important is Decision Making in the
Application of the Discipline to Personal Movement?*

*John Cheffers / Tom Evaul*

We have seen how the discipline of Human Movement can be applied in various professional endeavors. Equally as important is how an understanding of this discipline can be applied by individuals in making personal decisions. Alternatives concerning one's movement are continuously cropping up in daily life: to work out or not to work out; to walk across town or to take a cab; to go out and play tennis or to sit and watch the ball game on television; how to lift the box; when to pass the ball; where to go in case of a fire; what club to use on the tenth hole; or whether to play sports at all? These and many other decisions must be made frequently in life. What basis does a person have for making such decisions? What is required to make a rational and intelligent decision? How can a person go about it? How should a person go about it? And what does this all have to do with the discipline of Human Movement?

## WHO MAKES WHAT DECISIONS?

Some decision are made *for* human beings while other decisions are within the province of personal judgement and consequently are made *by* human beings.

To sustain life an individual needs oxygen, food, rest, and essential organic functioning. These decisions are in all essence made for people: They are the ground rules of living. In a different age it may be possible for people to select more efficient apparatus than natural hearts, lungs, noses, and so on, but in the twentieth century such choices are not available. Human beings are compelled to work within the framework of their congenitalia: The authority of ancestry is complete. Likewise, the young child has little decision-making power in the earlier socializing events of his existence. Although interesting research is currently focused upon the prospect of giving infants a much greater part to play in their own rearing, by and large, the young child has little say during the early part of life. A crucial issue in the growth and development of children is the maturation process by which they gain independence from parental and local environmental influences. By independence, we mean the capacity of an individual to make rational and meaningful decisions about personal activity. What is not intended or implied is ungrateful, wholesale disregard for family, school, or friends, which is an unfortunate phenomenon sometimes referred to as "brattism."

Most public educational institutions place control of decision making in the hands of outside expertise (teachers, coaches, judges, and politicians). In spite of pleas from liberal educators, most children are still subjected to authoritarian pressures that render decision-making capacities minimal and inadequate. Mosston (1) developed his spectrum of teaching styles around the cornerstone of decision making. He was interested in decision making at the preimpact, execution, and evaluation levels. His continuum of teaching styles entitled *From Command to Discovery* traced an educational journey from total teacher decision making to complete student decision making. His educational objective was to encourage teachers to employ styles of teaching that permitted unimpeded student growth toward independence and personal wisdom. An encouraging trend in high schools today is the movement toward permitting students to select activities in sports from a wide range of participatory events. This shift away from mass conformity appears to have had some effect in motivating young people to express deeper interest in their personal physical performances.

Although many decisions are made for us in life, the capacity each individual has to make important decisions is crucial in the developmental phases of adolescence and young adulthood. Inadequate decision making at these levels may result in eventual disillusionment, cynicism. and defeatism, which psychologists point out can bring about hallucination and depression in later life. The thrust of public education must be directed toward providing sufficient knowledge and cognitive skill so that young people can make decisions based upon sound arguments as well as emotional appeal. Sometimes sound arguments amount to little in the presence of crippling social pressures, but at least knowledge and intelligent preparation enables an enlightened, if injudicious, decision to be made. An unfortunate example of this is found in modern track and field. The international athlete today is faced with a decision, which on the one hand can traumatically affect his health, yet on the other, beneficially affect his performance. The taking of synthetic testosterone or anabolic steroids has become mandatory if athletes in the power events are to succeed in international competition. There is little doubt that the use of these hormones is essential if the athletes are to remain competitive. Yet, because of their established and suspected side effects, these hormones are banned by every reputable sporting body in the Olympic movement. The athlete has to make a decision, first, on the health question, second, on the career question, and third on the effects of defeat. Cooper (2) says "the ever present forces of change compel an endless updating of decisions and actions." Young athletes accept this statement and sometimes can be lured into taking such things as anabolic steroids to insure growth in their chosen sport. In a larger sense, however, change compels us to ask the very first question: What is decision making and does change automatically imply that new decisions have to be made with every change?

## THE NATURE OF DECISION MAKING

*What is decision making?* Richards and Greenlaw (3) maintain that decision making is making choices among alternatives after gathering information and processing it in order to select the appropriate solution. Feldman and Kanter (4) state "the decision problem is that of selecting a path which will move the system (an individual, computer program, or organization) from some initial state to some terminal state."

According to Tainiter (5), certain criteria are needed before a phenomenon can be called a decision. Tainiter lists the following:

1. The choice has to present the best average gain or the smallest average loss.
2. The choice has to result in the best overall state of natural harmony.
3. The choice has to reflect a continuum between the optimistic and the pessimistic viewpoint.

Although Tainiter's criteria relate specifically to economics, it does not take much imagination to transform his concepts to movement. Decision making is value laden if it is to be meaningful. It is highly unlikely, according to this viewpoint, that an individual would decide to run 10 miles a day in an effort to gain cardio-respiratory efficiency if that decision made the individual desperately unhappy or deprived him of social well being.

Raths et al. (6) make the case for including the values component with the thinking component in the process of decision making. They see comparing, summarizing, observing, classifying, interpreting, criticizing, assuming, and imagining as critical components in the decision-making process, and they infer that these processes cannot be divorced from the values domain.

It is clear that these definitions of decision making see a surface explanation advanced in the statement that decision making is choice among alternatives. It is also clear that these definitions recognize that decision making is not a simple process. Richards and Greenlaw (3) consider no definition of decision making complete without patient attention to the goals, values, psychological, sociological, intellectual, emotional, and environmental factors involved. Our only addition to this imposing list would be to include the physical factors.

## Types of Decisions

Ofstad (7) asserts that "to make a decision (means) to make a judgment what one ought to do in a certain situation after having deliberated on some courses of action." He assumes that all decisions are conscious choices among alternatives. Perhaps this is the first type of decision that people make. A second type of decision might be called *unconscious choices* that could range from unthinking conformity to unrealized inner turmoil. A third type is the decisions that are forced upon us—decisions where the only alternative is compliance or defiance. It is probably true to say that survival factors mandate acceptance of the obvious choice in these cases.

Most theorists favor Ofstad's view, but the alternatives cannot be ignored for they play an important role in the total Gestalt of every decision that is made. The decision to scale Mt. Everest, for instance, involves careful and deliberate planning. But it also involves essential decisions such as whether or not there is a need for supplementary oxygen, and perhaps some unconscious decisions, too, that could be motivated by ego satisfaction and unexplained rivalry.

Another way to categorize the types of decisions we make is to group them as simple or complex. Simple decisions refer to dichotomous choices such as yes–no, warm–cold, up–down, and right–wrong. Complex decisions involve multidimensional information gathered prior to the decision-making process and far-reaching outcomes projected after the decision has been made. For example, a young person's decision to play a game of "two on two" basketball with his friends after breakfast on the Wednesday following an examination is probably categorized as simple, whereas a decision to pursue a career in professional basketball is probably best seen as complex. As a child grows from infancy to adulthood, the decisions encountered move from the simple to the complex. It is probably necessary to help children gain the strength and skill of wise decision making through recognition of this need in curriculum and through cultivating classroom climates that allow for questioning and discovering answers.

## RESEARCH THEORIES OF DECISION MAKING

### Cooper: Forces and Processes

*What does research tell us about decision making?* Cooper (2) suggests there are two basic areas of understanding which must be analyzed carefully in the light of the data available. He calls one basic area the *forces* of decision making, and the second the *processes* of decision making.

1. A knowledge of the various forces of decision making is essential. By forces, he refers to the past, the present, the constraints, the environmental influences, and the interplay among these forces. These forces can be further subdivided into dimensions of the individual. The first, dynamics of the individual, refers directly to stability, self-image, and personal goals. Dynamics of the group in which the individual finds him or herself refers to such things as drive, organization, group maturity, group personality, and adherence to precedence. The dynamics of the environment constitutes a third force into which such concepts as progress, recognition, and internal and external pressures are included.

    By definition these forces generate both direction and magnitude which influence the decision accordingly. If the coach does not have sufficient money for meals on the road trip, the team has to settle for hamburgers and hot dogs. This cogent force would be classified as external, from the environment. If for three successive nights prior to an important game it was too cold to practice, this force would be classified as external, from the environment. The maturity curve of a group, especially during the teenage stage of development, strongly influences decisions about sex, drugs, and alcohol. These forces would be characterized by Cooper as dynamics of the group, whereas the counteracting stability and self-image of each member of the group would constitute forces characterized as dynamics of the individual. The ultimate decision made, according to Cooper, is a function of which forces from which category establish the greatest magnitude.

2. A knowledge of the various processes in decision making is necessary. By processes, Cooper means the techniques utilized, the number of parties involved, and the current status of background knowledge attained.

Certainly the manner in which decisions are arrived at is a critical variable in decision making. Many an enthusiast has lost a case because of dictatorial techniques in group settings even though she, and all others involved, acknowledge the superiority of her position. It appears to be a universal law that people will react unfavorably to presumption and abrasiveness on the part of one group member trying to dominate group decision making.

Cooper considers a knowledge of the forces and the processes of decision making pivotal in the world of commerce and management. We believe similar dynamics are at work in personal decision making in all matters relating to movement.

## Allport: Resolution of Disequilibrium

Allport (8) has contributed a model that conveys a strong message—the way people define their situation constitutes reality. Allport's model speaks to logical sequence in decision making with the prime motivator being feedback.

His theory is similar to those who maintain that dissonance, or a state of arousal, brings about a situation whereby decisions have to be made

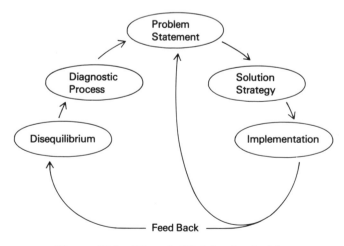

**Figure 13-1.** Allport's Model—the decision-making process.

for problem resolution. It is logical for a person to move to resolve any disequilibrium in life: The major activating medium needed to bring about resolution is the mechanism of feedback following a sequence of logical thought and development. This certainly appears to be the predominant process employed by teachers and coaches when handling sporting teams. It gives rational explanation, also, to personal dilemmas of dissonant individuals and their rash and sometimes antisocial behaviors.

## Vroom: Expectancy and Outcome

Vroom (9) designed a model for predicting what choice a person will make during the process of decision making. He included four major steps.

1. *Expectancy,* which is the individual's perceived and subjective notion that an action or activity which he undertakes will lead to some outcome or goal.

2. *A first level outcome,* which is a goal following the successful accomplishment of an initial effort.

3. *Instrumentalities,* which are the perceived expectations that the achievement of the first level outcome will lead to a desired second level outcome or goal.

4. *Valence,* which refers to the strength of the desire or need that the individual has for a particular outcome. The valence of each first level outcome is a continuously increasing function of the sum of the product of all second level outcomes plus the perception of its instrumentality for the attainment of the second level outcomes.

Vroom's model assumes that motivational understanding must consider goals people hope to accomplish and the extent to which they believe their actions are instrumental in producing these outcomes. Further, an individual will be motivated to choose actions that are perceived to be most desirable and that result in immediate satisfaction.

Vroom speaks to the multidimensional nature of decision making, assuming that all decisions are relatively complex, and sometimes unpredictable. What we as outsiders observe as talents in another person may not be perceived that way by the person concerned. So many times parents, teachers, and coaches are disappointed at decisions made by a youth because they have projected much greater expectations onto and attributed much stronger ambitions to the individual. Individual decision making is very much dependent upon process needs satisfaction; appar-

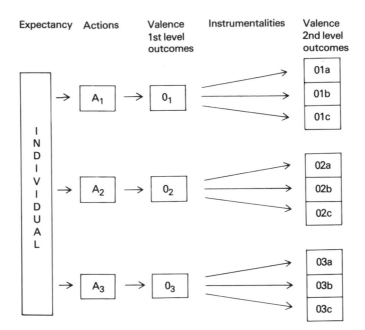

**Figure** 13-2. Vroom's Model—decision making.

ently there are levels of outcomes which gather strength, or lose potency, as the decision moves from one stage to another. If people are to develop their full potential through wise decision making, acceptance of Vroom's model implies a need for consistent and continuous feedback from internal and external sources.

## Berlynne: Discovery and Decision Making

Berlynne (10) infers that exploratory behavior, which is a cardinal component of decision making, contains three major concepts:

1. Epistemic curiosity,
2. Arousal,
3. Conceptual conflict.

By *epistemic curiosity* he means "a state of strong drive induced by conflict," which is best removed or reduced by the acquisition of knowledge. By *arousal* he refers to the reception of stimuli from any source that brings the organism from a state of boredom to an active state. By *conceptual conflict* he refers to discordance arising from incompatible symbolic response patterns such as beliefs, attitudes, thoughts, and ideas.

Berlynne cites many experiments to support his categorization. These categories direct human beings to important concepts relating to the pattern of actions they can expect from "discovering" behavior. He has, for instance, identified six major types of conflict—conflict which arises from placing a child in the multidimensional decision-making position of "discovering."

1. *Doubt,* which refers to confusion between what is real and what is imaginary. Do I have the ability to become an Olympic champion or not? Can I climb that tree or not?
2. *Perplexity,* which refers to a position where there are factors moving a person toward two mutually exclusive beliefs: I am involved in professional sport just for the money. My reason for playing professional sport is because I love the game. A surgeon enters his field to save lives. The surgeon selects partients by considering his time and their financial capabilities.
3. *Contradiction,* which occurs when a person is forced to accept two totally incompatible positions: Idealism in athletic competition—taking drugs to succeed. Upholding the principles of Christianity —supporting underhand strategies to subvert opposition and referees.
4. *Conceptual incongruity,* which is a situation that occurs when a person is expected to believe two incongruent facts: A mistaken coach's opinion from the sidelines—first-hand knowledge from the field.
5. *Confusion,* which results from unclear information: The basketball player whose sole training is four miles of swimming each day; a class which is given 36 intricate written instructions on a test where the teacher has left the room at the beginning of test.
6. *Irrelevance,* which is a position where a thought of no consequence is allowed to persist: The state of the weather to an athlete during the indoor season.

Berlynne infers that students' curiosities are stimulated by these methods which require an active searching out on the part of the learner. He believes that such methods as discovery and problem solving take the student beyond preconceived curricula limitations to a position where the student is involved in constructing the curriculum primarily as a result of conceptual conflict. Certainly conflict will arise during learning as soon as children are placed in a position where the specific goals are not clear and an active pursuit of discovery is required. Perhaps the very fact that a decision has to be made implies that a problem has arisen. By reversing this statement, it is possible, through the creation of a problem, to present the decision-making phenomenon to young people as an exercise in eliminating confusion. *Some educational theorists maintain that no real discovery takes place unless it is preceded by confusion and excellence in decision making.*

It is clear that during a game, confusion is not likely to result in immediate goal achievement, but confusion in the first half of the game may activate the changes that bring about a cohesive second half. Many times we have seen teams perform so badly in the early part of a competition that the reaction lifted the overall performance to unbelievable success by comparison.

## Aronson: "Jigsaw Puzzle" Method

Aronson (11) has designed a measure of teaching that he calls the *jigsaw puzzle* method. Each part of the group must complete its component task before the puzzle can be solved. In addition to supporting group cooperation and interdependence, this method of teaching implies that the real process of education is making sense out of confusion. On an individual basis, making sense out of confusion is achieved when wise decision making is possible and is accomplished.

## Parsons *et al.*: Dynamics of Decision Making

Parsons *et al.* (12) are concerned with a dynamic theory of action that attempts "to explain why one alternative rather than another was selected." They are convinced that there are limits to the variability in a range of alternatives. These limits are not only determined by knowledge but by individual capacities, social systems, and cultural boundaries. Perhaps Parsons *et al.* are suggesting that not all decisions are possible for the average person; that perhaps there are solutions to personal problems that are beyond everyone's reach. The implication here is that consultative effort or help from outside is needed in many instances of decision making. Such a position is incompatible with the philosophy of those who believe in "laissez faire" methods of teaching and decision making with people of all ages.

## Mancini and Martinek: Decision Sharing

Mancini (13) conducted an experiment on children's attitudes and interaction patterns to investigate two teaching models. One model had the teacher making all the decisions. The other required the children to share in the decision making process. Mancini found that children showed an increase in enjoyment of the program during the decision-sharing model. He also found that when children were given decision-making opportunities in a Human Movement program, there was a positive interaction between students and their teachers and an increase in student initiative.

Martinek (14) continued this investigation measuring self-concept and general motor skills as well. It was hypothesized that when children are given a share in decisions about their movement program, they enjoy improved self-concepts and perform better in overall skill development. He found this to be the case with self-concept but not so with motor skills. The research of Mancini and Martinek is expanded upon on page 344.

## DECISION MAKING AND PERSONAL MOVEMENT

*How is the discipline of Human Movement utilized in decision making?* The structure of the discipline of Human Movement provides both information important to making certain types of decisions and a framework for understanding the decision making process. In the discussion of why people move, it was concluded that people have needs to grow and mature in five dimensions (physical, social, emotional, intellectual, and spiritual). The existence of these needs provides the motivation for human behavior. In an effort to satisfy these needs, people move. They explore, manipulate, play, build, and do a host of other activities that involve movement. What movement to make, when, where, and how are all types of decisions the individual must make. If correct decisions are made, needs will be met; if not, they will go unfulfilled. For example, if a person desires to meet others of the opposite sex, the individual may learn forms of movement activities such as dancing, skiing, sailing, and the like. To the degree that the people the individual would like to meet participate in these activities, the need will be fulfilled. If, however, the person ends up on a sailboat with a crew all of the same gender, the need for social interaction with the opposite sex will be unfulfilled.

In making decisions, there are many factors that need to be taken into consideration. First, the people must be able to identify the need(s) they are attempting to satisfy. Next they must know how various forms of movement will affect themselves, others, or the environment. And finally, they must determine which effects will meet the need(s). This implies a thorough knowledge of the discipline, and particular skills in a variety of movement forms.

For example, people who wish to learn more about rocks and caves

(an intellectual need) may find out they must learn how to scale mountains and cliffs. This requires strength, endurance, balance, and a variety of other skills. With knowledge of the relationship of balance to base of support, strength to overload, and endurance to repetition they can select appropriate activities that will help develop these abilities. If they are ignorant of these factors, they can resort to trial and error practices which are often inefficient, and even dangerous.

The more people know about the discipline, the better prepared they are to make wise decisions. This does not mean that a person with knowledge will always make the best decision. The physician who smokes should know the potentially drastic effects of such behavior on the circulatory and respiratory systems, yet, he persists in the behavior. Apparently smoking fulfills a need that the individual doesn't know how to meet in any other way. Knowledge alone is not power. One must have an attitude to use this knowledge. However, there is very little chance of having power (e.g., making a good decision) without knowledge. It behooves people who desire to use movement as a means of meeting needs to learn as much as possible about the discipline. In this way they can select the best means of moving that will meet their needs.

The greater the knowledge and skill, the more alternatives people have to reach personal goals: If one way isn't available, another may be. If a person can't afford skiing or sailing, maybe skating or swimming will serve the same purpose. Knowing the physical, psychological, and social effects of each activity will help people make gratifying decisions.

The research indicates that we make decisions about our personal movement based on the quality of information we receive and the level of social-psychological well-being we enjoy. Decisions about personal movement are usually sound and productive when the only issues involved are availability and enjoyment. The decision to go skiing over a weekend is relatively simple and unencumbered by anything beyond financial restrictions or sensible safety regulations. The decision to undertake a five-day cross-country skiing tour requires different standards, however. Such considerations as employment, provisions, location, safety, skill levels, and cost are much more intricate and much more likely to produce confusion. In general, team-oriented individuals rarely can afford the luxury of making decisions using their own needs and desires as the sole consideration. Certainly strong leadership is needed and independent

**Figure 13-3.** Decisions: (*top*) To be alone; (*middle*) to share; (*bottom*) to compete. (*Top and bottom. Courtesy of the Argus Africa News Service; middle: Boston University Photo Service*)

decision making can enhance group achievement, but personal needs and goals are rarely satisfied if they are counterproductive to the group needs and goals.

Traditionally, the gymnasium, the indoor arena, and the playing field have fostered authoritarianism in decision making. Teachers, coaches, and mentors have tended to make all the decisions for their charges. Reasons for this have centered around the need to secure jobs, prevent accidents, and gain the best overall results from the majority of pupils. Surprisingly, however, models of democracy and decision sharing have given indication that they are as equally secure, safe, and productive as authoritarian models, and may even be more so.

## The Boston University Experiment

Professional preparation specialists at Boston University decided in the fall of 1972 to test the hypothesis that decision making by children is appropriate in physical education. Five hundred children from inner-city elementary schools were brought to the University's physical education facility for one hour per week. Two intact groups of children from similar environmental backgrounds were given different treatments. In one group the teacher made all the decisions, and in the other the children were given a genuine series of decisions which they could share with the teacher. In the first model the children were divided into groups of 8 to 10 staying with the one teacher throughout the year. In the second model the teachers were stationed at the respective apparatus with the children encouraged to move freely from one activity to another consulting with the teacher on choice of activity, strategy, and safety procedures. Teachers were trained in the second model to accept the children's initiative, yet still be very active in helping the children to make decisions. Both models were tested against a third or control group which did not take part in the program.

Careful measures were taken over a four year period beginning with attitudes and finishing with self-concept and motor skill measures. The Hawthorne effect was controlled for through the exciting physical education facility being used by both groups and the enthusiasm which developed in both groups through their weekly trips to the university. The same teachers were used in both models; these teachers were encouraged to show no difference in pleasantness or firmness in dealing with the students on either day. The curriculum, in so far as possible with the disparate teaching models, was kept constant. The results showed that the children enjoyed themselves in both models, but significantly more so in the decision-sharing model. Self-concept and motor skill tests showed that the students on both treatment days improved over students with similar environmental backgrounds who did not make the trip to Boston University. Differences between the two models confirmed similar findings of Dougherty (15). The children gained significantly higher self concept scores in the decision-sharing model, but were significantly less developed in motor skills. The explanation advanced by Martinek was plausible: When children are given freer rein in physical activity classes they feel more important and grow in psychosocial parameters, but teachers have considerably less say in the planning of their program, hence little systematic control over their physical program. The finding does not negate the importance of the decision-sharing model—rather it points to the need for variety in teaching models. The direct command style obviously has advantages in providing children with planned physical fitness growth and development. It is probably necessary for teachers to employ both models in appropriate and commensurate manner. There were many interesting factors which arose during the experiment, some of which are pertinent to the discussion. The techniques for introducing the students to the decision-sharing model varied. Initially, no information other than the following simple statements were used: "Children, the teachers are at each piece of apparatus and will help you. Be sensible, the gymnasium is yours, enjoy yourself." This resulted in much jollity with initial bursts of running and general enthusiasm, a high noise level, massing around some pieces of apparatus (especially the trampoline) and incessant mobility throughout. Only a very few children (less than 1%) needed to be apprehended, however, for misbehavior or dangerous activity, and later with restraints placed on the children for initial running, it was decided that a "controlled" group was needed to restrain the few who could not handle the freedom. This group was reconstituted each week as a result of current misdemeanors and its population did change. The rationale behind the institution of such a group was similar to that of society in its use of restraining influences (such as detainment centers, hospitals, and lockups)—some people simply cannot handle total freedom without resorting to antisocial behavior. In the fourth year of the project another approach was taken. Children were met by a teacher and taken in small groups to an initial piece of apparatus. From there the options were explained to them and an activity begun. It was then up to the children to make the decisions on their choice of activity, choice of apparatus, location, and time spent at each activity. The mobility continued, along with a plethora of activities, but this approach resulted in such responsible behavior on the part of the children that no "controlled" group was needed for the entire year. Apparently, children who are unsettled early in a class may not be able to recover personal management to the extent where they can effectively handle the freedom given to them. Perhaps we need to take our greatest care in the earlier norm-setting sessions prior to investing decision-sharing opportunities with children. The advocacy here is not to advise teachers "not to smile before Thanksgiving"; indeed, it is the opposite: children given the opportunity to be free will function better after the individual teacher explains their options and offers advice and quiet enthusiasm.

One very noticable difference between the two models is worth attention especially as it applies to discipline. During gymnastics in the first model, rowdy lines were universally evident. Teachers were constantly "shshing" kids: The youngsters' attention rarely focused on the performers in front and distractions were numerous. During the second model, however, children waited in line only if they wanted to perform the activity. As a result, they were aware of preceding performances, more patient in line, and more helpful to peers who were performing the activity with them. Indeed, very few lines were evident in the second model. The contrast in the two models in this regard was patent. But those traditionalists who need to keep the noise level to the inaudible would not be enamoured of the decision-sharing model. Children given the opportunity to express themselves physically rarely do so without expressing themselves in other dimensions at the same time. The important variable is not the noise level in a movement class, rather the busy occupation of all children investing personal time in the improvement and enjoyment of their physical skills.

Many lessons about movement expression can be learned from the continuing Boston University experiment. We do not need to overprotect children (no accidents of any consequence were reported from the decision-sharing model) but we *do* need to give some direction if their program is to be well balanced. They appear capable of learning responsibility while still enjoying themselves and developing sound self-concepts, provided that some direction is forthcoming from teachers in their individual curricula.

Another important lesson relates to discipline. Active, happy, busy children need a minimum of restraint and maximum of encouragement. Perhaps the penchant we physical educators have for martial authority and incessant program direction, and the reasons we entertain for this rigidity, are more imagined than real.


## IMPROVEMENT OF DECISION-MAKING SKILLS

Cooper (2) is particularly helpful in answering this question. He believes there are eight major components to improving personal decision making.

1. Possession of a broad general background. In order to control the "tunnel vision" for which some specialists strive, he recommends a broad, liberal-arts background, variety in personal reading, and avoidance of such statements as: "I can only speak on this (or that) topic. . . ." "I have no opinions on that. . . ." "I have only been trained in such and such. . . ." He believes that impressions are indelible so why pretend that scientific objectivity is totally attainable. Certainly the teacher, coach, or medical practitioner is well advised to have a broad background of learnings and experiences in addition to specialist skills. This is perhaps the strongest case for the retention of the conscientious generalist in a world that increasingly moves towards the exclusive model of specialism.

2. Possession of an adequate technical background. In order to perform the necessary technical duties and make intelligent decisions, people must possess technical expertise that is sometimes specific and sometimes general. The doctoral student is of little help in research without a background in design and statistics; the Olympic athlete is more likely to succeed with a knowledge of biomechanics than with a history of hocus pocus in his chosen sport; the musician needs hours of technical preparation before success is possible; the teacher is deficient without years of preparation in communicative and interaction skills, along with technical knowledges in the specialist subject areas. Few excuses can be found for professionals who are inadequately prepared in technical skills, and few enlightened decisions can be expected from them.

3. Possession of institutional awareness. Individuals must be awake to all the stimuli in the organization and institution around them. Some simple examples are given. "Where can the weight athletes work out . . . ?" "Where can the athletes go for good meals . . . ?" "Who has the keys . . . ?" "How does one secure clean towels . . . ?" "Where is the first aid kit . . . ?" "What is the schedule for next weekend . . . ?" "What time does the flight leave . . . ?" The professional who quickly and effectively learns the logistics of the immediate institution and its environment is more likely to succeed in making positive decisions, and much less likely to produce indecision and confusion.

4. Organization of self to use time well. Cooper cites hints from Carl Hegel:
   a. If you need help—find a busy person.
   b. Set some time aside to be by yourself, alone.

    c. Channel time demands of others so you can perform your own work.

    d. Expect others to be brief—be brief yourself with others' time.

    e. Plan your creative work when the mind is fresh and unencumbered.

    f. Itemize and file well in administration.

    g. Reason the "moment for action"—I have now reached the point of no return. . . .

    h. Learn from the success of others, and when you are successful, expect others to learn from you.

Hegel's hints are as practical and useful in the performance of personal movement as for their original intent—the office.

5. Full utilization of resources. In this day of technological progress, it is inefficient not to let machines do the "hack work." Many movement specialists, for instance, are either not familiar with or are afraid of the computer. A little time invested and some experiential success can change all that. The cultivation of an organization that invests trust and responsibility in appropriate and diverse channels is crucial. The overworked executive, coach, teacher, or parent is probably guilty of unnecessary clustering of duties, distrust toward others, and ego-massaging paranoia to the point where time is used poorly.

6. Development of skills in communication. Most misunderstandings arise from faulty communications. The skill of listening to other people is a key to the development of communication skills. Learning to conceptualize, to articulate in simple fashion while avoiding jargon and overly technical language, and to remain alert and open to others' suggestions and viewpoints are some other communicative skills that enhance productive decision making.

7. The learning of integrative skills. An individual's ability to communicate with other professions with differing philosophic beliefs immeasurably facilitates the decision-making process. Methods of receiving input from others are important also. Misunderstanding nonverbal signs and word reactions along with surface dogma are three common human errors that compound the difficulty of making productive decisions.

8. The development of an action personality. Whether they are ostentatious or quiet, Cooper (2) maintains that people with an action personality are decisive, confident, forthright, brave, and

mature. Eventually social psychologists may disagree with some of these adjectival descriptions of the successful personality, but one is tempted to take a second look at them when describing the successful leader in movement-oriented programs. To the letter, these adjectives describe action-inspiring leaders.

One would hope that the action personality encompasses empathy and understanding, and that perhaps all of these qualities can be developed through the influence of a balanced education.

## Helping Others Make Decisions

Cooper (2) lists some helpful hints:

1. Understand others' problems.
2. Ask yourself—Am I qualified to help them?
3. Time your intervention strategies well.
4. Check your personal motives.
5. Ask yourself What is your personal status with them—colleagueal, competitive, personal?
6. Think through which techniques are appropriate—executive, consultative, supportive, professional.
7. Establish your credibility through proving trustful and technically dependable.

The mere listing of helpful hints is probably insufficient, however, as personal application is so specific. When Rachmaninoff staggered under the charging fury of music critics over his first symphony, he collapsed into such depression that his family feared for his survival. Relief came not from family, acquaintances, friends, or professional colleagues, but from an unorthodox neurologist, Nikolai Dahl, who skillfully and patiently stimulated Rachmaninoff into composing his way out of the depression. The resultant second piano concerto is a masterpiece of romantic expression, a treasure the world might not have had but for the insight and skill of a man dedicated to helping others recover. Inherent in that recovery were essential decisions which, in sequence, provided the strength and confidence for the composer's rejuvenation needs. Literature has provided many lucid examples of people meeting other people's decision-making needs. Ken Kesey, in *One Flew Over the Cuckoo's Nest,* has written a modern classic illustrating deep interpersonal intervention. MacMurphy, the anti-hero, found himself in a situation where disturbed mental patients had lost all will to survive in the world at large; where they had tragically surrendered their rights to the normal processes of decision making in their daily existence. Through his alertness and intense commitment to individual dignity, he not too cautiously thwarted the efforts of a rigid, parasitic institution to enslave the minds and bodies of the pitiful inmates. This effort was not accomplished without personal tragedy, but his death was the impetus for others, particularly the lonely Indian giant, to grow sufficiently in stature to face the rigors of life with independence and resolution. This highly volatile and deeply moving story of intervention strengthens the case for human interdependence, and it points to the paramount need people have for wise decision-making capabilities.

MacMurhpy accomplished most of his goals through collective movement expression. The film version excellently prepared by L. Hauben and B. Goldman enhances an already compelling story and illustrates graphically MacMurphy's use of the liberating qualities of play: he taught Chief how to hold up his arms for those memorable scenes on the basketball court; he took the whole gang on a precarious and riotous fishing excursion; his interest in the world baseball series was contagious; he brought the joy of movement to a group of people who had been afraid to experience life.

The lessons learned from *One Flew Over the Cuckoo's Nest* can be applied far beyond the confines of a mental institution. Individuals are complex entities in a complex social web. The decisions they make are based upon their individual knowledge and conviction, and these decisions are their doorways to society. Certainly their decisions constitute their societal posture.

Perhaps it is true to say that the vast majority of our decisions (about work, play, recreation, sex, and so on) involve movement in a pivotal way. The phenomenon of decision making gives focus and reason to the application of the knowledge of the discipline of Human Movement to personal movement.

## References Cited

1. MOSSTON, MUSKA. *Teaching Physical Education.* Columbus, Ohio: Charles E. Merrill Book Co., 1967.
2. COOPER, JOSEPH D. *The Art of Decision Making.* Garden City, N.Y.: Doubleday and Co., Inc., 1961.
3. RICHARDS, MAX D., AND PAUL S. GREENLAW. *Management: Decisions and Behavior.* Homewood, Illinois: R. D. Irwin, 1972.
4. FELDMAN, JULIAN, AND HERSCHER E. KANTER. "Organizational Decision Making," in *Handbook of Organization*, James G. March (ed.) New York: Rand McNally, 1965.

5. TAINITER, M. *The Art and Science of Decision-Making.* New York: Time Table Press, 1971.

6. RATHS, LOUIS EDWARD *et al. Teaching for Thinking; Theory and Application,* Columbus, Ohio: Charles E. Merrill Book Co., 1967.

7. OFSTRAD, HARALD. *An Inquiry Into the Freedom of Decision.* Oslo: Norwegian Universities Press, 1961.

8. ALLPORT, GORDON W., *Becoming; Basic Considerations for a Psychology of Personality.* New Haven: Yale University Press, 1955.

9. VROOM, VICTOR HAROLD, AND PHILIP W. YETTON. *Leadership and Decision Making.* Pittsburgh: University of Pittsburgh Press, 1973.

10. BERLYNNE, D. E. *The Mind of Man.* Trans. by G. Thomas Rowland. Englewood Cliffs, N.J.: Prentice-Hall, Inc., 1971.

11. ARONSON, ELLIOTT. "The Jigsaw Puzzle Method of Teaching," *Psychology Today.* (May, 1975).

12. PARSONS, TALCOTT *et al. Toward a Theory of General Action.* Boston: Harvard University Press, 1967.

13. MANCINI, VICTOR. "A Comparison of Two Decision Making Models in an Elementary Human Movement Program Based on Attitudes and Interaction Patterns," Unpublished Doctoral dissertation, Boston University, 1974

14. MARTINEK, THOMAS J. "A Comparison of Vertical and Horizontal Models of Teaching in the Development of Specific Motor Skills and Self-Concept in Elementary Age Children." Unpublished Doctoral Dissertation. Boston University, 1976.

15. DOUGHERTY, NEIL JOSEPH, IV. "A Comparison of Command, Task, and Individual Program Styles of Teaching in the Development of Physical Fitness and Specific Motor Skills." Unpublished Doctoral Dissertation. Temple University, 1970.

# 14

## Do Human Beings Apply the Discipline to Gain Personal Fitness?

*John Cheffers*

On the surface the answer to this question may appear trivial. Surely individuals are interested in keeping all the home fires burning; surely they are interested in keeping the human machine in perfect running order.

There is a wealth of evidence to support the belief that physical fitness is a complex condition of the human organism that enables it to function at its optimum. Improved physical fitness results from participation in physical activity guided by certain principles. If we wish our organism to function optimally, to sustain life, to retain skills and maneuverability, and to obtain maximum enjoyment, the path is clear. We must engage in a program of regular total body activity, starting slowly, progressing gradually after a warmup, and permitting tapering down. We must consider the components of physical fitness (body composition, efficiency, endurance, skill). We must eat a balanced diet of necessary foods and necessary caloric intake, forever keeping in mind that the health of the circulatory, hormonal, neuromuscular and respiratory systems must have reasonable stress and appropriate rest. A "rule of thumb" is that an exercise episode lasting approximately one hour in duration, on a minimum of three days each week, using an intensity of physical expenditure ranking between 50 and 90% of maximum, with a caloric expenditure of around 300 calories per workout, is necessary if optimal physical fitness is to be maintained.

The copious research undertaken over the past 80 years is conclusive. Regular physical activity is necessary to both sustain and enrich life.

It would seem logical that this information would be sufficient to motivate most human beings to activity. We could expect them to set aside a proportion of each day for physical activity. People should automatically reach into the movement bag to grasp the essential that will sustain and enrich their comparatively short life span. Unfortunately, this is not the case.

In spite of the research evidence, the pleas of exercise physiologists, and the inclusion of physical education as a compulsory subject in the school curriculum, the sad reality is that less than 1% of Americans are physically fit (Cureton, 1969). Certainly, individuals can be seen jogging along river banks each morning. Others continue to play squash, handball, tennis, and other leisure sports well into their senior years. Statistics do not support any such positive statements about the bulk of citizenry. The average American spends life working in an occupation that requires little physical activity, or sitting mute in front of television, or eating unnecessary calories, or observing the intense efforts of a gifted few. People are effectively committing suicide in massive numbers. People have failed to take all the dimensions of the discipline of Human Movement into consideration for personal fitness endeavors. Their daily routines are determined by physical attributes, age, work, social status, a hierarchy of defense mechanisms, and the immediate environment

We cannot talk about the average human or his daily existence without accounting for the many dimensions that affect the daily profile. We are physical animals with bodies that have both structure and function. In addition, we have intellectual, social, emotional, and spiritual dimensions. Imbalance in any one of these dimensions can radically upset the whole scheme. The reason the pleas for physical fitness have fallen on deaf ears is because people will not change a complex existence consisting of many dimensions through input from a single dimension alone. The drawing power for an apple pie, a tumbler of beer, the comfort of the car, and the company of friends has proved to be considerably stronger than the well-intentioned resolve to exercise regularly, especially under adverse climatic and personal conditions. If we are to make headway in the business of convincing people that regular physical activity is vital for both optimal physical functioning and survival, first we have to explain the need, and second we have to include a strong sampling of activities from the many dimensions that affect a person's daily existence. The programs we offer, whether in school or in other institutions, must take into consideration a person's physical, intellectual, social, emotional, and spiritual dimensions. Perhaps we need to start applying knowledge from the discipline toward human fitness, of which physical fitness is only one important part.

## DIMENSIONS OF HUMAN FITNESS

### Physical

B. Don Franks offers a hierarchical model of the components of physical performance and fitness which is included in Figure 14-1. He is concerned that physical fitness programs include such components as endurance, cardiovascular, and neuromuscular activities in addition to the mastering of the many skills needed for life. The average school's allocation of two, 45-minute physical education periods each week will not substantially affect the actual bodily functioning of the child. We must incorporate into the meager school curriculum factors that will encourage

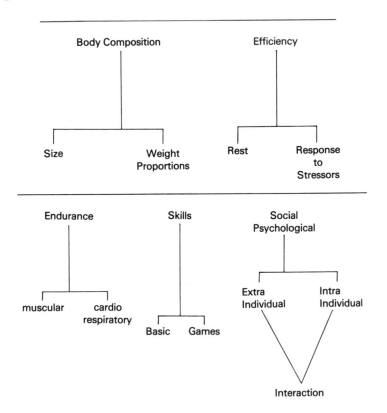

**Figure** 14-1. Components of Physical Fitness (According to B. Don Franks, 1974)

the students to gain a variety of interesting experiences. These factors must stimulate young people to continue to actively search out measures of physical expression that will keep their body functioning harmoniously. It is probably necessary for us to maintain institutions that will guarantee multifaceted opportunities for the physical involvement of the average citizen of any age. School physical education programs that emphasize universal dress codes and other trivia produce plasticity among young people and are the main culprits in demotivating students. Young people are so "turned off" by physical activity that they fail to recognize that growing inactivity is a form of suicide. The program of the physical dimension of human fitness should contain activities that encourage maximum mobility in joints and increase resistance to the musculature, the heart, and the lungs. An individual who never experiences perspiration, breathlessness, or body heat is highly deficient in the physical dimension of human fitness.

Several concepts or principles are offered that are relevant to improving physical fitness.

1. Use promotes function; lack of use results in deterioration.

2. Submitting the organism to greater work (overload) than it is used to improves fitness (providing the organism is healthy).

3. Progressively more work must be performed for continual improvement in fitness.

4. Improvements in physical fitness are specific to the type of training undertaken.

5. Sometimes fitness performance retrogresses before it improves.

6. People improve at different rates.

The individual's entry behavior levels must be carefully monitored. Medical examinations and appropriate work loads are essential. Testing used to evaluate the physical component include measures of endurance (Harvard Step Test, Maximal Oxygen uptake, and simple pulse recording devices), strength (the Predictive Indices of Berger, weight-training measures, dynamometer measures), power (sprint times, agility tests such as the Iowa test, jumping and throwing increments, and recovery measures), and flexibility (goniometers and body configuration tests). Although it is important for us to measure the results of our physical programs, we must be careful not to permit the tail to wag the dog. Some people are so concerned with comparative objective measures that they emphasize testing rather than program performance. For instance, it is not important that a person jogs around the block at a faster rate each day. What matters is that the jogging performance be carried out with effort commensurate with the physiological state of the organism at the time. Heavy colds, fatigue, or other bodily infections may reduce the overload for a single performance to a considerably less efficient time. Unfortunately, this important factor is ignored by many endurance activity coaches.

## Intellectual

To obtain intellectual fitness, human beings must be continuously challenged to develop their information processing ability. Such factors as creativity, problem solving, and the acquisition, interpretation, and retention of facts are important in this domain. Students of human fitness should be encouraged to learn about their body, to continuously process the cues given up by their body, and to intelligently plan appropriate activities for their body. The lack of understanding of the value of physical activity has produced the image of people rushing mindlessly around the exercise yard, and it has given rise to the term "jockism" with its unfortunate connotations. This hapless label has caused many an intellectual to avoid physical activity and then hinder the development of excellence in physical programming through preconceived biases and unfulfilled ambitions. Many of the disciplines in schools and colleges denigrate physical education. Programs in schools and outside institutions must permit a maximum of cognitive function if human fitness is to be maintained. Activities such as Vita Parcours encourage intellectual activity in a strong physical environment and are excellent additions to the physical repertoire. Orienteering, problem-solving activities like those proposed by Robert Lentz in his Project Adventure, and properly executed movement-education programs encourage maximal input of cognitive activity. Interdisciplinary programs involving bodily movement and mathematics, social studies, language arts, psycholinguistics, music, art, and drama must be included in any intelligently planned school curriculum. Intellectual fitness can be measured by intelligence tests but is probably more appropriately measured through accomplishment of performance objectives, i.e., evidence of a problem being solved or a task accomplished. The failure of school, and in particular of the personal fitness programs, to include intellectual challenge has resulted in boredom—that insidious disease of the current generation—which continues its stultifying path to general apathy and total oblivion.

## Social

Social fitness refers to an individual's ability to function in a group setting with a balance between the competitive and cooperative aspects of community living. Human beings depend on one another, and they are motivated by peer influences and cultural challenge to perform a plethora of activities. These activities have status, are ranked, are given social value, and are encouraged or discouraged; the physical appearance of individuals is judged likewise. The presence of another human being invariably alters the social system, bringing the individual into a climate for change. Adjustment, criticism, augmentation, and support are crucial factors in the performance of an individual's activity. The presence of a friend will make daily jogging, tri-weekly squash games, community pastimes, and regular leisure-time pursuits meaningful, enjoyable, and regular. The presence of a foe will tend to cause physical activity and performance to either diminish or exist in a climate of hostility. The presence of spectators has been found to assist in simple tasks but to deter performance in complicated tasks. Questions of self-image and self-confidence are important in relation to physical activity performed in public.

In a competitive climate where the community rewards favor only the gifted few, the bulk of citizenry recedes to inactive spectatorism. In a cooperative climate the assets of the gifted are used to facilitate the

**Figure 14-2.** Toward a 12-foot wall society: cooperation between, competition within. (*Courtesy of Jim Schaadt, Human Environment Institute, Boston University*)

performance of everybody. Unfortunately, today we live in a society dominated by punitive competition. Physical fitness programs that do not use cooperative group ventures tend to produce activity discrimination in society at large. An example is appropriate. A group will not be able to scale a 12-foot wall unless the skills of the gifted are used to help the less gifted. The strong are needed to support, elevate, reach initial securing positions, and close out the task. The weak are included as integral parts of the team and can, through input in many dimensions, add greatly to the solving of the problem—for it is only when all group members have scaled the wall that the task is classified as successful. By contrast the game of dodge ball (which for some reason enjoys universal indulgence in schools and institutions) reflects society's unfortunate emphasis upon elimination, discrimination, and the lowering of self-concept. The weak are eliminated first and delegated to an inferior spectatorial status. The strong who remain derive benefits from the continuing physical activity and enjoy and participate in the fruits of victory.

Our position is that the early socializing experiences in society today resemble the dodge ball model and as such account for the high proportion of inactive and lethargic citizenry. Social fitness can be measured with objective measures such as social distance scales, interaction analysis measures, and sociograms, but it is probably best measured experientially through the warmth of friendship and the evidence of team spirit and cooperation. Where a group is seen to be functioning harmoniously, measures of social fitness register strong.

## Emotional

Emotional fitness refers to the capacity of the individual to deal with arousal states that bring personality to a ready status. The capacity of a person to balance excitement with coolness in the face of psycho-physiological stress is a keen indication of emotional fitness. The eminent psychologist John Watson contended that we have three innate emotions, which he identified as love, fear, and rage. Whereas each of these strong emotions is easily recognizable to an individual, the many other causes for bodily arousal are less easily identified although they have a pivotal effect on the motivation of an individual to take action. Watson considered that these emotions were learned. Early theorists viewed the emotions as a physiological state that was brought about by the organism being energized and activated through immediate physical exertion. Endocrinologists assure us that the existence of norepinephrine, which is secreted by the adrenal glands, is a clear indication that physical action has just taken place. The immense feeling of well-being resulting from the presence of norepinephrine can be described as a high state of emotion.

Hans Selye's work on stress further underscores the need for us to consider seriously emotional activity as a prime means for activation in the physical domain. Daily, communications media produce written and pictorial evidence of the critical effect that physical activity has on the emotions of the spectators and participants in the world of sport. Baseball World Series games perenially lock two cities in a terminal struggle for supremacy that results in a social state that has accurately been described as "uncontained contagion." The effects of highly visible community models such as these cannot be ignored in the scheme of human fitness. Communications through body language, eye contact, and social role accentuate the importance that emotions have on the desire of an individual to partake in physical activity.

It is important for an individual to learn to maintain a balance between reasonable emotional involvement and reasonable emotional control. Imbalance results in an unfit emotional state that is neither appropriate nor desirable. The position taken in this text is that emotional fitness is crucial to human fitness. An activity program that does not provide opportunities for individuals to experience excitement, interest, and depression is probably bound for failure. Mentors can actually teach for emotional control by pointing out the rewards of competition and the necessity for continued effort following failure. Teachers can help children make the necessary and sometimes painful adjustments in their daily lives through courses such as ropes, gymnastics, and contact sports, and they can acquaint students with measures to help them push personal barriers much further back. The emotional satisfaction gained when an individual achieves undreamed of success is usually gratifying and positive. Sometimes it means that certain restrictive influences such as negative administrators, hard-nosed judicial decrees, and cynical parental controls need to be loosened. In our anxiety to protect children from risk, we frequently become overprotective and overindulgent. In the physiological domain, measures of testing emotions are through blood and gastro-intestinal sampling, and such external measures as biofeedback, lie detection, and galvanic skin response. Perhaps the finest evidence of emotional fitness is, however, the smile or the frown.

## Spiritual

Spiritual dimensions of fitness refer to the development of a positive value that balances the satisfaction of personal needs and interests with those of the community. With the breakdown of the family and the diminishing of the church's influence, schools and other institutions have had to pay closer attention to values clarification than at any other time in human history. Much of the conflict that arises in sports is spiritual in nature. Naturalists consider it a crime to abort nature, for instance, through the drawing of lines on the ground and the construction of stadiums and artificial facilities. They consider any human fitness dependent upon material substance as unnatural and undesirable, and decidedly temporary in nature. They prefer to gain personal fitness through adapting the body to the dictates of nature. Such activities as hiking, swimming, running, climbing, and mountaineering constitute their curriculum. A realist, on the other hand, recognizes the restrictions of civilization and seeks to do the best with what is available. This may be seen in weight training, small-court games, activities played on artificial surfaces, or in substitute physical fitness programs such as sit-ups, push-ups, jumping jacks, and so on.

It is evident that values fitness constitutes a balance between the natural and the necessary, and recognition by an individual of the appropriateness of the activity in hand. Universal principles tend to govern an activity curriculum which seeks to promote spiritual fitness. Universal participation, friendly competition, and illumination in place of elimination are examples that readily spring to mind. The importance of stressing inherent individual values and the maximizing of the constructive elements in human existence are stressed.

Values can be tested through activities designed to demonstrate preferred rankings. Simon *et al.* (2) have published a text containing many of these values clarification games. Other activities such as environmental tests, values auctions, and sensitivity procedures give valuable information. It is probably true, however, that values fitness or lack of it is clearly evident in the performance of the community at large. An environment that stresses winning at all costs, spectatorism, survival of the fittest, winner take all, "Bugger you Jack—I'm alright!" is best described as spiritually unfit.


## MULTIDIMENSIONAL FITNESS PROGRAMS

### The School Curriculum

Although many school teachers today are emphasizing the need for multidimensional fitness, most school curricula do not reflect this emphasis. Far too many public school curricula are centered around the acquisition of skills and the playing of games. Multidimensional fitness probably cannot be gained from a ballgame-oriented curriculum. The curriculum has to contain a pivotal organizing center from which multidimensional fitness can logically grow. Chapter 9 deals with the conceptual curriculum in much greater detail. Samples only are offered here. A tripartite structure is offered for your consideration.

**Understanding Movement**

This curriculum is centered around the learning of concepts or "big ideas" related to the body of knowledge of the discipline of human movement. It is conducted separately from the typical physical education system of lessons and is particularly suited to interdisciplinary focus. The emphasis lies in the understanding of the movement concept under study. The teaching of this section of the curriculum can also be interdisciplinary involving teachers from other subject areas. A unit on aggression is included to illustrate this idea.

## Interpretation of Aggression with Observation and Discussion

*Objectives*
1. The students will experience frustration to the point where discussion about the term *aggression* will be meaningful.
2. The students will participate in activities (game form) designed to produce frustration.
3. The students will discuss their feelings about the frustrating experiences, identifying either action or thoughts of aggression which arose from the activities.
4. The students will distinguish between their interpretation of aggression in others and the aggressive feelings that others actually expressed.

*Content Rationale*
1. It seems aggressive behavior occurs at some stage in all human beings.
2. Aggression is often produced by frustration.
3. It is wise to encourage children to accurately interpret their own aggressive behavior.

*Learning Experiences*
1. *Balloon on Plate*
   Relay formation or individual contest. The student will carry a plate with an inflated balloon on it from point *A* to point *B*. If the balloon is dropped, the student must start

again from point *A*. After successfully making the trip, the
student gives the plate and balloon to the next one in line.

2. *Lifesaver on a Toothpick*

Line formation. A lifesaver is passed down the line from
student to student by transferring it from toothpick to toothpick held by the student's teeth. No hands allowed. If lifesaver is dropped, it must be started from beginning. The
winning team goes to recess 10 minutes early; remaining
teams miss recess (stressful goal).

3. *Egg on Spoon*

Relay formation. An egg, which is balanced on a spoon held
between the teeth, must be carried from point *A* to point *B*.
The spoon and egg are then given to the next student. If the
egg is dropped, student must begin again at point *A* (likely
to produce aggression in parents as well).

4. *Water in Cup*

Relay formation. Student must carry a cup of water from
point *A* to point *B* without spilling it. The team which finishes relay first with the most water remaining in the cup
wins. The remaining teams clean up floor.

*Evaluation*

1. Discussion involving class during or at end of activities.
2. Children will be given opportunity to describe in words, writing, or through artistic media, feelings experienced during
   activities. Other children will be asked whether their opinions
   were commensurate.

## Applying Movement

This curriculum is centered around the application of movement in
the learning of sports motor skills as applied to inclusive games and challenges. Included in this section are lead-up activities to major and minor
games, gymnastics, dance, track, swimming, etc. This should lead to inter-
mural activities for all who can be persuaded to join in. Games for the
gifted few can be added in nonclass time. Miller *et al.* (3) have included
many such games.

Emphasis here is on promoting sound intellectual, social, emotional,
and value-fitness principles in the developing child at the elementary
level. Attempts to educate parents can come also through sending home
report cards that reflect this emphasis.

Table 14-1 gives a simple example of such an instrument.

### Table 14-1. Report of Progress in Physical Education*

Name _____        Grade 4 ___ 5 ___ 6 ___

| Items | Sept.–Jan. | Jan.–June | Comments |
|---|---|---|---|
| **Physical** Fitness Skills | | | |
| **Intellectual** Activity knowledge Tests | | | |
| **Social** Leadership Cooperation | | | |
| **Emotional** Enthusiasm Control of feelings | | | |
| **Spiritual (Values)** Respect (personal, property) Effort | | | |

*Scoring Key:
1. Above average
2. Average
3. Needs attention

Parent Signature: _____

Parent Comments: _____

### Enjoying Movement

This curriculum is centered around providing lifetime activity experiences which help children make intelligent decisions about the extent of their movement participation. It is hoped that this participation will last for many years. Such curriculum items as cycling, bowling, hiking, camping, skiing, boating, and climbing are planned. The provision for relatively inexpensive equipment helps promote universal involvement, and the opportunity for interdisciplinary activity is great.

Table 14-2 contains a sample of an interdisciplinary learning experience conducted by the Human Environment Institute of Boston University at Sargent Camp, Peterborough, New Hampshire.

**Table 14-2. Interdisciplinary Studies through Environmental Education**

*Schedule of Activities*

All activities will originate at Northern Lodge

*Friday, November 7*

| | |
|---|---|
| 4:00—5:30 p.m. | Scrounging Around |
| 6:00 p.m. | Dinner |
| 7:00 p.m. | Introductory Activities |
| 7:45—8:45 p.m. | Sardines Activity |
| 9:00 p.m. | Movement & Creative Expression |
| 9:45 p.m. | The Wellington |
| 10:15 p.m. | Social Hour |

*Saturday, November 8*

7:30 a.m.            Breakfast

8:30–11:00 a.m.     *Group I*     A. Watershed Laboratory and Percolation Test
B. Solar Panel and Telescope
C. Meadow Trail and Bird Blind
D. Adventure Course
E. Aesthetic Expression

*Group II*     B. Solar Panel and Telescope
C. Meadow Trail and Bird Blind
D. Adventure Course
E. Aesthetic Expression
A. Watershed Laboratory and Percolation Test

*Group III*     D. Adventure Course
E. Aesthetic Expression
A. Watershed Laboratory and Percolation Test
B. Solar Panel and Telescope
C. Meadow Trail and Bird Blind

*Group IV*     E. Aesthetic Expression
A. Watershed Laboratory and Percolation Test
B. Solar Panel and Telescope
C. Meadow Trail and Bird Blind
D. Adventure Course

*Schedule of Activities (cont.)*

| | |
|---|---|
| 11:00 a.m. | Environmental Auction |
| 12:00–12:15 p.m. | Lunch |
| | In-Depth Activity, selected from: |
| | 1. Adventure Course |
| | 2. Solving a Problem—Water Testing |
| | 3. Orienteering |
| | 4. Triangulation and Map Making |
| | 5. Forest Community |
| | 6. Stake-A-Claim |
| 2:30–2:45 p.m. | Exploration of Follow-Up Activities related to above |
| 2:45–4:00 p.m. | Planning Session |
| 4:00 p.m. | Departure |

## A Personal Curriculum

Success at school probably is not sufficient to guarantee continued growth toward human fitness once the student has left this structured environment. The most valuable curriculum any school can embrace is one that develops personal habits leading young people into postures of self-discipline. Human fitness is a form of self-discipline as well as a lifetime pursuit, and it is intensely personal. Some examples of outstanding personal fitness curricula are available but the overall statistical picture is gloomy. Included here is a personal multidimensional fitness schedule developed by Gerd Lutter of Plymouth State College, New Hampshire. Lutter developed this schedule with a view to including opportunities for personal growth in all five dimensions, with the schedule on the left of each page reflecting an ideal schedule, and the one on the right reflecting a schedule of practical validity in the author's daily existence.

### Developing Physical Fitness*

When concerned with the task of developing fitness, the questions that come to mind immediately are fitness for what, and how will I develop this fitness. In my particular case the answers are closely related to my lifestyle and my work, as they are for most people. At this particular time I am employed as an Instructor/Coach at Plymouth State College. I am the coach of the varsity soccer as well as the track and field team and also instruct our "major activities" of basketball, soccer, track and field, and tennis. My fitness goals are then to maintain a high level of fitness in these activities so that I can maintain my ability to demonstrate these activities and also to be able to compete with the better amateurs in New

---

*This section was written by Gerd Lutter, soccer and track coach at Plymouth State College, New Hampshire, and it is reprinted with the author's permission.

Hampshire in the sports of basketball, tennis and soccer. I would also like to maintain a high level of fitness because I am convinced of the benefits of fitness and also because of my very competitive nature . . . I hate to lose to anybody in anything. . . . To be a winner I must maintain a high level of fitness. I can stand to compete in something every day. I thrive on competition—I find it exciting.

To answer the question of how I will develop and maintain my fitness, I will include in my schedule a variety of activities that are strenuous and are designed to develop the various fitness components as presented to our *Fitness Institute* by Don Franks, namely those related to body composition, efficiency, endurance, skill, and to the socio-psychological (Table 14-2). Plymouth State's excellent athletic facilities will facilitate my desire to keep fit. Some of these facilities include an indoor track, swimming pool, basketball courts, handball and paddleball courts, as well as a conditioning room and a wrestling room.

In developing my fitness and in making up these two workout schedules I will try to follow a number of guidelines that reflect my attitude and feelings toward fitness and activity Some of these are:

1. I will try to overload to make for improvement.

2. I will play the game or practice the activity in which I would like to become more efficient.

3. I will try to eat, sleep, rest, and exercise in "moderation."

4. I will test myself from time to time to check my fitness status.

5. I will weigh myself daily.

6. I will try to begin every activity with a warm-up and follow it with a warm-down.

7. When beginning a new activity I will try to ease into it . . . not overdo an activity not done before or not done in a while to avoid possible muscular problems.

8. I will do those activities that are fun as well as those that are challenging to me.

9. I will vary the activities to tax the different parts of my body as well as to avoid boredom.

10. I will try to follow days of hard workouts with days of light workouts.

11. I will try to be a good sport.

12. I will try to use sports to relieve tensions and anxieties, not to increase them.

## Table 14-2. Developing Physical Fitness

| *The Ideal Workout Schedule* | *The Practical Workout Schedule* |
| --- | --- |

### Monday

*Time:* 10:00 AM—?
     3:00 PM—?
*Activity*: Rowing (Single Shell)
Rowing on Newfound Lake . . . in the morning when the lake is smooth and peaceful. . . . Row about 2½ miles at slow pace.

*Rationale:*

Good activity for strength of upper body as well as legs. Very enjoyable under the circumstances. The strength developed could carry over to tennis and track.

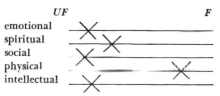

*Activity:* Basketball
Play basketball in gym with players of my ability. Five on five. Play until tired. Keep score.

*Rationale:*

This is one of my favorite activities. . . . I love this game. Endurance, composition, skill, socio-psych.

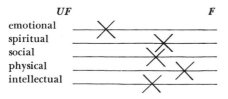

*Time:* Afternoon sometime about 1:30
*Activity:* Jogging
Jog around the athletic fields (2½ miles) at about 6 minute pace

*Rationale:*

Normally only activity available because of heavy usage of college facilities . . . also little time available during schoolday.

It's a good cardio-respiratory endurance activity. Weight control (body composition).

Good carry-over to basketball, soccer, tennis, and track which are my concern

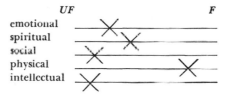

Table 14-2 (Cont.)

## Tuesday

*Time:* 10:00 AM
*Activity:* Tennis
Play tennis match with Art (PSC Tennis Coach). 3 sets. Warm-up with easy hitting.

*Rationale:*
    Art is a good challenge, enjoy playing with him . . . skill development.

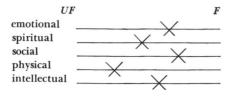

*Time:* 1:30 to 2:15
*Activity:* Jogging, Universal Gym
Jog-run three and a half miles . . . use 1st mile for warm-up . . . run last ½ mile hard, warm-down with walk
    Light series on all 10 stations of U.G.

*Rationale:*
    Strength, endurance, body composition, carry-over to tennis, soccer, track, baseball.

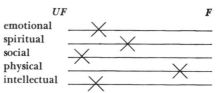

## Wednesday

*Activity:* Running
    Warm-up with some light calisthenics and stretching of legs and back.
    Run the college cross-country course. 1st mile slow, 2nd and 3rd mile at faster but comfortable pace . . . run the last·1½ miles at good pace . . . pushing it.

*Rationale:*
    Running the college cross-country course is a pleasant and enjoyable experience . . . it's a beautiful course . . . wooded, secluded . . . with a number of good challenging hills.
    This workout will help develop endurance (muscular, cardio-respiratory) which will carry over to tennis, track, soccer, basketball, etc., in which I want to stay competitive.

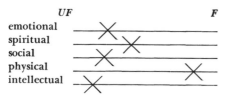

*Activity:* Tennis, Universal Gym
    Tennis match with anyone I can find. Probably warm-up with easy hitting. After match go through all ten stations on universal gym. . . . One set with 10 reps.

*Rationale:* Tennis for skill development in that particular sport and also for some muscular endurance.
    The universal gym work will help promote overall strength and favorably affect body composition. Will help develop strength for other sports.

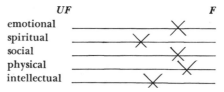

## Thursday

*Activity:* Tennis (in morning)
Play tennis with Rod Laver. Have him help me on strategy and technique. Play a set to point out my shortcomings.

*Rationale:* I am very much interested in improving my tennis skills. . . . I'm sure that Rod could help me. Rod seems like a nice guy. . . . I think I would enjoy playing with him and in having him help me. Just being on the court with him would be very exciting and inspirational.

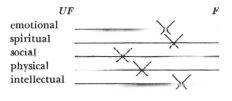

*Activity:* Basketball, Universal Gym
Play basketball pick-up game with anyone in gym for about an hour or until tired.
Follow with universal gym work. On all stations. . . . One set of 10 reps. Overload or same as last session.

*Rationale:* Basketball is a good activity for the development of agility, balance, leg strength quickness . . . and the way I play, endurance.
On the universal gym I can develop my strength . . . arms, legs, abdominal, as well as back and chest.

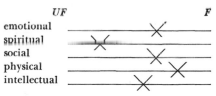

## Friday

*Activity:* Cross Country Skiing
Take backpack along with lunch for picnic . . . ski the Waterville Valley, N.H. C.C. course . . . a delightful experience . . . take wife and son and make it a family outing. Ski about 5–6 miles . . . take time.

*Rationale:* Terrific overall conditioner . . . reinforces vascular system . . . total body strengthening. Employs arm and leg muscles. Good family activity. I enjoy such outings with the family.

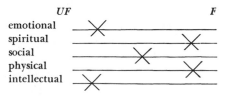

*Activity:* Running
Run the college cross country course. 4.4 miles in about 30 minutes . . . run at comfortable pace for first mile. FARTLEK for last 3.4 miles.

*Rationale:* This is an enjoyable way for me to get a workout alone. Finding someone to work out with is a problem for me many times. I also like to set my own pace when I run.
This is a good cardio-vascular endurance activity. It also helps develop my leg strength. Helps keep my weight down.

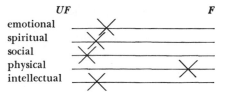

Table 14-2 (Cont.)

### Saturday

*Activity:* Square Dancing

This is a lively activity that I enjoy doing. This also involves my wife and close friends of the family.

*Rationale:*

Good family activity. Good recreation . . . lots of fun.

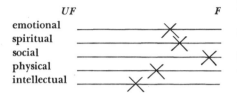

*Activity:* Basketball

Play pick-up games with whoever happens to be in the gym. Play for 1 to 2 hours.

*Rationale:*

Saturday finds many good pick-up games going on in the college gym. I enjoy playing in these games.

Tremendous workout . . . vascular, muscular workout.

One of my fitness goals is to maintain basketball fitness and the best way to do this is to play basketball.

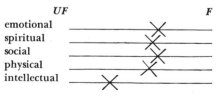

### Sunday

*Activity:* None planned

*Rationale:*

One day a week (Sunday) I would like to spend with the family . . . although no specific activity is planned for, we might still do some fun activity.

*Activity:* None planned
*Rationale:* same as ideal schedule.

### Monday

*Activity:* Rowing

Single scull rowing on Newfound Lake (N.H.). Row for about 1½ to 2 hours. Nice easy pace with emphasis on enjoyment. If I feel up to it . . . push last half mile back to boathouse.

*Rationale:* Benefits heart, muscle power, coordination. This sort of activity makes one feel close to nature.

*Activity:* Soccer

Play with the team during their practice; will also play in soccer activity classes.

*Rationale:* I enjoy playing the game. It is one of the activities in which I would like to maintain a degree of fitness.

Good activity for stamina, agility, balance, leg strength, etc.

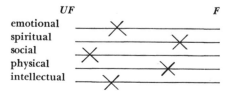

## Tuesday

*Activity:* Golf (in the early morning)

Play 18 holes with Gary Player. Gary Player is the golfer most admired by me. He is a good golfer as well as a good athlete. Playing with him would be a good golf education. It would also be very inspirational. We would not use cars but walk the course for the exercise.

To make the foursome complete, I would also ask my two golfing cronies, Art and John, to join us.

*Rationale:*

I enjoy playing golf especially in the early morning when there are few people on the course, when the grass is still wet and everything is quiet.

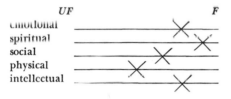

*Activity:* Swimming

Swim laps in the pool. Four laps of freestyle (crawl), four laps backstroke, four breaststroke, four butterfly. Swim at a comfortable pace. Finish with some diving.

*Rationale:* Swimming is another enjoyable activity for me. It is taxing while at the same time it has a loosening effect on my muscles. After playing soccer the day before, it will help me recover from the aches and pains incurred.

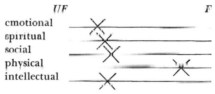

## Wednesday

*Activity:* Soccer

Play in a practice scrimmage with the "Boston Minutemen."

*Rationale:* This would be very inspirational . . . I would certainly "hustle" and play hard. I would get a good vascular and muscular fitness type workout.

I would also get a good insight into a professional team's tactics.

Soccer is one of my favorite activities.

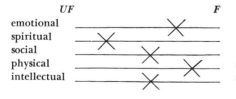

*Activity:* Paddleball

Play with Jim Smith. Best out of three games.

*Rationale:* Jim is available for play most of the time. He is the best player in the college.

Paddleball is a demanding game. It requires an ability to change direction as in tennis, soccer, and basketball.

A good workout in a short time.

I also enjoy the game and enjoy the challenge of playing Jim Smith.

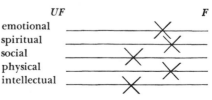

## Thursday

*Activity:* Running—Swimming

Run FARTLEK for about 4 miles on the college C.C. course.

Follow with a relaxing swim in the lake.

*Rationale:*

Good vascular endurance activity. Leg strength developer.

I intend to run early in the morning and on a delightful, beautiful wooded path.

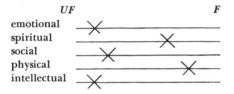

*Activity:* Running—Swimming

Exactly the same as ideal schedule.

*Rationale:* Same.

## Friday

*Activity:* Skiing (downhill)

Skiing the afternoon at Waterville Valley.

*Rationale:*

It's an invigorating activity, exciting and enjoyable.

Good for developing balance, leg strength, courage-confidence.

Good change of pace in workout schedule.

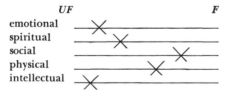

*Activity:* Tennis

Play tennis with someone of equal skill. Compete . . . best out of 3 sets.

*Rationale:*

Enjoy the game and am stimulated by competition.

This is one of my fitness goals.

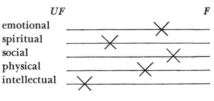

### *References*

Class Notes, SED MH 713 Institute on Physical Fitness, Boston University.

Fleishman, Edward. *The Structure and Measurement of Physical Fitness.* Englewood Cliffs, N.J.: Prentice-Hall, 1965.

Homola, Samuel. *Muscle Training for Athletes.* West Nyack, N.Y.: Parker Publishing Co., 1968.

Olson, Edward. *Conditioning.* Columbus, Ohio: Charles Merrill Publishing Co., 1968.

## Conclusion

In making up these two "fitness schedules," I selected activities that contributed to my social, intellectual, and spiritual fitness as well as to my physical fitness. Unfortunately, the activities selected for my "practical schedule" tilted very heavily toward the physical aspect of total fitness. This I tried to avoid in my ideal schedule. The ideal schedule does make for a more complete development.

In the ideal schedule, I selected a greater variety of activities with ideal partners, opponents, and teammates to increase my chances of an "all around" development. The time of workouts are also better on the ideal schedule. On the ideal schedule I also tried to select activities that make me look forward to the next day, activities that make me feel excited about life.

In reviewing these two schedules, I realize that the intellectual fitness aspect is most neglected. As it is, I know quite a bit about most of the activities selected and have had previous experience in these activities as either a teacher or participant.

The best "all around" activity on either of the schedules seems to be square dancing, which is a little bit of a surprise.

If there is a pattern to the schedules that can be detected, it is probably a pattern of alternating team and individual activities and a pattern of hard workouts followed by easier workouts.

It can also be seen that I have included a lot of strenuous activities such as running, rowing, swimming, etc. I have been doing such activities for a long time. I enjoy punishing myself somewhat. I obtain a tremendous feeling of satisfaction from having pushed myself, which always seems to make it worthwhile. It also lets me know where I stand in my fitness. About two hours after such hard workouts, I get a feeling of tranquility . . . a feeling of well-being that I find difficult to describe.

I have also included a lot of competitive activities; again, I enjoy these. I don't put pressure on myself and although I play hard to win, losing does not upset me emotionally but it does spur on my efforts to stay fit.

Lutter has clearly demonstrated his use of the discipline in application to personal fitness. Clear direction in this chapter is to suggest that human fitness does result from application of the knowledge outlined in the Discipline of Human Movement, provided the full scope of the discipline structure is used. Physical fitness alone is inadequate—human fitness results from healthy growth in intellectual, social, emotional, and values dimensions as well.

# Bibliography

*Adult Physical Fitness.* President's Council of Physical Fitness. U.S. Government Printing Office, Washington, D.C. 20402.

ASTRAND, P. O. AND K. RODAHL. *Textbook of Work Physiology.* New York: McGraw Hill Book Co., 1970.

BERGER, RICHARD A. *Conditioning for Men.* Boston: Allyn and Bacon, 1972.

CHEFFERS, J. T. F., E. AMIDON, AND KEN D. RODGERS. *Interaction Analysis: An Application to Nonverbal Activity.* Minneapolis, Minnesota: Paul S. Amidon and Associates, 1974.

CURETON, T. K. "Comparison of Various Factor Analyses of Cardiovascular-respirator Test Variables," *Research Quarterly,* 37 (1966): 317–25.

CURETON, T. K. *The Physiological Effects of Exercise Programs on Adults.* Springfield, Ill.: C. C. Thomas, 1969.

DEVRIES, H. A. *Physiology of Exercise for Physical Education and Athletes.* Dubuque, Iowa: W. C. Brown, 1966.

*Exercise and Fitness.* Chicago: Athletic Institute, 1960.

*Exercise and Fitness.* Chicago: Athletic Institute, 1969.

*Exercise in the Prevention, in the Evaluation, and in the Treatment of Heart Disease. Journal of South Carolina Medical Association,* 65 (1969): sup.

FRANKS, DON B., AND HELGA DEUTSCH. *Evaluating Performance in Physical Education.* New York: Academic Press, 1973.

FRANKS, DON B. 3 excellent papers available from the author, College of HPER, Temple University, Philadelphia, Pa.
   (1) "Components of Physical Fitness and Performance"
   (2) "Cardiovascular Function"
   (3) "Review of Effects of Regular, Vigorous Physical Activity with Implications for Exercise Prescription"

FRANKS, DON B. (ed). *Exercise and Fitness—1969.* Chicago: Athletic Institute, 1969.

GILLIS, JAMES, AND ANTHONY LANSTON. Various papers and programs, Human Environment Institute, School of Education, Boston University, Boston 02215.

HARRISON, CLARKE H. *Physical Fitness Newsletters,* Available from University of Oregon, Eugene, Oregon 97403.

*Health and Fitness in the Modern World.* Chicago: Athletic Institute, 1969.

HOLLOSZY, J. O. "Biochemical Adaptations to Exercise: Aerobic Metabolism," in J. Wilmore (ed.), *Exercise and Sport Sciences Reviews,* Vol. 1. New York: Academic Press, 1973.

HOMEL, STEVEN R., AND TOM EVAUL. *Understanding Human Behavior: A Needs Approach.* The Authors—Temple University, Philadelphia, Pennsylvania, 1968.

MILLER, A. G., J. T. F. CHEFFERS, AND VIRGINIA WHITCOMB. *Physical Education: Teaching Human Movement in Elmentary Schools,* 4th ed. Englewood Cliffs, N.J.: Prentice-Hall, Inc., 1974.

MORGAN, RICHARD L. *Psychology: An Individualized Course,* rev. ed. Sunnyvale, Cal.: Westinghouse Learning Press, 1972.

Physical Activity and Cardiovascular Health. *Canadian Medical Association Journal,* 96 (1967): 695–915.

POLLOCK, M. L., R. JANEWAY, AND H. B. LOFLAND. "Effects of Frequency of Training on Serum Lipids, Cardiovascular Function, and Body Composition," in B. Franks (ed). *Exercise and Fitness.* Chicago: Athletic Institute, 1969.

ROHNKE, KARL, AND ROBERT LENTZ. *Adventure Curriculum: Physical Education.* Project Adventure, rev. ed., Hamilton Wenham High School, Mass. 1974.

SIMON SIDNEY et al. *Values Clarification: A Handbook of Practical Strategies for Teachers and Students.* New York: Hart Publishing Co., 1972.

WILMORE. J. (ed). *Exercise and Sports Science Review,* Vol. 1. New York: Academic Press, 1974.

# PART IV

*Human Movement:*
*Generative and Integrated*

# 15

## How Does the Discipline of
## Human Movement Change?

*Leonard Zaichkowsky*

One of the most obvious phenomena of the modern era is change.*
It characterizes every phase of life. In a broad sense, change implies
realigning existing regularities in some way by modifying existing regularities, by eliminating one or more regularities, or by producing new
ones. Change can be initiated simply by a dislike on the part of an individual for an existing regularity, or by a number of other forces. These
forces will be discussed later as *agents of change.*

Grossman (1) points out that change historically was slow to transpire,
and it is only during the last 150 years that tremendous changes in
everyday life have taken place throughout the world. Before the latter
part of the eighteenth century, life, for the average person, remained
relatively constant. Today, however, most of us are caught up in the
process of change either as agents (those who initiate change), or as individuals affected by change from an external force.

Historically, the discipline of Human Movement, has been slow to
change. However, in recent years it has undergone fundamental changes.
What are some of these changes? What are the characteristics of change?
What brings about change? The present chapter discusses the concept of
change and attempts to provide answers to these questions.

*Change is discussed in a sociological context in Chap. 6 and from a self-change
viewpoint in Chap. 8.

## THE CHARACTERISTICS OF CHANGE

The first characteristic of change is *rate*. Change may occur very slowly, rapidly, or sputter along and gradually fade. For example, historically, major rule changes in games such as baseball, football, basketball, and hockey have been difficult, if not impossible, to implement. It has only been in the last few years that innovative changes (such as the designated hitter in baseball and changes in football's kicking game) have occurred. Expansion of the four major professional sports was also slow to occur. For decades football, baseball, hockey, and basketball maintained the same teams in their respective leagues with only occasional franchise changes. In recent years all of the major professional sports have expanded or have formed competing leagues.

Track and field as well as tennis are also examples of sports whose major concepts have undergone recent drastic change. Track has introduced the professional tour and tennis has initiated team tennis. Rather drastic rapid changes are often referred to as *revolutionary*. Rather slow changes, or changes not of a major nature, are referred to as *evolutionary*.

Another characteristic of change is *direction*. It is rare that change occurs simply for the sake of change, thus the direction of change must come under careful scrutiny. Planners of change usually rely heavily on research reports as well as on insight before plunging into change. For example, the owners of expansion teams as well as the owners of teams in newly formed professional leagues have relied on some objective reports of the dollar market before making their investments.

A third characteristic of change is *volume*. Whenever there is a successful change experience, there is a "snowballing effect"; that is, similar groups aspire to make the same changes. When professional football achieved success by introducing the "already old" American Football League, the other major professional sports expanded. When they too experienced success, along came the World Hockey Association, World Football League, and now there is even talk of a World Baseball League.

A fourth characteristic of change is *quality*, which requires a value judgment. The produced changes may be judged as good or bad depending upon one's point of view. There are many sports fans who believe that expansion in the various sports has created a "watered-down" product, and hence has been bad. In addition, the formation of new leagues has spiraled athletes' salaries, making the same opponents of expansion critical of ticket prices. On the other hand, the proponents of expansion indicate that more fans in new cities have been provided with opportunities to see their favorite sport and sports heroes, and this is necessarily good. The athletes themselves see expansion as a positive change, since it has provided opportunities for more to play professional sports. The new leagues have placed the athlete in a better bargaining position for salaries. For them this is a positive change.

A way of conceptualizing a system of change is shown schematically in Figure 15-1.

## THE AGENTS OF CHANGE

Something has to precipitate or initiate change. The initiator is referred to as the change agent. A number of change agents have been functioning in the discipline of Human Movement, and they will be discussed. Emphasis will be placed on those agents which have contributed the most to change, namely research and technology. Discussion will also center around the change agents of government, university scholars, and the teacher.

**Figure 15-1**

| Characteristics of Change | Agents of Change | Focus of Change |
|---|---|---|
| 1. Rate | 1. Research | |
| 2. Direction | 2. Technology | Human behavior, |
| 3. Volume | 3. University scholars | Attitudes, etc. |
| 4. Quality | 4. Government laws | |
| | 5. Teachers | |

Modified from Unruh and Turner (1970).

### Research

Undoubtedly research findings over the past 35 years have contributed greatly to changes in Human Movement. Research has also directly or indirectly contributed to the effectiveness of the other change agents (technology, government laws, university scholars, and teachers) and vice versa. Hence it can be said that these change agents interact.

Before fully discussing the contributions of research, let us first define research. Gantz (2) provides us with an informal definition of research. "Actually research means finding out things for oneself. It often means trying out things just to see what happens. It is an outlet for that most precious human quality, curiosity." Kerlinger (3) in providing a definition of scientific research states, "Scientific research is systematic, controlled, empirical, and critical investigation of hypothetical propositions about the presumed relations among natural phenomena."

From these two definitions, we might conclude that research involves testing a hypothesis that one is curious about. When certain findings occur because of systematic, well-controlled, and empirical (submitted to objective test) research, change may be an outcome. Again change should not come about simply for the sake of change but to improve physical, mental, and social well-being.

Research in the field of Human Movement may concern itself with either *basic research* or *applied research*. Basic research aims to enlarge the pool of knowledge common to all professions. It does not have any immediate application; however, in many cases the researcher searches for laws and principles that govern many situations, rather than a specific situation. Applied research, on the other hand, is concerned with applying knowledge immediately to the field. The distinction between basic and applied research is not always clear-cut. However, most researchers in the field of Human Movement engage in research that is toward the applied end of the basic-applied research continuum (Figure 15-2).

The specific contributions of research to change in Human Movement

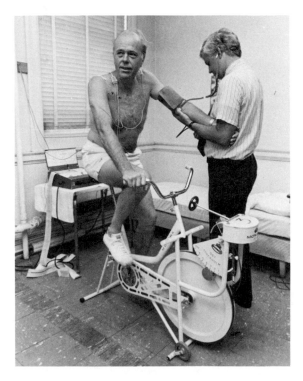

**Figure 15-2.** Research findings enhance human movement. (*Courtesy of the Boston University Photo Service*)

are innumerable. It is also probably safe to say that research in the area of Human Movement has, on the whole, been evolutionary rather than revolutionary. For purposes of illustration let us look at some research findings that have contributed to changes in Human Movement.

In 1954, Kraus and Hirschland (4) published the results of a fitness test (Kraus-Weber test) given to 4,458 American and 3,156 European children. The American children showed the highest failure rate (57.9 percent) when compared to Austrian (9.5 percent), Swiss (8.9 percent), and Italian (8.0 percent) children. The results of this research prompted President Dwight D. Eisenhower to establish the President's Council on Youth Fitness in 1956. Since that time the United States government has maintained an interest in the fitness of America's youth.

It is, however, rare to see change occur largely as a result of the findings of one study. More often, change occurs as a result of a series of studies which have similar findings.

For example, the use of weight training in the preparation of athletes is a relatively new concept brought about by a combination of observation and systematic research findings. For years very few athletes took part in weight training for fear of becoming "muscle bound." Now in order to be successful at almost any sport, athletes, both male and female, must engage in some type of resistance training. Also, rather than using weights only during the preseason, many athletes have found it beneficial to use weights during the season.

Another situation in which research has contributed to change is the specificity of practice. Numerous studies have demonstrated that the practice drill used for motor-skill learning must closely resemble the actual situation in order to be effective. Shooting baskets in practice without a defensive player is not at all like the game situation and hence not as effective as using a defensive player during the drill.

Research then, has been a major change agent in human movement and will continue to be so if members of the profession show a willingness to conduct important research studies. Not everyone feels capable or comfortable in conducting research, and this is to be expected. However, it is most important that everyone in the profession make an attempt to stay abreast of current research findings. Publications such as the *Research Quarterly, Journal of Motor Behavior, Medicine and Science in Sports, Abstracts of Research Papers* from the AAHPER Convention, and *Completed Research in Health, Physical Education, and Recreation* are examples of what should be read. Other publications which discuss research findings include *Research in Dance, The Athletic Journal, Scholastic Coach,* and a series entitled *What Research Tells the Coach.* This series includes research findings for baseball, distance running, swimming, wrestling, and football.

As well as these research publications, research reports are always held at state, district, and national AAHPER conventions. Conventions sponsored by the American College of Sports Medicine, North American Society for the Psychology of Sport and Physical Activity, and the Canadian Association for Health, Physical Education, and Recreation also have excellent research studies reported.

## Technology

*How has technology contributed to change in Human Movement?* The tremendous strides in technology during the last two decades have contributed immeasurably to change in the discipline of Human Movement. It would be difficult to find any aspect of Human Movement not affected in some way by technological innovation.

Technology has brought about a decrease in manual labor. This has contributed toward a less fit individual, since physical exertion has become minimized. Rather than walking to work or riding bicycles, workers ride in their cars or on rapid transit systems. Manual labor on the job itself has also been reduced in most situations. Although technology in general has contributed to positive change in Human Movement, the above example is one in which technology has perhaps done us a disservice.

The positive aspect of recent technological advancement is the wide assortment of innovative products, equipment, supplies, and materials that have allowed athletes to train more effectively, receive better coaching, and break records. For example, excellent compact training devices such as the Exergenie, Universal Gym, and Nautilus have contributed a great deal to change in methods of strength and endurance training. Fiberglass poles as well as foam landing pads (in place of metal poles and sand or sawdust pits) have contributed to record-breaking performances in pole-vaulting events.

The advent of videotape equipment as well as the increased use of all filming equipment has resulted in better coaching and improved learning on the part of the athlete because of feedback. Very few amateur or professional athletes fail to use film in attempting to better their performance.

Research opportunities and sophistication have also increased because of technology. Exercise physiologists are capable of rapidly analyzing gases and monitoring vital human functions while exercising because of modern equipment. Kinesiologists are able to record subtle muscle movements via electromyographic machines. Researchers in motor learning are able to train individuals to relax through biofeedback machines. As well as providing research opportunities, technology has produced sophisticated computers that are capable of rapidly analyzing research data.

Technology has also made rapid, extended travel very easy. This along with technological advances in mass communication has allowed individuals in all parts of the world to benefit from innovative change.

## Government

*How has government and the passage of laws contributed to change in Human Movement?* Recently the government has produced what could be termed a revolutionary change in the discipline of Human Movement through legislation commonly referred to as Title IX. In essence, this legislation has mandated that women be given "equal" opportunity to participate in scholastic and collegiate athletics. Although Title IX affects more than just athletic financing and participation, it has definitely produced change in female athletic programs. Many schools are providing budgetary allowances for athletic directors, coaches, and athletic scholarships. This governmental action has made it possible for girls to enjoy the same benefits that boys have had for years.

Similar government laws such as affirmative action, designed to prevent discrimination against minorities and women, have also contributed to the formation of coeducational offerings from unified departments of physical education rather than from antiquated men's and women's departments.

The President's Council on Physical Fitness is another example of government involvement in Human Movement change. Change is also brought to the schools through the National Defense Education Act and the Elementary and Secondary School Act by providing funds to schools and colleges for certain services.

The government contributes indirectly to change in the field by awarding thousands of dollars annually for research projects in the form of grants.

## Scholars

*How have university scholars contributed to change in Human Movement?* University scholars, in their constant quest for wider knowledge, contribute to change in Human Movement primarily through conducting research and writing or the publication of their material. Their writings generally have a powerful impact on some of the other agents of change such as technology and the government. Change occurs because of the scholars' interest in research on teaching techniques, learnings, and human interaction. In many ways and situations university scholars have provided the research leadership that has labeled them as irritants to the status quo and a threat to tradition.

## Teachers

*How have teachers contributed to change in Human Movement?* The teacher has not and should not be the least of the change agents. Whenever an improvement in instruction or an imaginative project is attempted, change is implied. Over the years teachers have relied on their own initiative and imagination to bring about change. With strong training on the part of recent graduates, perhaps more positive change can occur because of the teachers' familiarity with research, technology, laws, and communication with university scholars. Without the desire to change on the part of the everyday practitioner, our profession faces a dim future. We cannot maintain credibility with the public if we practice archaic and outmoded methods of teaching. The alternative then is to be willing to be informed about change and to experiment in order to bring about these changes.

## THE FOCUS OF CHANGE

Change is not a simple process because not everyone affected by change will support it. Many people are conservative by nature and are reluctant to try new ideas. Others are simply indifferent to change, or do not wish to be tied up in bureaucratic red tape. Change may bring about insecurity and fear. These human inhibitors of change exist because change is generally directed towards them and their behavior. Change cannot take place without first changing the attitudes and behavior of people. Curriculum change in schools requires that teachers realize the need for change and be willing to implement it. The students must also be supportive of innovations. Human behavior then is the primary target group at which change is directed.

## THE INITIATION OF CHANGE

As stated in the beginning of the chapter, change in the discipline of Human Movement has been slow in transpiring or evolutionary rather than revolutionary. However, there are many new people in the profession, young people who have the potentiality for becoming change agents.

There are also creative, perceptive teachers or coaches, who are bored with detail, routine, and repetitiveness. They too can be agents of change. These characteristics are not innate in an individual; they can be developed.

In initiating change it is not only important that one have courage or creativity. It is equally important that the objectives of change are clearly spelled out, preferably in behavioral terms so that they can be evaluated. Support systems must be available from the financial community and others. If support is not available, proposed change may be doomed to failure. When change has finally been implemented, it is important that constant feedback be obtained so that evaluation can take place.

This chapter has stressed the importance and the necessity for change in the discipline of Human Movement. It will also end on that note. Our discipline cannot survive without change; we ourselves must initiate change. Numerous areas require change. The priorities, however, differ for each of us. By being adequately prepared as professionals and willing to engage in and utilize research, the future professional in Human Movement can seek out priorities and implement necessary change.

## References Cited

1. GROSSMAN, L. *The Change Agent.* New York: AMACOM (American Management Associations), 1974.
2. GANTZ, B. "The Relevance of Research to Teaching," in B. Gantz (ed.), *Learning Theory and Personality Research Applied to Teaching.* New York: Selected Academic Readings, Inc., 1965.
3. KERLINGER, F. N. *Foundations of Behavioral Research.* New York: Holt, Rinehart, and Winston, 1973.
4. KRAUS, H., AND R. HIRSCHLAND. "Minimum Muscular Fitness Tests in School Children." *Research Quarterly*, 25 (1954): 178.
5. UNRUH, A., AND H. E. TURNER. *Supervision for Change and Innovation.* Boston: Houghton Mifflin Co., 1970.

# 16

## How is the Discipline of Human Movement Interdependent with Other Disciplines?

*John Cheffers* / *Lois Smith*

The thesis of this text is strong: the discipline of Human Movement is, like History, a compelling example of the integrative discipline. The body of knowledge of Human Movement is integral to and interdependent with many other disciplines. In the words of Rudolph Laban (1), "There is no emotion or intellectual action without bodily movement manifestation or vice versa." Siedentop (2) describes it as an approach that "takes the primary focus out of the realm of educational programs and into the realm of the value free discipline."

Acceptance of this viewpoint sets at rest the perennial argument that Human Movement is a homeless waif wandering amid the generous embraces of paternal, settled, and relatively complete academic families. No longer do hapless physical educators have to defend their academic emphasis through peripheral attachment to other more prestigious disciplines such as Anatomy, Physiology, Psychology, Physics, Chemistry, Sociology, and Anthropology. The study of Human Movement is, in and of itself, a scholarly pursuit. Indeed, specialists from other disciplines constantly study the fundamental concepts of the body of knowledge of Human Movement. No area of human endeavor can exist on input from a single discipline alone. In fact, every area must utilize movement of some kind, be it movement so fine as making the digital adjustments on the stem of a violin or so gross as the scaling of a mountain peak. Certainly it appears that those applying the discipline of Human Movement through gross motor patterns (the physical educators, the dance educators, the recreators, and the fitness exponents) have enjoyed considerably less prestige than those applying the discipline of Human Movement through fine motor patterns (the surgeons, the lapidaries, the musicians, the artisans, and the crafts people). The reasons for this discrimination are varied and not without some foundation, especially in situations where those entrusted with the teaching of gross motor patterns are seen lumbering from swivel chair to activity area with cigar, whistle, verbal commands, and intransigent policies on attendance and uniforms in tow. Fortunately, discerning people have begun to realize that the application of the discipline is multifaceted and central to the advancement of humankind.

Professionals who draw from the discipline and integrate their efforts with other disciplines and professions are more productive. The physical therapist who incorporates play movements is much more effective in helping young children to rehabilitate. The orthopedic specialist who studies the exact nature of the performance of a skill is strong in both diagnosis and recovery prognosis. The baseball pitcher who understands flight, air resistance, spin, and the summation of forces in conjunction with basic socio psychological principles is well prepared for the winning performance. Although the body of knowledge of Human Movement is developed and validated through research and logical analysis, most of its verification is received through professional application. As professionals apply the principles of any discipline, they become aware of the need to go to other disciplines for fundamental as well as supplemental information. In addition, they apply knowledge more effectively through using techniques gleaned through other professions.

We have paraphrased the words of a prominent American dean of education:

> As a young teacher in a small private school my duties entailed teaching English to the senior students and coaching the school football team. It took me six months to realize that I was a popular mentor in football, but an unpopular task master in the classroom. It was only when I began transferring the same methodology and enthusiasm I freely showed on the playing arena into the English classroom that things began to change. I encouraged peer teaching, problem solving, small-group activity, and put away the musty academic robes. The students began to experience success and I changed, too, from an expectant stentorian purist to an encourager and facilitator, helping the students with their ongoing performance rather than threatening them with reprisals before their effort had even begun.
>
> ROBERT DENTLER, Dean of the School of Education, Boston University, 1974

This man, as a young teacher, had called upon the techniques available in one profession to enhance the productivity of his efforts in another. We suggest that similar experiences await all those who are prepared to look around them with unjaundiced eyes and alert, perceptive minds. Some educators (including physical educators) have successfully integrated movement with other subject areas, but most have avoided interdisciplinary focus because of insecurity, restrictions of time, resistance from other subject areas, or just plain apathy.

We suggest that as the United States tightens its fiscal buckle during the 1970's and 1980's, the period of splendid isolation will end. The time is ripe for the conceptual curriculum with an interdisciplinary focus.

Perhaps we can best illustrate this vital concept with an example drawn from a five-day residential field experience organized by Boston University involving 350 seventh- and eighth-grade children from the Boston and Brookline school systems (3). Funded by the Chapter 636, Section 8, Magnet Schools Integration Program conducted by the Bureau of Equal Opportunity, this project (known as *Magnet Movement Athletics*) sought to bring urban and suburban children together for school with a difference at a camp 150 miles north of Boston. Although the prime purpose was to bring together children from widely differing ethnic and socioeconomic backgrounds, it was realized that the week-long experience had to be strong and motivating in curriculum as well as recreation. It was not planned as an extension of summer camp, but rather as an integrated, interdisciplinary learning experience representing unusual and rarely used experiences during the normal school time. Students of environmental education will be interested in a skeletal outline of the program.

## "THE GREAT EXPERIMENT"*

### Agassiz Village II—"Satellite City"

During the early 1970's the major urban areas of New England such as Portland, Augusta, and Boston have grown rapidly to the point where it is difficult to find any more space to expand. The cities are overcrowded and housing is deteriorating rapidly. Jobs are scarce because many industries and businesses have moved to the suburbs. The best land has been used and prices are very high. Taxes are high and going up. Transportation systems are not good—roads are crowded, railroad and bus service is inadequate. Many difficult problems exist in the metropolitan areas.

The states of Maine and Massachusetts have joined together in an attempt to solve the problems of urban overcrowding. They have decided to fund the development of an experimental new city at Agassiz Village II, Maine, and you have been selected to be one of the first citizens of

*Written by James Gillis, Director Human Environment Institute, Boston University.

the new community. If the "Great Experiment" is successful, many more may be built.

The governors of Maine and Massachusetts have been advised that the best way to design the new city is by letting the new citizens draw up the plan. The city will be expected to be a model example with little pollution of air and water, low unemployment, plenty of parks and open space, good housing, and a vibrant community spirit. Therefore, a group of planning consultants (the staff) has been sent along with you (the new citizens) to aid in your efforts to design the new city.

The activities the staff has created for you to participate in are all designed to help your community reach some decisions about what your city will be like. Some activities will be oriented toward helping you decide the locations of such things as housing, community buildings, parks and industry. Other activities will aid you in setting up a scheme for your town government, job development, city services, and cultural activities.

Since it is difficult to have you all work in one group, it has been necessary to separate you into smaller groups of 32. Each group of 32 citizens will be required to develop its own plan for the city, and on the last day of your visit to Agassiz Village, each group will present its plan to the whole group.

In developing your plan, you might consider the following:

1. Initial housing for 200 people (you).
2. Sites for future housing for 1,800 more people (a total of 2,000 people).
3. Business and industry to provide good jobs.
4. Community services
   a. fire department
   b. law enforcement
   c. waste disposal
   d. post office
   e. churches
   f. schools
   g. town hall
   h. other
5. Parks and open space.
6. Transportation system (such as roads, busses, bicycle paths, hiking trails, etc.).
7. Stores and commercial services.
8. Food sources (gardens, farms, fish ponds, etc.).
9. Other.

Remember that everyone needs some kind of job, and that for the city to be a pleasant place to live everyone must be able to have the necessary community services.

In order to plan your new satellite city (Agassiz Village II), you will have to survey the situation very carefully. You will need to know the physical features: rocks, fields, trees, water, soil, types of plants and animals, flat versus hilly terrain, etc. You will need to consider the location of buildings, gardens, roads, and so on. It is also important to consider the economy of the area: how does everybody make money? Also very important—how is Agassiz Village II governed—who runs it? You should think about how people will work together: for example, will each of you build your own house alone, or will you work together to help each other build the houses? Will you each have a separate garden, or will you have a cooperative garden?

The problems you are considering for Agassiz Village II are problems common to all communities. Every city and town is facing these problems —and more. How can you create a better community? Perhaps your plan will do away with poverty, discrimination, pollution, and overcrowding. Perhaps your new city would be a really nice place to live.

## MAJOR PROGRAM COMPONENTS

*Program Centers*

Monday, 1:00–4:00 p.m.: Adventure Initiative Tasks for all teams of eight with team guides

A. Orienteering:   Map and compass skills
    four teams of eight—separate courses

B. Transection/Survey:   Major physical terrain of Agassiz
                                      Village
    four teams of eight—four compass directions

C. Quadrant Inventory/Analysis:   Intensive study of selected
                                                      areas
    four teams of eight—two separate areas per team

D. Adventure Course:   Building self-confidence and team trust
    four teams of eight—separate equipment-activities

E. Trips to Environment/Economy Sites (4)
    four teams of eight—Hatchery; Game farm; Fire look-out;
                                      Shaker Village; Lumber Mills.

F. Mine Study:   Natural mineral resource possibility
    four teams of eight—small teams each mine

G. Values clarification component—auction of values

Friday, 9:00–11:30 a.m.:   Present plans for the structure of
                                        Agassiz Village II

*Evening Activities (For schedule, see page 394)*
Social Interaction through Mime
Social Interaction through Dance
Social Interaction through Games
Language Communication through Movement
Project Plan Development
Recreational Activities
Film Analysis

Programs such as these do not originate without careful preparation by staff and students. Ideally the children should be prepared at school during class periods prior to going to camp, and should apply the camp experiences long after they return. Subject areas such as Biology, Geography, Botany, Geology, Social Studies, and Zoology are directly involved. If the most is to be made of the interdisciplinary experience, language arts, physical education, health education, dance, and journalism must also be directly involved.

Teachers and parents were used in the Boston University program to supplement the staff that was comprised mostly of graduate and undergraduate Human Movement majors. These students underwent extensive preparation in Boston and at the camp site. Specialists in Mineralogy, Biology, Orienteering, and soil analysis were consulted along with experts from the Hamilton-Wenham Project Adventure which specializes in bringing the scope and methodology of the Outward Bound movement into the range of the average school child. The result was a very successful multidisciplinary, integrative experience that received near universal approval. The Boston University students who conducted the program learned invaluable skills for future application and, more importantly, developed a positive, informed, and active attitude toward interdisciplinary and integrative curricular effort. The students from the two public schools systems, after experiencing initial culture shock, settled in to express very positive attitudes toward the total program. The students' ability to grasp the cognitive concepts was continuously evidenced by their ability to apply those knowledges in group problem-solving tasks.

As we move into the latter stages of the twentieth century, scholars and professionals will be tearing down the walls that have allowed discipline areas to isolate themselves. So much redundancy has recently been located that future directions mandate a genuine interdisciplinary focus. The comparative new discipline called Social Psychology is a classic example of this trend.

Another possibility of an interdisciplinary program exists at the college or university level. By providing, encouraging, and even requiring students to participate in studies from a variety of disciplines, and by encouraging faculty to offer interdisciplinary studies, the breadth and depth

## "The Great Experiment" Schedule, Human Environment Institute, Boston University School of Education

| Monday | Tuesday | Wednesday | Thursday | Friday |
|---|---|---|---|---|
| | 7:15 Wake Up | 7:15 Wake Up | 7:15 Wake Up | 7:15 Wake Up |
| | 8:00 Breakfast | 8:00 Breakfast | 8:00 Breakfast | 8:00 Breakfast |
| Travel: Arrive Agassiz Village | 9:00   Grp / Cnt: 1 A, 2 B, 3 C, 4 D, 5 E, 6 F | 9:00   Grp / Cnt: 1 C, 2 D, 3 E, 4 F, 5 A, 6 B | 9:00   Grp / Cnt: 1 E, 2 F, 3 A, 4 B, 5 C, 6 D | 9:00 Present Plans: 1, 2, 3, 4, 5, 6 Wrap up |
| Bunk Assignments | 12:00 | | | |
| 12:30 Lunch | 12:30 Lunch | 12:30 Lunch | 12:30 Lunch | 12:30 Lunch |
| 1:00 Adventure Initiative Tasks | 1:00   Grp / Cnt: 1 B, 2 C, 3 D, 4 E, 5 F, 6 A | Grp / Cnt: 1 D, 2 E, 3 F, 4 A, 5 B, 6 C | Grp / Cnt: 1 F, 2 A, 3 B, 4 C, 5 D, 6 E | 1:30   LEAVE |
| 4:00 | 4:00   Initiative Tasks (all) | 4:00   and/or Recreation Games | 4:00 | TRAVEL |
| 4:00–5:15 Sports and/or | | | | |
| 5:30 Supper | 5:30 Supper | 5:30 Supper | 5:30 Supper | |
| 6:30 "The Great Experiment" | 6:30 Social Interaction & Communication Mime Dance Games | 6:30 Mime Dance Games | 6:30 Complete Team Plan | |
| 7:30 Mime Dance Games | 9:00 | 9:00 | 9:30 Campfire | |
| 9:00 | | | | |

**Figure 16-1.** Movement and intellectual/emotional activity: *(top)* trusting; *(center)* padding; *(bottom)* figuring. (*Courtesy of Jim Schaadt, Human Environment Institute, Boston University*)

**Table 16-1. Sample Matrix of Interdependence:
An Intercurricular Matrix for Schools**

| Physical Activity | Science | Language Arts |
| --- | --- | --- |
| 12-foot wall: Group negotiates scaling a wall as one unit in time limitation | Gravity: levers Forces: Motion Anatomy: Physiology Engineering | Drama: Poetry Communication (V and NV): Journal Writing |
| 15 kilometer run | Levers: Meteorology Physiology: Newtons 1 and 3: | Listening: Journal Writing Reading |
| Trampoline: an eight bounce routine | Gravity; Work: Stability: Projectiles: Vibration: | Describing Communicating Analyzing |
| Basketball: Preparation for and execution of offensive play | Newtons 1, 2 and 3: Stability: Work: Vibration: Gravity Projectiles | Describing Communicating (V and NV) |
| Ski Jump: Preparations and execution | Friction: Gravity Force: Stability Aerodynamics: Flow Meteorology: Body as a projectile | Describing Communicating Reading |
| Electric fence: All members exit from triangular rope compound in time limitation | Energy: Work: Gravity: Anatomy Physiology: Levers | Describing Communicating Poetry Drama |
| Diving: Reverse 1½ from tower-pike position | Gravity: Buoyancy: Gyration: Meteorology: Leverage Metals: Newton 1,2,3 | Journal Writing Communication Poetry: Drama |

of professional preparation is increased. For example, Figures 16-2 and 16-3 describe the passage of a hypothetical student through college and the professional careers which would benefit from interdisciplinary focus.

We present, here, a sample of an intersubject matrix to illustrate

| Social Studies | Math | Music |
|---|---|---|
| Leadership: | Measuring: | Singing: |
| Conformity: | Math sentences: | Tempo: |
| Cooperation: | Force Quantities | Chanting: |
| Geog. and History | Time: Space | |
| Geography: | Graphing | Singing |
| History: | Measuring | Humming |
| Social Needs: | time | Rhythm. |
| Solitude | | |
| History: | Force: Time: | Rhythm |
| Social Needs: | Space: | Percussion: |
| Fear: | Geometry: | Chanting |
| Safety | Proportions: | |
| | Numbers | |
| Competition, | Sets & subsets | Rhythm |
| Cooperation, | Numbers: | |
| Task analysis | Graphing: time | Rhymes |
| Racial equality | Space: force | |
| Goal orientation | Flow | |
| History: Social | Graphing: | Dancing |
| Needs: Trust: | Measuring: | Singing |
| Fear: Competition | Geometry: | Chanting |
| Self and others | Cartography | Rhythm |
| | Time: Space | |
| Energy needs | Measuring | Rhythm |
| & supplies | Sets, time, | Singing |
| Freedom | number | |
| Conformity | Algebra | |
| Leadership task | Geometry | |
| Analysis | | |
| History: | Geometry | Dancing |
| Geography: | Measuring | Rhythm |
| Social Needs | Proportion | |
| | Time | |

ideas which schools can use to initiate the interdisciplinary curriculum (Table 16-1).

It is important to realize that the physical educator is, under these circumstances, merely one member of a team. The movement curriculum

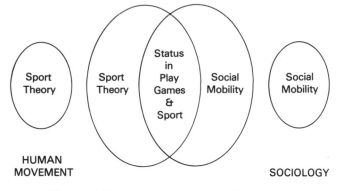

Figure 16-2. Example of interdisciplinary substance.

can and will be taught by many other specialists as well. In turn, physical educators will be called upon to teach basic concepts relating to Math, Language Arts, Science, Music, and many other subject areas (4).

The preparation of professionals to bring about the integrative focus will necessitate changes at the tertiary education levels, also.

*What would a university or college structure look like which embraced the essential theory of this text and what would happen to the student entering this expanded learning and growing environment?*

1. The body of knowledge of the discipline of Human Movement would be taught in colleges of Liberal Arts, where the other disciplines are studied.

2. All application of the discipline of Human Movement would be taught in the professional schools—Education, Medicine, Fine and Applied Arts, Management, Public Communication, Nursing, and so on.

3. The interdisciplinary aspect would focus upon the interdependence of knowledge among and within disciplines and the interprofessional aspect would focus on the interdependence of applications among and within professions.

A Department of Human Movement would exist in the College of Liberal Arts with such curriculum content as: Essentials of Nonlocomotive Motion; Exercise and Training Effect; Psychology of Play; Why People Move; Cultural Patterns in Human Movement; Analysis of Fine Movement Forms; Theory of Sport; Mechanics of Movement; and so on.

Interdisciplinary staff utilization could be obtained using the essential integrative skills of specialists in Anatomy, Psychology, Anthropology, Sociology, Physics and Mathematics. Such specialists could be developed from within Human Movement through outreach scholarships or lured from the disciplines through an interest in movement. Figure 16-2 gives an example of overlapping that occurs in the disciplines.

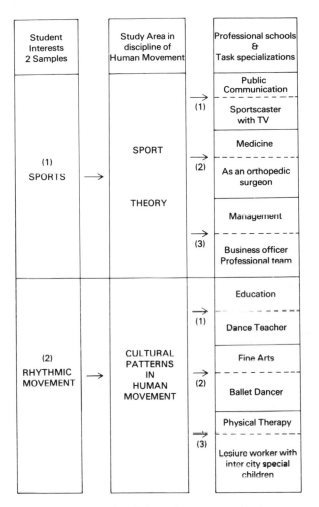

**Figure 16-3.** Possible pathways to professions from the discipline.

Students from all the professional schools would study the discipline of Human Movement then return to apply the knowledges to their professional applications. Figure 16-3 traces several possible pathways to bring this application about.

In similar fashion to the interdisciplinary focus, an interprofessional focus would develop among those applying the knowledge gained from the discipline. Examples of this have already been given in "The Great Experiment" (pp. 390-94) and the intersubject matrix (pp. 396-97). For this input to be fully operable, the walls of the professional schools would, like the disciplines, need to be appropriately permeable.

Figure 16-4 explains how the preparation of the multiprofessional could be traced. A student, for instance, may enter college with some vague goal of becoming a swimming coach. In order to coach in the

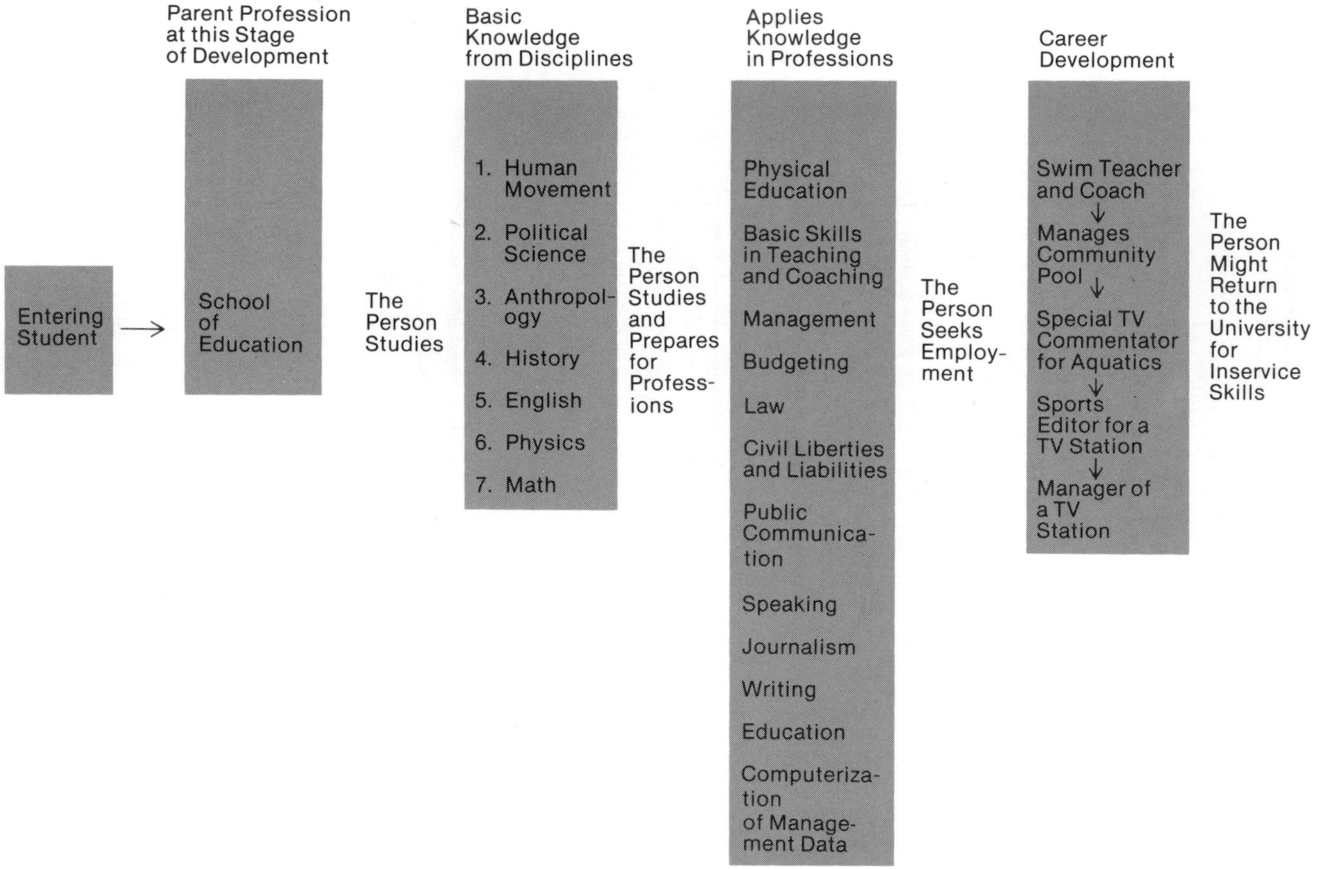

Parent Profession
at this Stage
of Development

Basic Knowledge
from Disciplines

Applies Knowledge
in Professions

Career Development

The Person Studies

Entering Student → School of Education

The Person Studies and Prepares for Professions

1. Human Movement
2. Political Science
3. Anthropology
4. History
5. English
6. Physics
7. Math

Physical Education

Basic Skills in Teaching and Coaching

Management

Budgeting

Law

Civil Liberties and Liabilities

Public Communication

Speaking

Journalism

Writing

Education

Computerization of Management Data

The Person Seeks Employment

Swim Teacher and Coach →
Manages Community Pool →
Special TV Commentator for Aquatics →
Sports Editor for a TV Station →
Manager of a TV Station

The Person Might Return to the University for Inservice Skills

**Figure 16-4.** Preparing multi-skilled professionals: A sample

public schools, he is required to become a certified teacher. Hence he enters the School of Education to study physical education. He is required to gain basic knowledge in a cross section of disciplines and professions as part of his program. This would include the traditional general education disciplines of Mathematics, English, History, and the like and the traditional physical education program with its emphasis on the teaching and coaching of basic skills, the structures and function of the body, and the mechanics of movement. In addition it would include the acquisition of special skills in other professions such as Management, Law, Communication, and Education.

This broad-based education would prepare him to move well beyond his initial goal of being a swimming coach. Although his first job may be that of a humble swimming teacher and coach, he may move into the job of manager of a pool, or special television commentator for aquatics, or manager of the community center or manager of the television station. The broad-based educational background has prepared him to move far in his professional endeavors. Surely in the process it will be necessary for him to acquire more training in certain areas. Thus, opportunity must be provided for him to return to school to deepen and broaden his professional expertise. Continuing a lifelong education provided it is available or viable serves this purpose.

We are convinced that the schools, youth agencies, industrial and community institutions of tomorrow will move in the direction of greater sophistication and multi-dimensional effort in curriculum and instruction. Knowledges gained in one dimension will more readily be incorporated in other dimensions. In like manner to the knowledge explosion of the 1940's, 1950's and 1960's, the successful combining of knowledge and applications across disciplines and professions will produce a geometric rather than an arithmetic advance in the discipline of Human Movement and its applications for the remainder of the twentieth century.


## References Cited

1. DE LABAN, JUANA. "Modus Operandi," *Quest* 2 (April 1964): 13.

2. SIEDENTOP, DARYL. *Physical Education: An Introductory Analysis.* Dubuque, Iowa: W. Brown Company, 1972.

3. CHEFFERS, J. T. F., ANN S. BATCHELDER, AND LINDA D. ZAICHKOWSKY. "Achieving Racial Integration through Movement Oriented Programs," *Research in Education* (ERIC), 1976.

4. GALLAHUE, DAVID L., PETER H. WERNER, AND GEORGE C. LUEDKE. *A Conceptual Approach to Moving and Learning.* New York: Wiley, 1975.

*Indexes*

# Name Index

# Subject Index

414